LITERARY CRITICISM

An Introduction
to Theory and Practice

Third Edition

Charles E. Bressler

Houghton College

Prentice
Hall

Upper Saddle River, New Jersey 07458

Library of Congress Cataloging-in-Publication Data

Bressler, Charles E.
    Literary criticism : an introduction to theory and practice / Charles
E. Bressler.— 3rd ed.
       p. cm.
Includes bibliographical references and index.
    ISBN 0-13-033397-2
    1. Criticism.   I. Title.
    PN81 .B666 2002
    801'.95—dc21   2002074510

Once again, for Darlene, my best friend and loving wife, and
Heidi, my much loved daughter

VP, Editor-in-Chief: Leah Jewell
Senior Acquisitions Editor: Carrie Brandon
Editorial Assistant: Jennifer Migueis
VP, Director of Production and Manufacturing: Barbara Kittle
Senior Managing Editor: Ann Marie McCarthy
Senior Production Editor: Shelly Kupperman
Prepress and Manufacturing Manager: Nick Sklitsis
Prepress and Manufacturing Buyer: Sherry Lewis
Director of Marketing: Beth Mejia
Senior Marketing Manager: Rachel Falk
Marketing Assistant: Christine Moodie
Cover Design Director: Robert Farrar-Wagner
Cover Art: Theodore J. Murphy, "Before the Fall," 2001, oil, 10" × 11".

For permission to use copyrighted material, grateful acknowledgment
is made to the copyright holders listed on pages 312–313, which are
considered an extension of this copyright page.

This book is set in 10/12 Palatino and was printed
and bound by Courier Companies, Inc.
The cover was printed by The Lehigh Press, Inc.

 © 2003, 1999, 1994 by Pearson Education, Inc.
Upper Saddle River, New Jersey 07458

Printed in the United States of America
10 9 8 7 6 5 4 3 2

ISBN: 0-13-033397-2

Pearson Education LTD., London
Pearson Education Australia PTY, Limited, Sydney
Pearson Education Singapore, Pte. Ltd
Pearson Education North Asia Ltd, Hong Kong
Pearson Education Canada, Ltd., Toronto
Pearson Educación de Mexico, S.A. de C.V.
Pearson Education – Japan, Tokyo
Pearson Education Malaysia, Pte. Ltd
Pearson Education, Upper Saddle River, New Jersey

Contents

10 Cultural Poetics   179
or New Historicism

11 Cultural Studies   197

Literary Selections   214

Foreword

Early in Mark Twain's *The Adventures of Huckleberry Finn*, we learn about Tom Sawyer's gang and his "deep laid" plans, for Tom and his inner circle of friends dedicate one memorable occasion to working out such details: the name of the gang, its objectives, its general line of business—its modus operandi. But there are problems, namely, problems of interpretation. After all, not everybody defines "gang" the same way. These interpretive problems are not insurmountable, so we discover, but they are real, at least for a few enchanted moments in the narrative:

> "Now," says Ben Rogers, "what's the line of business of this Gang?"
>
> "Nothing only robbery and murder," Tom said.
>
> "But who are we going to rob?—houses, or cattle, or—"
>
> "Stuff! stealing cattle and such things ain't robbery; it's burglary," says Tom Sawyer. "We ain't burglars. That ain't no sort of style. We are highwaymen. We stop stages and carriages on the road, with masks on, and kill the people and take their watches and money."
>
> "Must we always kill the people?"
>
> "Oh, certainly. It's best. Some authorities think different, but mostly it's considered best to kill them—except some that you bring to the cave here, and keep them till they're ransomed."
>
> "Ransomed? What's that?"
>
> "I don't know. But that's what they do. I've seen it in books; and so of course that's what we've go to do."
>
> "But how can we do it if we don't know what it is?"
>
> "Why, blame it all, we've got to do it. Don't I tell you it's in the books? Do you want to go to doing different from what's in the books, and get things all muddled up?"

It is difficult to argue that Tom Sawyer, under any circumstances, is a reliable reader of literary texts. Yet amidst this already "muddled up" but delightfully humorous conversation, Tom is right about one thing: books carry a certain cultural authority. They can and do influence the way a person understands human experience, even if that same person makes no claim to be an avid reader. Tom Sawyer is certainly not the model reader, nor was he ever the model student. But his cocksure knowledge of books, however boyishly obtained, is telling nonetheless.

Readers are still intensely interested in understanding "what's in the books." It is a task, in fact, made all the richer and at the same time more difficult, given the great variety of critical approaches to literary texts, and the decades of theoretical debates, political wrangling, and culture wars. In her book *West of Everything*, Jane Tompkins has accurately described such conflicts in the discipline as "academic shootouts" (230). Even in the late afternoon of theory, however, the dust has not settled. Terry Eagleton's admonition is as true now as it was when he first offered it: "Hostility to theory usually means an opposition to other people's theories and an oblivion of one's own" (*Literary Theory,* viii). But just what constitutes "theory" and its various uses is still a hotly debated subject, yet one worth pursuing.

Not all critics share Eagleton's views on the subject. Denis Donoghue asserts, "If theory is merely experimental or, as we say, heuristic, we do well to take it to mind if not to heart, and give it a run for whatever money we risk on it. But if it is offered to us as a creed or a vision or a doctrine, we should approach it much more skeptically and estimate the consequence of taking it to heart and soul." In Shakespearean criticism, for instance, Donoghue contends that Eagleton's commitments to "theory" have amounted to what he calls a "New Thematics": the "queering" of "one discipline—literary criticism—with the habits of another—social science or moral interrogation" (*The Practice of Reading* 66–67). This one tension is only representative of the many that exist in response to "what's in the books," that persistent question.

Charles Bressler's *Literary Criticism, Third Edition,* invites readers not only into the debate but also into the larger literary conversation. Like the two previous editions, this one is written on the assumption that too often literary theory is a subject only for professional critics and academicians. While this new edition makes it even more possible for students to work with complex theoretical configurations, it is not at all phobic about literary power. Bressler's goal is to introduce students to the practice of literary reading in all its variety, not to indoctrinate.

Chapter 1 addresses two of the most central questions in the college literature classroom: How we read and why? To help students answer these questions, Bressler provides a working definition of literature, including its epistemological and ontological components. His discussion also attempts to relate literary study to the relationship between public and private values.

Chapter 2 traces the historical developments of literary criticism, from Plato to the present. This chapter is designed to help students relate to and participate in the historical debate about such important subjects as representation, truth, beauty, nature, form, meaning, gender, class, and audience, among others. Chapter 2 explores some of the important early influences on what is now modern and postmodern literary theory. What is important about this chapter is that it alerts students to the intellectual risks of developing a merely contemporary diet of ideas.

Chapters 3 through 11 of *Literary Criticism, Third Edition,* investigate the main critical "schools" that have developed to the present: respectively, New Criticism, Reader-Response Criticism, Structuralism, Deconstruction, Psychoanalytic Criticism, Feminism, Marxism, Cultural Poetics (or New Historicism), and Cultural Studies, which has been expanded to include a more detailed discussion of Postcolonialism.

Literary Criticism, Third Edition, is designed to equip teachers and students to enter into a more meaningful conversation about literary texts. To this end, this revised edition includes a new, updated glossary of critical terms, new student essays, an updated bibliography, and a list of useful Web sites and links. The Internet listings will provide students new and exciting avenues for literary research. All of the revisions to the new edition are intended to help students sharpen their critical thinking skills and develop a voice in critical discussions. To enable students to become more informed readers of literature, the third edition also includes a Questions for Analysis section at the end of each chapter. This section reinforces the point that all good research writing and discussion begins with one good, well-focused question.

It is not the goal of this book to substitute for any important primary readings. Instead, this text intends to engage students in a series of mutual introductions to primary and secondary works in literary studies. It is hoped that students then will decide "what's in the books," with the added awareness that it is only through rereading them over a lifetime that makes answers even possible.

Daniel H. Strait
Asbury College
Wilmore, Kentucky

To the Reader

Like the first two editions, this new edition of *Literary Criticism* is designed as a supplemental text for introductory courses in both literature and literary criticism. In all three editions, the purpose of this text has always remained the same: to enable students to approach literature from a variety of practical and theoretical perspectives and to equip them with a theoretical and a practical understanding of how critics develop their interpretations. Its overall aim is to take the mystery out of working with and interpreting texts.

Like the first and second editions, the third edition holds to several key premises. First, I assume that there is no such thing as an "innocent" reading of a text. Whether our responses to a text are emotional and spontaneous or well reasoned and highly structured, all of our interpretations are based on underlying factors that cause us to respond in a particular way. What elicits these responses, and how a reader makes sense out of a text, is what really matters. It is the domain of literary theory to question our initial and all our further responses, our beliefs, our values, our feelings, and our eventual, overall interpretation. To understand why we respond to a text in a certain way, we must first understand literary theory and criticism.

Second, since our responses to any text have theoretical bases, I presume that all readers have a literary theory. Consciously or unconsciously, as readers we have developed a mind-set that fits or encompasses our expectations when reading any text. Somehow we all seem able to make sense of a text. The methods we use to frame our personal and public interpretations directly involve us in the process of literary criticism and theory and automatically make us practicing literary critics, whether we know it or not!

My third assumption rests on the observation that each reader's literary theory and accompanying methodology is either conscious or unconscious, complete or incomplete, informed or ill-informed, eclectic or unified. Since an unconscious, incomplete, ill-informed, and eclectic literary theory more frequently than not leads to illogical, unsound, and haphazard interpretations, I believe that a well-defined, logical, and clearly articulated theory will enable readers to develop their own methods of interpretation, permitting readers, in fact, to order, clarify, and justify their appraisals of a text in a consistent and rational manner.

Unfortunately, many readers cannot articulate their own literary theory and have little knowledge of the history and development of the ever-evolving principles of literary criticism. It is the goal of this book to introduce such students to literary theory and criticism, its historical development, and the various theoretical positions or schools of criticism that will enable them as readers to make conscious, informed, and intelligent choices about their own methods of interpretation.

Like the first two editions, this new edition introduces students to the basic concerns of literary theory in Chapter 1, which now includes a more expansive definition of *literature* itself. Chapter 2 places literary theory and criticism in historical perspective, starting with Plato and ending with modern-day theorists. Chapters 3 to 11 have all been revised, adding new terminology where appropriate. These chapters present the eleven major schools of criticism that have been developed in the twentieth century: New Criticism, Reader-Response Criticism, Structuralism, Deconstruction, Psychoanalytic Criticism, Feminism, Marxism, Cultural Poetics or New Historicism, and Cultural Studies, with an expanded discussion of Postcolonialism, including African American and Gender Studies. To maintain consistency and for ease of study, each of these chapters is identically organized. We begin with a brief **Introduction** followed by the **Historical Development** of each school of criticism. The **Assumptions** section, which sets forth the philosophical principles on which each school of criticism is based, is next. The **Methodology** section follows and serves as a "how-to" manual for explaining the techniques used by the various schools of criticism to formulate their interpretations of a text based upon their philosophical assumptions. All chapters in the third edition have received careful editing, with added terminology and scope of coverage. Throughout each of these sections, all **key terms** are in boldface type and are included in the new **Glossary** that appears at the back of this edition.

After the Methodology section, there is an expanded **Questions for Analysis** section in Chapters 3 through 11. This feature provides students with key questions to ask of a text in order to view that text from the perspective of the school of criticism under discussion. Some of the questions also ask students to apply their new-found knowledge to a particular text. Following this section is the **Student Essay** introduction, which poses critical questions to prepare students to read the example essay at the end of the Chapter. As in the first two editions, this undergraduate **Student Essay** provides an example for analysis, in which a student applies the principles and methods of interpretation of the school of criticism under discussion to one of nine primary texts in the **Literary Selections**. All of these primary texts can be found at the back of this edition.

Following the Student Essay warm-up is an updated **Further Reading** section. More comprehensive than in the first two editions, these selected references complement the more extensive **References** section found at the end of the text. After the Further Reading section, an updated **Web Sites** section appears that provides additional avenues of exploration for each of the schools of criticism. It is often the case that these World Wide Web addresses include links to other sites, thus providing opportunities to venture into the ever-expanding world of literary theory.

Since *Literary Criticism* is an introductory text, the explanations of the various schools of criticism should not be viewed as exhaustive but as a first step toward an understanding of some rather difficult concepts, principles, and methodologies. Similarly, the student essays should not be viewed as literary masterpieces but as undergraduate attempts to employ differing literary theories. Instructors and students alike should feel free to critique these essays and explore both their strengths and weaknesses. After reading each of the chapters in this new edition, it is hoped that readers will continue their own investigations of literary theory by exploring advanced theoretical texts and the primary works of both theoretical and practical critics.

ACKNOWLEDGMENTS

Believing in the intertextuality of texts, I readily acknowledge that the creation of this text involved an intricate web of relationships with many people. First, to those students who enrolled in my literary criticism classes, I say a big thank you. Your thoughtful questions, your oral presentations, and your countless written essays helped me crystallize my thinking about many complex theoretical issues of literary criticism. Without you, this book could not have been written. In particular, I wish to thank those students who contributed new essays for this edition: Jennifer Douglas, Conie Krause, Lori Huth, and Wendy Rader. I am also deeply grateful to Christopher Smith and Jonathan Sponsler for their many hours exploring literary sites on the World Wide Web. To Houghton College I am also thankful. By generously awarding me several mini-sabbaticals, released time from teaching, and a laptop computer, you have made this book possible. Special thanks must go to my academic dean, Dr. Ron Oakerson, for his continued moral and academic support. In addition, my fellow faculty members of the Department of English and Communication have also encouraged me in my research and writing. Thank you one and all, with special thanks to Willis Beardsley for his ever-faithful friendship and help. Words of gratitude must also be expressed for my editor at Prentice Hall, Carrie Brandon. Her gentle prodding, her kind words, her superb editing, and all her other professional advice have been extremely appreciated. Special thanks to senior production editor Shelly Kupperman, to copyeditor Diane Garvey Nesin, and to proofreader Genevieve Coyne for their guidance and helpful suggestions. I'd also like to thank the reviewers of the third edition: George Evans Light, Mississippi State University; Cornelia Wells, William Paterson University; Philip J. Burns, Worcester State College; Edward A. Shannon, Ramapo College; Rachel Crawford, University of San Francisco; Connie R. Phillips, Warner Pacific College; Alison M. Perry, University of Colorado at Boulder; Howard A. Kerner, Polk Community College; and Jose M. Blanco, Miami-Dade Community College. Most of all, I must express my undying love and appreciation to my best friend and wife, Darlene: you are my first and most loved editor, my life's companion, and my joy. Thanks for allowing me freedom from the many chores of life to pursue countless hours of research and writing to complete this project. And to my daughter, Heidi, know that you are the apple of my eye. Your personal encouragement to keep on keeping on has always been and will forever be eternally appreciated. Without the help of all of these excellent students, colleagues, and companions, this book would not have been conceived or written. Any errors in this text, however, are solely mine.

Charles E. Bressler
Houghton, New York

✒ *1* ✑

Defining Criticism, Theory, and Literature

Literary theory has permeated our thinking to the point that it has defined for our times how discourse about literature, as well as about culture in general, shall proceed. Literary theory has arrived, and no student of literature can afford not to come to terms with it.

Thomas McLaughlin, *Critical Terms for Literary Study*

EAVESDROPPING ON A LITERATURE CLASSROOM

Having assigned her literature class Flannery O'Connor's short story "A Good Man Is Hard to Find" and knowing O'Connor's canon and her long list of curious protagonists, Professor Sally Blackwell could not anticipate whether her students would greet her with silence, bewilderment, or frustration when asked to discuss this work. Her curiosity would soon be satisfied, for as she stood before the class, she asked a seemingly simple, direct question: "What do you believe O'Connor is trying to tell us in this story? In other words, how do you, as readers, interpret this text?"

Although some students suddenly found the covers of their anthologies fascinating, others shot up their hands. Given a nod from Professor Blackwell, Alice was the first to respond. "I believe O'Connor is trying to tell us the state of the family in rural Georgia during the 1950s. Just look at how the children, June Star and John Wesley, behave. They don't respect their grandmother. In fact, they mock her."

"But she deserves to be mocked," interrupted Peter. "Her life is one big act. She wants to act like a lady—to wear white cotton gloves and carry a purse—but she really cares only for herself. She is selfish, self-centered, and arrogant."

"That may be," responded Karen, "but I think the real message of O'Connor's story is not about family or one particular character, but about a philosophy of life. O'Connor uses the Misfit to articulate her personal view of life. When the Misfit says Jesus has thrown 'everything off balance,'

O'Connor is really asking each of her readers to choose his or her own way of life or to follow the teachings of Jesus. In effect, O'Connor is saying we all have a choice: to live for ourselves or to live for and through others."

"I don't think we should bring Christianity or any other philosophy or religion into the story," said George. "Through analyzing O'Connor's individual words—words like *tall, dark,* and *deep*—and noting how often she repeats them and in what context, we can deduce that O'Connor's text, not O'Connor herself or her view of life, is melancholy and a bit dark. But to equate O'Connor's personal philosophy about life with the meaning of this particular story is somewhat silly."

"But we can't forget that O'Connor is a woman," said Betty, "and an educated one at that! Her story has little to do with an academic or pie-in-the-sky, meaningless philosophical discussion, but a lot to do with being a woman. Being raised in the South, O'Connor would know and would have experienced prejudice because she is a woman. And as we all know, the Southern male's opinion of women is that they are to be kept 'barefoot, pregnant, and in the kitchen.' Seemingly, they are to be as nondescript as Bailey's wife is in this story. Unlike all the other characters, we don't even know this woman's name. How much more nondescriptive could O'Connor be? O'Connor's message, then, is simple: Women are oppressed and suppressed. If they open their mouths, if they have an opinion, and if they voice that opinion, they will end up like the grandmother, with a bullet in their head."

"I don't think that's her point at all," said Barb. "I do agree that she is writing from personal experience about the South, but her main point is about prejudice itself—prejudice against African Americans. Through the voice of the Grandmother we see the Southern lady's opinion of African Americans: They are inferior to whites, uneducated, poor, and basically ignorant. O'Connor's main point is that we are all equal."

"Yes, I agree," said Mike. "But if we look at this story in the context of all the other stories we have read this semester, I see a theme we have discussed countless times before: appearance versus reality. This is O'Connor's main point. The grandmother acts like a lady—someone who cares greatly about others—but inwardly she cares only for herself. She's a hypocrite."

"I disagree. In fact, I disagree with everybody," announced Daniel. "I like the grandmother. She reminds me of my grandmother. O'Connor's grandmother is a bit self-centered, but whose old grandmother isn't? Like my grandma, O'Connor's grandmother likes to be around her grandchildren, to read and to play with them. She's funny, and she has spunk. And she even likes cats."

"But, Professor Blackwell, can we ever know what Flannery O'Connor really thinks about this story?" asked Jessica. "After all, she's dead, and she didn't write an essay titled "What 'A Good Man Is Hard to Find' Really Means." And since she never tells us its meaning, can't the story have more than one meaning?"

Professor Blackwell instantly realized that Jessica's query—Can a story have multiple meanings?—is a pivotal question not only for English professors and their students but also for anyone who reads any text.

CAN A TEXT HAVE MORE THAN ONE INTERPRETATION?

A quick glance at the discussion of O'Connor's "A Good Man Is Hard to Find" in Professor Blackwell's classroom reveals that not all readers interpret texts in the same way. In fact, all of the eight students who voiced their understandings of the story gave fundamentally different interpretations. Was only one of these eight interpretations correct and the remaining seven wrong? If so, how does one arrive at the correct interpretation? Put another way, if there is only one correct interpretation of a text, what are the **hermeneutical principles** (the rules of interpretation) readers must use to discover this interpretation?

On the other hand, if a work can have multiple interpretations, are all such interpretations valid? Can and should each interpretation be considered a satisfactory and legitimate analysis of the text under discussion? In other words, can a text mean anything a reader declares it to mean, or are there guiding principles for interpreting a text that must be followed if a reader is to arrive at a valid interpretation? And who, anyway, can declare that one's interpretation is valid or legitimate? English professors? Professional critics? Published scholars? Or any reader?

You might also ask, Need a reader be thinking of any of these particulars when reading a text? Can't one simply enjoy a novel, for example, without considering its interpretation? Need one be able to state the work's theme, discuss its structure, or analyze its tone in order to enjoy the act of reading the novel itself?

These and similar questions are the domain of **literary criticism:** the act of studying, analyzing, interpreting, evaluating, and enjoying a work of art. At first glance the study of literary criticism appears daunting and formidable. Jargon such as **hermeneutics**, **Aristotelian poetics**, **deconstruction**, and a host of other intimidating terms confront the would-be **literary critic**. Nevertheless, the actual process or act of literary criticism is not as ominous as it may first appear.

HOW TO BECOME A LITERARY CRITIC

When the students in Professor Blackwell's class were discussing O'Connor's short story "A Good Man Is Hard to Find," each of them was directly responding to the instructor's initial question: What do you believe O'Connor is trying to tell us in and through this story? Although not all responses were radically different, each student viewed the story from a unique perspective. For example, some students expressed a liking for the grandmother, but others thought her a selfish, arrogant woman. Still others believed O'Connor was voicing a variety of philosophical, social, and cultural concerns, such as the place of women and African Americans in Southern society, or adherence to tenents of Christianity and the teachings of Jesus Christ as the basis for one's view of life, or the structure of the family in rural Georgia in the 1950s. All had an opinion about and therefore an interpretation of O'Connor's story.

When Professor Blackwell's students stated their personal interpretations of O'Connor's story, they had become practicing literary critics. All of them had already interacted with the story, thinking about their likes and dislikes of the various characters; their impressions of the setting, plot, and structure; and their overall assessment of the story itself, whether that assessment was a full-fledged interpretation that seeks to explain every facet of the text or simply bewilderment as to the story's overall meaning.

None of the students, however, had had formal training in literary criticism. None knew the somewhat complicated language of literary theory. And none were acquainted with any of the formal schools of literary criticism.

What each student had done was to have read the story. The reading process itself produced within the students an array of responses, taking the form of questions, statements, opinions, and feelings evoked by the text. These responses coupled with the text itself are the concerns of formal literary criticism.

Although these students may need to master the terminology, the many philosophical approaches, and the diverse methodologies of formal literary criticism to become trained literary critics, they automatically became literary critics as they read and thought about O'Connor's text. They needed no formal training in literary theory. By mastering the concepts of formal literary criticism, these students, like all readers, can become critical readers who are better able to understand and articulate their own reactions and analyze those of others to any text.

WHAT IS LITERARY CRITICISM?

Matthew Arnold, a nineteenth-century literary critic, describes literary criticism as "A disinterested endeavor to learn and propagate the best that is known and thought in the world." Implicit in this definition is that literary criticism is a disciplined activity that attempts to describe, study, analyze, justify, interpret, and evaluate a work of art. By necessity, Arnold would argue, this discipline attempts to formulate aesthetic and methodological principles on which the critic can evaluate a text.

When we consider its function and its relationship to texts, literary criticism is not usually considered a discipline in and of itself, for it must be related to something else—that is, a work of art. Without the work of art, the activity of criticism cannot exist. And it is through this discerning activity that we can knowingly explore the questions that help define our humanity, critique our culture, evaluate our actions, or simply increase our appreciation and enjoyment of both a literary work and our fellow human beings.

When analyzing a text, literary critics ask basic questions such as these about the philosophical, psychological, functional, and descriptive nature of the text itself:

- Does a text have only one correct meaning?
- Is a text always didactic; that is, must a reader learn something from every text?
- Does a text affect each reader in the same way?
- How is a text influenced by the culture of its author and the culture in which it is written?
- Can a text become a catalyst for change in a given culture?

Since the time of the Greek philosophers Plato and Aristotle and continuing to the present day, critics and readers have been hotly debating the answers to these and similar questions. By asking questions of O'Connor's or any other text and by contemplating answers, we too can participate in this debate. We can question, for example, the grandmother's motives in O'Connor's "A Good Man Is Hard to Find," for wanting to take her cat on the family's vacation. Or we can ask if the presence of the Misfit and his companions is the primary reason the grandmother experiences her **epiphany**. No matter what question we may ask concerning O'Connor's text, we are participating in an ongoing discussion of the value and enjoyment of O'Connor's short story while simultaneously engaging in literary criticism and functioning as practical literary critics.

Traditionally, literary critics involve themselves in either theoretical or practical criticism. **Theoretical criticism** formulates the theories, principles, and tenets of the nature and value of art. By citing general aesthetic and moral principles of art, theoretical criticism provides the necessary framework for practical criticism. **Practical criticism** (also known as **applied criticism**) applies the theories and tenets of theoretical criticism to a particular work. Using the theories and principles of theoretical criticism, the **practical critic** defines the standards of taste and explains, evaluates, or justifies a particular piece of literature. A further distinction is made between the practical critic who posits that there is only one theory or set of principles a critic may use when evaluating a literary work—the **absolutist critic**—and the **relativistic critic**, one who uses various and even contradictory theories in critiquing a text. The basis for either kind of critic, or any form of criticism, is literary theory. Without theory, practical criticism could not exist.

WHAT IS LITERARY THEORY?

When reading O'Connor's "A Good Man Is Hard to Find," we necessarily interact with the text, asking many specific, text-related questions and, often times, rather personal ones as well. For example, such questions as these may concern us, the readers:

- What kind of person is the grandmother? Is she like my grandmother or any grandmother I know?
- What is the function or role of June Star? John Wesley? Bailey? The mother?
- Why was the grandmother taking Pitty Sing, the cat, on the family vacation?
- What is the significance of the restaurant scene at The Tower?
- Right before she is shot, what does the grandmother recognize about the Misfit? What is the significance of this recognition?

Such questions immediately involve us in practical criticism. What we tend to forget during the reading of O'Connor's short story or any other text, however, is that we have read other literary works. Our response to any text, then—or the principles of practical criticism we apply to it—is largely a conditioned or socially constructed one; that is, how we arrive at meaning in fiction is in part determined by our past experiences. Consciously or unconsciously, we have developed a mind-set or framework that accommodates our expectations when reading a novel, short story, poem, or any other type of literature. In addition, what we choose to value or uphold as good or bad, moral or immoral, or beautiful or ugly within a given text actually depends on this ever-evolving framework. When we can clearly articulate our mental framework when reading a text and explain how this mind-set directly influences our values and aesthetic judgments about the text, we are well on our way to developing a coherent, unified **literary theory**—the assumptions (conscious or unconscious) that undergird one's understanding and interpretation of language, the construction of meaning, art, culture, aesthetics, and ideological positions.

Because anyone who responds to a text is already a practicing literary critic and because practical criticism is rooted in the reader's preconditioned expectations (his or her mind-set) when actually reading a text, every reader espouses some kind of literary theory. Each reader's theory may be conscious or unconscious, whole or partial, informed or ill informed, eclectic or unified. An incomplete, unconscious, and therefore unclear literary theory leads to illogical, unsound, and haphazard interpretations. On the other hand, a well-defined, logical, and clearly articulated theory enables readers to develop a method by which to establish principles that enable them to justify, order, and clarify their own appraisals of a text in a consistent manner.

A well-articulated literary theory also assumes that an innocent reading of a text or a sheerly emotional or spontaneous reaction to a work cannot exist, for theory questions the assumptions, beliefs, and feelings of readers, asking why they respond to a text in a certain way. According to a consistent literary theory, a simple emotional or intuitive response to a text does not explain the underlying factors that caused such a reaction. What elicits that response, or how the reader constructs meaning through or with the text, is what matters.

MAKING MEANING FROM TEXT

How we as readers construct meaning through or with a text depends on the mental framework each of us has developed concerning the nature of reality. This framework or **worldview** consists of the assumptions or presuppositions that we all hold (either consciously or unconsciously) about the basic makeup of our world. For example, we all struggle to find answers to such questions as these:

- What is the basis of morality or ethics?
- What is the meaning of human history?
- Is there an overarching purpose for humanity's existence?
- What is beauty? Truth? Goodness?
- Is there an ultimate reality?

Interestingly, our answers to these and other questions do not remain static, for as we interact with other people, our environment, our culture, and our own inner selves, we are continually shaping and developing our personal philosophies, rejecting former ideas and replacing them with newly discovered ones. It is our dynamic answers—including our doubts and fears about these answers—that largely determine our response to a literary text.

Upon such a conceptual framework rests literary theory. Whether that framework is well reasoned or simply a matter of habit and past teachings, readers respond to works of art via their worldview. From this philosophical core of beliefs spring their evaluations of the goodness, worthiness, and value of art itself. Using their worldviews either consciously or unconsciously as a yardstick by which to measure and value their experiences, readers respond to individual works of literature, ordering and valuing each separate or collective experience in each text based on the system of beliefs housed in their worldviews.

THE READING PROCESS AND LITERARY THEORY

The relationship between literary theory and a reader's personal worldview is best illustrated in the act of reading itself. When reading, we are constantly interacting with the text. According to Louise M. Rosenblatt's text *The Reader, the Text, the Poem* (1978), during the act or event of reading,

> A reader brings to the text his or her past experience and present personality. Under the magnetism of the ordered symbols of the text, the reader marshals his or her resources and crystallizes out from the stuff of memory, thought, and feeling a new order, a new experience, which he/she sees as the poem. This becomes part of the ongoing stream of the reader's life experience, to be reflected on from any angle important to him or her as a human being.

Accordingly, Rosenblatt declares that the relationship between the reader and the text is not linear, but **transactional;** that is, it is a process or event that takes place at a particular time and place in which the text and the reader condition each other. The reader and the text transact, creating meaning, for meaning does not exist solely within the reader's mind or within the text, Rosenblatt maintains, but in the transaction between them. To arrive at an interpretation of a text (what Rosenblatt calls the **poem**), readers bring their own "temperament and fund of past transactions to the text and live through a process of handling new situations, new attitudes, new personalities, [and] new conflicts in value. They can reject, revise, or assimilate into the resource with which they engage their world." Through this transactional experience, readers consciously and unconsciously amend their worldview.

Because no literary theory can account for all the various factors included in everyone's conceptual framework, and because we as readers all have different literary experiences, there can exist no **metatheory**—no one overarching literary theory that encompasses all possible interpretations of a text suggested by its readers. And too, there can be no one correct literary theory, for in and of itself, each literary theory asks valid questions of and about a text, and no one theory is capable of exhausting all legitimate questions to be asked about any text.

The valid and legitimate questions asked about a text by the various literary theories differ, often widely. Espousing separate critical orientations, each theory focuses primarily on one element of the interpretative process, although in practice different theories may address several areas of concern in interpreting a text. For example, one theory may stress the work itself, believing that the text alone contains all the necessary information to arrive at an interpretation. This theory isolates the text from its historical or sociological setting and concentrates on the literary forms found in the text, such as figures of speech, word choice, and style. Another theory may attempt to place a text in its historical, political, sociological, religious, and economic setting. By placing the text in historical perspective, this theory asserts that its adherents can arrive at an interpretation that both the text's author and its original audience would support. Still another theory may direct its chief concern toward the text's audience. It asks how the readers' emotions and personal backgrounds affect each reader's interpretation of a particular text. Whether the primary focus of concern is psychological, linguistic, mythical, historical, or from any other critical orientation, each literary theory establishes its own theoretical basis and then proceeds to develop its own methodology whereby readers can apply the particular theory to an actual text.

Although each reader's theory and methodology for arriving at a text's interpretation differs, sooner or later groups of readers and critics declare allegiance to a similar core of beliefs and band together, thereby founding **schools of criticism**. For example, critics who believe that social and historical concerns must be highlighted in a text are known as Marxist critics, whereas reader-response critics concentrate on readers' personal reactions to the text. Because new points of view concerning literary works are continually evolving, new schools of criticism—and therefore new literary theories—will continue to develop. One of the more recent schools to emerge in the 1980s and 1990s, New Historicism or Cultural Poetics, declares that a text must be analyzed through historical research that assumes that history and fiction are inseparable. The members of this school, known as New Historicists, hope to shift the boundaries between history and literature and thereby produce criticism that accurately reflects what they believe to be the proper relationship between the text and its historical context. Still other newly evolving schools of criticism, such as postcolonialism, African American studies, and gender studies, continue to emerge and challenge previous ways of thinking about and critiquing texts.

Because the various schools of criticism (and the theories on which they are based) ask different questions about the same work of literature, these theoretical schools provide an abundance of options from which readers can choose to broaden their understanding not only of texts but also of their society, their culture, and their own humanity. By embracing literary theory, we learn about literature, but importantly, we are also taught tolerance for other people's beliefs. By rejecting or ignoring theory, we are in danger of canonizing ourselves as literary saints who possess divine knowledge and who can therefore supply the one and only correct interpretation for a given text. When we oppose, disregard, or ignore literary theory, we are in danger of blindly accepting our often unquestioned prejudices and assumptions. By embracing literary theory and literary criticism (its practical application), we can participate in that seemingly endless historical conversation about the nature of humanity and of humanity's concerns as expressed in literature. In the process, we can begin to question our concepts of ourselves, our society, and our culture and how texts themselves help define and continually redefine these concepts.

WHAT IS LITERATURE?

Because literary criticism presupposes that there exists a work of literature to be interpreted, we could assume that formulating a definition of literature would be simple. This is, however, not the case. For centuries, writers, literary historians, and others have debated about but have failed to agree on a definition for this term. Some assume that literature is simply anything that is written, thereby declaring a city telephone directory, a cook book, and a road atlas to be literary works along with *David Copperfield* and the *Adventures of Huckleberry Finn*. Derived from the Latin *littera*, meaning "letter," the root meaning of the word *literature* refers primarily to the written word and seems to support this broad definition. Yet such a definition eliminates the important oral traditions upon which much of our literature is based, including Homer's *Iliad* and *Odyssey*, the English epic *Beowulf*, and many Native American legends, among many other examples.

To solve this difficulty, others choose to define *literature* as an art, thereby leaving open the question of its being written or oral. This definition further narrows its meaning, equating literature to works of the imagination or creative writing. To emphasize the imaginative qualities of literature, some critics choose to use the German word for literature, *Wortkunst*, instead of its English equivalent, for *Wortkunst* automatically implies that the imaginative and creative aspects of literature are essential components of the word *literature* itself. By this definition, written works such as a telephone directory or a cook book can no longer be considered literature; these kinds of works are superseded by poetry, drama, fiction, and other imaginative writing.

Although the narrowing of the definition of literature accomplished by equating it to the defining terms of art seemingly simplifies what can and cannot be considered a literary work, such is not the case. That the J. Crew and Victoria's Secrets clothes catalogues are imaginative (and colorful) writing is unquestioned, but should they then be considered works of literature? Or should Madonna's book *Sex* or the lyrics of the West Coast rap song "Cop Killer," spoken and sung by Ice Tea, be called literary works? Is Madonna's text or the rap an imaginative or a creative work? If so, can or should either be considered a work of literature? Specifying and narrowing the definition of literature to a "work of art" does not, then, immediately provide consensus or a consistent rule about how to declare a text a "work of literature."

Whether one accepts the broad or narrow definition, many argue that a text must have certain peculiar qualities before it can be dubbed "literature." Those who hold this view believe that an artist's creation or secondary world often mirrors the author's primary world, the world in which the writer lives and moves and breathes. Because reality or the primary world is highly structured, so must be the secondary world. To achieve this structure, the artist must create plot, character, tone, symbols, conflict, and a host of other elements or parts of the artistic story, with all of these elements working in a dynamic relationship to produce a literary work. Some would argue that it is the creation of these elements—how they are used and in what context—that determines whether a piece of writing is literature.

Still other critics add the "test of time" criterion to their essential components of literature. If a work such as Dante's *Divine Comedy* withstands the passage of time and is still being read centuries after its creation, it is deemed valuable and worthy to be called literature. This criterion also denotes literature's functional or cultural value: If people value a written work, for whatever reason, they often declare it to be literature whether or not it contains the prescribed elements of a text.

What this work may contain is a peculiar aesthetic quality—that is, some element of beauty—that distinguishes it as literature from other forms of writing. **Aesthetics,** the branch of philosophy that deals with the concept of the beautiful, strives to determine the criteria for beauty in a work of art. Theorists such as Plato and Aristotle declare that the source of beauty is inherent within the art object itself; other critics, such as David Hume, say that beauty is in the eye of the beholder. And some contemporary theorists argue that one's perception of beauty in a text rests in the dynamic relationship between the object (the text) and the perceiver (the reader) at a given moment in time. Wherever the criteria for judging beauty of a work of art finally resides, most critics agree that a work of literature does have an appealing aesthetic quality.

While distinguishing literature from other forms of writings, this appealing aesthetic quality directly contributes to literature's chief purpose: telling a story. Although it may simultaneously communicate facts, literature's primary aim is to tell a story. The subject of this story is particularly human, describing and detailing a variety of human experiences, not stating facts or bits and pieces of information. For example, literature does not define the word *courage*, but shows us a courageous character acting courageously. By so doing, literature concretizes an array of human values, emotions, actions, and ideas in story form. It is this concretization that allows us to experience vicariously the stories of a host of characters. Through these characters we observe people in action, making decisions, struggling to maintain their humanity in often inhumane circumstances, and embodying for us a variety of values and human characteristics that we may embrace, discard, enjoy, or detest.

LITERARY THEORY AND THE DEFINITION OF LITERATURE

Is literature simply a story that contains certain aesthetic and literary qualities that all somehow pleasingly culminate in a work of art? If so, can texts be considered **artifacts** that can be analyzed, dissected, and studied to discover their essential nature or meaning? Or does a literary work have **ontological** status; that is, does it exist in and of itself, perhaps in a special **neo-Platonic** realm? Or must it have an audience, a reader, before it becomes literature? And can we define the word *text*? Is it simply print on a page? If pictures are included, do they automatically become part of the text? Who determines when print becomes a work of art? The reader? The author? Both?

The answers to these and similar questions have been long debated, and the various responses make up the corpus of literary theory. Providing the academic arena in which those interested in literary theory (literary theorists) can posit philosophical assumptions as to the nature of the reading process, the **epistemological** nature of learning, the nature of reality itself, and a host of related concerns, literary theory offers a variety of methodologies that enable readers to interpret a text from different and often conflicting points of view. Such theorizing empowers readers to examine their personal worldviews, to articulate their individual assumptions about the nature of reality, and to understand how these assumptions directly affect their interpretation not only of a work of art but also of the definition of literature itself.

Although any definition of literature is debatable, most would agree that an examination of a text's total artistic situation would help us decide what constitutes literature. This total picture of the work involves such elements as the work itself (an examination of the fictionality or secondary world created within the story), the artist, the universe or world the work supposedly represents, and the audience or readers. Although readers and critics will emphasize one, two, or even three of these elements while de-emphasizing the others, such a consideration of a text's artistic situation immediately broadens the definition of literature from the concept that it is simply a written work that contains certain qualities to a definition that must include the dynamic interrelationship of the actual text and the readers. Perhaps, then, the literary competence of the readers themselves helps determine whether a work should be considered literature. If this is so, then a literary work may be more functional than ontological, its existence and therefore its value being determined by its readers and not by the work itself.

Overall, the definition of literature depends on the particular kind of literary theory or school of criticism that the reader or critic espouses. For formalists, for example, the text and text alone contains certain qualities that make a particular piece of writing literature. On the other hand, for reader-response critics, the interaction and psychological relationships between the text and the reader help determine whether a document should be deemed literary. A working knowledge of literary theory can thus help all readers formulate their ever-developing definition of literature and what they believe constitutes a literary work.

THE FUNCTION OF LITERATURE AND LITERARY THEORY

Critics continually debate literature's chief function. Tracing their arguments to Plato, many contend that literature's primary function is moral, its chief value being its usefulness for cultural or societal purposes. But others, like Aristotle, hold that a work of art can be analyzed and broken down into its various parts, with each part contributing to the overall enjoyment of the work itself. For these critics, the value of a text is found within the text itself or is inseparably linked to the work itself. In its most simple terms, the debate centers around two concerns: Is literature's chief function to teach (extrinsic) or to entertain (intrinsic)? In other words, can we read a text for the sheer fun of it, or must we always be studying and learning from what we read?

Such questions and their various answers lead us directly to literary theory, for literary theory concerns itself not only with ontological questions (whether a text really exists), but also with epistemological issues (how we know or ways of knowing). When we ask, then, if literature's chief function is to entertain or to teach, we are really asking epistemological questions. Whether we read a text to learn from it or to be entertained, we can say that once we have read a text we "know" that text.

We can know a text, however, in two distinct ways. The first way involves the typical literature classroom analysis. When we have studied, analyzed, and critiqued a text and arrived at an interpretation, we can then confidently assert that we know the text. On the other hand, when we stay up all night turning the pages of P. D. James's mystery novel *Death in Holy Orders* to discover who the murderer is, we can also say that we know the text, for we have spent time devouring its pages, lost in its secondary world, consumed by its characters, and by novel's end eagerly seeking the resolution of its tensions. Both methods—one with its chief goal to learn, the other to entertain—involve similar yet distinct epistemological endpoints: to know a text, but in two different ways.

The French verbs *savoir* and *connaître* can both be translated "to know" and can highlight for us the difference between these two epistemological goals or ways of knowing a text. *Savoir* means "to analyze" (from the Greek *analuein,* to undo) and "to study." The word is used to refer to knowing something that is the object of study and assumes that the object, such as a text, can be examined, analyzed, and critiqued. Knowledge or learning *about* is the ultimate goal.

Connaître, on the other hand, implies that we intimately know or have experienced the text. Interestingly, *connaître* is used for knowing people and refers also to knowing an author's canon. Both knowing persons and knowing all a writer's works imply intimacy, learning the particular qualities of one person or author, ins and outs of each. Indeed, it is this intimacy that one often experiences while reading a mystery novel all night long. It is knowing or knowledge *of* that the word means.

To know how to analyze a text, to discuss its literary elements, and to apply the various methodologies of literary criticism means that we know that text (*savoir*). To have experienced the text, to have cried with or about its characters, to have lost time and sleep immersed in the secondary world of the text, and to have felt our emotions stirred also means that we know that text (*connaître*). From one way of knowing, we learn facts or information; from the other, we encounter and participate in an intimate experience.

At times, however, we have actually known the text from both these perspectives, *savoir* and *connaître*. While analyzing and critiquing a text (*savoir*), we have at times (and perhaps more often than not) simultaneously experienced it, becoming emotionally involved with its characters' choices and destinies (*connaître*) and imagining ourselves to be these characters— or at least recognizing some of our own characteristics dramatized by the characters.

To say that we know a text is no simple statement. Underlying our private and public reactions and our scholarly critiques and analyses is our literary theory, the fountainhead of our most intimate and our most public declarations. The formal study of literary theory therefore enables us to explain our responses to any text and allows us to articulate the function of literature in an academic and a personal way.

BEGINNING THE FORMAL STUDY OF LITERARY THEORY

This chapter has stressed the importance of literary theory and criticism and its relationship to literature and the interpretative processes. And it has also articulated the underlying premises of why a study of literary theory is essential:

- Literary theory assumes that there is no such thing as an innocent reading of a text. Whether our responses are emotional and spontaneous or well reasoned and highly structured, all such interactions with and about a text are based on some underlying factors that cause us to respond to that text in a particular fashion. What elicits these responses or how a reader makes sense of a text is at the heart of literary theory.

- Because our reactions to any text have theoretical bases, all readers must have a literary theory. The methods we use to frame our personal interpretations of any text directly involve us in the process of literary criticism and theory, automatically making us practicing literary critics.

- Many readers have a literary theory that is more often than not unconscious, incomplete, ill informed, and eclectic; therefore their interpretations can easily be illogical, unsound, and haphazard. A well-defined, logical, and clearly articulated literary theory enables readers to consciously develop their own methods of interpretation, permitting them to order, clarify, and justify their appraisals of a text in a consistent and logical manner.

It is the goal of this text to enable readers to make such conscious, informed, and intelligent choices, and in doing so, refine their own methods of literary interpretation and more precisely understand their personal and public reactions to a text. To accomplish this goal, the text will introduce readers to literary theory and criticism, its historical development, and the various theoretical positions or schools of criticism, enabling readers to become knowledgeable critics of their own and others' interpretations. By becoming acquainted with diverse and often contradictory approaches to a text, readers will broaden their perspectives not only about themselves but also about others and the world in which they live.

FURTHER READING

Culler, Jonathan. *Literary Theory: A Very Short Introduction*. Oxford: Oxford University Press, 1997.

Eagleton, Terry. *Literary Theory: An Introduction*. 2nd ed. Minneapolis: University of Minnesota Press, 1996.

Groden, Michael, and Martin Kreiswirth, eds. *The Johns Hopkins Guide to Literary Theory and Criticism*. Baltimore: Johns Hopkins University Press, 1994.

Harmon, William, and C. Hugh Holman. *A Handbook to Literture*. 8th ed. New York: Macmillan, 2000.

Lodge, David, ed. *Modern Criticism and Theory: A Reader*. 2nd ed. New York: Longman, 1999.

Makaryk, Irena R., ed. *Encyclopedia of Contemporary Literary Theory: Approaches, Scholars, Terms (Theory/Culture)*. Toronto: University of Toronto Press, 1993.

Reiss, Timothy J. *The Meaning of Literature*. Ithaca: Cornell University Press, 1992.

Richter, David H. *Falling into Theory: Conflicting Views of Reading Literature*. Boston: Bedford, 1994.

Ryan, Michael. *Literary Theory: A Practical Introduction*. Malden, MA: Blackwell, 1999.

Tyson, Lois. *Critical Theory Today: A User-Friendly Guide*. New York: Garland, 1999.

℘ *2* ℘

A Historical Survey of Literary Criticism

It's hard to organize literature.

Irving Howe

INTRODUCTION

Questions about the value, the structure, and even the definition of litera-ture undoubtedly arose in all cultures as people heard or read works of art. Such practical criticism probably began with the initial hearing or reading of the first literary works. It is the Greeks of the fifth century B.C., however, who first articulated and developed the philosophy of art and life that serves as the foundation for most theoretical and practical criticism. These fifth-century Athenians questioned the very act of reading and writing itself, while pondering the purpose of literature. By so doing, these early critics began a debate about the nature and function of literature that continues to the pres-ent day. What they inaugurated was the formal study of literary criticism.

From the fifth-century B.C. to the present, numerous critics—such as Plato, Dante, Wordsworth, Derrida, and a host of others—have developed principles of criticism that have had a major influence on the continuing discussion of lit-erary criticism. By examining these critics' ideas, we can gain an understand-ing of and participate in this critical debate, while acquiring an appreciation for and a working knowledge of both practical and theoretical criticism.

PLATO (*CA.* 427–347 B.C.)

Alfred North Whitehead, a modern British philosopher, once quipped that "all of Western philosophy is but a footnote to Plato." Although others have indeed contributed to Western thought, it was Plato's ideas, expressed in his *Ion, Crito, The Republic*, and other works, that laid the foundation for many, if not most, of the pivotal issues of philosophy and literature: the concepts of truth, beauty, and goodness; the nature of reality; the structure of society; the nature and relations of being (ontology); questions about how we know what we know (epistemology); and ethics and morality. Since Plato's day, such ideas have been debated, changed, debunked, or simply accepted. None, however, have been ignored.

Before Plato, only fragmentary comments about the nature and value of literature can be found. In the plays and writings of the comic dramatist Aristophanes, a contemporary of Plato, a few tidbits of practical criticism arise, but no clearly articulated literary theory. It is Plato who systematically begins for us the study of literary theory and criticism.

The core of Platonic thought resides in Plato's doctrine of essences, ideas, or forms. Ultimate reality, he states, is spiritual. This spiritual realm, which Plato calls **The One**, is composed of "ideal" forms or absolutes that exist whether or not any mind posits their existence or reflects their attributes. It is these ideal forms that give shape to our physical world, for our material world is nothing more than a shadow, a replica, of the absolute forms found in the spiritual realm. In the material world we can therefore recognize a chair as a chair because the ideal chair exists in this spiritual realm and preceded the existence of the material chair. Without the existence of the ideal chair, the physical chair, which is nothing more than a shadow or replica (representation, imitation, reflection) of the ideal chair, could not exist.

Such an emphasis on philosophical ideals earmarks the beginning of the first articulated literary theory and becomes the foundation for literary criticism. Before Plato and his Academy, Greek culture ordered its world through poetry and the poetic imagination; that is, by hearing such epics as the *Iliad* and *Odyssey* or by attending the play cycles, the Greeks saw good characters in action performing good deeds. From such stories, they formulated their theories of goodness and other similar standards, thereby using the presentational mode for discovering truth: observing good characters acting justly, honorably, and courageously and inculcating these characteristics within themselves. With the advent of Plato and his Academy, however, philosophical inquiry and abstract thinking usurped the narrative as a method for discovering truth. Not by accident, then, Plato places above his school door the words, "Let no one enter here who is not a geometer" (a master of geometry; one skilled in formal logic and reasoning). All his students had to value the art of reason and abstraction as opposed to the presentational mode for discovering truth.

This art of abstract reasoning and formal logic not only usurps literature's role as an evaluating mode for discerning truth but also condemns it. If ultimate reality rests in the spiritual realm, and the material world is only a shadow or replica of the world of ideals, then according to Plato and his followers, poets (those who compose imaginative literature) are merely imitating an imitation when they write about any object in the material world. Accordingly, Plato declares that a poet's craft is "an inferior who marries an inferior and has inferior offspring," for the poet, declares Plato, is one who is now two steps removed from ultimate reality. These imitators of mere shadows, contends Plato, cannot be trusted.

While condemning poets for producing art that is nothing more than a copy of a copy, Plato also argues that poets produce their art irrationally, relying on untrustworthy intuition rather than reason for their inspiration. He writes, "For the poet is a light and winged and holy thing, and there is no invention in him until he has been inspired and is out of his senses, and then the mind is no longer in him." Because such inspiration opposes reason and asserts that truth can be attained intuitively, Plato condemns all poets.

Thus, because poets are untrustworthy and damned, their works can no longer be the basis of the Greeks' morality or ethics; for Plato argues, lies abound in the works of poets, critical lies about the nature of ultimate reality and dangerous lies about human reality. In the *Iliad*, for example, the gods lie and cheat and are one of the main causes of suffering among humans; even the mortals in these works steal, complain, and hate each other. Such writings, contends Plato, set a bad example for Greek citizens and may even lead normally law-abiding people down paths of wickedness and immorality. In *The Republic*, Plato ultimately concludes that the poets must be banished.

In a later work, Plato recants the total banishment of poets from society; seemingly, he recognizes society's need for poets and their craft to "celebrate the victors" of the state. Plato asserts that only those poets "who are themselves good and also honourable in the state" can be tolerated. In making this statement, Plato decrees poetry's function and value in and for his society: to sing the praises of loyal Greeks. Accordingly, poets must be supporters of the state or risk exile from their homeland. Being mere imitators of reality—in effect, good liars—these artisans and their craft must be religiously censured.

By directly linking politics and literature in a moral and reasoned worldview, Plato in his Academy founded a complex theory of literary criticism that initiated the debate, still ongoing, on the value, nature, and worth of the artist and literature itself.

ARISTOTLE (384–322 B.C.)

Whereas literary criticism's concern with morality began with Plato, its emphasis on the elements of which a work is composed began with Aristotle, Plato's famous pupil. Rejecting some of his teacher's beliefs about the nature of reality, Aristotle opts for a detailed investigation of the material world.

The son of a medical doctor from Thrace, Aristotle reveled in the physical world. After studying at the Academy and mastering the philosophy and the techniques of inquiry taught there, he founded the Lyceum, a school of scientific and philosophical thought and investigation. Applying his scientific methods of investigation to the study of literature, Aristotle answers Plato's accusations against poetry in a series of lectures known as the *Poetics*. Unlike **exoteric treatises** meant for general publication, the *Poetics* is an **esoteric work**, one meant for private circulation to those who attended the Lyceum. It therefore lacks the unity and coherence of Aristotle's other works, but it remains one of the most important critical influences on literary theory and criticism.

Aristotle's *Poetics* has become the cornerstone of Western literary criticism. By applying his analytic abilities to a definition of tragedy, Aristotle began in the *Poetics* a discussion of the components of a literary work that continues to the present day. Unfortunately, many critics and scholars mistakenly assume that the *Poetics* is a how-to manual, defining and setting the standards for literature (particularly tragedy) for all time. Aristotle's purpose, however, was not to formulate a series of absolute rules for evaluating a tragedy, but to state the general principles of tragedy, as he viewed them in his time, while at the same time responding to many of Plato's doctrines and arguments.

Even his title, the *Poetics,* reveals Aristotle's purpose, for in Greek the word *poetikes* means "things that are made or crafted." Like a biologist, Aristotle dissects tragedy to discover its component or crafted parts.

At the beginning of the *Poetics*, Aristotle notes that "epic poetry, tragedy, comedy, dithyrambic poetry, and most forms of flute and lyre playing all happen to be, in general, imitations." All seemingly differ in how and what they imitate, but Aristotle agrees with Plato that all the arts are imitations. In particular, the art of poetry exists because people are imitative creatures who enjoy such imitation. Whereas Plato contends that this is a pleasure that can undermine the structure of society and all its values, Aristotle strongly disagrees. His disagreement is basically a metaphysical argument concerning the nature of imitation itself. Whereas Plato posits that imitation is two steps removed from the truth or realm of the ideal (the poet imitating an object that is itself an imitation of an ideal form), Aristotle contends poetry is more universal, more general than things as they are. For, "it is not the function of the poet to relate what has happened, but what may happen—what is possible according to the law of probability or necessity." It is the historian, not the poet, who writes of what has already happened. The poet's task, declares Aristotle, is to write of what could happen. "Poetry, therefore, is a more philosophical and a higher thing than history: for poetry tends to express the universal, history the particular." In arguing that poets present things not as they are but as they should be, Aristotle rebuffs Plato's concept that the poet is merely imitating an imitation, for Aristotle's poet, with his emphasis on the universal, actually attains something nearer to the ideal than does Plato's.

In Aristotle's view, not all imitations by poets are the same, for "writers of greater dignity imitated the noble actions of noble heroes; the less dignified sort of writers imitated the actions of inferior men." "Comedy," writes Aristotle, "is an imitation of base men [. . .] characterized not by every kind of vice but specifically by 'the ridiculous,' some error or ugliness that is painless and has no harmful effects." It is to tragedy, written by poets imitating noble actions and heroes, that Aristotle turns his major attention.

Aristotle's complex definition of **tragedy** has perplexed and frustrated many readers:

> Tragedy is, then, an imitation of a noble and complete action, having the proper magnitude; it employs language that has been artistically enhanced by each of the kinds of linguistic adornment, applied separately in the various parts of the play; it is presented in dramatic, not narrative form, and achieves, through the representation of pitiable and fearful incidents, the catharsis of such pitiable and fearful incidents.

When put in context with other ideas in the *Poetics*, this complex definition highlights Aristotle's chief contributions to literary criticism:

1. Tragedy, or a work of art, is an imitation of nature that reflects a high form of art in exhibiting noble characters and noble deeds, the act of imitation itself giving us pleasure.
2. Art possesses form; that is, tragedy, unlike life, has a beginning, a middle, and an end, with each of the parts being related to every other part. A tragedy, then, is an organic whole, with its various parts all formally interrelated.
3. In tragedy, concern for form must be given to the characters as well as to the structure of the play, for the tragic hero must be "a man who is not eminently good and just, yet whose misfortune is brought about not by vice or depravity, but by some error or frailty. He must be one who is highly renowned and prosperous." In addition, all tragic heroes must have a tragic flaw, or **hamartia**, that leads to their downfall in such a way as not to offend the audience's sense of justice.
4. The tragedy must have an emotional effect on its audience and "through pity and fear" effect a **catharsis**; that is, by the play's end, the audience's emotions should be purged, purified, or clarified. (What Aristotle really meant by *catharsis* is debatable; see glossary entry under catharsis for further details).
5. The universal, not the particular, should be stressed, for unlike history, which deals with what happens, poetry or tragedy deals with what could happen and is therefore closer to perfection or truth.

6. The poet must give close attention to diction or language itself, be it in verse, prose, or song; but ultimately, it is the thoughts expressed through language that are of the utmost concern.

Interestingly, nowhere in the *Poetics* does Aristotle address the didactic value of poetry or literature. Unlike Plato, whose chief concern is the subject matter of poetry and its effects on the reader, Aristotle emphasizes literary form or structure, examining the component parts of a tragedy and how these parts must work together to produce a unified whole.

From the writings of philosopher–artists, Plato and Aristotle, arise the concerns, questions, and debates that have spearheaded the development of most literary criticism. By addressing different aspects of these fifth-century critics' ideas and concepts, other literary critics from the Middle Ages to the present have formulated theories of literary criticism that force us to ask different, but also legitimate, questions of a text. Nevertheless, the shadows of Plato and Aristotle loom over much of what these later theorists espouse.

HORACE (65–8 B.C.)

With the passing of the glory that was Greece and its philosopher–artists came the grandeur of Rome and its chief stylist, Quintus Horatius Flaccus or, simply, Horace. Friend of Emperor Augustus and many other members of the Roman aristocracy, Horace enjoyed the wealth and influence of these associates. In a letter to the sons of one of his friends and patrons, Maecenas, Horace articulated what became the official canon of literary taste during the Middle Ages, the Renaissance, and much of the Neoclassic period. By reading this letter and his *Ars Poetica* [The Art of Poetry], any Roman aristocrat, any medieval knight, and even Alexander Pope himself could learn the standards of good or proper literature.

Although Horace was probably acquainted with Aristotle's works, his concerns are quite different. Whereas both Plato and Aristotle decree that poets must, and do, imitate nature, Horace declares that poets must imitate other poets, particularly those of the past and especially the Greeks. Less concerned with **metaphysics** than his predecessors, Horace establishes the practical do's and don'ts for a writer. To be considered a good writer, he maintains, one should write about traditional subjects in unique ways. In addition, the poet should avoid all extremes in subject matter, diction (word choice), vocabulary, and style. Gaining mastery in these areas could be achieved by reading and following the examples of the classical Greek and Roman authors. For example, because authors of antiquity began their epics in the middle of things, all epics must begin **in medias res**. Above all, writers should avoid appearing ridiculous and must therefore aim their sights low, not attempting to be a new Virgil or Homer.

Literature's ultimate aim, declares Horace, is *"dulce et utile,"* to be "sweet and useful"; the best writings, he argues, both teach and delight. To achieve this goal, poets must understand their audience: The learned reader may want to be instructed, whereas others may simply read to be amused. The poet's task is to combine usefulness and delight in the same literary work.

Often oversimplified and misunderstood, Horace opts for giving the would-be writer practical guidelines for the author's craft, while leaving unattended and unchallenged many of the philosophical concerns of Plato and Aristotle. For Horace, a poet's greatest reward is the adulation of the public.

LONGINUS (FIRST CENTURY A.D.)

Although his date of birth and national origin remain controversial, Longinus garners an important place in literary history for his treatise *On the Sublime*. Probably a Greek, Longinus often peppers his Greek and Latin writings with Hebrew quotations, making him the first literary critic to borrow from a different literary tradition and earning him the title of the first comparative critic in literary history.

Unlike Plato, Aristotle, and Horace, who focus respectively on a work's essence, the constituent parts of a work, and literary taste, Longinus concentrates on single elements of a text, and he is the first critic to define a literary classic.

One cannot accurately judge a literary work, he argues, unless one is exceedingly well read. A well-read critic can evaluate and recognize what is great or what Longinus calls sublime: "For that is really great which bears a repeated examination, and which it is difficult or rather impossible to withstand, and the memory of which is strong and hard to efface." Longinus also contends that all readers are innately capable of recognizing the sublime, for "Nature has appointed us to be no base or ignoble animals [. . .] for she implants in our souls the unconquerable love of whatever is elevated and more divine than we." When our intellects, or emotions, and our wills harmoniously respond to a given work of art, we know we have been touched by the sublime.

Until the late seventeenth century, few people considered Longinus' *On the Sublime* important or had even read it. By the eighteenth century, its significance was recognized, and the treatise was quoted and debated by most public authors. Emphasizing the author (one who must possess a great mind and a great soul), the work itself (a text that must be composed of dignified and elevated diction while simultaneously disposing the reader to high thoughts), and the reader's response (the reaction of a learned audience in large part determines the value or worth of any given text), Longinus' critical method foreshadows New Criticism, reader-response, and other schools of twentieth-century criticism.

DANTE ALIGHIERI (1265–1321)

Born in Florence, Italy, during the Middle Ages, Dante is one of the most significant contributors to literary criticism since Longinus and the appearance of *On the Sublime* approximately 1000 years earlier. Like Longinus, Dante's concern is the proper language for poetry.

Banished from his native Florence for political reasons, Dante wrote many of his works in exile, including his masterpiece *The Divine Comedy* (written during the last twenty years of his life). As an introduction to the *Paradiso*, the third and last section of the *Commedia*, Dante wrote a letter to Can Grande della Scala explaining his literary theory. Known today as *Letter to Can Grande della Scala*, this work states that the language spoken by the people (the vulgar tongue or the vernacular) is an appropriate and beautiful language for writing.

Until the publication of Dante's works, Latin was the universal language, and all important works—such as histories, Church documents, and even government decrees—were written in this official Church tongue. Only frivolous or popular works appeared in the vulgar language of the common people. But in his *Letter*, Dante asserts and establishes that the vernacular is an excellent vehicle for works of literature.

In the *Letter*, Dante also notes that he uses multiple levels of interpretation or symbolic meaning in *The Divine Comedy*. Since the time of St. Augustine and throughout the Middle Ages, the Church fathers had followed a tradition of **allegoric reading** of Scripture that interpreted many of the Old Testament laws and stories as symbolic representations (allegories) of Christ's actions. Such a semiotic interpretation—reading of signs—had been applied only to Scripture. Until Dante's *Commedia*, no secular work had used these principles of symbolic interpretation.

Praising the lyric poem and ignoring a discussion of genres, Dante established himself as the leading, if not the only, significant critic of the Middle Ages. Because he declared the common tongue an acceptable vehicle of expression for literature, literary works found an ever-increasing audience.

SIR PHILIP SIDNEY (1554–1586)

The paucity of literary criticism and theory during the Middle Ages is more than made up for by the abundance of critical activity during the Renaissance. One critic of this period far excels all others: Sir Philip Sidney.

The representative scholar, writer, and gentleman of Renaissance England, Sidney is usually considered the first great English critic–poet. His work *An Apology for Poetry* (published 1595; originally *Defence of Poesy*) is the definitive formulation of Renaissance literary theory and the first influential piece of literary criticism in English history. With Sidney begins the English tradition and history of literary criticism.

As evidenced in *An Apology for Poetry*, Sidney is eclectic, borrowing and often amending the theories of Plato, Aristotle, Horace, and a few of his contemporary Italian critics. He begins his criticism by quoting from Aristotle: He writes, "Poesy therefore is an art of imitation, for so Aristotle termeth it in his word **mimesis**, that is to say, a representing, counterfeiting, or figuring forth." Eight words later, however, he adds a Horatian note, declaring poesy's chief end to be "to teach and delight." Like Aristotle, Sidney values poetry over history, law, and philosophy; but he takes Aristotle's idea one step further in declaring that poetry, above all the other arts and sciences, embodies truth.

Unlike critics before him, Sidney best personifies the Renaissance period when he dictates his literary precepts. After ranking the different literary genres and declaring all to be instructive, he declares poetry to excel all. He mocks other genres (tragicomedy, for example) and adds more dictates to Aristotelian tragedy by insisting on unity of action, time, and place.

Throughout *An Apology for Poetry*, Sidney stalwartly defends poetry against those who would view it as a mindless or immoral activity. By the essay's end, a passionate and somewhat platonically inspired poet places a curse on all those who do not love poetry. Echoes of such emotionality reverberate throughout the centuries in English literature, especially in British romantic writings of the early 1800s.

JOHN DRYDEN (1631–1700)

More than any other English writer, poet laureate, dramatist, and critic John Dryden embodies the spirit and ideals of the Neoclassical period, the literary age that follows Sidney and the Renaissance. Dr. Samuel Johnson attributes to Dryden "the improvement, perhaps the completion of our meter, the refinement of our language, and much of the correctness of our sentiments." The most prolific writer of the Restoration (the name given to that period of English literature from 1660 to 1700), Dryden excelled in almost all genres.

His lasting contribution to literary criticism, *An Essay of Dramatic Poesy* (1668), highlights his genius in most of these genres.

The structure of Dryden's *An Essay of Dramatic Poesy* reflects his brilliance: During a naval battle between the English and the Dutch, four men are floating down a barge on the Thames River, each supporting a different aesthetic theory among those prominently espoused in Renaissance and Neoclassical literary criticism. The Platonic and Aristotelian debate concerning the nature or inherent condition of art as an imitation of nature itself begins the discussion. Nature, argues one debater, must be imitated directly, whereas another declares that writers should imitate the classical authors such as Homer, for such ancient writers were the best imitators of nature. Through the voice of Neander, Dryden presents the benefits of both positions.

A lengthy discussion then ensues over the Aristotelian concept of the three unities of time, place, and action within a drama. Should the plot of a drama take place during one twenty-four-hour cycle (time)? And in one location (place)? Should it be only a single plot, with no subplots (action)? The position that a drama must keep the three unities unquestionably wins the debate.

Other concerns center on the following:

1. The language or diction of a play, with the concluding emphasis being placed on "proper" speech;
2. Issues of decorum—that is, whether violent acts should appear on the stage, with the final speaker declaring it would be quite "improper";
3. The differences between the English and French theaters, with the English drama winning out for its diversity, its use of the stage, and its Shakespearian tradition; and
4. The value of rhymed as opposed to blank verse in the drama, with rhymed verse the victor—although Dryden later recanted this position and wrote many of his tragedies in blank verse.

A reflection of his age in his life and works, Dryden sides with politesse (courteous formality), clarity, order, decorum, elegance, cleverness, and wit as controlling characteristics of literary works.

ALEXANDER POPE (1688–1744)

Born into a Roman Catholic family in a Protestant-controlled England, born a healthy infant but soon deformed and twisted in body by spinal tuberculosis, and born at the beginning of the Neoclassical age (English literature from 1660 to 1798) and becoming its literary voice by age twenty, Alexander Pope embodies in his writings eighteenth-century thought and literary criticism. His early poems such as *The Rape of the Lock,* "Eloisa to Abelard," and "Pastorals" establish him as a major British poet, but with the publication of his *Essay on Criticism* (1711), he becomes for all practical purposes the "literary pope" of England.

Unlike previous literary critics and theorists, Pope in this essay directly addresses the critic rather than the poet, as he undertakes to codify Neoclassical literary criticism. Toward the end of the essay, however, he does speak to both critics and poets.

According to Pope, the golden age of criticism is the classical age, the age of Homer, Aristotle, Horace, and Longinus. They are the writers who discovered the laws of a harmonious and ordered nature. It is the critic and the poet's task first to know and then to copy these authors and not nature, for "To copy nature is to copy them [the classical authors]."

Pope asserts that the chief requirement of a good poet is natural genius, coupled with a knowledge of the classics and an understanding of the rules of poetry (literature). Such knowledge must be tempered with politeness and grace, for "Without good breeding truth is disapproved/ That only makes superior sense beloved."

Natural genius and good breeding being established, the critic/poet must then give heed to certain rules, says Pope. To be a good critic or poet, one must follow the established traditions as defined by the ancients. Not surprisingly, Pope spells out what these rules are and how they should be applied to eighteenth-century verse. Great concern for poetic diction, the establishment of the heroic couplet as a standard for verse, and the personification of abstract ideas, for example, became fixed standards, whereas emotional outbreaks and free verse were *extraordinaire* and considered unrefined.

Governed by rules, restraint, and good taste, poetry, as defined by Pope, seeks to reaffirm truths or absolutes already discovered by the classical writers. The critic's task is clear: to validate and maintain classical values in the ever-shifting flux of cultural change. In effect, the critic becomes the custodian and defender of good taste and cultural values.

By affirming the imitation of the classical writers and through them of nature itself, and by establishing the acceptable or standard criteria of poetic language, Pope grounds his criticism in both the **mimetic** (imitation) and **rhetoric** (patterns of structure) literary theories. By the end of the 1700s, however, a major shift in literary theory occurs.

WILLIAM WORDSWORTH (1770–1850)

By the close of the eighteenth century, the world had witnessed several major political rebellions, among them the American and French Revolutions, along with extreme social upheavals and prominent changes in philosophical thought. During this age of rebellion, a paradigmatic shift occurred in how people viewed the world. Whereas the eighteenth-century valued order and reason, the emerging nineteenth-century worldview emphasized intuition as a proper guide to truth. The eighteenth-century mind likened the world to a great machine, with all its parts operating harmoniously, but in the nineteenth-century, the world was perceived as a living organism that was always growing and eternally becoming. The city housed the centers of art and literature and set the standards of good taste for the rationalistic mind of the eighteenth century. In contrast, the emerging nineteenth-century citizen saw rural places as fundamental, as the setting in which a person could discover the inner self. Devaluing the empirical and rationalistic methodologies of the previous century, the nineteenth-century thinker believed that truth could be attained by tapping into the core of our humanity or our transcendental natures, best sought in our original or natural setting.

Such radical changes found their spokesperson in William Wordsworth. Born in Cockermouth, Cumberlandshire, and raised in the Lake District of England, Wordsworth completed his formal education at St. John's College, Cambridge, in 1791. After completing his grand tour of the Continent, he published *Descriptive Sketches* and then met one of his literary admirers and soon-to-be friends and coauthors, Samuel T. Coleridge. In 1798 Wordsworth and Coleridge published *Lyrical Ballads*, a collection of poems that heralded the beginning of British romanticism. In the ensuing fifteen-year period, Wordsworth wrote most of his best poetry, including *Poems in Two Volumes*, *The Excursion, Miscellaneous Poems*, and *The Prelude*. But it is *Lyrical Ballads* that ushers in the Romantic age in English literature.

In an explanatory preface written as an introduction to the second edition of *Lyrical Ballads*, Wordsworth espouses a new vision of poetry and the beginnings of a radical change in literary theory. His purpose, he notes, is "to choose incidents and situations from common life, and [. . .] describe them in language really used by [people] in situations [. . .] the manner in which we associate ideas in a state of excitement." Like Aristotle, Sidney, and Pope, Wordsworth concerns himself with the elements and subject matter of literature, but changes the emphasis: Common men and women people his poetry, not kings, queens, and aristocrats, for in "humble and rustic life" the poet finds that "the essential passions of the heart find a better soil in which they can attain their maturity, are less under restraint, and speak a plainer and more emphatic language."

Not only does Wordsworth suggest a radical change in subject matter but he also dramatically shifts the focus of poetry's "proper language." Unlike Pope and his predecessors, Wordsworth chooses "language really used by [people]"—everyday speech, not the inflated poetic diction of heroic couplets, complicated rhyme schemes, and convoluted figures of speech placed in the mouths of the typical eighteenth-century character. Wordsworth's rustics, such as Michael and Luke in his poetic narrative "Michael," speak in the simple, everyday diction of their trade.

In addition to reshaping the focus of poetry's subject and language, Wordsworth redefines poetry itself: "For all good poetry is the spontaneous overflow of powerful feelings." Unlike Sidney, Dante, and Pope, who decree that poetry should be restrained, controlled, and reasoned, Wordsworth now highlights poetry's emotional quality. Imagination, not reason or disciplined thought, becomes its core.

In altering poetry's subject matter, language, and definition, Wordsworth redefines the role of the poet. The poet is no longer the preserver of civilized values or proper taste, but "he is a man speaking to men: a man [. . .] endowed with more lively sensibility, more enthusiasm and tenderness, who has a greater knowledge of human nature and a more comprehensive soul than are supposed to be common among mankind." Wordsworth's poet "has acquired a greater readiness and power in expressing what he thinks and feels, and especially those thoughts and feelings which, by his own choice, or from the structure of his own mind, arise in him without immediate external excitement." Such a poet need no longer follow a prescribed set of rules, for this artist may freely express his or her own individualism, valuing and writing about feelings that are peculiarly the artist's.

Because he defines poetry as "the spontaneous overflow of powerful feelings [. . .] [taking] its origin from emotion recollected in tranquility," Wordsworth's new kind of poet crafts a poem by internalizing a scene, circumstance, or happening and "recollects" that occasion with its accompanying emotions at a later time when the artist can shape the remembrance into words. Poetry, then, is unlike biology or one of the other sciences, for it deals not with something that can be dissected or broken down into its constituent parts, but primarily with the imagination and feelings. Intuition, not reason, reigns.

What then of the reader? What part does the audience play in such a process? Toward the end of the "Preface to *Lyrical Ballads*," Wordsworth writes, "I have one request to make of my reader, which is, that in judging these poems he would decide by his own feelings genuinely, and not by reflection upon what will probably be the judgement of others." Wordsworth apparently hopes that his readers' responses to and opinions of his poems will not depend on critics who would freely dispense their evaluations. Wordsworth wants his readers to rely on their own feelings and their own imaginations, as they grapple with the same emotions the poet felt when he first saw and then later "recollected in tranquility" the subject or circumstances of the poem itself. Through poetry, declares Wordsworth, the poet and the reader share such emotions.

This subjective experience of sharing emotions leads Wordsworth away from the preceding centuries' mimetic and rhetorical theories of criticism and toward a new development in literary theory: the **expressive school**, which emphasizes the individuality of the artist and the reader's privilege to share in this individuality. By expressing such individuality and valuing the emotions and the imagination as legitimate concerns in poetry, Wordsworth lays the foundation for English romanticism and broadens the scope of literary criticism and theory for both the nineteenth and twentieth centuries.

HIPPOLYTE ADOLPHE TAINE (1828–1893)

Wordsworth's romanticism, with its stress on intuition as a guide to learning ultimate truth and its belief that emotions and the imagination form the core of poetry's content, dominated literature and literary criticism throughout the first three decades of the nineteenth century, and its influence still continues today. With the rise of the Victorian era in the 1830s, reason, science, and a sense of historical determinism began to supplant Romantic thought. The growing sense of historical and scientific determinism finally found its authoritative voice and culminating influence in Charles Darwin and his text *On the Origin of Species*, published in 1859. Humankind was now demystified, for we finally knew our origins and understood our physiological development; science, it seemed, had provided us with the key to our past and an understanding of the present, and would help us determine our future if we relied on the scientific method in all our human endeavors.

Science's methodology, its philosophical assumptions, and its practical applications found an admiring adherent and a strong voice in French historian and literary critic Hippolyte Taine. Born in Vouziers, France, Hippolyte Taine was a brilliant but unorthodox student at the École Normale Supérieure in Paris. After finishing his formal education, he taught in various schools throughout France, continuing his investigations in both aesthetics and history. During the 1850s, he published various philosophical and aesthetic treatises, but his chief contribution to literary criticism and history is *The History of English Literature*, published in 1863. In this work, Taine crystallizes what is now known as the historical approach to literary analysis.

In the introduction to *The History of English Literature*, Taine uses a scientific simile to explain his approach to literary criticism:

> What is your first remark on turning over the great, stiff leaves of a folio, the yellow sheets of a manuscript,—a poem, a code of laws, a declaration of faith? This, you say was not created alone. It is but a mould, like fossil shell, an imprint, like one of those shapes embossed in stone by an animal which lived and perished. Under the shell there was an animal, and behind the document there was a man. Why do you study the shell, except to represent to yourself the animal? So do you study the document only in order to know the man.

For Taine, then, a text is like a fossil shell that naturally contains the likeness of its inhabiter, who in this case is the author. To study only the text (discovering its date of composition or the accuracy of its historical references or allusions, for example) without considering the author and his or her inner psyche would therefore result in an incomplete analysis. An investigation of both the text and the author, Taine believed, would result in an accurate understanding of the literary work.

Taine asserts that to understand any literary text, we must examine the environmental causes that joined together in its creation. He divides such influences into four main categories: race, milieu, moment, and dominant faculty. By race, Taine posits that authors of the same race, or those born and raised in the same country, share peculiar intellectual beliefs, emotions, and ways of understanding. By examining each author's inherited and learned personal characteristics, Taine believes we will then be able to understand more fully the author's text. In addition, we must also examine the author's milieu or surroundings. English citizens, he believed, respond differently to life than do French or Irish citizens. Accordingly, by examining the culture of the author, Taine proposes that we would understand more fully the intellectual and cultural concerns that inevitably surface in an author's text. Further, Taine maintains that we must investigate an author's epoch or moment—that is, the time period in which the text was written. Such information reveals the dominant ideas or worldview held by people at that particular time and therefore helps us identify and understand the characters' actions, motivations, and concerns more fully than if we did not have such information. Finally, Taine decrees we must examine each author's individual talents that make him or her different from others who share similar characteristics of race, milieu, and moment. For Taine, a work of art is "the result of given causes" and can best be represented by using the following formula: race + milieu + moment + dominant faculty = work of art. Taine argues that we cannot therefore appreciate art as it "really" is without considering all four of his stated elements.

Ultimately, for Taine, the text becomes a literary object that can be dissected to discover its meaning. By examining the actual text itself, the circumstances of place and race, the historical times in which the text was written, and each author's individual talents, we will realize, Taine asserts, that no text is written in a vacuum, but is instead the result of its history.

MATTHEW ARNOLD (1822–1888)

In the "Preface to *Lyrical Ballads,*" Wordsworth declares that "poetry is the breath and finer spirit of all knowledge; it is the impassioned expression which is the countenance of all science." Such a lofty statement concerning the nature and role of poetry finds an advocate in Matthew Arnold, the self-appointed voice for English Victorianism, the literary epoch immediately following Wordsworth's romanticism.

Born during the Romantic era, Matthew Arnold was the son of an English educator. Following in his family's tradition, Arnold attended Oxford, and upon graduation accepted a teaching position at Oriel College. He spent most of his professional life (nearly 35 years) as an inspector of schools. By age 35, he had already written the majority of his poetry, including "Dover Beach," "The Scholar-Gipsy," and "Sohrab and Rustum," some of his most famous poems.

During Arnold's early career, reactions against Wordsworth's romanticism and its adherents began to occur. Writers, philosophers, and scientists began to give more credence to empirical and rationalistic methods for discovering the nature of their world rather than to Wordsworthian concepts of emotion, individualism, and intuition as pathways to truth. With the publication of Charles Darwin's *On the Origin of Species* in 1859 and the writings of philosopher and sociologist Herbert Spencer (1820–1903) and German theologian and philosopher David Friedrich Strauss (1808–1874), science seemingly usurped the place of Wordsworth's "religion of nature" and the beliefs of most other traditional religions. At the same time, however, philosophy became too esoteric and therefore less relevant as a vehicle for understanding reality for the average Victorian. Into this void stepped Arnold, proclaiming that poetry can provide the necessary truths, values, and guidelines for society.

Fundamental to Arnold's literary criticism is his reapplication of classical criteria to literature. Quotes and borrowed ideas from Plato, Aristotle, Longinus, and other classical writers pepper his criticism. From Aristotle's *Poetics*, for example, Arnold adapts his idea that the best poetry is of a "higher truth and seriousness" than history—or any other human subject or activity, for that matter. Like Plato, Arnold believes that literature reflects the society in which it is written and thereby heralds its values and concerns. Like Longinus, he attempts to define a classic and decrees that such a work belongs to the "highest" or "best class." And in attempting to support many of his other ideas, he also cites the later "classical" writers such as Dante, Shakespeare, and Milton.

For Arnold, poetry—not religion, science, or philosophy—is humankind's crowning activity. He notes, "More and more [human]kind will discover that we have to turn to poetry to interpret life for us, to console us, to sustain us. Without poetry, our science will appear incomplete; and most of what now passes with us for religion and philosophy will be replaced by poetry." And in the best of this poetry, he declares, we find "in the eminent degree, truth and seriousness." Equating "seriousness" with moral excellence, Arnold asserts that the best poetry can and does provide standards of excellence, a yardstick by which both Arnold and his society should judge themselves.

In his pivotal essays "The Study of Poetry" and "The Function of Criticism at the Present Time," Arnold crystallizes his critical position. Like Plato's critic, Arnold reaffirms but slightly amends the social role of criticism: creating "a current of true and fresh ideas." To accomplish this goal, the critic must avoid becoming embroiled in politics or any other activity that would lead to a form of bias, for the critic must view society disinterestedly, keeping aloof from the world's mundane affairs. In turn, such aloofness will benefit all of society, for the critic will be able to pave the way for high culture—a prerequisite for the poet and the writing of the best poetry.

How then may the best poetry be achieved or discovered? By establishing objective criteria whereby we can judge whether any poem contains or achieves, in Aristotelian terms, "higher truth or seriousness." The critic's task is "to have always in one's mind lines and expressions of the great masters, and to apply them as a touchstone to other poetry." By comparing the newly written lines to classical poems that contain elements of the "sublime," the critic will instantly know whether a new poem is good or bad.

In practice, such apparent objectivity in criticism becomes quite subjective. Whose judgments, for example, shall we follow? Shall lines written by Homer and Dante be considered excellent? How about Sidney's or even Aristophanes'? Need the critic rank all past poets in an attempt to discover who is great and who is not in order to create a basis for such comparisons and value judgments? And whose moral values shall become the yardstick with which we judge poetry? Arnold's only?

Such "objective" touchstone theory redefines the task of the literary critic and introduces a subjective approach in literary criticism. No longer the interpreter of a literary work, the critic now functions as an authority on values, culture, and tastes. This new literary "watchdog" must guard and defend high culture and its literature, while simultaneously defining what high culture and literature really are.

Decreeing the critic to be the preserver of society's values and poetry to be its most important activity, Arnold became the recognized spokesperson for Victorian England and its literature. By taking Wordsworth's concept of the poet one step further, Arnold separated both the critic and the poet from society in order to create a type of poetry and criticism that could supposedly rescue society from its baser elements and preserve its most noble characteristics.

HENRY JAMES (1843–1916)

While Arnold was decreeing how poetry would rescue humanity from its baser elements and would help lead us all to truth, literary works were also being written in other genres, particularly the novel. Throughout both the Romantic and Victorian eras, for example, people in England and America were reading such works as *Wuthering Heights, Vanity Fair, The House of the Seven Gables*, and *Great Expectations*. Few, however, were providing for either the writers or the readers of this genre a body of theory or criticism comparable to that continually being formulated for poetry. As Henry James notes in his critical essay "The Art of Fiction" in 1884, the English novel "had no air of having a theory, a conviction, a consciousness of itself behind it—of being the expression of an artistic faith, the result of choice and comparison." It was left to James himself to provide us with such a theory.

Born in New York City in 1843, Henry James enjoyed the privileges of education, travel, and money. Throughout his early life, he and his family (including his brother William, the father of American pragmatic philosophy) traveled to the capitals of Europe, visiting the sites and meeting the leading writers and scholars of the day. Having all things European early injected into his life and thoughts, James believed he wanted to be a lawyer and enrolled in Harvard Law School. He quickly discovered that writing, not law, captivated him and abandoned law school for a career in writing. By 1875, the early call of Europe on his life had to be answered, and James, a bachelor for life, settled permanently in Europe and began in earnest his writing career.

Noted for his short stories—"The Real Thing," "The Beast in the Jungle," and "The Jolly Corner," to name a few—and his novels—*The American, The Portrait of a Lady, The Bostonians*, and *The Turn of the Screw,* among others—James's favorite theme is the conflict he perceives between Europe and America. The seasoned aristocracy with its refined manners and taste is often infiltrated in his stories by the naive American who seemingly lacks refined culture and discernment. Though a very involved practicing writer, James was also concerned with developing a theory of writing, particularly for the novel. Indeed, in his critical essay "The Art of Fiction," he provides us with the first well-articulated theory of the novel in English literature.

James states in "The Art of Fiction" that "a novel is in its broadest definition a personal, a direct impression of life: that, to begin with, constitutes its value, which is greater or less according to the intensity of the impression"; furthermore, "the only obligation to which in advance we may hold a novel, without incurring the accusation of being arbitrary, is that it be interesting. The ways in which it is at liberty to accomplish this result [are] innumerable." From the start, James's theory rejects the romantic notion of either Wordsworth or Coleridge that the reader suspend disbelief while reading a text. For James, a text must first be realistic, a representation of life as it is and one that is recognizable to its readers. Bad novels, declares James, are either romantic or scientific; good novels show us life in action and, above all else, are interesting.

Bad novels, James continues, are written by bad authors, whereas good novels are written by good authors. Unlike weak authors, good writers are good thinkers who can select, evaluate, and imaginatively utilize the "stuff of life" (the facts or pictures of reality) in their work. These writers also recognize that a work of art is organic. The work itself is not simply the amassing of realistic data from real life experiences but has a life of its own that grows according to its own principles or themes. The writer must acknowledge this fact and distance himself or herself from directly telling the story. Shunning the omniscient, third-person narrator as a vehicle for telling a story, James asserts that a more indirect point of view is essential so that the author shows characters, actions, and emotions to readers rather than telling us about them. By showing rather than telling us about his characters and their actions, James believes that he creates a greater illusion of reality than if he were to present his story through one point of view or one character. Ultimately, however, the reader must decide the worth of the text, and "nothing of course, will ever take the place of the good old fashion liking of a work of art or not liking it: the most improved criticism will not abolish that primitive, that ultimate test."

Thanks to Henry James, the genre of the novel became a respectable topic for literary critics. With his emphasis on realism and "the stuff of life," James formulated a theory of fiction that is still discussed and debated today.

MODERN LITERARY CRITICISM

Matthew Arnold's death in 1888 (and to a lesser degree Henry James's death in 1916) marked a transitional period in literary criticism. Like Dryden, Pope, and Wordsworth before him, Arnold was the recognized authority and leading literary critic of his day, and it is his theories and criticism that embody the major ideas of his era. With the passing of Arnold, the predominance of any one person or set of ideas representing a broad time period or literary movement ends. After Arnold, literary theory and criticism become splintered and more diversified, with no one voice speaking ex cathedra or no one theory tenaciously held by all. At the end of the nineteenth century, most critics emphasized either a biographical or historical approach to the text. Using Taine's historical interests in a text and Henry James's newly articulated theory of the novel, many critics investigated a text as if it were the embodiment of its author or a historical artifact. No single, universally recognized voice dominates literary theory in the years that follow Arnold or James. Instead, many distinctive literary voices give rise to a host of differing and exciting ways to examine a text.

What follows in the twentieth century is a variety of schools of criticism, with each school asking legitimate, relevant but different questions about a text. Most of these schools abandon the **holistic approach** to literary study, which investigates, analyzes, and interprets all elements of the artistic situation, in favor of concentrating on one or more specific aspects. For example, modernism (and, in particular, the New Criticism, the first critical movement of the twentieth century) wishes to break from the past and seemingly disavow cultural influences on a work of literature. The text, these critics declare, will interpret the text. On the other hand, Cultural Poetics, a school of criticism that first appeared in the 1980s and continues to develop its underlying assumptions and methodologies to the present day, argues that most critics' historical consciousness must be reawakened because, in reality, the fictional text and its historical and cultural milieu are amazingly similar. For these critics, a reader can never fully discern the truth about a historical or a literary text since truth itself is perceived differently from one era to another. The text-only criticism of the early and mid twentieth century therefore appears biased and incomplete to those espousing the principles of Cultural Poetics.

In the remaining chapters of this book, we will examine eleven of the most prominent schools of twentieth-century interpretation. For each of these diverse schools, we will note the tenets of the philosophy underlying their literary theory. Most, if not all, have borrowed ideas, principles, and concerns from the literary critics and theories already discussed. We will examine closely what they borrow from these past schools of criticism, what they amend, and what concepts they add. We will also note each school's historical development, examining how new schools of criticism often appear as a reaction to previously existing ones.

After explaining each school's historical development, its working assumptions, and its methodology, we will then examine a student-written essay that interprets a text from the point of view of the particular school of criticism under discussion. A close examination of such essays will allow us to see how the theories of the various schools of criticism can be applied directly to a text and, simultaneously, to evaluate the different emphases of each critical school.

In becoming acquainted with these schools of criticism, we also undertake to examine our own theory of interpretation and to articulate our own principles of criticism. We will then come to realize that there is no such thing as an innocent reading of a text, for all readings presuppose either a conscious or unconscious, articulated and well-informed or piecemeal and uninformed reading of a literary work. An informed and intelligent reading is by far the better option.

FURTHER READING

Adams, Hazard. *Critical Theory Since Plato.* 2nd ed. New York: Harcourt, 1992.

Adams, Hazard, and Leroy Searle, eds. *Critical Theory Since 1965.* Parkland, FL: University Press of Florida, 1986.

Atkins, G. Douglas, and Laura Morrow, eds. *Contemporary Literary Theory.* Amherst: University of Massachusetts Press, 1989.

Con Davis, Robert, and Ronald Schleifer, eds. *Contemporary Literary Criticism and Theory: Literary and Cultural Studies.* 4th ed. Boston: Addison-Wesley, 1998.

Cuddon, J. A., and Claire Preston. *A Dictionary of Literary Terms and Literary Theory.* 4th ed. Oxford: Blackwell, 1998.

Docherty, Thomas. *Alterities: Criticism, History, Representation.* Oxford: Oxford University Press, 1996.

Harland, Richard. *Literary Theory From Plato to Barthes: An Introductory History.* New York: Palgrave, 1999.

Hutner, Gordon, ed. *The American Literary History Reader.* Oxford: Oxford University Press, 1995.

Leitch, Vincent B., ed. *The Norton Anthology of Theory and Criticism.* New York: Norton, 2001.

Rice, Philip, and Patricia Waugh, eds. *Modern Literary Theory: A Reader.* 4th ed. London: Edward Arnold, 2001.

Selden, Raman, and Peter Widdowson. *A Reader's Guide to Contemporary Literary Theory.* 4th ed. Upper Saddle River: Prentice, 1997.

Wimsatt, William K., and Cleanth Brooks. *Literary Criticism: A Short History.* New York: Knopf, 1964.

3

New Criticism

And though one may consider a poem as an instance of historical or ethical documentation, the poem itself, if literature is to be studied as literature, remains finally the object for study. A poem should always be treated as an organic system of relationships, and the poetic quality should never be understood as inhering in one or more factors taken in isolation.

Cleanth Brooks and Robert Penn Warren, *Understanding Poetry,*
1938

INTRODUCTION

Sacramental Vision

Sometimes in my dream	
he is still alive.	
We stand at the fence	
talking about the garden.	
"Plant kohlrabi," he says,	5
and I remember the way	
he'd slice white wafers	
from the bulb, offering	
them to me balanced	
on his knife blade.	10
I would eat again	
that sharp sacrament	
and join myself	
to that good world	
he walks, but I wake	15
in time	
and know my flesh is one	
with frailty. The garden	
I must tend is dark	
with weeping, grown up	20
in widow's weeds.	

John Leax, *The Task of Adam,* 1985

If John Leax's poem "Sacramental Vision" were to be taught in most high school or introductory-level college literature courses, the instructor would probably begin the discussion with a set of questions that contain most, if not all, of the following: What is the meaning of the title? What is the title's relationship to the rest of the poem? Who is the *he* in line two? What is *kohlrabi*? What is a *sacrament*? Are there other words in the text that need to be defined? What words connote sharpness? How are these words related to the garden discussed in the poem? Is Leax discussing any particular garden, or all gardens in general? Can this word be an allusion to some other garden in the canon of Western literature? Is Leax establishing any other relationships between words or concepts in the text? What of the poem's physical structure? Does the arrangement of the words, phrases, or sentences help establish relationships among them? What is the poem's tone? How do you know this is the tone? What tensions does Leax create in the poem? What ambiguities? Based on the answers to these, what does the poem mean? In other words, what is the poem's form or its overall meaning and interpretation?

Upon close examination of these discussion questions, a distinct pattern or methodology quickly becomes evident. This interpretive model begins with a close analysis of the poem's individual words, including both denotative and connotative meanings, and then moves to a discussion of possible allusions within the text. Following this discussion, the critic searches for any patterns developed through individual words, phrases, sentences, figures of speech, and allusions. The critic's sharp eye also notes any **symbols**, either **public** or **private** images that represent or stand for something else, used by the poet. Other elements for analysis include point of view, tone, and any other poetic device that will help the reader understand the dramatic situation. After ascertaining how all the above information interrelates and coalesces in the poem, the critic can declare what the poem means. The poem's overall meaning or form, then, depends solely on the text in front of the reader. No library research, no studying of the author's life and times, and no other extraneous information is needed; the poem itself contains all the necessary information to discover its meaning.

This method of analysis became the dominant school of thought during the first two thirds of the twentieth century in most high school and college literature classes and in British and American scholarship. Known as **New Criticism**, this approach to literary analysis provides the reader with a formula for arriving at the correct interpretation of a text using only the text itself. Such a formulaic approach gives both the beginning student of literature and academicians a seemingly objective approach for discovering a text's meaning. Using New Criticism's clearly articulated methodology, any intelligent reader, say its adherents (called **New Critics**), can uncover a text's hitherto hidden meaning.

New Criticism's theoretical ideas, terminology, and critical methods are, more often than not, disparaged by present-day critics who themselves are introducing new ideas concerning literary theory. Despite its current unpopularity, New Criticism stands as one of the most important English-based contributions to literary critical analysis. Its easily repeatable principles, teachability, and seemingly undying popularity in the literature classroom and in some scholarly journals have enabled New Criticism to enrich theoretical and practical criticism while helping generations of readers to become **close readers** of texts.

The term *New Criticism* came into popular use to describe this approach to understanding literature with the 1941 publication of John Crowe Ransom's *The New Criticism*, which contained Ransom's personal analysis of several of his contemporary theorists and critics. Ransom himself was a Southern poet, a critic, and one of the leading advocates of this evolving movement. While teaching at Vanderbilt University in the 1920s, Ransom, along with several other professors and students, formed the Fugitives, a group that believed in and practiced similar interpretative approaches to a text. Other sympathetic groups, such as the Southern Agrarians (also in Nashville, Tennessee), soon formed. In *The New Criticism*, Ransom articulates the principles of these various groups and calls for an **ontological critic**, one who will recognize that a **poem** (used as a synonym in New Criticism for any literary work) is a concrete entity, as is Leonardo da Vinci's *Mona Lisa* or the score of Handel's *Messiah* or any chemical element, such as iron or gold. Like these concrete objects, a poem can be analyzed to discover its true or correct meaning independent of its author's intention or of the emotional state, values or beliefs of either its author or reader. Because this claim rests at the center of the movement's critical ideas, it is not surprising that the title of Ransom's book quickly became the official name for this approach to literary analysis.

Called modernism, formalism, aesthetic criticism, textual criticism, or ontological criticism throughout its long and successful history, New Criticism does not represent a coherent body of critical theory and methodology espoused by all its followers. At best, New Criticism and its adherents (New Critics) are an eclectic group, each challenging, borrowing, and changing terminology, theory, and practices from one another while asserting a common core of basic ideas. Their ultimate unity stems from their opposition to the prevailing methods of literary analysis found in academia in the first part of the twentieth century.

HISTORICAL DEVELOPMENT

At the beginning of the twentieth century (often said to mark the start of **modernism** or the modernist period), historical and biographical research dominated literary scholarship. Criticism's function, many believed, was to discover the historical context of a text and to ascertain how the authors' lives influenced their writings. Such **extrinsic analysis** (examining elements outside the text to uncover the text's meaning) became the norm in the literature departments of many American universities and colleges. Other forms of criticism and interpretation were often intermingled with this prominent emphasis on history and biography. For example, some critics believed we should appreciate the text for its beauty. For these **impressionistic critics**, how we feel and what we personally see in a work of art are what really matters. Others were more philosophical, arguing a naturalistic view of life that emphasizes the importance of scientific thought in literary analysis. For advocates of **naturalism**, human beings are simply animals who are caught in a world that operates on definable scientific principles and who respond somewhat instinctively to their environment and internal drives. Still other critics, the **New Humanists**, valued the moral qualities of art. Declaring that human experience is basically ethical, these critics demanded that literary analysis be based on the moral values exhibited in a text. Finally, remnants of nineteenth-century **romanticism** asserted themselves. For the romantic scholar, literary study concerns itself with the artists' feelings and attitudes exhibited in their work. Known as the **expressive school**, this romantic view values the individual artist's experiences as evidenced in a text.

Along with impressionism, the New Humanism, and naturalism, this romantic view of life and art was rejected by the New Critics. In declaring the objective existence of the poem, the New Critics assert that only the poem itself can be objectively evaluated, not the feelings, attitudes, values, and beliefs of the author or the reader. Because they concern themselves primarily with an examination of the work itself and not its historical context or biographical elements, the New Critics belong to a broad classification of literary criticism called **formalism**. As formalists, the New Critics espouse what many call "the text and text alone" approach to literary analysis.

Their approach to textual criticism automatically leads to multiple and divergent views about the elements that constitute what the New Critics call the poem. Because many of the practitioners of this formalistic criticism disagree with each other concerning the various elements that make up the poem, and also hold differing approaches to textual analysis, it is difficult to cite a definitive list of critics who consider themselves New Critics. However, we can group together critics who hold to some of the same New Critical assumptions of poetic analysis. Among this group are John Crowe Ransom, René Wellek, W. K. Wimsatt, and R. P. Blackmur, I. A. Richards, Robert Penn Warren, and Cleanth Brooks. Thanks to the publication of the 1938 college text *Understanding Poetry: An Anthology for College Students* by Brooks and Warren, New Criticism emerged in American universities as the leading form of textual analysis throughout the late 1930s until the early 1960s.

Although New Criticism emerged as a powerful force in the 1940s, its roots stem from the early 1900s. Two British critics and authors, T. S. Eliot and I. A. Richards, helped lay the foundation for this form of formalistic analysis. From Eliot, New Criticism borrows its insistence that criticism be directed toward the poem, not the poet. The poet, declares Eliot, does not infuse the poem with his or her personality and emotions, but uses language in such a way as to incorporate within the poem the impersonal feelings and emotions common to all humankind. Poetry is not, then, the freeing of the poet's emotions, but an escape from them. Because the poem is an impersonal formulation of common feelings and emotions, the successful poem unites the poet's impressions and ideas with those common to all humanity, producing a text that is not a mere reflection of the poet's personal feelings.

The New Critics also borrow Eliot's belief that the reader of poetry must be instructed in literary technique. A good reader perceives the poem structurally, maintains Eliot, resulting in good criticism. Such a reader must necessarily be trained in reading good poetry (especially the poetry of the Elizabethans, John Donne, and other metaphysical poets), and be well acquainted with established poetic traditions. A poor reader, on the other hand, simply expresses his or her personal emotions and reactions to a text. Such a reader is untrained in literary technique and craftsmanship. Following Eliot's lead, the New Critics declare that there are both good and bad readers and good and bad criticism. A poor reader and poor criticism, for example, may argue that a poem can mean anything its reader or its author wishes it to mean. On the other hand, a good critic and good criticism would assert that only through a detailed structural analysis of a poem can the correct interpretation arise.

Eliot also lends New Criticism some of its technical vocabulary. Thanks to Eliot, for example, the term **objective correlative** has become a staple in poetic jargon. According to Eliot, the only way of expressing emotion through art is by finding an objective correlative: a set of objects, a situation, a chain of events, or reactions that can effectively awaken in the reader the emotional response the author desires without being a direct statement of that emotion. When the external facts are thus presented in the poem, they somehow come together (correlate) and immediately evoke an emotion. The New Critics readily adopted and advanced this indirect or impersonal theory of the creation of emotions in poetry.

From Eliot's British contemporary I. A. Richards, a psychologist and literary critic, New Criticism borrows a term that has become synonymous with its methods of analysis, **practical criticism.** In an experiment at Cambridge University, Richards distributed to his students copies of poems without such information as the authors, dates, and oddities of spelling and punctuation, and asked them to record their responses. From these data he identified the difficulties that poetry presents to its readers: matters of interpretation, poetic techniques, and specific meanings. Then, from this analysis, Richards devised an intricate system for arriving at a poem's meaning, including a minute scrutiny of the text—it is this close scrutiny or **close reading** of a text that has become synonymous with New Criticism.

From Eliot, Richards, and other critics, New Criticism borrows, amends, and adds its own ideas and concerns. Although few of its advocates would agree on many tenets, definitions, and techniques, there exists a core of assumptions, which allows us to identify adherents of this critical approach to texts.

ASSUMPTIONS

New Criticism begins by assuming that the study of imaginative literature is valuable; to study poetry or any literary work is to engage oneself in an **aesthetic experience** (the effects produced on an individual when contemplating a work of art) that can lead to truth. However, the truth discoverable through an aesthetic experience is distinguishable from the truth that science provides us. Science speaks propositionally, telling us whether a statement is demonstrably either true or false. Pure water, in the language of science, freezes at 32 degrees Fahrenheit, not 30 or 31. Poetic truth, on the other hand, involves the use of the imagination and intuition, a form of truth that, according to the New Critics, is discernable only in poetry. In the aesthetic experience alone we are cut off from mundane or practical concerns, from mere rhetorical, doctrinal, or propositional statements. Through an examination of the poem itself, we can ascertain truths that cannot be perceived through the language and logic of science. Both science and poetry, then, provide different but valid sources of knowledge.

Like many other critical theories, New Criticism's theory begins by defining its object of concern, in this case a poem. (New Critics use the word *poem* synonymously with *work of art;* however, their methodology works most efficiently with poetry rather than any other genre.) New Critics assert that a poem has **ontological** status; that is, it possesses its own being and exists like any other object. In effect, a poem becomes an artifact, an objective, self-contained, autonomous entity with its own structure. As W. K. Wimsatt declares, a poem becomes a "verbal icon."

Having declared a poem an object in its own right, the New Critics then develop their **objective theory of art**. For them, the meaning of a poem must not be equated with its author's feelings or stated or implied intentions. To believe that a poem's meaning is nothing more than an expression of the private experiences or intentions of its author is to commit a fundamental error of interpretation, which the New Critics call the **Intentional Fallacy**. Because they believe that the poem is an object, New Critics claim that every poem must also be a *public* text that can be understood by applying the standards of public discourse, not simply the private experience, concerns, and vocabulary of its author.

That the poem is somehow related to its author cannot be denied. In his essay "Tradition and the Individual Talent," T. S. Eliot states the New Critical position on the relationship between the author and his or her work. The basis of Eliot's argument is an analogy. We all know, he says, that certain chemical reactions occur in the presence of a **catalyst**, an element that causes, but is not affected by, the reaction. For example, if we place hydrogen peroxide, a common household disinfectant, in a clear bottle and expose it to the sun's rays, we will no longer have hydrogen peroxide. Acting as a catalyst, the sun's rays will cause a chemical reaction to occur, breaking down the hydrogen peroxide into its various parts, while the sun's rays remain unaffected.

Similarly, the poet's mind serves as a catalyst for the reaction that yields the poem. During the creative process, the poet's mind, serving as the catalyst, brings together the experiences of the author's personality (not the author's personality traits or attributes), into an external object and a new creation: the poem. It is not the personality traits of the author that coalesce to form the poem, but the experiences of the author's personality. In apparently distinguishing between the personality and the mind of the poet, Eliot asserts that the created entity, the poem, is about the experiences of the author that are similar to all of our experiences. By structuring these experiences, the poem allows us to examine them objectively.

Dismissing the poet's stated or supposed intentions as a means of discovering the text's meaning, the New Critics give little credence to the biographical or contextual history of a poem. If the Intentional Fallacy is correct, then unearthing biographical data will not help us ascertain a poem's meaning. Likewise, trying to place a poem in its social or political context will tell us much social or political history about the time when the poem was authored; although such information may indeed help in understanding the poem, its real meaning cannot reside in this extrinsic or outside-the-text information.

Of particular importance to the New Critics, however, is the etymology of individual words. Because the words of a poem sometimes change meaning from one time period to another, the critic often needs to conduct historical research, discovering what individual words meant at the time the poem was written. The *Oxford English Dictionary* (a dictionary that cites a word's different historical meanings chronologically) becomes one of the critic's best friends.

Placing little emphasis on the author, the social context, or a text's historical situation as a source for discovering a poem's meaning, the New

Critics also assert that a reader's emotional response to the text is neither important nor equivalent to its interpretation. Such an error in judgment, called the **Affective Fallacy**, confuses what a poem *is* (its meaning) with what it *does*. If we derive our standard of criticism, say the New Critics, from the psychological effects of the poem, we are then left with impressionism or, worse yet, relativism (believing that a poem has innumerable valid interpretations).

Where, then, can we find the poem's meaning? According to the New Critics, it does not reside in the author, the historical or social context of the poem, or even in the reader. Because the poem itself is an artifact or an objective entity, its meaning must reside within its own structure. Like all other objects, a poem and its structure can be analyzed scientifically. Accordingly, careful scrutiny reveals that a poem's structure operates according to a complex series of laws. By closely analyzing this structure, the New Critics believe that they have devised a methodology and a standard of excellence that we can apply to all poems to discover their correct meaning. It is the critic's job, they conclude, to ascertain the structure of the poem, to see how it operates to achieve its unity, and to discover how meaning evolves directly from the poem itself.

New Criticism sees the poet as an organizer of the content of human experience. Structuring the poem around the often confusing and sometimes contradictory experiences of life, the poet crafts the poem in such a way that the text stirs its readers' emotions and causes its readers to reflect on the poem's contents. As an artisan, the poet is most concerned with effectively developing the poem's structure, for the artist realizes that the meaning of a work emerges from its structure. The poet's chief concern, maintain the New Critics, is how meaning is achieved through the various and sometimes conflicting elements operating in the poem itself.

The chief characteristic of the poem—and therefore of its structure—is coherence or interrelatedness. Borrowing their ideas from the writings of Samuel T. Coleridge, the New Critics posit the **organic unity** of a poem—that is, the concept that all parts of a poem are interrelated and interconnected, with each part reflecting and helping to support the poem's central idea. Such organic unity allows for the harmonization of conflicting ideas, feelings, and attitudes, and results in the poem's oneness. Superior poetry, declare the New Critics, achieves such oneness through **paradox, irony**, and **ambiguity**. Because such tensions are necessarily a part of everyone's life, it is only fitting and appropriate, say the New Critics, that superior poetry present these human experiences while at the same time showing how these tensions are resolved within the poem to achieve its organic unity.

Because the poem's chief characteristic is its oneness, New Critics believe that a poem's form and content are inseparable. For the New Critics, however, **form** is more than the external structure of a poem; a poem's form encompasses, but rises above, the usual definition of poetic structure (that is, whether or not the poem is a Shakespearian or Petrarchan sonnet, or a lyric, or any other poetic structure having meter, rhyme, or some other poetic pattern). In New Criticism, form is the overall effect the poem creates. Because all the various parts of the poem combine to create this effect, each poem's form is unique. When all the elements of a poem work together to form a single, unified effect—the poem's form—New Critics declare that the poet has written a successful poem, one that has organic unity.

Since all good and successful poems have organic unity, it would be inconceivable to try to separate a poem's form and its content, maintain the New Critics. How can we separate what a poem says from how it says it. Because all the elements of a poem, both structural and aesthetic, work together to achieve a poem's effect or form, it is impossible to discuss the overall meaning of a poem by isolating or separating form and content.

To the New Critic, it is therefore inconceivable to believe that a poem's interpretation is equal to a mere paraphrased version of the text. Labeling such an erroneous belief the **Heresy of Paraphrase**, New Critics maintain that a poem is not simply a statement that is either true or false, but a bundle of harmonized tensions and resolved stresses, more like a ballet or musical composition than a statement of prose. No simple paraphrase can equal the meaning of the poem, for the poem itself resists through its inner tensions any prose statement that attempts to encapsulate its meaning. Paraphrases may help readers in their initial understanding of the poem, but such prose statements must be considered working hypotheses that may or may not lead to a true understanding of the poem's meaning. In no way should paraphrased statements about a poem be considered equivalent to the poem's structure or form, insist the New Critics.

METHODOLOGY

Believing in the thematic and structural unity of a poem, New Critics search for meaning within the text's structure by finding the tensions and conflicts that must eventually be resolved into a harmonious whole and inevitably lead to the creation of the poem's chief effect. Such a search first leads New Critics to the poem's diction or word choice. Unlike scientific discourse with its precision of terminology, poetic diction often has multiple meanings and can immediately set up a series of tensions within the text. For example, many words have both a **denotation**, or dictionary meaning, and **connotation(s)**, or implied meanings. A word's denotation may be in direct conflict with its connotative meaning determined by the context of the poem. In addition, it may be difficult to differentiate between the various denotations of a word. For example, if someone writes that "a *fat* head enjoys the *fat* of the land," the reader must note the various denotative and connotative differences of the word *fat*. At the start of poetic analysis, then, conflicts or tensions exist by the very nature of poetic diction. This tension New Critics call **ambiguity**. At the end of a close reading of the text, however, all such ambiguities will be resolved.

Even on a surface level of understanding or upon a first reading, a poem, from a New Critic's perspective, is a reconciliation of conflicts, of opposing meanings and tensions. Its form and content are indivisible, so it is the critic's job to analyze the poetic diction to ascertain such tensions. Although various New Critics give a variety of names to the poetic elements that make up a poem's structure, all agree that the poem's meaning is derived from the oscillating tensions and conflicts that are brought to the surface through the poetic diction.

For example, Cleanth Brooks claims that the chief elements in a poem are **paradox** and **irony**, two closely related terms that imply that a word or phrase is qualified or even undercut by its context. Other critics use the word **tension** to describe the opposition or conflicts operating within the text. For these critics, tension implies the conflicts between a word's denotation and its connotation, between a literal detail and a figurative one, and between an abstract and a concrete detail.

Because conflict, ambiguity, or tension controls the poem's structure, the meaning of the poem can be discovered only by analyzing contextually the poetic elements and diction. Further, because context governs meaning, meanings of individual words or phrases are therefore context-related and unique to the poem in which they occur. It is the job of the critic, then, to unravel the various apparent conflicts and tensions within each poem and to show that, ultimately, the poem has organic unity, thereby showing that all parts of the poem are interrelated and support the poem's chief paradox. This paradox, which New Critics often call *form* or overall effect, can usually be expressed in one sentence that contains the main tension and the resolution of that tension. It is this "key idea" to which all other elements of the poem must relate.

Although most New Critics would agree that the process of discovering the poem's form is not necessarily linear (for advanced readers often see ambiguities and ironies upon a first reading of a text), New Criticism provides the reader with a distinct methodology to help uncover the paradox or chief tension. These guided steps allow both novices and advanced literary scholars together to enter the discussion of a text's ultimate meaning, each contributing to the poem's interpretation. From a New Critical perspective, one begins the journey of discovering a text's correct interpretation by reading the poem several times and by carefully noting the work's title (if it has one) and its relationship to the text. Then, by following the prescribed steps listed here, a reader can ascertain a text's meaning. The more practice one has at following this methodology, and the more opportunities one has to be guided by an advanced reader and critic, the more adept one will undoubtedly become at textual analysis.

Step 1   Examine the text's diction. Consider the denotation, connotations, and etymological roots of all words in the text.

Step 2   Examine all allusions found within the text by tracing their roots to the primary text or source, if possible.

Step 3   Analyze all images, symbols, and figures of speech within the text. Note the relationships, if any, among the elements, both within the same category (between images, for example) and among the various elements (between an image and a symbol, for example).

Step 4   Examine and analyze the various structural patterns that may appear within the text, including the technical aspects of **prosody**. Note how the poet manipulates metrical devices, grammatical constructions, tonal patterns, and syntactic patterns of words, phrases, or sentences. Determine how these various patterns interrelate with each other and with all elements discussed in steps 1 to 3.

Step 5   Consider such elements as tone, theme, point of view, and any other element—dialogue, foreshadowing, narration, parody, setting, and so forth—that directly relates to the text's dramatic situation.

Step 6   Look for interrelationships of all elements, noting where tensions, ambiguities, or paradoxes arise.

Step 7   After carefully examining all of the above, state the poem's chief, overarching tension and explain how the poem achieves its dominant effect by resolving all such tensions.

All poems are unique; thus the process of uncovering a poem's chief tension is unique. By using the prescribed methodology of New Criticism, New Critics believe that readers can justify their interpretations of a text with information gleaned from the text alone while enjoying the aesthetic process that allows them to articulate the text's meaning.

According to such New Critical principles, a **good critic** examines a poem's structure by scrutinizing its poetic elements, rooting out and showing its inner tensions, and demonstrating how the poem supports its overall meaning in reconciling these tensions into a unified whole. By implication, **bad critics** are those who insist on imposing extrinsic evidence, such as historical or biographical information, on a text to discover its meaning. These critics fail to realize that the text itself elicits its own meaning. They flounder in their analysis, declare the New Critics, because such critics believe more often than not that a text can have multiple meanings.

Asserting that a poem has ontological status, the New Critics believe that a text has one and only one correct interpretation and that the poem itself provides all the necessary information for revealing its meaning. By scrutinizing the text and thus giving it a **close reading**, and by providing readers with a set of norms that will assist them in discovering the correct interpretation of the text, New Criticism provides a teachable, workable framework for literary analysis.

QUESTIONS FOR ANALYSIS

To apply the assumptions and methodology of New Criticism to a given text, one can begin by asking the following questions:

- If the text has a title, what is the relationship of the title to the rest of the poem? Before answering this question, New Critical theory and practice assume that the critic has read the text several times.
- What words, if any, need to be defined?
- What words and their etymological roots need to be scrutinized?
- What relationships or patterns do you see among any words in the text?
- What are the various connotative meanings words in the text may have? Do these various shades of meaning help establish relationships or patterns in the text?
- What allusions, if any, are in the text? Trace these allusions to their appropriate sources and explore how the origins of the allusion help elucidate meaning in this particular text.
- What symbols, images, and figures of speech are used? What is the relationship between any symbol or image? Between an image and another image? Between a figure of speech and an image? A symbol?
- What elements of prosody can you note and discuss? Look for rhyme, meter, and stanza patterns.
- What is the tone of the work?
- From what point of view is the content of the text being told?
- What tensions, ambiguities, or paradoxes arise within the text?
- What do you believe the chief paradox or irony is in the text?
- How do all the elements of the text support and develop the text's chief paradox?

SAMPLE ESSAY

In the sample student essay that follows, note how the student uses the tenets of New Criticism to arrive at an interpretation of John Keats's ode "To Autumn." Be able to explain how the student uncovers ambiguities and tensions within the poem, and how the student uses these elements to develop the overarching paradox. Note especially how all the elements of the text that the student cites support his stated chief paradox.

FURTHER READING

Brooks, Cleanth. "My Credo: Formalist Critics." *Kenyon Review* 13 (1951): 72–81.

———. *The Well Wrought Urn: Studies in the Structure of Poetry.* New York: Harcourt, 1975.

Brooks, Cleanth, and Robert Penn Warren, eds. *Understanding Poetry.* New York: Holt, 1938.

Empson, William. *Seven Types of Ambiguity.* 3rd ed. London: Hogarth, 1984.

Ransom, John Crowe. *The New Criticism.* New York: New Directions, 1941.

Richards, I. A. *Practical Criticism.* 1929. London: Routledge & Kegan Paul, 1964.

———. *Principles of Criticism.* London: Routledge & Kegan Paul, 1964.

Wellek, René, and Austin Warren. *Theory of Literature.* Rev. ed. New York: Harcourt, 1977.

Wimsatt, W. K., and Monroe C. Beardsley. *The Verbal Icon.* Lexington: University of Kentucky Press, 1954.

Winters, Yvor. *In Defense of Reason.* Denver: Swallow Press, 1947.

WEB SITES FOR EXPLORATION

www.ipl.org/ref/litcrit/
   The Internet Public Library's (IPL) *Online Literary Criticism Collection* links 745 critical and biographical Web sites about authors and their works. One of the best research tools on the Web, it can be searched by author name, title, nationality, or literary period.

www.sou.edu/English/Hedges/Sodashop/RCenter/Theory/Explaind/ncritexp.htm
   An excellent explanation of New Criticism

www.mcauley.acu.edu.au/staff/simonr/new_criticism.htm
   A solid introductory lecture to New Criticism

www.cnr.edu/home/bmcmanus/poetry1.html
   A good introduction to New Criticism, plus many good links to other sites!

www.wsu.edu/~delahoyd/new.crit.html
   Another good introductory source

www.leaderu.com/ftissues/ft9308/articles/young.html
An excellent overview of New Criticism

✂ **Student Essay** ✂

Keats's "To Autumn":
Verses of Praise for a Malicious Season?

Written in September of 1891, Keats's ode "To Autumn" describes the work and effect of Autumn on specific aspects of nature. At first glance, the combined verses of Keats sing the praises of a season bestowed with the ability to "bless" (line 3). What seems an ode praising a good-intentioned season, however, in actuality is a paradoxical commentary on the sometimes harsh reality of the beneficial cycle of life. In this cycle, Autumn has the seemingly malevolent job of preparing nature for a wintry death.

Stanza one introduces the reader to a personified character, Autumn, whose personality perfectly fits her job. Stanza two then portrays the guilt faced by Autumn while performing an ostensibly destructive task. By mingling positive images with images of death, stanza three provides hope for life in spring after Autumn and winter have passed. In the end, Autumn's role in the cycle of life is to be a bleak but necessary part of the intricate and beautiful cycles of the seasons.

"To Autumn" is an ode, "a single, unified strain of exalted lyrical verse, directed to a single purpose, and dealing with one theme. The term connotes certain qualities of both manner and form. The ode is elaborate, dignified, and imaginative" (Harmon, *A Handbook to Literature*, 7th ed., p. 358). In addition, the word *autumn* has its origin in the Middle English word *autumpne*, meaning any period of maturity, or the beginning of a decline. When these two definitions are synthesized, "To Autumn" becomes an elaborate, dignified, and imaginative strain of unified verse about either a period of maturity or the beginning of a decline. The combination of these words—autumn and ode—embodies the major paradox around which the poem derives its meaning and effect. In the poem, Autumn is the vehicle that brings about a period of decline, while the ode's tone of praise suggests that somehow Autumn's function is beneficial.

In stanza one, Autumn's first attribute mentioned is her "mists" (line 1). Autumn uses these mists in an attempt to hide her actions that may and will threaten other parts of nature. She apparently recognizes that nature must remain unsuspecting of her approach and her final actions so that she [Autumn] can accomplish her work without frightening nature, and in particular, summer. The second of Autumn's characteristics mentioned in this stanza is her mellowness (line 1, "mellow"), suggesting Autumn's ability to pleasantly intoxicate her environs. Since *mellow* also implies a relaxed or genial mood, Autumn is thus lulling nature, etherizing her, before Autumn prepares to do the rest of her work.

"To load and bless" in line three perfectly exemplifies the overarching paradox of the entire ode. "Load" is followed directly in the text by "bless," both of these being effects of Autumn on nature. In this combination of infinitives, the order and word choice suggest that nature is blessed to have been loaded. The word *loaded*, however, has the somewhat negative connotation of being overfilled, being weighted or tampered with, thus implying a trick or trap. Such fecundity and such blessing therefore serve as a mask to lull nature into accepting its prescribed destiny.

Though the remainder of stanza one contains images that seem to praise Autumn, upon close examination such images connote more harm than good. For example, Autumn, under the guise of benevolence, acts to "bend" (line 5) the mossed cottage-trees with unbearable weight, "swell" (line 7) the gourds as if bruised by a violent strike, and "plump" (line 7) the hazel shells as though fattening them for slaughter. The verbs *bend*, *swell*, and *plump* clearly connote destruction—the breaking of a tree branch, the bursting of a gourd, the swelling of a shell. The season whose job it is "to load and bless" (line 3) has indeed deceived all of nature into accepting its approaching death!

Even the "bees" (line 9) are lured by "later flowers" (line 9) from their wintry slumber in "clammy cells" (line 11) where they had been safe for the season from cold. Autumn produces these "later flowers" as a trap for the bees that come out, thinking that "warm days will never cease" (line 10). Now that the bees have been seduced from their sleep by Autumn's masterful deception and masquerade, they will be killed in the days that follow by winter's cold. Once again a seemingly gracious gesture on the part of Autumn has proved deadly.

To carry out such treachery, Autumn must possess a certain amount of apparent apathy toward her work (or at least disguised indifference) and its overall effect. Stanza two encapsulates this attitude. Line 14 pictures the character of Autumn "sitting careless on a granary floor," while "thy [Autumn's] hair [is] soft-lifted by the winnowing wind" (line 15). Such an image of peace amidst approaching death directly relates to the ode's major paradox. While Autumn, disguised by both mists and benevolence, carefully plots the death of summer and even herself, she is able to find peace in the seasons' demise, knowing that death is just one part of the cycle of life. Knowledge of this fact enables her to relax while she works.

Three other images in the second stanza serve to develop further the concept of Autumn's finding peace while preparing all nature for death.

Autumn now appears "on a half-reap'd furrow sound asleep./ Drows'd with the fume of poppies" (lines 16–17). In this image Keats pictures an attempt by nature and Autumn to escape their coming doom. Emitting perfume, the poppies lull Autumn to sleep in an attempt to delay their own unavoidable destruction and, ironically, Autumn's too. But their destruction is unavoidable, for even as Autumn sleeps, its work continues, as seen in Keats's next image when he writes, "while thy hook/ Spares the next swath and all its twinèd flower" (lines 17–18). The harvest will be gathered, the storehouse will be filled, and the cycle of the seasons will not be delayed or avoided despite any person's efforts or even those of nature herself.

Keats now presents his third image of Autumn's finding peace with her assigned task in lines 19–20, for Autumn is successful in keeping her "laden head" (line 20) "steady [. . .] across a brook" (line 20). Although Autumn is guilty of bringing about death and although her head is "laden" and apparently heavy with this guilt, she finds peace within herself, believing something is redeemable about her work. She thus marches on, "steady" about her work, knowing that contrary to her seemingly destructive actions, her work is not in vain.

Lines 21 and 22 contain another image of Autumn's coming to grips with the guilt of her actions. Now her personage has a "patient look" (line 21) while the "last oozings" (line 22) are squeezed from the apples and other fruits "ripeness to the core" (line 6). Describing Autumn as "patient," Keats creates the impression that she is at peace with the destruction of the fruit. The image of the "cider-press" (lines 21–22) also contains the first hint of true benefit from her work. The cider that is squeezed from the fruit is a pleasantry to other participants in nature's continuing drama. Hence, instead of being another image solely of death and destruction, this time Keats presents a positive element. Until now, Keats has presented Autumn as deceitful and seemingly uncaring and unfeeling, but now her apparent destructive labors actually begin to prove productive.

The first line of stanza three marks the major turning point of the poem. Line 24 asks, "Where are the songs of Spring? Ay, where are they?" Through these questions, Keats develops a tone of lament, suggesting that the songs of spring are to be desired over the destruction of Autumn, implying the beauty and the joy of spring and the songlessness and loss of Autumn. Line 24, however, modifies this lament, for here Keats emphatically declares that Autumn too has her songs: "Think not of them, thou has thy music too." The tone of lament developed throughout stanzas one and two now changes to one of rejoicing as Autumn is reassured of her own beauty and music. Until this point in the ode, the words, the images, the figures of speech, and their overall patterns and interrelationships all seemingly criticize Autumn for her preparations of death. At this turning point in the text, her task does not change, but Keats finally presents Autumn's work as part of nature's continuous cycle of change and renewal.

In lines 25 through 33, Keats introduces several images of Autumn that are consistent with her work of destruction and her previously developed personality as presented in stanzas one and two. Ironically, these images of death are now connected to and triumphantly modified by images of life, birth, and rebirth. The first of these images appears in line 25, where Keats observes that "barrèd clouds bloom the soft-dying day." Paradoxically, the "barrèd clouds," an image of an imposing and sometimes deadly storm, "*bloom* the soft-dying day" [italics added]. Now, an image of death created by the clouds blooms or gives birth, not to any day, but to a "soft-dying" one. Yes, notes Keats, the day must die as must the season, but the day's death is "soft" and gentle, connoting a good and positive aspect of death itself. Similarly, the "stubble-plains" in line 26 are now given a "rosy-hue"; that is, the harvested and therefore somewhat barren plains are no longer only an image of death. These once fruitful but now empty fields are rosy, exhibiting their own beauty, somewhat like the "soft-dying day" of the previous line.

Paralleling the "soft-dying day" and the now "rosy-hue[d]" plains is Keats's description in the next three lines of the ode of "in a wailful choir the small gnats mourn/ Among the river sallows, [and] borne aloft/ Or sinking as the light wind lives or dies." In picturing the "gnats" choir mourning their and all nature's impending doom, Keats adds words that connote hope and life and joy, for this choir floats in "the light wind" that "lives or dies," a wind that carries the gnats from the river willows into the sky. Paradoxically mixed with the images of death, then, are words and images that connote hope, that all is not lost, that something is and will be gained from apparent loss, that even in dying there is cause for rejoicing.

And all of nature's creatures seem to join in the chorus of Autumn, really an ode to joy, for in the last stanza "gnats" sing, "lambs loud bleat," "hedge-crickets sing," "the redbreast whistles," and "swallows twitter." Such a cooperation among the members of nature is expected, for Keats has prepared us for this cooperation in the opening line of the ode. As the ode begins, we note that at the start of the fall season, Autumn is "conspiring" with its "close bosom-friend," the sun, to produce the "Season of mists and mellow fruitfulness." Now, at the end of Autumn, all of nature's creatures are rejoicing. Seemingly, all of nature is celebrating the end of the season, the end of Autumn. Such music contains both notes of mourning and joy. Like the season itself, many creatures will die, the grass will wither, and no fruit will grow on the trees. But with Autumn's passing comes winter, and when winter too passes, spring will come again. As Autumn prepares all for death, winter allows nature her much needed rest. But from death, from resting, issues life again.

So sing ye animals of Autumn, sing in the midst of impending death, for Autumn is just one season of four that creates the life of nature. Just as Autumn and the sun conspire to produce luscious fruit, just as the animal choir of late Autumn joins to produce Autumn's final ode to joy, so all nature—all its four seasons—are necessary cycles in nature's ever-repeating process of life in death and death in life. Although Autumn is the harbinger of death, because she comes, all will live again.

DALE SCHUURMAN

4

Reader-Response
Criticism

The Muse is an enigmatic lady. Ever since Aristotle we have tried to penetrate her mysteries, yet still she eludes us.

Norman Holland, *Dynamics of Literary Response*

INTRODUCTION

Once I said to myself it would be a thousand times better for Jim to be a slave at home where his family was, as long as he'd *got* to be a slave, and so I'd better write a letter to Tom Sawyer and tell him to tell Mis Watson where he was. But I soon give up that notion, for two things: she'd be mad and disgusted at his rascality and ungratefulness for leaving her, and so she'd sell him straight down the river again; and if she didn't, everybody naturally despises an ungrateful nigger, and they'd make Jim feel it all the time, and so he'd feel ornery and disgraced. And then think of *me*! It would get all around that Huck Finn helped a nigger to get his freedom; and if I was to ever see anybody from that town again I'd be ready to get down and lick his boots for shame. That's just the way: a person does a low-down thing, and then he don't want to take no consequences of it. Thinks as long as he can hide it, it ain't no disgrace. That was my fix exactly. The more I studied about this the more my conscience went to grinding me, and the more wicked and low-down and ornery I got to feeling. And at last, when it hit me all of a sudden that here was the plain hand of Providence slapping me in the face and letting me know my wickedness was being watched all the time up there in heaven, whilst I was stealing a poor old woman's nigger that hadn't ever done me no harm, and now was showing me there's One that's always on the lookout, and ain't agoing to allow no such miserable doings to go only just so fur and no further, I most dropped in my tracks I was so scared. Well, I tried the best I could to kinder soften it up somehow for myself by saying I was brung up wicked, and so I warn't so much to blame; but something inside of me kept saying, "There was the Sunday school, you could a gone to it; and if you'd a done it they'd a learn't you there that people that acts as I'd been acting about that nigger goes to everlasting fire."

It made me shiver. . . .

Mark Twain, *Adventures of Huckleberry Finn*, Chapter 31

In a college-level, introductory literature course, several class members are voicing their interpretations of Chapter 31 of Mark Twain *Adventures of Huckleberry Finn* (1885), part of which is quoted at the beginning of this chapter. Student A declares that Huck Finn's struggle is obvious; he is simply debating whether he should listen to his feelings and keep Jim's whereabouts a secret, or listen to his conscience, which dictates that he must report the slave's location to Miss Watson, Jim's lawful owner. This chapter, asserts Student A, illustrates the novel's unifying theme: Huck's struggle to obey his innately good feelings versus his obeying the abstract commandments of an institutionalized system, his society. What unites all the chapters in the text and is now highlighted and climaxed in this chapter, maintains Student A, is Huck's realization that his inner feelings are correct and his society-dominated conscience is wrong. He accordingly opts for declaring Jim's humanity and thus tears up the letter he has written to Miss Watson.

Student B objects, declaring that Student A's interpretation is not relevant for the 2000s. Student A is correct, claims Student B, when she notes that Huck chooses to obey his conscience and disavow his allegiance to society's dictates. This is indeed Twain's chief purpose in *Huckleberry Finn*. The novel's significance, however, rests in how it can be applied today. Prejudice, she contends, still exists in our college town. We, like Huck, must see the humanness in all our citizens.

Student C affirms that both Student A and Student B have made valid criticisms. What they overlook, however, is the change that now takes place in Huck himself. No longer will we see, maintains Student C, a Huck who will play dirty tricks on Jim or even consider hurting him in any way. We now have a Huck who has positioned himself against his society and will not retreat from his stance. In the rest of the novel, declares Student C, we will observe this more mature and directed Huck as he responds to Jim's personal needs.

With a quiver in his voice, Student D remarks that Huck reminds him of his friend George. One day when he and George were walking down the hall of their high school on their way to their eleventh-grade biology class, they passed a group of students who began cursing and throwing milk cartons at them. "Go home, Jap," "USA all the way," and other derogatory comments came their way. Then George retorted, "Cut it out, guys. Pete has feelings too. Should we call some of you tow-heads, carrot tops, or other names because of how you look and because of your ancestors?" Like George, says Student D, Huck hates prejudice no matter where he finds it. Being on the side of the oppressed, he chooses to guard his friend's dignity and self-worth. He therefore destroys the letter to Miss Watson and will eventually help Jim obtain his freedom.

Each of these four students sees something slightly different in Twain's passage. Consciously or unconsciously, each of their interpretations rests upon different theoretical assumptions and their corresponding interpretative methodologies. Of the four interpretations, Student A's is the most theoretically distinct approach to the passage. Seeing an overall textual unity, this student presupposes that the text is autonomous; it must interpret itself with little or no help from historical, societal, or any other extrinsic factors, with all its parts relating back to its central theme. Utilizing the tenets of New Criticism, Student A posits the organic unity of the text. For this student, learning and applying literary terminology and searching for the correct interpretation are of utmost importance.

Unlike Student A, who applies a given set of criteria to the text in an attempt to discover its meaning, Students B, C, and D become participants in the interpretive process, actively bringing their own experiences to bear upon the text's meaning. Student B's interpretation, for example, highlights the theoretical difference between a text's meaning (the author's intentions) and its significance or relevance to present-day readers. Student C's approach begins filling in the gaps in the text, hypothesizing how Huck Finn will act in the pages yet unread based on Huck's decision not to write to Jim's owner. Whether Student C is correct or not, and whether she will have to alter some of her presently held ideas about Jim, remains an open question. Student D's theoretical framework objectifies the text and its meaning based on the reader's personal experiences with prejudice.

Although Students B, C, and D differ in their various approaches, none view the text as an objective entity that contains its own meaning (as does Student A). For these students, the text does not and cannot interpret itself. To determine a text's meaning, these students believe they must become active readers and participants in the interpretive process. The various theoretical assumptions and methodologies they used to discover the text's meaning exemplify **reader-response criticism.**

HISTORICAL DEVELOPMENT

Although reader-response criticism rose to prominence in literary analysis in the early 1970s and still influences much contemporary criticism, its historical roots can be traced to the 1920s and 1930s. Such precise dating, however, is artificial, for readers have obviously been responding to what they have read and experienced since the dawn of literature itself. Even the classical writers Plato and Aristotle were aware of and concerned about the reader's (or viewer's) reactions. Plato, for example, asserts that watching a play could so inflame the passions of the audience that the viewers would forget that they were rational beings and allow passion, not reason, to rule their actions. Similarly, in the *Poetics*, Aristotle voices concern about the effects a play will have on the audience's emotions. Will it arouse the spectators' pity or fear? Will these emotions purge the viewer? Will they cleanse a spectator of all emotions by the play's end? Such interest in audience response to the artistic creation dominates much literary criticism.

Underlying both Plato's and Aristotle's concerns about audience response—as well as the concern of many critics who follow in their paths—is the assumption that the audience (or the reader) is passive. As if watching a play or reading a book were a spectator sport, readers sit passively, absorbing the contents of the artistic creation and allowing it to dominate their thoughts and actions. From this point of view, the reader brings little to the play or text. The text provides all that is needed to interpret itself.

From Plato's time until the beginning of the romantic movement in British literature in the early 1800s, such a passive view of the reader existed. Although many critics recognized that a text did indeed have an effect upon its readers, criticism concerned itself primarily with the text. With the advent of romanticism, emphasis shifted from the text to the author. The author now became the genius who could assimilate truths that were unacknowledged or unseen by the general populace. And as the nineteenth century progressed, concern for the author continued, with literary criticism stressing the importance of the author's life, times, and social context as chief aids in textual analysis.

Nevertheless, by the 1920s, emphasis in textual analysis once again shifted to the text. With the advent of the New Criticism, the text became autonomous—an objective entity that could be analyzed and dissected. If studied thoroughly, the New Critics believed, the text would reveal its own meaning. Extrinsic factors, such as historical or social context, mattered little. Now considered a verbal icon, the text itself, declared the New Critics, contains what is needed to discover its meaning. We need only master the technical vocabulary and the correct techniques to unlock it.

However, while positing the autonomy of the text and declaring it to be an **autotelic artifact**, the New Critics did acknowledge the effects a text could have on its readers. Studying the effects of a literary work, they decreed, was not the same as studying the text itself. This emphasis on the objective nature of the text once again created a passive reader who did not bring personal experiences or private emotions to bear in a textual analysis.

I. A. Richards

In the midst of New Criticism's rise to dominance in the field of textual analysis—a dominance which would last for more than 30 years—one of its two early pioneers, I. A. Richards (T. S. Eliot being the other) became interested in the reading process itself. Using a decidedly reader-response approach to textual analysis, Richards distributed to his classes at Cambridge

University copies of short poems of widely diverse aesthetic and literary value, without citing their authors and titles and with various editorial changes that updated spelling and pronunciation. He then asked his students to record their free responses to and evaluations of each of these short texts. What surprised Richards was the wide variety of seemingly incompatible and contradictory responses.

After collecting and analyzing these responses, Richards published his findings, along with his own interpretations of the short texts, in *Principles of Literary Criticism* (1925). Underlying Richards's text is his assumption that science, not poetry or any other literary genre, leads to truth—that is, science's view of the world is the correct one. Poems, on the other hand, can produce only "pseudo-statements" about the nature of reality. But such pseudo-statements, declares Richards, are essential to the overall psychological health of each individual. In fact, according to Richards, human beings are basically bundles of desires called **appetencies**. In order to achieve psychic health, one must balance these desires by creating a personally acceptable vision of the world. Richards observes that religion was once able to provide this vision, but has now lost its effectiveness to do so. Borrowing from the thoughts of the nineteenth-century poet Matthew Arnold, Richards decrees that poetry, above all other art forms, can best harmonize and satisfy humankind's appetencies and thereby create a fulfilling and intellectually acceptable worldview.

After creating this substantially affective system of analysis, which gives credence to a reader's emotional response to a text, Richards then abandons this same reader-response approach in his analysis of his students' responses. Like the New Critics who were to follow him in the next several decades, he asserts that "the poem itself" contains all the necessary information to arrive at the "right" or "more adequate" interpretation. Through textual analysis—that is, by closely examining the poem's diction, imagery, and overall unity—Richards believes a reader can arrive at a better (more correct) interpretation of a poem than one derived from personal responses to a text.

Despite this seemingly complete departure from his initial reader-response methodology, Richards does recognize the contextual nature of reading poems, for he acknowledges that a reader brings to the text a vast array of ideas amassed through life's experiences, including previous literary experiences, and applies such information to the text. By so doing, the reader is no longer the passive receiver of knowledge but an active participant in the creation of a text's meaning.

Louise M. Rosenblatt

In the 1930s, Louise M. Rosenblatt further developed Richards's earlier assumptions concerning the contextual nature of the reading process. In her text *Literature as Exploration* (1937), Rosenblatt asserts that both the reader and the text must work together to produce meaning. Unlike the New Critics, she shifts the emphasis of textual analysis away from the text alone and views the reader and the text as partners in the interpretative process.

In the late 1930s, however, Rosenblatt's ideas seemed revolutionary, too abstract, and simply off the beaten, critical path. Although New Criticism dominated literary practice for the next 30 years or so, Rosenblatt continued to develop her ideas, culminating her critical work with the publication of *The Reader, the Text, the Poem* (1978). In this work, she clarifies her earlier ideas and presents what has become one of the main critical positions held by many theorists and practical critics today.

According to Rosenblatt, the reading process involves both a reader and a text. The reader and the text participate in or share a **transactional experience:** The text acts as a stimulus for eliciting various past experiences, thoughts, and ideas from the reader, those found in both our everyday existence and in past reading experiences. Simultaneously, the text shapes the reader's experiences by functioning as a blueprint, selecting, limiting, and ordering those ideas that best conform to the text. Through this transactional experience, the reader and the text produce a new creation, a poem. For Rosenblatt and many other reader-response critics, a **poem** is now defined as the result of an *event* that takes place during the reading process, or what Rosenblatt calls the "aesthetic transaction." No longer synonymous with the word *text*, a poem is created each time a reader transacts with a text, be that transaction a first reading or any one of countless rereadings of the same text.

For Rosenblatt, readers can and do read in one of two ways: *efferently* or *aesthetically*. When we read for information—for example, when we read the directions for heating a can of soup—we are engaging in **efferent reading**. During this process, we are interested only in newly gained information, not in the actual words themselves. When we engage in **aesthetic reading**, we experience the text. We note its every word, its sounds, its patterns, and so on. In essence, we live through the transactional experience of creating the poem.

When reading aesthetically, we involve ourselves in an elaborate give-and-take encounter with the text. Though the text may allow for many interpretations by eliciting and highlighting different past experiences of the reader, it simultaneously limits the valid meanings the poem can acquire. For Rosenblatt, a poem's meaning is, therefore, not a smorgasbord of infinite interpretations but a transactional experience, in which several different yet probable meanings emerge and thereby create a variety of "poems."

What differentiates Rosenblatt's and all reader-response critics from other critical approaches (especially New Criticism) is their purposive shift in emphasis away from the text as the sole determiner of meaning and toward the significance of the reader as an essential participant in the reading process and the creation of meaning. Such a shift negates the formalists' assumption that the text is autonomous and can therefore be scientifically analyzed to discover its meaning. No longer, then, is the reader passive, merely applying a long list of learned, poetic devices to a text in the hope of discovering its intricate patterns of paradox and irony, which, in turn, will lead, supposedly, to the one correct interpretation. For reader-response critics, the reader is an active participant along with the text in creating meaning. It is from the **literacy experience** (an event that occurs when a reader and print transact), they believe, that meaning evolves.

ASSUMPTIONS

Like most approaches to literary analysis, reader-response criticism does not provide us with a unified body of theory or a single methodological approach for textual analysis. What those who call themselves reader-response critics, reader-critics, or audience-oriented critics share is a concern for the reader. Believing that a literary work's interpretation is created when a reader and a text interact and/or transact, these critics assert that the proper study of textual analysis must consider both the reader and the text, not simply a text in isolation. For these critics,

Reader + Text = Meaning (Poem)

Only in context, with a reader actively involved in the reading process with the text, can meaning emerge.

Meaning, declare reader-response critics, is context-dependent and intricately associated with the reading process. Like literary theory as a whole, several theoretical models and their practical applications exist to explain the reading process—or how we make sense of printed material. Using these models, we can group the numerous approaches to the literacy experience into three broad categories. Each category emphasizes a somewhat different philosophy, a body of assumptions, and a methodology to explain what these various critics believe happens when a reader interacts or transacts with printed material.

Although each model espouses a different approach to textual analysis, all hold to some of the same presuppositions and concerns and ask similar questions. All, for example, focus directly on the reading process. What happens, they ask, when a person picks up printed material and reads it?

Put another way, their chief interest is what occurs when a text and a reader interact or transact. During this exchange, reader-response critics investigate and theorize whether the reader, the text, or some combination finally determine the text's interpretation. Is it the reader who manipulates the text, they ponder, or does the text manipulate the reader to produce meaning? Does some word, phrase, or image trigger in the reader's mind a specific interpretation, or does the reader approach the text with a conscious or unconscious collection of learned reading strategies that systematically impose an interpretation on the text?

Such questions then lead reader-response critics to a further narrowing and developing of terminology. They ask, for example, what is a text? Is it simply the words or symbols on a page? How, they ask, can we differentiate between what is actually in the text and what is in the mind of the reader? And who is this reader, anyway? Are there various kinds of readers? Is it possible that different texts presuppose different kinds of readers?

In addition, what about a reader's response to a text? Are the responses equivalent to the text's meaning? Can one reader's response, they speculate, be more correct than some other reader's, or are all responses of equal validity? Although readers respond to the same text in a variety of ways, why is it, they ask, that often times many readers individually arrive at the same conclusions or interpretations of the same text?

Reader-response critics also ask questions about another person, the author. What part, if any, does the author play in a work's interpretation? Can the author's attitudes toward the reader, they wonder, actually influence a work's meaning? And if a reader knows the author's clearly stated intentions for a text, does this information have any part in creating the text's meaning, or should an author's intentions for a work simply be ignored?

The concerns, then, of reader-response critics can best be summarized in one question: What is and what happens during the reading process? The answer to this question, however, is perplexing, for it involves investigating such factors as

- The reader—including his or her view of the world, background, purpose for reading, knowledge of the world, knowledge of words, and other such factors;
- The text, with all its various linguistic elements; and
- Meaning, or how the text and the reader interact or transact so that the reader can make sense of the printed material.

How reader-response critics define and explain each of these elements will in fact determine their approach to textual analysis. Furthermore, their definitions and explications also help determine what constitutes a valid interpretation of a text for each critic.

Although many reader-response critics allow for a wide range of legitimate responses to a text, most agree that reader-response criticism does not mean that any and all interpretations are valid or of equal importance. The boundaries and restrictions placed upon possible interpretations of a text will vary, depending upon how the critic defines the multiple elements of the reading process. It is these definitions and assumptions that allow us to group reader-response critics into several broad subgroups.

METHODOLOGY

Although reader-response critics employ a wide variety of critical approaches—from those espousing their own particular and modified form of New Criticism to postmodern practitioners such as deconstructionists—most adherents of reader-response theory and practice fall into three distinct groups. While members within each group may differ slightly, each group espouses its own distinct theoretical and methodological concerns. Student B's interpretation at the beginning of this chapter represents the focus of the first group.

Like all reader-response critics, this group believes that the reader must be an active participant in the creation of meaning; but for these critics, the text has more control over the interpretative process than does the reader. A few of these critics lean toward New Critical theory, asserting that some interpretations are more valid than others. Others differentiate between a text's meaning and its significance. For them, the text's meaning can be synonymous with its author's intention, while its significance can change from one context or historical period to another. Notwithstanding these variations, the majority of critics in this first group belong to the school known as **structuralism**.

Structuralism

Basing their ideas upon the writings of Ferdinand de Saussure, the founder of modern linguistics, structuralists often approach textual analysis as if it were a science. The proponents of structuralism—Roland Barthes, Gerard Genette, Roman Jakobson, Claude Lévi-Strauss, Gerard Prince, and Jonathan Culler in his early works—look for specific codes within the text that allow meaning to occur. These codes or signs embedded in the text are part of a larger system that allows meaning to occur in all facets of society, including literature. For example, when we are driving a car and we see a red light hanging above an intersection, we have learned that we must stop our car. Or when we hear a fire engine or an ambulance siren, we have learned that we must drive our car to the side of the road. Both the red light and the sirens are signs or codes in our society that provide us with ways of interpreting and ordering our world.

According to structuralist critics, a reader brings to the text a predetermined system for ascertaining meaning (a complex system of signs or codes like the sirens and the red light) and applies this sign system directly to the text. The text becomes important because it contains signs or signals to the reader that have preestablished and acceptable interpretations. Many structuralists are therefore more concerned about the overall system of meaning a given society has developed than with textual analysis itself and concentrate their efforts on what a reader needs to know about interpreting any sign (such as a road sign or a word) in the context of acceptable societal standards. Because of this emphasis, structuralists seem to push both the text and the reader to the background and concentrate their attention on a linguistic theory of communication and interpretation. Since structuralism has become a springboard for many other modern theories of literary criticism, its significance to literary theory and practical criticism will be explored at length in the next chapter. Meanwhile, the ideas of one leading structuralist, Gerard Prince, will illustrate the methodology of structuralism.

Gerard Prince   In the 1970s, Gerard Prince helped develop a specific kind of structuralism known as **narratology**, which is the process of analyzing a story using all the elements involved in its telling, such as narrator, voice, style, verb tense, personal pronouns, audience, and so forth. Prince noted that critics often ask questions about the story's point of view—omniscient, limited, first person, and so on—but rarely do they ask about the person to whom the narrator is speaking, the **narratee**. Usually, the narratee is not the actual person reading the text, for Prince argues that the narrative itself— that is, the story—produces the narratee. By first observing and then analyzing various signs in the text, such as pronoun reference; direct address ("Dear reader"); gender, race, and social class references; and writing style, Prince believes it is possible not only to identify the narratee but also to classify stories based on the different kinds of narratees created by the texts themselves. Such narratees may include the **real reader** (person actually reading the book), the **virtual reader** (the reader to whom the author believes he or she is writing), and the **ideal reader** (the one who explicitly and implicitly understands all the nuances, terminology, and structure of a text).

Although such an approach relies heavily on textual analysis, Prince's concerns about the reader place him in the reader-response school of criticism. Other structuralists such as Jonathan Culler who distance themselves from Prince and this kind of close reliance upon the text to generate meaning will be discussed in Chapter 5.

Phenomenology

Student C represents the second major group of reader-response critics. For the most part, these theorists follow Rosenblatt's assumption that the reader is involved in a transactional experience when interpreting a text. Both the text and the reader, they declare, play somewhat equal parts in the interpretative process. For them, reading is an event that culminates in the creation of the poem.

Many adherents in this group—George Poulet, Wolfgang Iser, Hans Robert Jauss, Roman Ingarden, and Gaston Bachelard—are often associated with phenomenology. **Phenomenology** is a modern philosophical tendency that emphasizes the perceiver. Objects can have meaning, phenomenologists maintain, only if an active consciousness (a perceiver) absorbs or notes their existence. In other words, objects exist if, and only if, we register them in our consciousness. Rosenblatt's definition of a poem directly applies this theory to literary study. The true poem can exist only in the reader's consciousness, not on the printed page. When reader and text transact, the poem and therefore meaning are created; they exist only in the consciousness of the reader. Reading and textual analysis now become an aesthetic experience, wherein both the reader and the text combine in the consciousness of the reader to create the poem. Like Student C's interpretation at the beginning of the chapter, the reader's imagination must work, filling in the gaps in the text and conjecturing about characters' actions, personality traits, and motives. The ideas and practices of two reader-response critics, Hans Robert Jauss and Wolfgang Iser, will serve to illustrate phenomenology's methodology.

Hans Robert Jauss   Writing toward the end of the 1960s, the German critic Hans Robert Jauss emphasized that a text's social history must be considered when interpreting the text. Unlike New Critical scholars, Jauss declares that critics must examine how any given text was accepted or received by its contemporary readers. Espousing a particular kind of reader-response criticism known as **reception theory**, Jauss asserts that readers from any given historical period devise for themselves the criteria whereby they will judge a text. Using the term **horizons of expectation** to include all of a historical period's critical vocabulary and assessment of a text, Jauss points out that how any text is evaluated from one historical period to another (from the Age of Enlightenment to the Romantic period, for example), necessarily changes. For example, Alexander Pope's poetry was heralded as the most nearly perfect poetry of its day, for heroic couplets and poetry that followed prescribed forms were judged superior. During the Romantic period, however, with its emphasizes on content, not form, the critical reception of Pope's poetry was not as great.

Accordingly, Jauss argues that since each historical period establishes its own horizons of expectation, the overall value and meaning of any text can never become fixed or universal, for readers from any given historical period establish for themselves what they value in a text. A text, then, does not have one and only one correct interpretation because its supposed meaning changes from one historical period to another. A final assessment about any literary work thus becomes impossible.

For Jauss, the reader's reception or understanding and evaluation of a text matters greatly. Although the text itself remains important in the interpretive process, the reader, declares Jauss, plays an essential role.

Wolfgang Iser   The German phenomenologist Wolfgang Iser borrows and amends Jauss's ideas. Iser believes that any object—a stone, a house, or a poem—does not achieve meaning until an active consciousness recognizes or registers this object. It is thus impossible to separate what is known (the object) from the mind that knows it (human consciousness). Using these phenomenological ideas as the basis for his reader-response theory and practice, Iser declares that the critic's job is not to dissect or explain the text, for once a text is read, the object and the reader (the perceiver) are essentially one. Instead, the critic's role is to examine and explain the text's effect on the reader.

Iser, however, differentiates two kinds of readers: the **implied reader** who "embodies all those predispositions necesary for a literary work to exercise its effect—predispositions laid down, not by an empirical outside reality, but by the text itself. Consequently, the implied reader [. . .] has his or her roots firmly planted in the structure of the text" (Iser 1978); and the **actual reader**, the person who physically picks up the text and reads it. It is this reader as opposed to the text's reader who comes to the text shaped by particular cultural and personal norms and prejudices. By positing the implied reader, Iser affirms the necessity of examining the text in the interpretive process; at the same time, by acknowledging the actual reader, Iser declares the validity of an individual reader's response to the text.

Like Jauss, Iser disavows the New Critical stance that a text has one and only one correct meaning and asserts that a text has many possible interpretations. For Iser, texts, in and of themselves, do not possess meaning. When a text is **concretized** by the reader (the phenomenological concept whereby the text registers in the reader's consciousness), the reader automatically views the text from his or her personal worldview. Since texts, however, do not tell the reader everything that needs to be known about a character, a situation, a relationship, and other such textual elements, readers must automatically fill in these "gaps," using their own knowledge base, grounded as it is in a worldview. In addition, each reader creates his or her *horizons of expectation*—that is, a reader's expectations about what will or may or should happen next. (Note the variation in meaning Iser gives this term compared with Jauss, who coined it). These horizons of expectation change frequently, for at the center of all stories is conflict or dramatic tension, often resulting in sudden loss, pain, unexpected joy or fear, and at times great fulfillment. Such changes will cause a reader to modify his or her horizons of expectation to fit a text's particular situation. For example, when, in Chapter 31 of the *Adventures of Huckleberry Finn,* Huck declares that he will not write a letter to Miss Watson telling her the location of Jim, Huck openly chooses to side with Jim against the precepts of Huck's society. A reader may then assume that Huck will treat Jim differently, for now Jim, the slave, has a chance to become a free man. According to Iser, the reader has now established horizons of expectation. When, however, in just a few short chapters, Tom Sawyer talks Huck into chaining Jim to a table, the reader may reformulate his or her horizons of expectation, for Huck is not treating Jim as a free man, but once again as a slave.

In making sense of the text, in filling in the text's gaps, and in continually adopting new horizons of expectation, the reader uses his or her own value system, personal and public experiences, and philosophical beliefs. According to Iser, each reader makes "concrete" the text, each concretization is therefore personal, allowing the new creation—the text's meaning and effect on the reader—to be unique.

For Iser, the reader is an active, essential player in the text's interpretation, writing part of the text as the story is read and concretized and, indispensibly, becoming its coauthor.

Subjective Criticism

Student D represents the third group of reader-response critics who place the greatest emphasis on the reader in the interpretative process. For these psychological or subjective critics, the reader's thoughts, beliefs, and experiences play a greater part than the actual text in shaping a work's meaning. Lead by Norman Holland and David Bleich, these critics assert that we shape and find our self-identities in the reading process.

Norman Holland   Using Freudian psychoanalysis as the foundation for his theory and practices formulated in the early 1970s, Norman Holland believes that at birth we receive from our mothers a primary identity. We personalize this identity through our life's experiences, transforming it into our own individualized **identity theme** that becomes the lens through which we see the world. Textual interpretation then becomes a matter of working out our own fears, desires, and needs to help maintain our psychological health.

Like Rosenblatt, Holland asserts that the reading process is a transaction between the text and the reader. The text is indeed important, for it contains its own themes, its own unity, and its own structure. A reader, however, transforms a text into a private world, a place where one works out (through the ego) his or her fantasies, which are in fact mediated by the text so that they will be socially acceptable.

For Holland, all interpretations are therefore subjective. Unlike New Criticism, his reader-response approach asserts that there exists no such thing as a correct intepretation. From his perspective, there are as many valid interpretations as there are readers, for the act of interpretation is a subjective experience.

David Bleich   The founder of "subjective criticism," David Bleich (1978) agrees with Holland's psychological explanation of the interpretive process, but Bleich devalues the role the text plays, denying its objective existence. Meaning, Bleich argues, does not reside in the text but is *developed* when the reader works in cooperation with other readers to achieve the text's collective meaning (what Bleich calls "the interpretation"). Only when each reader is able to articulate his or her individual responses about the text within a group, then and only then can the group, working together, negotiate meaning. Such communally motivated negotiations ultimately determine the text's meaning.

For Bleich, the starting point for interpretation is the reader's responses to a text, not the text itself. Bleich states, however, that these responses do not constitute the text's meaning because meaning cannot be found within a text or within responses to the text. Rather, a text's meaning must be *developed* from and out of the reader's responses, working in conjunction with other readers' responses and with past literary and life experiences. In other words, Bleich differentiates between the reader's response(s) to a text (which for Bleich can never be equated to a reader's interpretation) and the reader's interpretation or meaning, which must be developed communally in a classroom or similar setting.

The key to developing a text's meaning is the working out of one's responses to a text so that these responses will be challenged and amended and then accepted by one's social group. Subjective critics like Bleich assert that when reading a text, a reader may respond to something in the text in a bizarre and personal way. These private responses will, through discussion, be pruned away by members of the reader's social group. Finally, the group will decide what is the acceptable interpretation of the text. As in Student D's interpretation cited at the beginning of this chapter, the reader responds personally to some specific element in the text, seeks to objectify this personal response, and then declares it to be an interpretation of the text. However, only through negotiations with other readers (and other texts), can one develop the text's meaning.

A Two-Step Methodology

Although reader-response critics all believe the reader plays a part in discovering a text's meaning, just how small or large a part is debatable. Espousing various theoretical assumptions, these critics must necessarily have different methodologies for textual analysis. According to the contemporary critic Steven Mailloux, however, reader-response critics all share a two-step procedure, which they then adapt to their own theories. These critics all show that a work gives a reader a task or something to do, and they represent the reader's response or answer to that task.

Returning, for example, to Student D: At the beginning of the chapter, Student D's argument shows that he saw something in the text that triggered his memories of his friend George. His task is to discover what in the text triggered his memory and why. He moves, then, from the text to his own thoughts, memories, and past experiences. These personal experiences temporarily overshadow the text, but he realizes that his personal reactions must in some way become acceptable to his peers. He therefore compares George to Huck and himself to Jim and thereby objectifies his personal feelings while at the same time having his interpretation deemed socially respectable in his **interpretative community**—a term coined by the reader-response critic Stanley Fish to designate a group of readers who share the same interpretive strategies.

Because the term *reader-response criticism* allows for so much divergence in theory and methods, many twentieth-century schools of criticism, such as deconstruction, feminism, Marxism, and New Historicism, declare their membership in this broad classification. Each of these approaches to textual analysis provides its own ideological basis to reader-response theory and develops its unique methods of practical criticism. Such an eclectic membership, however, denotes the continued growth and ongoing development of reader-response criticism.

QUESTIONS FOR ANALYSIS

Since reader-response critics use a variety of methodologies, no particular listing of questions can encompass all their concerns. Nevertheless, by asking the following questions of a text one can participate in both the theory and practice of reader-response criticism:

- Who is the actual reader?
- Who is the implied reader?
- Who is the ideal reader?
- Who is the narratee?
- What are some gaps you see in the text?
- Can you list several horizons of expectations and show how they change from a particular text's beginning to its conclusion?
- Using Jauss's definition of horizons of expectation, can you develop first on your own and then with your classmates an interpretation of a particular text?
- Can you articulate your identity theme as you develop your personal interpretation of a particular text?
- Using Bleich's subjective criticism, can you state the difference between your response to a text and your interpretation?
- In a classroom setting, develop your class's interpretive strategies for arriving at the meaning of a particular text.

SAMPLE ESSAY

After reading the sample student essay that follows, be able to identify the narratee and the implied and the ideal reader. In addition, be able to identify which one of the various subgroups of reader-response criticism the student uses to write this essay. Is the text, the reader + the text, or the reader of most importance for this critic in her methodology and philosophy? In addition, can you point out the distinctive personal strategies or moves the author makes to arrive at her interpretation? Can you identify the interpretive community to which the author belongs? Does she belong to more than one interpretive community? Be able to cite references from her text to support your answers. Also note the style of the essay. From what point of view does the author write the essay? Why? Finally, what is the tone of the essay? How does the author establish this tone, and do you believe it is effective?1

FURTHER READING

Bleich, David. *Subjective Criticism*. Baltimore: Johns Hopkins University Press, 1978.

Fish, Stanley. *Is There a Text in This Class?* Cambridge: Harvard University Press, 1980.

Holland, Norman N. *5 Readers Reading*. New Haven, CT.: Yale University Press, 1975

———. *Holland's Guide to Psychoanalytic Psychology and Literature.* Oxford: Oxford University Press, 1990.

Iser, Wolfgang. *The Implied Reader: Patterns of Communication in Prose Fiction from Bunyan to Beckett.* Baltimore: Johns Hopkins University Press, 1974.

———. *The Act of Reading.* Baltimore: Johns Hopkins University Press, 1978.

Jauss, Hans Robert. *Aesthetic Experience and Literary Hermeneutics.* Minneapolis: University of Minnesota Press, 1982.

Mailloux, Steven. "Learning to Read: Interpretation and Reader-Response Criticism." *Studies in the Literary Imagination* 12 (1979): 93–108.

McGregor, Graham, and R. S. White, eds. *Reception and Response: Hearer Creativity and the Analysis of Spoken and Written Texts.* London: Routledge, 1990.

Miller, J. Hillis. *Theory Now and Then.* Hemel Hempstead: Harvester Wheatsheaf, 1991.

Rosenblatt, Louise M. *Literature as Exploration.* New York: Noble, 1938.

———. *The Reader, the Text, the Poem.* Carbondale: Southern Illinois University Press, 1978.

———. "Towards a Transactional Theory of Reading." *Journal of Reading Behavior* 1 (1969): 31–47.

Suleiman, Susan, and Inge Crosman, eds. *The Reader in the Text: Essay on Audience and Interpretation.* Princeton: Princeton University Press, 1980.

Tompkins, Jane, ed. *Reader-Response Criticism: From Formalism to Post-Structuralism.* Baltimore: Johns Hopkins University Press, 1980.

WEB SITES FOR EXPLORATION

www.cas.usf.edu/JAC/122/olson.html
A conversation with one of the leading reader-response critics, Stanley Fish

www.cnr.edu/home/bmcmanus/readercrit.html
A good overview of reader-response criticism plus excellent links to other sites

www.xenos.org/essays/litthry4.htm
An excellent overview of Stanley Fish's reader-response theory

www.br.cc.va.us/vcca/i11chur.html
The significance of Louise Rosenblatt

www.clas.ufl.edu/users/nnh/online.htm
Provides articles and links of Norman Holland's works

www.standford.edu/group/SHR/4-1/text/holland.commentary.html
A solid discussion of reader-response theory

www.ualberta.ca/~dmiall/FORMALSM.HTM
Provides an overview of reader-response theories

ᘯ Student Essay ᘯ

"Ethan Brand's" Challenge to Me

Nathaniel Hawthorne's short story "Ethan Brand" presents a challenge, evoking in me identification with Joe's innocent, tender perusal of humanity and with Ethan Brand's relentless intellectual pursuits for the unpardonable sin. While I value a childlike faith in my theistic worldview, I also endeavor to pursue my understanding of life and God through vigilant refinement of my intellect. This short story contradicts my fundamental doctrinal beliefs by positing an unpardonable sin while challenging me to delve into the apparent dichotomy between faith and reason that proves Ethan Brand's demise.

Joe's role in the story diametrically opposes that of Ethan Brand through his portrayal as a boy still untouched by the cynicism of life's unfairness and full of compassion for the rest of humanity. Initially, Hawthorne describes Joe as "more sensitive than the obtuse, middle-aged clown [his father]," a statement that makes me question my personality as a child. My parents recall that as a baby I used to stare so intently at people that they wondered what I knew and what I was thinking. This characterization of Joe also reminds me that children can be the most astute observers of humanity, able to perceive beyond the facades we wear. Beyond his sensitivity, Joe acts "timorous and imaginative," reminding me of my own tendency both now and when I was younger to wander into a world of my own making, one far removed from reality. My memories of childhood include many games of "pilot," in which the hay shoot in my family's barn served as the perfect place to yell "Geronimo!"

Tenderness and compassion for Ethan Brand fashion Joe into a Christlike figure because of his ability to have "an intuition of the bleak and terrible loneliness in which this man had enveloped himself." During his formative years, the Bible describes Jesus' encounters with teachers of the Jewish law and their amazement at his understanding and insight. At the age of twelve, when his parents accidentally left him in Jerusalem after the Passover feast, Jesus acts surprised that their search for him did not begin in the temple, a place Jesus called his Father's house. Through his discussions with the teachers and treatment of his parents, Jesus shares Joe's gift of heightened insight and sensitivity beyond that of adults. Joe's tender disposition prompts me as well to examine my behavior in everyday life, to attempt to see others' needs, and to respond with sensitivity.

Because I am a Christian theist, this story takes on particular significance for me because of Ethan Brand's assertion that he has found the unpardonable sin, an act so terrible that even God's mercy cannot forgive it. His discovery, that the unpardonable sin lies in "an intellect triumphed over the sense of brotherhood with man and reverence for God," also brings into focus the dichotomy of faith and reason, an issue that Christians throughout the centuries have sought to reconcile. Instead of an unpardonable sin, I posit that Brand has actually come to terms with the issue of original sin. Oswald Chambers, a well-known theologian, defines original sin in this fashion: the disposition of sin is not immorality and wrong-doing, but the disposition of self-realization—I am my own god. This disposition may work out in decorous morality or in indecorous immorality, but it has one basis, my claim to my right to myself. Before Brand's quest began, he recalls his view of the heart of humanity as "a temple, originally, and however, desecrated, still to be held sacred by a brother." Through his many years of toil, however, Brand transforms from loving humanity to exhibiting a cold detachment, which allows him to use a young girl named Esther in a psychological experiment that "wasted, absorbed, and perhaps annihilated her soul."

Even though Brand's deeds seem horrible and fiendish, I find a strange kinship in admitting the corruptness of my own human nature and in struggling between childlike faith and intellectual development. Joe demonstrates the magnetism of evil because he sees something in Brand's face that scares him and attracts him simultaneously. Many times I have personally experienced the allure of a particular sin, mysteriously desiring both to commit it and not to commit it. Admitting the sinfulness of my own nature to myself surfaces most particularly when Ethan Brand points to his own heart as the location of the unpardonable sin. His action reminds me of my condition as a member of the human race cursed by original sin, but also brings reassurance that, contrary to Brand, I have experienced God's forgiveness and can rejoice in my redemption. This story also evokes the words *Kyrie eleison*, "Lord have mercy," as another confirmation that my faith rests on grace and a belief in God's mercy extended through Christ's death and resurrection.

Intellect opposes faith in Ethan Brand's experience by producing a literal hardening of heart that cuts him off from communion with the human race and relationship with God. Before Brand even enters the story, Hawthorne contrasts his strange musing with the strictly businesslike thoughts of Bartram, implying that the mind can become a dangerous tool when used too much to contemplate the human condition. In attempting to explain the unpardonable sin, Brand places it almost entirely in the intellectual realm, or rather the intellect, severing the relationship with the ear and invalidating faith. Brand's elevated state of thought in fact makes the townspeople's vulgarity so crude to him that he begins to question whether they or he possess the unpardonable sin. His confidence returns, though, when he recalls the callousness with which he subjected Esther, thereby crushing her spirit. To codify his transformation, the process of his "vast intellectual development, which, in its progress, disturbed the counterpoise between mind and heart" leads to a heart that becomes "withered," "contracted," "hardened," even "perished!" Instead of participating in humanity as a "brother-man," Brand watches as a "cold observer."

The dichotomy between faith and intellect conflicts with my worldview in several ways, the first being the supposition that intellect could ever produce a sin incapable of being forgiven—if one indeed desires forgiveness. Holy Scripture states, "If we confess our sin, God is faithful and just to forgive us our sins and cleanse us from all unrighteousness" (1 John 1:9), and also declares that "as far as east is from west, so far has he removed our transgressions from us" (Psalms 103:12). Rather than separating faith and reason, I choose to view them both as avenues to worship God, as we are commanded to "Love the Lord your God with all your heart and with all your soul and with all your mind" (Matthew 22:37) and to "take captive every thought to make it obedient to Christ" (2 Cor. 10:5). One of the paradoxes of Christianity requires coming to God with childlike faith while retaining the value of the intellect he has given us. In examining truth, the Church today has largely avoided intellectual pursuit when, in fact, this study should be valued as a means of discovering truth not explicitly stated in Scripture.

Other associations arise throughout the story that also apply to contemporary culture and to my personal faith. Recounting the dog spinning in countless circles to chase its elusive tail parallels the confusion of the postmodern condition in its endless questioning without an absoute moral or spiritual center. Another image, the fire in the kiln, appears in the story as a symbol of evil, but I associate fire, in part, with the prophet Malachi's description of the Lord as "a refiner's fire" that purifies Christians like "gold and silver" (Malachi 3:2). Even Brand's disintegration into lime provides a glimpse of mortality and leads to the question of what legacy I will leave.

Hawthorne's short tale essentially challenges me to embody Joe's tenderness, inquisitiveness, and imagination, and to continue attempting to resolve the dichotomy of faith and reason. My Christian faith impacts my reading of this story by answering the text's question of the existence of an unpardonable sin and in dealing with my frustration at the Church's sometimes facile answers to life's difficult questions, answers offered instead of delving into these questions and facing the paradoxes of reason necessarily held by a worldview based on faith. Though the story does not provide a response or resolution to Brand's demise, I am thankful to be able to evaluate this work through the lens of my worldview and emerge with new knowledge and a different perspective.

JENNIFER DOUGLAS

5

Structuralism

In its resolute artificiality, literature challenges the limits we set to the self as an agent of order and allows us to accede, painfully or joyfully, to an expansion of self. But that requires, if it is to be fully accomplished, a measure of awareness of the modes of ordering which are the components of one's culture, and it is for that reason that I think a structuralist poetics has a crucial role to play [. . .] in advancing an understanding of literature as an institution [. . .] and in promoting the richest experience of reading.

Jonathan Culler, "Structuralism and Literature"

INTRODUCTION

Having narrowed her list of job candidates to two, the personnel director of a large computer company instructed her secretary to invite each applicant for a job interview. Both candidates seemed equally qualified for the position. Applicant A had graduated from an Ivy League university, earning a B.S. in accounting and business, while Applicant B, also a graduate of an Ivy League institution, earned a B.S. in business administration. Each had received outstanding references from his professors and business mentors; each had scored in the 95th percentile on the Graduate Record Examination (GRE). The personnel director's choice, no doubt, would be difficult.

On the day of the interview, Applicant A arrived wearing a black suit, a white cotton shirt, a subdued but somewhat bright cranberry tie, a pair of highly polished black wing tips, and an appropriate smile and short haircut. Applicant B arrived a few minutes after Applicant A's interview had begun. Wearing a green fatigue shirt, a pair of stonewashed jeans, and black suede, open-toed Birkenstocks, Applicant B brushed back his long hair and wondered why the first candidate's interview was lasting more than an hour. After another fifteen minutes had passed, Applicant A finally exited through the main doors, and the secretary ushered Applicant B into the director's office. Eighteen minutes later, Applicant B passed by the secretary's desk and left the building, his interview apparently being over.

Shortly thereafter, the personnel director buzzed for her secretary to come to her office. Upon his entering, the director responded, "Please send

Applicant A the contract. He will represent our business well. Also, mail Applicant B an I'm-sorry-but letter. Evidently he doesn't understand our image, our values, and our standards. Jeans, no tie, and long hair, in this office and for this company! Never!"

Applicant A's ability to grasp what his future employer valued earned him his job. Through the language of fashion (**language** used here in its broad sense as any system of codes or signs that convey meaning), Applicant A demonstrated to the personnel director his understanding of the company's image and its concern for appropriate dress and physical appearance. Applicant B, however, silently signaled his lack of understanding of the company's values and public image through his tie-less and seemingly inappropriate attire. While Applicant B failed to master those fashion codes that represented his understanding of the company's standards, Applicant A demonstrated his command of the language of fashion and his potential to learn other similar intricate systems or languages used in such areas as economics, education, the sciences, and social life in general. Through his mastery of these codes and his ability (either consciously or unconsciously) to analyze and employ them correctly in a given situation, Applicant A demonstrated his knowledge of structuralism.

Flourishing in the 1960s, **structuralism** is an approach to literary analysis grounded in **structural linguistics**, the science of language. By utilizing the techniques, methodologies, and vocabulary of linguistics, structuralism offers a scientific view of how we achieve meaning not only in literary works but also in every form of communication and social behavior.

To understand structuralism, we must trace its historical roots to the linguistic writings and theories of Ferdinand de Saussure, a Swiss professor and linguist of the late nineteenth and and early twentieth centuries. It is his scientific investigations of language and language theory that provide the basis for structuralism's unique approach to literary analysis.

HISTORICAL DEVELOPMENT

Pre-Saussurean Linguistics

Throughout the nineteenth and early twentieth centuries, **philology**, not **linguistics**, was the science of language. Its practitioners, **philologists**, described, compared, and analyzed the languages of the world to discover similarities and relationships. Their approach to language study was **diachronic**; that is, they traced language change throughout long expanses of time, discovering, for example, how a particular phenomenon, such as a word or sound, in one language had changed **etymologically** or **phonologically** over several centuries and whether a similar change could be noted in other languages. Using a cause-and-effect relationship as the basis for their research, the philologists' main emphasis was the historical development of languages.

Such an emphasis reflected the nineteenth-century philologists' theoretical assumptions on the nature of language. Language, they believed, mirrored the structure of the world it imitated and therefore had no structure of its own. Known as the **mimetic theory of language**, this linguistic hypothesis asserts that words (either spoken or written) are symbols for things in the world, each word having its own **referent**—the object, concept, or idea that is represented and/or symbolized by that word. According to this theory, the symbol (a word) equals a thing:

$$\text{Symbol} = \text{Thing}$$
$$\text{(word)}$$

Saussure's Linguistic Revolution

In the first decade of the 1900s, a Swiss philologist and teacher, Ferdinand de Saussure (1857–1913), began questioning these long-held ideas and, by so doing, triggered a reformation in language study. Through his research and innovative theories, Saussure changed the direction and subject matter of linguistic studies. His *Course in General Linguistics*, a compilation of his 1906-11 lecture notes published posthumously by his students, is one of the seminal works of modern linguistics and forms the basis for structuralist literary theory and practical criticism. Through the efforts of this pioneer of modern linguistics, nineteenth-century philology evolved into the more multifaceted science of twentieth-century linguistics.

Saussure began his linguistic revolution by affirming the validity and necessity of the **diachronic** approach to language study utilized by such nineteenth-century philologists as the Grimm brothers and Karl Verner. Using this diachronic approach, these linguists discovered the principles governing consonantal pronunciation changes that occurred in Indo-European languages (the language group to which English belongs) over many centuries. While not abandoning a diachronic examination of language, Saussure introduced the **synchronic** approach, a method that proceeds by focusing on a language at one particular time—a single moment—and that emphasizes the whole state of a particular language at that time. Attention is on how the language and its parts function, not on tracing the historical development of a single element, as would occur in a diachronic analysis. By highlighting the activity of the language system and how it operates rather than its evolution, Saussure drew attention to the nature and composition of language and its constituent parts. For example, along with examining the phonological antecedents of the English sound *b*, as in the word *boy* (a diachronic analysis), Saussure opened a new avenue of investigation, asking how the *b* sound is related to other sounds in use at the same time by speakers of Modern English (a synchronic analysis). This new concern necessitated a rethinking of language theory and a re-evaluation of the aims of language research, and finally resulted in Saussure's articulating the basic principles of modern linguistics.

Unlike many of his contemporary linguists, Saussure rejected the mimetic theory of language structure. In its place, he asserted that language is primarily determined by its own internally structured and highly systematized rules. These rules govern all aspects of a language, including the sounds its speakers will identify as meaningful, grouping various combinations of these sounds into words, and how these words may be arranged to produce meaningful communication within a given language.

The Structure of Language

According to Saussure, all languages are governed by their own internal rules that do not mirror or imitate the structure of the world. The basic build block of language is the **phoneme**—the smallest, meaningful (significant) sound in a language. The number of phonemes differs from language to language, with the least number of total phonemes for any one language being around nine and the most in the mid sixties. American English, for example, consists of approximately forty-three to forty-five phonemes, depending on the specific dialect being spoken. Although native speakers of American English are capable of producing phonemes found in other languages, it is these forty-five distinct sounds that serve as the building blocks of American English. For example, the first sound heard in the word *pin* is the /p/ phoneme, the second /I/, and the last /n/. A phoneme can be identified in writing by enclosing the **grapheme**—the written symbol that represents the phoneme's sound—in virgules or diagonal lines.

Although each phoneme makes a distinct sound that is meaningful and recognizable to speakers of a particular language, in actuality a phoneme is composed of a family of nearly identical speech sounds called **allophones**. For instance, in the word *pit*, the first phoneme is /p/, and in the word *spin*, the second phoneme is also /p/. Although the /p/ appears in both words, its pronunciation is slightly different. To validate this statement, simply hold the palm of your hand about two inches from your mouth and pronounce the word *pit* followed immediately by the word *spin*. You will quickly note the difference. These slightly different pronunciations of the same phoneme are simply two different allophones of the phoneme /p/.

How phonemes and allophones arrange themselves to produce meaningful speech in any language is not arbitrary, but is governed by a prescribed set of rules developed through time by the speakers of a language.

For example, in Modern American English (1755–present), no English word can end with the two phonemes /m/ and /b/. In Middle English (1100–1500), these phonemes could combine to form the two terminal sounds of a word, resulting, for example, in the word *lamb*, where the /m/ and /b/ were both pronounced. Over time, the rules of spoken English have changed so much that when *lamb* appears in Modern English, /b/ has lost its phonemic value. The study of the rules governing the meaningful units of sound in a linguistic system is called **phonology**, whereas the study of the production of these sounds is known as **phonetics**.

In addition to phonemes, another major building block of language is the **morpheme**, the smallest part of a word that has lexical or grammatical significance. (**Lexical** refers to the base or root meaning of a word; **grammatical** refers to those elements of language that express relationships between words or groups of words, such as the **inflections** {-ed}, {-s}, and {-ing} that carry tense, number, gender, and so on). Like the phoneme, the number of lexical and grammatical morphemes varies from language to language. In American English, the number of lexical morphemes far outdistances the relatively handful of grammatical morphemes (ten or so). For instance, in the word *reaper*, {reap} is a lexical morpheme, meaning "to ripple flax" and {-er} is a grammatical morpheme, meaning "one who." (Note that in print morphemes are placed in braces.) All words must have a lexical morpheme (hence their great number), whereas not every word need have a grammatical morpheme. How the various lexical and grammatical morphemes combine to form words is highly rule-governed and is known in modern linguistics as the study of **morphology**.

Another major building block in the structure of language is the actual arrangement of words in a sentence—its **syntax**. Just as the placement of phonemes and morphemes in individual words is a rule governed activity, so is the arrangement of words in a sentence. For example, although native speakers of English would understand the sentence "John threw the ball into the air," such speakers would have difficulty ascertaining the meaning of "Threw the air into the ball John." Why? Native speakers of a language have mastered which strings of morphemes are permitted by syntactic rules and which are not. Those that do not conform to these rules do not form English sentences and are called **ungrammatical**. Those that do conform to the established syntactic structures are called **sentences** or **grammatical sentences**. In most English sentences, for example, the subject ("John") precedes the verb ("threw"), followed by the complement ("the ball into the air"). Although this structure can at times be modified, such changes must follow tightly prescribed rules of syntax if a speaker of English is to be understood.

Having established the basic building blocks of a sentence—*phonemes, morphemes,* and *syntax*—language also provides us with one additional body of rules to govern the various interpretations or shades of meaning such combinations of words can evoke: **semantics**. Unlike morphemes (the meanings of which can be found in the dictionary) and unlike the word stock of a language—its **lexicon**—the **semantic features** (the properties of words that show facets of meaning) are not so easily defined. Consider, for example, the following sentences:

"Danny is a nut."
"I found a letter on Willard Avenue."
"Get a grip, Heidi."

To understand each of these sentences, a speaker or reader needs to understand the semantic features that govern an English sentence, for each of the above sentences has several possible interpretations. In the first sentence, the speaker must grasp the concept of metaphor, in the second, lexical ambiguity, and in the third, idiomatic structures. Unless these semantic features are consciously or unconsciously known and understood by the reader or listener, problems of interpretation may arise. As with the other building blocks of language, an understanding of semantics is necessary for clear communication in any language.

Langue and Parole

By age five or six, native speakers of English or any other language have consciously and unconsciously mastered their language's complex system of rules or its **grammar**—their language's phonology, morphology, syntax, and semantics—which enables them to participate in language communication. They have not, however, mastered such advanced elements as all the semantic features of their language, nor have they mastered its **prescriptive grammar**, those rules, for example, of English grammar often invented by eighteenth- and nineteenth-century purists who believed that there were certain constructions that all educated people should know and employ, such as using the nominative form of a pronoun after an intransitive linking verb as in the sentence, "It is *I*." What these five- or six-year-old native speakers of a language have learned Saussure dubs **langue**, the structure of the language that is mastered and shared by all its speakers.

While langue emphasizes the social aspect of language and an understanding of the overall language system, an individual's actual speech utterances and writing Saussure calls **parole**. A speaker can generate countless examples of individual utterances, but these will all be governed by the language's system, its langue. It is the task of the linguist, Saussure believes, to infer a language's langue from the analysis of many instances of parole. In other words, for Saussure, the proper study of linguistics is the system (langue), not the individual utterances of its speakers (parole).

Saussure's Redefinition of a *Word*

Having established that languages are systems that operate according to verifiable rules and that they need to be investigated both diachronically and synchronically, Saussure then re-examined philology's definition of a *word*. Rejecting the long-held belief that a word is a symbol that equals a thing (its referent), Saussure proposed that words are **signs** made up of two parts: the **signifier** (a written or spoken mark) and a **signified** (a concept):

$$\text{Sign} = \frac{\text{Signifier}}{\text{Signified}}$$

For example, when we hear the sound *ball*, the sound is the signifier and the concept of a ball that comes to our minds is the signified. Like the two sides of a sheet of paper, the linguistic sign is the union of these two elements. As oxygen combines with hydrogen to form water, Saussure says, so the signifier joins with the signified to form a sign that has properties unlike those of its parts. Accordingly, for Saussure a word does not represent a referent in the objective world but a sign. Unlike previous generations of philologists who believed that we perceive things (word = thing) and then translate them into units or meaning, Saussure revolutionizes linguistics by asserting that we perceive signs.

Furthermore, the linguistic sign, declares Saussure, is arbitrary: the relationship between the signifier (*ball*) and the signified (the concept of *ball*) is a matter of convention. The speakers of a language have simply agreed that the written or spoken sounds or marks represented by *ball* will equal the concept *ball*. With few exceptions, proclaims Saussure, there is no natural link between the signifier and the signified, nor is there any natural relationship between the linguistic sign and what it represents.

If, as Saussure maintains, there is no natural link between the linguistic sign and the reality it represents, how do we know the difference between one sign and another? In other words, how does language create meaning? We know what a sign means, says Saussure, because it differs from all other signs. By comparing and contrasting one sign with other signs, we learn to distinguish each individual sign. Individual signs, then, can have meaning (or signify) only within their own langue.

For Saussure, meaning is therefore relational and a matter of difference. Within the system of sound markers that comprise our language, we know *ball*, for instance, because we differentiate it from *hall*, *tail*, and *pipe*. Likewise, we know the concept "bug" because it differs from the concepts "truck," "grass," and "kite." As Saussure declares, "In language there are only differences."

Since signs are arbitrary, conventional, and differential, Saussure concludes that the proper study of language is not an examination of isolated entities but the system of relationships among them. He asserts, for example, that individual words cannot have meaning by themselves. Because language is a system of rules governing sounds, words, and other components, individual words obtain their meaning only within that system. To know language and how it functions, he declares, we must study the system (langue), not individual utterances (parole) that operate according to the rules of langue.

For Saussure, language is the primary sign system whereby we structure our world. Language's structure, he believes, is not unlike that of any other sign system of social behavior, such as fashion, table manners, and sports. Like language, all such expressions of social behavior generate meaning through a system of signs. Saussure proposed a new science called **semiology** that would study how we create meaning through these signs in all our social behavioral systems. Since language was the chief and most characteristic of all these systems, Saussure declared, it was to be the main branch of semiology. The investigation of all other sign systems would be patterned after language, for like language's signs, the meaning of all signs is arbitrary, conventional, and differential.

Although semiology never became the important new science Saussure envisioned, a similar science was being proposed in America almost simultaneously by philosopher and teacher Charles Sanders Peirce. Called **semiotics**, this science borrowed linguistic methods utilized by Saussure and applied them to all meaningful cultural phenomena. Meaning in society, this science of signs declares, can be systematically studied, both in studying how this meaning occurs and in understanding the structures that allow it to operate. Distinguishing among the various kinds of signs, semiotics continues to develop today as a particular field of study. Because it uses structuralist methods borrowed from Saussure, *semiotics* and *structuralism* are terms often used interchangeably, although the former denotes a distinct field of study, while the latter is more an approach and method of analysis.

ASSUMPTIONS

Borrowing the linguistic vocabulary, theory, and methods from Saussure and to a smaller degree from Peirce, structuralists—their studies being variously called structuralism, semiotics, stylistics, and narratology, to name a few—believe that codes, signs, and rules govern all human social and cultural practices, including communication. Whether that communication is the language of fashion, sports, education, friendships, or literature, each is a systematized combination of codes (signs) governed by rules. Structuralists want to discover these codes, which they believe give meaning to all our social and cultural customs and behavior. The proper study of meaning—and therefore reality—they assert, is an investigation of the system behind these practices, not the individual practices themselves. To discover how all the parts fit together and function is their aim.

Structuralists find meaning, then, in the relationship among the various components of a system. When applied to literature, this principle becomes revolutionary. The proper study of literature, for the structuralists, now involves an inquiry into the conditions surrounding the act of interpretation itself (how literature conveys meaning), not an in-depth investigation of an individual work. Since an individual work can express only those values and beliefs of the system of which it is a part, structuralists emphasize the system (langue) whereby texts relate to each other, not an examination of an isolated text (parole). They believe that a study of the system of rules that govern literary interpretation becomes the critic's primary task.

Such a belief presupposes that the structure of literature is similar to the structure of language. Like language, so say the structuralists, literature is a self-enclosed system of rules that is composed of language. Literature, like language, needs no outside referent except its own rule-governed, but socially constrained, system. Before structuralism, literary theorists discussed the literary conventions—that is, the various genres or types of literature, such as the novel, the short story, or poetry. Each genre, it was believed, had its own conventions or acknowledged and acceptable way of reflecting and interpreting life. For example, in poetry, a poet could write in nonsentences, using symbols and other forms of figurative language to state a theme or to make a point. For these prestructuralist theorists, the proper study of literature was an examination of these conventions and of how either individual texts used applicable conventions to make meaning or how readers utilized these same conventions to interpret the text. Structuralists, however, seek out the system of codes that they believe convey a text's meaning. For them, how a text convenes meaning rather than what meaning is conveyed is at the center of their interpretative methodology—that is, how a symbol or a metaphor, for example, imparts meaning is now of special interest. For instance, in Nathaniel Hawthorne's "Young Goodman Brown," most readers assume that the darkness of the forest equates with evil and images of light represent safety. Of particular interest to the structuralist is *how* (not *that*) darkness comes to represent evil. A structuralist would ask why darkness more frequently than not represents evil in any text and what sign system or code is operating that allows readers to interpret darkness as evil intertextually or in all or most texts they read. To the structuralist, how a symbol or any other literary device functions is of chief importance, not how literary devices imitate reality or express feelings.

In addition to emphasizing the system of literature and not individual texts, structuralism also claims it demystifies literature. By explaining literature as a system of signs encased in a cultural frame that allows that system to operate, say the structuralists, a literary work can no longer be considered a mystical or magical relationship between the author and the reader, the place where author and reader share emotions, ideas, and truth. A scientific and an objective analysis of how readers interpret texts, not a transcendental, intuitive, or transactional response to any one text, leads to meaning. Similarly, an author's intentions can no longer be equated to the text's overall meaning, for meaning is determined by the system that governs the writer, not an individual author's own quirks. And no longer can the text be autonomous, an object whose meaning is contained solely within itself. All texts, declare structuralists, are part of the shared system of meaning that is **intertextual**, not text specific; in other words, all texts refer readers to other texts. Meaning, claim the structuralists, can therefore be expressed only through this shared system of relations, not in an author's stated intentions or the reader's private or public experiences.

Declaring both isolated text and author to be of little importance, structuralism attempts to strip literature of its magical powers or so-called hidden meanings that can only be discovered by a small, elite group of highly trained specialists. Meaning can be found, it declares, by analyzing the system of rules that comprise literature itself.

METHODOLOGIES

Like all other approaches to textual analysis, structuralism follows neither one methodological strategy nor one set of ideological assumptions. Although most structuralists use many of Saussure's ideas in formulating their theoretical assumptions and foundations for their literary theories, how these assumptions are employed when applied to textual analysis vary greatly. A brief examination of five structuralists or subgroups will help highlight structuralism's varied approaches to textual analysis.

Claude Lévi-Strauss

One of the first scholar–researchers to implement Saussure's principles of linguistics to narrative discourse in the 1950s and 1960s was the anthropologist Claude Lévi-Strauss. Attracted to the rich symbols in myths, Lévi-Strauss spent years studying myths from throughout the world. Myth, he assumed, possessed a structure like language. Each individual myth was therefore an example of parole. What he wanted to discover was myth's langue, its overall structure that allows individual examples (parole) to function and have meaning.

After reading countless myths, Lévi-Strauss identified recurrent themes running through all of them. Such themes transcended culture and time, speaking directly to the minds and hearts of all people. These basic structures, which he called **mythemes**, were similar to the primary building blocks of language, the phonemes. Like phonemes, these mythemes find meaning in and through their relationships within the mythic structure. And like phonemes, such relationships often involve oppositions. For example, the /b/ and /p/ phonemes are similar in that they are pronounced by using the lips to suddenly stop a stream of air. They differ or oppose one another in only one aspect: whether the air passing through the wind pipe does or does not vibrate the vocal cords; during actual speech, vibrating vocal cords produce /b/ and nonvibrating /p/. Similarly, a mytheme finds its meaning through opposition. Hating or loving one's parents, falling in love with someone who does or who does not love you, and cherishing or abandoning one's children all exemplify the dual or opposing nature of mythemes. The rules that govern how these mythemes may be combined constitute myth's structure or grammar. The meaning of any individual myth, then, depends on the interaction and order of the mythemes within the story. Out of this structural pattern will come the myth's meaning.

When applied to a specific literary work, the intertextuality of myth becomes evident. For example, in Shakespeare's *King Lear*, King Lear overestimates the value and support of children when he trusts, Regan and Goneril, his two oldest daughters, to take care of him in his old age. He also underestimates the value and support of children when he banishes his youngest and most-loved daughter, Cordelia. Like the binary opposition that occurs between the /b/ and /p/ phonemes, the binary opposition of underestimating versus overestimating love automatically occurs when reading the text, for such mythemes have occurred in countless other texts and immediately ignite emotions within the reader.

Like our unconscious mastery of our language's langue, we also master myth's structure. Our ability to grasp this structure, says Lévi-Strauss, is innate. Like language, myths are simply another way we classify and organize our world.

Roland Barthes

Researching and writing in response to Lévi-Strauss was his contemporary, the eminent French structuralist Roland Barthes. Barthes' contribution to structuralist theory is best summed up in the title of his most famous text, *S/Z*. In Balzac's *Sarrasine*, Barthes noted that the first *s* is pronounced as the *s* in *snake*, and the second as the *z* in *zoo*. Both phonemes, /s/ and /z/ respectively, are a **minimal pair**—that is, both are produced by using the same articulatory organs and in the same place in the mouth, the difference being that /s/ is **unvoiced** (no vibration of vocal cords) and /z/ is **voiced** (vibration of vocal cords when air is blowing through the breath channel). Like all minimal pairs—/p/ and /b/, /t/ and /d/, and /k/ and /g/, for example—this pair operates in what Barthes calls "binary opposition." Even within a phoneme, binary opposition exists, for a phoneme is, as Saussure reminded us, a class of nearly identical sounds called allophones, which differ **phonetically**, that is, by slightly changing the pronunciation but not altering the recognizable phoneme. Borrowing and further developing Saussure's work, Barthes then declares that all language is its own self-enclosed system based upon binary operations (difference).

Barthes then applies his assumption that meaning develops through difference to all social contexts, including fashions, familial relations, dining, and literature, to name a few. When applied to literature, an individual text is simply a message—a parole—that must be interpreted by using the appropriate codes or signs or binary operations that form the basis of the entire system, the langue. Only through recognizing the codes or binary operations within the text, says Barthes, can the message encoded within the text be explained. For example, in Nathaniel Hawthorne's "Young Goodman Brown" most readers intuitively know that Young Goodman Brown will come face to face with evil when he enters the forest. Why? Because one code or binary operation that we all know is that light implies good and dark evil. Thus Brown enters the *dark* forest and leaves the *light* of his home, only to find the "false light" of evil emanating from the artificial light—the fires that light the baptismal service of those being inducted into Satan's legions. By finding other binary oppositions within the text and showing how these oppositions interrelate, the structuralist can then decode the text, thereby explaining its meaning.

Such a process abandons or dismisses the importance of the author, any historical or literary period, or particular textual elements or genres. Rather than discovering any element of truth within a text, this methodology shows the process of decoding a text in relationship to the codes provided by the structure of language itself.

Valdimir Propp

Expanding Lévi-Strauss' linguistic model of myths, a group of structuralists called **narratologists** began another kind of structuralism: **structuralist narratology**, the science of narrative. Like Saussure and Lévi-Strauss, these structuralists illustrate how a story's meaning develops from its overall structure, its langue, rather than from each individual story's isolated theme. Using this idea as his starting point, the Russian linguist Valdimir Propp investigated Russian fairy tales to decode their langue. According to his analysis, which appears in his work *The Morphology of Folktale* (1968), all folk or fairy tales are based upon thirty-one fixed elements, or what Propp calls functions, which will occur in a given sequence. Each function identifies predictable patterns or functions that central characters, such as the hero, the villain, or the helper, will enact to further the plot of the story. Any story may use any number of these elements, such as "accepting the call to adventure," "recognizing the hero," "the punishing of the villain," among others, but each element will occur in its logical and proper sequence.

Applying Propp's narratological principles to specific literary works is both fun and obvious. For example, in Twain's *Adventures of Huckleberry Finn*, Huck, the protagonist, is given a task to do: free Jim. His evil enemy (the villain), society, tries to stop him. But throughout the novel, various helpers appear to propel the plot forward, until the hero's task is completed, and he successfully frees Jim and flees from his enemy.

Tzvetan Todorov and Gerard Genette

Another narratologist, the Bulgarian Tzvetan Todorov declares that all stories are composed of grammatical units. For Todorov, the syntax of narrative or how the various grammatical elements of a story combine is essential. By applying a rather intricate grammatical model to narrative—dividing the text into semantic, syntactic, and verbal aspects—Todorov believes he can discover the narrative's langue and establish a grammar of narrative. He begins by asserting that the grammatical clause, and in turn, the subject and verb, is the basic interpretative unit of each sentence and can be linguistically analyzed and further dissected into a variety of grammatical categories to show how all narratives are structured. An individual text (parole) interests Todorv as a means to describe the overall properties of literature in general (langue).

Other narratologists, such as Gerard Genette and Roland Barthes, have also developed methods of analyzing a story's structure to uncover its meaning, each building upon the former work of another narratologist and adding an additional element or two. Genette, for example, believes that **tropes** or figures of speech require a reader's special attention. Barthes, on the other hand, points readers back to Todorov and provides more linguistic terminology with which to examine a story.

Although these narratologists provide us with various approaches to texts, all furnish us with a **metalanguage**—words used to describe language—so that we can understand *how* a text means, not *what* it means.

Jonathan Culler

By the mid-1970s, Jonathan Culler became the voice of structuralism in America and took structuralism in yet another direction. In his work *Structuralist Poetics*, Culler declared that abstract linguistic models used by narratologists tended to focus on parole, spending too much time analyzing individual stories, poems, and novels. What was needed, he believed, was a return to an investigation of langue, Saussure's main premise.

According to Culler, readers, when given a chance, will somehow make sense out of the most bizarre text. Somehow, readers possess **literary competence**. Through experiences with texts, Culler asserts, they have internalized a set of rules that govern their acts of interpretation. Instead of analyzing individual interpretations of a work, we must spend our time, Culler insists, on analyzing the act of interpretation itself. We must shift the focus from the text to the reader. How, asks Culler, does interpretation take place in the first place? What system underlies the very act of reading that allows any other system to operate?

Unlike other structuralists, Culler presents a theory of reading. What, he asks, is the internalized system of literary competence readers use to interpret a work? In other words, how do they read? What system guides them through the process of interpreting the work, of making sense of the spoken or printed word?

Culler asserts that three elements undergird any reading, for instance, of a poem:

- that a poem should be unified,
- that it should be thematically significant, and
- that this significance can take the form of reflection in poetry.

Accordingly, Culler then seeks to establish the system, the langue, that undergirds the reading process. By focusing on the act of interpretation itself to discover literature's langue, Culler believes he is returning structuralism to its Saussurean roots.

A Model of Interpretation

Many structuralist theories abound, but a core of structuralists believe that the primary signifying system is best found as a series of binary oppositions that the reader organizes, values, and then uses to interpret the text. Each binary operation can be pictured as a fraction, the top half (the numerator) being what is more valued than its related bottom half (the denominator). Accordingly, in the binary operation *light/dark*, the reader has learned to value light *over* dark, and in the binary operation *good/evil* the reader has similarly valued good *over* evil. How the reader maps out and organizes the various binary operations and their interrelationships found within the text but already existing in the mind of the reader will determine for that particular reader the text's interpretation.

No matter what its methodology, structuralism emphasizes form and structure, not the actual content of a text. Although individual texts must be analyzed, structuralists are more interested in the rule-governed system that underlies texts rather than the texts themselves. How texts mean, not what texts mean, is their chief interest.

QUESTIONS FOR ANALYSIS

- What are the various binary oppositions or operations that operate in Nathaniel Hawthorne's "Ethan Brand" or any other story of your choosing. After you map out these oppositions, show *how* the text means, not *what* it means.
- What mythemes are evident in Robert Browning's "My Last Duchess"? How do these mythemes show the intertextuality of this particular text with other literary texts you have read?
- How do the various semantic features contained in a text of your choosing directly relate to the codes, signs, or binary oppositions you find in the text?
- Using a text you have selected, can you apply at least three different methods of structuralism to arrive at how the text achieves its meaning? In the final analysis, is there a difference among the three methodologies in how the text achieves its meaning?
- Can you choose another sign system—sports, music, classroom etiquette—and explain the codes that generate meaning?

SAMPLE ESSAY

In the student essay that follows, note how the interpretation of James Thurber's short story "The Secret Life of Walter Mitty" revolves around two major binary oppositions or tensions and several minor but interlated tensions. After citing the secondary tensions, be able to explain the intricate web of relationships among both the dominant and the secondary binary oppositions. Can you map out a listing of these binary oppositions upon which the interpretation is based? In addition, consider also the actual essay itself as a literary text. What binary oppositions—both major and minor— unite this text? Be able to cite specific examples from the essay to prove your ideas.

FURTHER READING

Barthes, Roland. *Critical Essays.* Trans. R. Howard. Evanston, IL: Northwestern University Press, 1972.

———. *Mythologies.* Trans. Annette Lavers. New York: Hill and Wang, 1972.

Culler, Jonathan. *Structuralist Poetics: Structuralism, Linguistics, and the Study of Literature.* New York: Cornell University Press, 1975.

Genette, Gerard. *Narrative Discourse.* Trans. Jane Lewin. Ithaca: Cornell University Press, 1980.

Hawkes, Terence. *Structuralism and Semiotics.* Berkley: University of California Press, 1977.

Jakobson, Roman. "Linguistics and Poetics." *Style in Language.* Ed. Thomas Sebeok. Cambridge: MIT Press, 1960. 350–77.

Jameson, Fredic. *The Prison House of Language: A Critical Account of Structuralism and Russian Formalism.* Princeton: Princeton University Press, 1972.

Lévi-Strauss, Claude. *Structural Anthropology.* Trans. Claire Jacobson and Brooke Schoepf. London: Allen Lane, 1968.

Propp, Vladimir. *The Morphology of the Folktale.* Trans. Laurence Scott. Austin: University of Texas Press, 1968.

Saussure, Ferdinand de. *Course in General Linguistics.* New York: McGraw, 1966.

Scholes, Robert. *Structuralism in Literature: An Introduction.* New Haven: Yale University Press, 1974.

———. *Semiotics and Interpretation.* New Haven: Yale University Press, 1982.

Todorov, Tzvetan. *The Fantastic: A Structural Approach to a Literary Genre.* Trans. Richard Howard. Ithaca: Cornell University Press. 1977.

WEB SITES FOR EXPLORATION

www.brockku.ca/english/courses/4F70/struct.html
  A good review of the basic elements of structuralism plus a solid application to literary theory

www.classics.cam.ac.uk/Faculty/structuralism.html
  A mini-guide to structuralism and its hermeneutics

www.xrefer.com/entry/344812
  An excellent overview of structuralist theory

www.panix.com/~squigle/vcs/structuralism.html
  An excellent review of both structuralism and poststructuralism

http://192.148.225.23
  A solid review of structuralism

www.colorado.edu/English/ENGL201Klages/levi-strauss.html
  A review of the structuralist principles of Claude Lévi-Strauss

✥ Student Essay ✥

Will the Real Walter Mitty Please Wake Up:
A Structuralist's View of "The Secret Life of Walter Mitty"

In "The Secret Life of Walter Mitty" by James Thurber, Mitty is a henpecked, insignificant, and insecure husband who runs from his reality to a world of fantasy created in his mind. Once there, he is superior, confident, and capable of handling any occasion.

This interpretation of the short story is built on two prominent binary oppositions, supported by others, and interwoven within the structure of the story. The most obvious binary opposition occurs as Mitty moves in and out of his fantasies and is indicated by ellipses before and after each fantasy. It is through the binary opposition of fantasy versus reality that we see the second predominant opposition of superior versus inferior.

The story begins with a commander of a Navy hydroplane shouting orders to a lieutenant. "We're going through!" he declares with a cool voice and a cold eye as he stands up to a hurricane. "Full Strength in No. 3 turret!" he yells. "The Old Man ain't afraid of Hell!" his inferior officers boast. Commander Mitty is fearless and feared; to his crew he is superior. The irony of this fantasy, though, is that the superior commander does not know that hydroplanes do not have turrets. Suddenly, readers can see another binary opposition related to superior/inferior, that of knowledge versus ignorance. But whom do we blame: the commander or Walter Mitty?

Abruptly, in the next paragraph, the cold commander is gone and Walter Mitty's wife is yelling at him for driving too fast. Reality has once again returned to Walter Mitty along with his nagging wife, who is now the superior one. She scolds him for driving too fast, much like a mother would scold a child for wiping his nose on his sleeve. She then reminds him to get overshoes to keep his feet dry because he's "not a young man any longer," introducing the tension of youth versus age.

Driving past a hospital catapults Mitty into another fantasy, in which he is an awed medical doctor who saves the life of a millionaire banker. This is not just any millionaire; he is a close friend of Roosevelt. Dr. Mitty is elevated far beyond the most coveted men in America. Even the two specialists cannot compare to the superiority of Dr. Mitty who, by the way, is also an author of an extraordinary book about streptothricosis, a disease no dictionary has yet defined. When an important machine breaks during the surgery, Dr. Mitty leaps to the rescue calling for a fountain pen that he promptly sticks into the correct place to replace a faulty piston. The two specialists are so unnerved by the surgery that they can only turn the scalpel over to Mitty. Again, Dr. Mitty is superior and almost godlike. He is capable and confident; that is, until a parking-lot attendant yells at him for driving in the wrong lane.

Reality hits again, however, and the superior Dr. Mitty finds himself an inferior to a young, grinning, and cocky parking-lot attendant, displaying again the tension between youth and age, with youth in this case being superior. A tension between confidence and insecurity unveils itself, as Walter Mitty remembers trying to take off his snow chains and finds he cannot. "Next time," he thinks to himself, "I'll wear my right arm in a sling; they won't grin at me then." The attendants would simply conclude that a bum arm was the reason for his inability. As Mitty berates himself for forgetting what it was he needed to get from the store, the tension or binary opposition between confidence and insecurity reappears. Feelings of inferiority lead Mitty to fear his wife's reprimand.

Thinking about his forgetfulness plus the added stimulus of a newsboy causes Mitty once again to lose himself in yet another fantasy. This time he is a criminal, capable of shooting anyone at three hundred feet with his left hand. There is no fear in Mitty as he sits in the witness chair, not of the prosecutor or of the judge. Mitty the Murderer exhibits the binary opposition of strength versus weakness, another superior/inferior relative, as he defies the law and punches the district attorney in the chops for pushing a pretty, young, dark-haired girl away from Mitty's arms. Ignorance versus knowledge reappears at this point when Mitty the Murderer examines his gun "expertly" and declares that the Webley-Vickers 50.80 is his. What Mitty does not realize is that a Webley-Vickers is a motorcycle.

Next we observe Mitty the Murderer mumbling "puppy biscuits" and being laughed at by a passer-by. Reality and the feelings of inferiority that accompany it surround Mitty, as he rushes off to the place where he is to meet his wife.

Waiting for his wife, Mitty picks up a newspaper. As soon as he reads the headlines about the Germans, he becomes a World War II bomber pilot. Now Captain Mitty awakens from a deep sleep by a panicky sergeant whom he swiftly sends to bed, declaring that he will fly the bomber alone. But first he pours himself a spot of brandy. "I never see a man could hold his brandy like you, sir," the sergeant says. Mitty's superiority apparently has no boundaries. He is confident, capable, and fearless until his wife startles him with a tap on the shoulder.

"I've been looking all over this hotel for you," Mrs. Mitty scolds with superiority. She continues to nag and question him, until Mitty unexpectedly confronts her. "I was thinking," he declares. "Does it ever occur to you that I am sometimes thinking?" Is it possible that the confident, superior, and capable man of Mitty's fantasies is emerging into reality? We'll never know, for Mrs. Mitty immediately squashs him back into inferiority with her superiority by attributing his assertiveness to a fever.

As both husband and wife leave, Mitty crosses over into fantasy one last time. Waiting for his wife while she goes into a store, Mitty leans against a wall and lights a cigarette. Instantly, Mitty confronts an enemy, not his wife this time, but a firing squad. With fearless confidence, he rips the blindfold from his eyes and meets death face to face. Mitty the Fearless stands "erect and motionless, proud and disdainful, Walter Mitty the Undefeated, inscrutable to the last," at least in his fantasies!

The binary opposition of fantasy versus reality dominates Walter Mitty's life. In his fantasies, he is everything he cannot be in reality: strong, confident, and superior—traits that society values in a person. The binary oppositions of strength/weakness, youth/age, knowledge/ignorance, and confidence/insecurity support the other dominant tension of superior versus inferior. These tensions appear again and again in both Mitty's fantasies and his reality. Within the world of fantasy, Mitty is superior to everyone, both great and small. Within the real world, however, he is superior to no one, including his own wife.

CONIE KRAUSE

ᔰ *6* ᖲ

Deconstruction

We need to interpret interpretations more than to interpret things.

Montaigne (as quoted in Jacques Derrida's essay,
"Structure, Sign, and Play," 1966)

STRUCTURALISM AND POSTSTRUCTURALISM:
TWO VIEWS OF THE WORLD

Throughout the 1950s and 1960s, a variety of different forms of structuralism dominated European and American literary theory: the French structuralism of Roland Barthes, the Russian structuralist narratology of Vladimir Propp, and Jonathan Culler's American brand of structuralist poetics, to name a few. While the application of structuralist principles varies from one theoretician to another, all believe that language is the primary means of **signification** (how we achieve meaning through linguistic signs and other symbols) and that language comprises its own rule-governed system to achieve such meaning. Although language is the primary sign system, it is not the only one. Fashions, sports, dining, and other activities all have their own language or codes whereby the participants know what is expected of them in a particular situation. When dining at a restaurant, for example, connoisseurs of fine dining know that it is inappropriate to drink from a finger bowl. Similarly, football fans know that it is appropriate to shout, scream, and holler to support their team.

From a structuralist perspective, such expectations highlight that all social and cultural practices are governed by rules or codes. Wishing to discover these rules, structuralists declare that the proper study of reality and meaning is the system behind such individual practices, not the individual practices themselves. Like football or fine dining, the act of reading is also a cultural and a social practice that contains its own codes. Meaning in a text resides in these codes that the reader has mastered before he or she even picks up an actual text. For the structuralist, the proper study of literature is an inquiry into the conditions surrounding the act of interpretation itself, not an investigation of the individual text.

Holding to the principles of Ferdinand de Saussure, an early pioneer of modern linguistics, structuralists seek to discover the overall system (langue) that accounts for an individual interpretation (parole) of a text. Meaning and the reasons for meaning can be both ascertained and discovered.

With the advent of **deconstruction** theory in the late 1960s, however, the structuralist assumption that a text's meaning can be discovered through an examination of its structural codes was challenged and replaced by the maxim of undecidability: a text has many meanings and, therefore, no definitive interpretation. Rather than providing answers about the meaning of texts or a methodology for discovering how a text means, deconstruction asks a new set of questions, endeavoring to show that what a text claims it says and what it actually says are discernibly different. By casting doubt on most previously held theories, deconstruction declares that a text has an almost infinite number of possible interpretations. Further, declare some deconstructionists, the interpretations themselves are just as creative and important as the text being interpreted.

With the advent of deconstruction and its challenge to structuralism and other prior theories, a paradigmatic shift occurs in literary theory. Before deconstruction, literary critics—New Critics, some reader-response theorists, structuralists, and others—found meaning *within* the literary text or the codes of the various sign systems within the world of the text and the reader. The most innovative of these theorists, the structuralists, provided new and exciting ways to discover meaning, but nonetheless, these theorists maintained that meaning could be found. Underlying all the predeconstructionist suppositions about the world is a set of assumptions called **modernism** (or the modern worldview), which provided the philosophical, ethical, and scientific bases for humankind for about 300 years. With the coming of deconstruction, however, these long-held beliefs were challenged by **poststructuralism**, a new basis for understanding and guiding humanity (its name denoting that it historically comes after or *post* structuralism). Often, historians, anthropologists, literary theorists, and other scholars use the term **postmodernism** synonymously with deconstruction and poststructuralism, although the term *postmodernism* was coined in the 1930s and has broader historical implications outside the realm of literary theory than do the terms *poststructuralism* or *deconstruction*. To place this discussion and the somewhat turbulent reception of deconstruction (the first of several poststructural schools of criticism) in context, a working understanding of modernism and postmodernism is necessary.

MODERNITY

For many historians and literary theorists alike, the Enlightenment or the Age of Reason (18th century) is synonymous with modernism. That its roots predate this time period is unquestioned, with a few scholars even dating its beginnings to 1492, coincident with Columbus's journeys to the Americas, and its overall spirit lasting until the middle of the twentieth century. At the center of this view of the world lie two prominent features: a belief that reason is humankind's best guide to life, and that science, above all other human endeavors, could lead humanity to a new promised land. Philosophically, modernism rests on the foundations laid by René Descartes (1596–1650), a French philosopher, scientist, and mathematician. Ultimately, declares Descartes, the only thing one cannot doubt is one's own existence. Certainty and knowledge begin with the self. "I think, therefore I am" thus becomes the only solid foundation upon which knowledge and a theory of knowledge can be built. For Descartes, the rational essence freed from superstition, from human passions, and from one's oftentimes irrational imagination will allow humankind to discover truth about the physical world.

While Descartes's teachings elevated to new heights the individual's rational essence and humankind's ability to reason, the scientific writings and discoveries of both Francis Bacon and Sir Isaac Newton allowed science to be likewise coronated. Thanks to Francis Bacon (1561–1626), the scientific method has become part of everyone's elementary and high school education. It is through experimentation, in the doing of experiments, in making inductive generalizations, and in verifying the results that one can discover truths about the physical world. And thanks to Sir Isaac Newton (1642–1727), the physical world is no longer a mystery but a mechanism that operates according to a system of laws that can be understood by any thinking, rational human being who is willing to apply the principles of the scientific method to the physical universe.

Armed with an unparalleled confidence in humankind's capacity to reason—the ability to inquire and to grasp necessary conditions essential for seeking out such undoubtable truths as provided by mathematics—and the assurance that science can lead the way to a complete understanding of the physical world, the Enlightenment (read modern) scholar was imbued with a spirit of progress. Anything the enlightened mind set as its goal, so these scholars believed, was attainable. Through reason and science, all poverty, all ignorance, and all injustice would be finally banished.

Of all Enlightenment people, Benjamin Franklin (1706–1790) may best exemplify the characteristics of modernity. Gleaned from self-portraits contained in his *Autobiography*, Franklin is the archetypal modern philosopher-scientist. Self-assured, Franklin declares that he literally "pulled himself up by his own bootstraps," overcoming poverty and ignorance through education to become America's first internationally known and respected scientist-philosopher-statesman. Believing in the power and strength of the individual mind, he delighted in the natural world and decided early in life to know all possible aspects of his universe. Accordingly, he abandoned superstitions and myths and placed his trust in science to lead him to truths about his world. Through observations, experiments, and conclusions drawn upon the data discovered under the scientific method, Franklin believed he could obtain and know the necessary truths for guiding him through life.

Like Descartes, Franklin does not abandon religion and replace it with science. Holding to the tenets of deism, he rejects miracles, myths, and much of what he called religious superstitions. What he does not reject is a belief in the existence of God. He asserts, however, that God leaves it to humanity, to each individual, to become the master of his or her own fate. According to Franklin, individuals must find salvation within themselves. By using one's God-given talent for reason, and joining these rational abilities to the principles of science, each person, declares Franklin, can experience and enjoy human progress.

For Franklin and other enlightened minds, truth is to be discovered scientifically, not through the unruly and passionate imagination or through one's feelings or intuition. Indeed, what is to be known and discovered via the scientific method is reality: the physical world. All people, declares Franklin, must know this world objectively and must learn how to investigate it to discover its truths.

Self-assured, self-conscious, and self-made, Franklin concludes that all people possess an essential nature. It is humanity's moral duty to investigate this nature contained within ourselves and also to investigate our environment through rational thinking and the methods of science so that we can learn and share the truths of the universe. By devoting ourselves to science and to the magnificent results that will necessarily follow, Franklin proclaims that human progress is inevitable and will usher in a new golden age.

Franklin and modernity's spirit of progress permeated humankind's beliefs well into the twentieth century. For several centuries modernity's chief tenets—that reality can be known and investigated and that humanity possesses an essential nature characterized by rational thought—became the central ideas upon which many philosophers, scientists, educators, and writers constructed their worldviews. In particular, writers and literary theoreticians—New Critics, structuralists, and others—believed that texts possessed some kind of objective existence and therefore could be studied and analyzed, with appropriate conclusions to follow from such analyses. Whether a text's actual value and meaning was intrinsic or extrinsic was debatable; nevertheless, an aesthetic text's meaning could be discovered. With the formulation of deconstruction, the first major poststructuralist or postmodern school of criticism, the belief in the objective reality of not only texts but also objective reality itself becomes questionable.

POSTSTRUCTURALISM OR POSTMODERNISM

What is truth? How can truth be discovered? What is reality? Is there an objective reality on which we can all agree? If so, how can we best investigate this reality so that all humanity can understand the world in which we live and prosper from such knowledge? Until the late 1960s (with a few notable exceptions), the worldview espoused by modernity and symbolized by Benjamin Franklin provided acceptable and workable answers to these questions. For Franklin and other modern thinkers, the primary form of discourse is like a map. The map itself is a representation of reality as known, discovered, and detailed by humanity. By looking at a map, a traveler with these assumptions can see a delineated view of the world and therefore a basically accurate picture of reality itself: the mountains, the rivers, the plains, the cities, the deserts, and the forests. By placing his or her trust in this representation of reality, the traveler can then plot a journey, feeling confident in the accuracy of the map and its depictions. For the modern mind, objective reality as pictured on the map was knowable and discoverable by any intelligent person who wished to do so.

With the inception of deconstruction, in Jacques Derrida's poststructural view of the world in the mid-1960s, however, modernity's understanding of reality is challenged and turned on its head. For Derrida and other postmodernists, there is no such thing as "objective reality." For these thinkers, all definitions and depictions of truth are subjective, simply creations of human minds. Truth itself is relative, depending on the nature and variety of cultural and social influences in one's life. Because these poststructuralist thinkers assert that many truths exist, not one, they declare that modernity's concept of one objective reality must be disavowed and replaced by many different concepts, each a valid and reliable interpretation and construction of reality.

Postmodernist thinkers reject modernity's representation of discourse (the map) and replace it with the collage. Unlike the fixed, objective nature of a map, a collage's meaning is always changing. Whereas the viewer of a map relies on and obtains meaning and direction from the map itself, the viewer of a collage actually participates in the production of meaning. Unlike a map, which allows one interpretation of reality, a collage permits many possible meanings: the viewer (or "reader") can simply juxtapose a variety of combinations of images, thereby constantly changing the meaning of the collage. Each viewer, then, creates his or her own subjective picture of reality.

To say postmodernism popped onto the American literary scene with the coming of Derrida to America in 1966 would, of course, be inaccurate. Although historians disagree about who actually coined the term, there is general agreement that the word first appeared in the 1930s. In fact, however, its seeds had already germinated far earlier in the writings of Friedrich Nietzsche (1844–1900). As Zarathustra, the protagonist of Nietzsche's *Thus Spake Zarathustra* (1891), proclaims the death of God, simultaneously the death knell begins to sound for the demise of objective reality and ultimate truth. World Wars I and II, a decline in the influence of Christianity and individualism, and the appearance of a new group of theologians lead by Thomas Altizer, who in the 1950s echoed Nietzsche's words that God is dead, all contributed to the obsolescence of objective reality and of the autonomous scholar who seeks to discover ultimate reality.

Beginning in the 1960s and continuing to the present, the voices of the French philosopher Jacques Derrida, the French cultural historian Michel Foucault, the aesthetician Jean-Francois Lyotard, and the ardent American pragmatist Richard Rorty, professor of humanities at the University of Virginia, declare univocally the death of objective truth. These leading articulators of postmodernism assert that modernity failed because it searched for an external point of reference—God, reason, science, among others—on which to build a philosophy. For these postmodern thinkers, there is no such point of reference, for there is no ultimate truth or inherently unifying element in the universe and thus no ultimate reality.

According to postmodernism, all that is left is difference. We must acknowledge, they say, that each person shapes his or her own concepts of reality. Reality, then, becomes a human construct that is shaped by each individual's dominant social group. There exists no center, nor one lone, encompassing objective reality, but as many realities as there are people. Each person's interpretation of reality will necessarily be different. No one has a claim to absolute truth; therefore, tolerance of each other's points of view becomes the postmodern maxim.

Since postmodern philosophy is constantly being shaped, reshaped, defined, and articulated by its adherents, no single voice can adequately represent it or serve as an archetypal spokesperson, as Franklin can for modernity. However, by synthesizing the beliefs of Derrida, Foucault, Lyotard, and Rorty, we can hypothesize what this representative postmodern thinker would possibly espouse:

> I believe, like my forebears before me, that we, as a race of people, will see progress, but only if we all cooperate. The age of the lone scholar, working diligently in the laboratory, is over. Cooperation among scholars from all fields is vital. Gone are the days of individualism. Gone are the days of conquest. Now is the time for tolerance, understanding, and collaboration.
>
> Since our knowledge always was and always will be incomplete, we must focus on a new concept: holism. We must realize that we all need each other, including all our various perspectives on the nature of reality. We must also recognize that our rationality, our thinking processes, is only one of many avenues that can lead to an understanding of our world. Our emotions, our feel-

ings, and our intuition can also provide us with valid interpretations and guidelines for living.

And we have finally come to realize that no such thing as objective reality exists; there is no ultimate truth, for truth is perspectival, depending upon the community and social group in which we live. Since many truths exist, we must learn to accept each other's ideas concerning truth, and we must learn to live side by side, in a pluralistic society, learning from each other while celebrating our differences.

We must stop trying to discover the undiscoverable—absolute truth—and openly acknowledge that what may be right for one person may not be right for another. Acceptance, not criticism; open-mindedness, not closed-mindedness; tolerance, not bigotry; and love, not hatred, must become the guiding principles of our lives. When we stop condemning ourselves and others for "not having truth," then and only then we can spend more time interpreting our lives and giving them meaning, as together we work and play.

When such principles are applied to literary interpretation, the postmodernist realizes that no such thing as *the* meaning—or, especially, the *correct* meaning—of an aesthetic text exists. Like looking at a collage, meaning develops as the reader interacts with the text, for meaning does not reside within the text itself. And since each reader's view of truth is perspectival, the interpretation of a text that emerges when a reader interacts with a text will necessarily be different from every other reader's interpretation. For each text, then, there exists an almost infinite number of interpretations, or at least as many interpretations as there are readers.

HISTORICAL DEVELOPMENT

Deconstruction: Its Beginnings

The term *deconstruction* first emerged on the American literary stage in 1966 when Jacques Derrida (b.1930), a French philosopher and teacher, read his paper "Structure, Sign, and Play" at a Johns Hopkins University symposium. In the essay, Derrida questioned and disputed the metaphysical assumptions held to be true by Western philosophy since the time of Plato, and thus inaugurated what many critics believe to be the most intricate and challenging method of textual analysis yet to appear.

Derrida himself, however, would not want deconstruction construed as either a critical theory, a school of criticism, a mode or method of literary criticism, or a philosophy. Nowhere in Derrida's writings does he state the encompassing tenets of his critical approach, nor does he ever present a codified body of deconstructive theory or a practical methodology. Although he gives his views in bits and pieces throughout his canon, Derrida believes that he cannot develop a formalized statement of his "rules for reading, interpretation, and writing." Unlike a unified treatise, Derrida claims, his approach to reading and literary analysis is more a "strategic device" than a methodology, more a strategy or approach to literature than a school or theory of criticism. Such theories of criticism, he believes, must identify with a body of knowledge that adherents decree to be true or to contain truth. It is this assertion, that truth or a core of metaphysical ideals actually exists and can be believed, articulated, and supported, that Derrida wishes to dispute and "deconstruct"—his device is deconstruction.

Because deconstruction utilizes previously formulated theories from other schools of criticism, coins many words for its newly established ideas, and challenges beliefs long held in Western culture, many students, teachers, and even critics avoid studying its ideas, fearing the supposed complexity of its analytical apparatus. By organizing deconstruction and its assumptions into three workable areas of study rather than plunging directly into some of its complex terminology, we can begin to grasp this approach to textual analysis. To understand deconstruction and its strategic approach to a text, we must first gain a working knowledge of the historical and philosophical roots of structuralism, a linguistic approach to textual analysis that gained critical attention and popularity in the 1950s and 1960s (see Chapter 5 for a detailed analysis of structuralism). It is from this school of criticism that Derrida borrows the basis of and the starting point for his deconstructive strategy. After examining structuralism, we must then investigate the proposed radical changes Derrida makes in Western philosophy and metaphysics. Such changes, Derrida readily admits, literally turn Western metaphysics on its head. Finally, we must master the new terminology, coupled with the new philosophical assumptions and their corresponding methodological approaches to textual analysis, of deconstruction if we wish to understand and utilize this approach to interpreting a text.

Structuralism at a Glance

Derrida begins formulating his strategy of reading by critiquing Ferdinand de Saussure's *Course in General Linguistics*. In the early part of the twentieth century, Saussure, the founder of modern linguistics, dramatically shifted the focus of linguistic science. It is his ideas concerning language that form the core of structuralism, the critical body of literary theory from which Derrida borrows many of the major philosophical building blocks of deconstruction.

According to Saussure, structural linguistics and structuralism itself rest on a few basic principles. First, language is a system of rules. These rules govern its every aspect, including individual sounds that comprise a word (the *t* in *cat*, for example), small units that join together to form a word (*garden* + *er* = *gardener*), grammatical relationships between words (such as the rule that a singular subject must combine with a singular verb—for example, in the sentence *John eats ice cream*, the singular subject, *John*, agrees in number with the singular verb, *eats*), and the relationships among all words in a sentence, such as the relationship between the phrase *under a tree* and all remaining words in the sentence *Mary sits under a tree to eat her lunch*. Consciously and unconsciously, every speaker of a language learns these rules and knows when they are broken. Speakers of English know, for example, that the sentence *Simon grew up to be a brilliant doctor* seems correct and thereby follows the rules of the English language, but that the sentence *Simon up grew a brilliant doctor* is somehow incorrect and violates the rules of English. These rules that comprise a language and which we learn both consciously and unconsciously Saussure dubs **langue**. Saussure recognizes that individual speakers of a language evidence langue in their individual speech utterances, which he calls **parole**. It is the task of the linguist, Saussure believes, to infer a language's langue from the analysis of many instances of parole.

Emphasizing the systematized nature of language, Saussure then asserts that all languages are composed of basic units or **emes**. The job of a linguist is to identify these paradigms (models) or relationships among symbols (the letters of the alphabet, for example) in a given language. This task becomes especially difficult when the emes in the linguist's native language and those in an unfamiliar language under investigation differ. Generally, linguists must first recognize and understand the various emes in their native language. For example, one eme in all languages is the individual sounds that comprise words. The number of distinct and significant sounds (**phonemes**) that comprise a language ranges from eight or nine to about sixty-seven. English, for instance, has approximately forty-five phonemes. Telling the difference among sounds, knowing when any alteration in the pronunciation of a phoneme changes the meaning of a group of phonemes (that is, a word), or knowing when a simple variation in a phoneme's pronunciation is linguistically insignificant can, at times, be difficult. For example, in English the letter *t* represents the sound /t/, but is there one distinct pronunciation for this sound whenever and wherever it appears in an English word? Is the *t* in the word *tip*, for instance, pronounced the same as the *t* in *stop*? Obviously not—the first *t* is **aspirated** or pronounced with a greater force of air than the *t* in *stop*. In either word, however, a speaker of English could still identify the /t/ as a phoneme or a distinct sound. If we then replace the *t* in *tip* with a *d*, we now have *dip*, the difference between the two words being the sounds /t/ and /d/. With further analysis, we find that these sounds are pronounced in the same location in the mouth, but with one difference: /d/ is **voiced** or pronounced with the vocal cords vibrating, whereas /t/ is **unvoiced** with the vocal cords remaining basically still. It is this difference between the sounds /t/ and /d/ that allows us to say that

/t/ and /d/ are phonemes or distinct sounds in English. Whether the eme is a sound, or a minimal unit of grammar such as the adding of an -*s* in English to form most plurals, or any other distinct category of a language, Saussure's basic premise operates: Within each eme, distinctions depend on differences.

The idea that distinctions or meaning in language depends on differences within each eme radically changes some primary concepts that linguists who preceded Saussure accepted as fundamental. Before Saussure, linguists believed that the structure of language was **mimetic**, merely mimicking the outside world. Language had no structure of its own; it simply copied its structure from the reality exhibited in the world in which it was utilized. Saussure denies that language is intrinsically mimetic and demonstrates that it is primarily determined by its own internal rules, such as **phonology** (individual sounds), **grammar** (the principles and rules of a language), and **syntax** (how words combine within an utterance to form meaning). In addition, these rules are highly systematized and structured. Furthermore, and most importantly, Saussure argues that the **linguistic sign** (Saussure's linguistic replacement for the word *word*) that comprises language itself is both arbitrary and conventional. For example, most languages have different words for the same concept. For instance, the English word *man* is *homme* in French. And in English we know that the meaning of the word *pit* exists not because it possesses some innate acoustic quality but because it differs from *hit*, *wit*, and *lit*. In other words, the linguistic sign is composed of two parts: the **signifier**, the spoken or written constituent such as the sound /t/ and the orthographic (written) symbol *t*, and the **signified**, the concept signaled by the signifier. It is this relationship between the signifier (the word *dog*, for example) and the signified (the concept or the reality behind the word *dog*) that Saussure maintains is arbitrary and conventional. The linguistic sign is thus defined by differences that distinguish it from other signs, not by any innate properties.

Believing that our knowledge of the world is shaped by the language that represents it, Saussure is insistent about the arbitrary relationship between the signifier and the signified. In establishing this principle, he undermines the long-held belief that there is some natural link between the word and the thing it represents. Saussure argues, however, that it is only *after* a signifier and the signified are linked that some kind of relationship exists between these two linguistic elements, although the relationship itself is both arbitrary and conventionalized. Ultimately, meaning in language for Saussure resides in a systematized combination of sounds that rely chiefly on the differences among these signs, not on any innate properties within the signs themselves. It is this concept that meaning in language is determined by the differences among the language signs that Derrida borrows from Saussure as a key building block in the formulation of deconstruction.

Derrida's Interpretation of Saussure's Sign

Derridean deconstruction begins with and emphatically affirms Saussure's decree that language is a system based on differences. Derrida agrees with Saussure that we can know the meaning of signifiers through and because of their relationships and their differences among themselves. Unlike Saussure, Derrida also applies this reasoning to the signified. Like the signifier, the signified can also be known only through its relationships and its differences among other signifieds. Furthermore, declares Derrida, the signified cannot orient or make permanent the meaning of the signifier, for the relationship between the signifier and the signified is both arbitrary and conventional. Accordingly, signifieds often function as signifiers. For example, in the sentence *I filled the glass with milk*, the spoken or written word *glass* is a signifier; its signified is the concept of a *container* that can be filled. However, in the sentence *The container was filled with glass*, the spoken or written word *container*, a signified in the previous sentence, is now a signifier, its signified being the concept of an object that can be filled.

ASSUMPTIONS

Transcendental Signified

Believing that signification is both arbitrary and conventional, Derrida now begins his process of turning Western philosophy on its head: He boldly asserts that the entire history of Western metaphysics from Plato to the present is founded on a classic, fundamental error. The great error is in searching for what Derrida calls a **transcendental signified**, an external point of reference upon which one may build a concept or philosophy. Once found, this transcendental signified would provide ultimate meaning since it would be the origin of origins, reflecting itself and, as Derrida says, providing a "reassuring end to the reference from sign to sign." It would, in essence, guarantee to those who believe in it that they do exist and have meaning. For example, if we posit that *I* or *self* is a transcendental signified, then the concept of *self* becomes the unifying principle upon which I structure my world. Objects, concepts, ideas, or even people only take on meaning in my world if I filter them through my unifying, ultimate signified: *self*.

Unlike other signifieds, the transcendental signified would have to be understood without comparing it to other signifieds or signifiers. In other words, its meaning would originate directly with itself, not differentially or relationally as does the meaning of all other signifieds or signifiers. Thus a transcendental signified functions as or provides the *center* of meaning, allowing those who believe in one or more of them to structure their ideas of reality around such centers of truth. A center of meaning by definition could not subject itself to structural analysis, for by so doing it would lose its place as a transcendental signified to another center. For example, if I declare the concept *self* to be my transcendental signified and then learn that my mind or self is composed of the id, the ego, and the superego, I could no longer hold the *self* or *I* to be my transcendental signified. In the process of discovering the three parts of my conscious and unconscious mind, I have both structurally analyzed and "de-centered" *self*, thus negating it as a transcendental signified.

Logocentrism

According to Derrida, Western metaphysics has invented a variety of terms that function as centers: *God, reason, origin, being, essence, truth, humanity, beginning, end,* and *self,* to name a few. Each can operate as a concept that is self-sufficient and self-originating and can serve as a transcendental signified. This Western proclivity for desiring a center Derrida names **logocentrism**: the belief that there is an ultimate reality or center of truth that can serve as the basis for all our thoughts and actions.

That we can never totally free ourselves from our logocentric habit of thinking and our inherited concept of the universe Derrida readily admits. To "de-center" any transcendental signified is to be caught up automatically in the terminology that allows that centering concept to operate. For example, if the concept *self* functions as my center and I then discover my unconscious self, I automatically place in motion what Derrida calls a "binary opposition" (two opposing concepts): the *self* and the *unconscious self*. By de-centering and questioning the *self*, I cause the *unconscious self* to become the new center. By questioning the old center, I establish a new one.

Such logocentric thinking, declares Derrida, has its origin in Aristotle's principle of noncontradiction: A thing cannot both have a property and not have a property. Thanks to Aristotle, maintains Derrida, Western metaphysics has developed an "either-or" mentality or logic that inevitably leads to dualistic thinking and to the centering and de-centering of transcendental signifieds. The process of logocentric thinking, asserts Derrida, is natural for Western readers, but problematic.

Binary Oppositions

Since the establishing of one center of unity automatically means that another is de-centered, Derrida concludes that Western metaphysics is based on a system of **binary operations** or conceptual oppositions. For each center, there exists an opposing center (God/humankind, for example). In addition, Western philosophy decrees that in each of these binary operations or opposing centers, one concept is superior and defines itself by its opposite or inferior center. We know *truth*, for instance, because we know *deception*; we know *good* because we know *bad*. It is to the creation of these hierarchal binaries as the basis for Western metaphysics that Derrida objects.

Phonocentrism

To Derrida, conceptual opposition is such a fragile basis for believing what is really real that he wants to dismantle the structure it has made. The binary oppositions on which Western metaphysics has built itself since Plato are structured, Derrida declares, such that one element will always be **privileged** (be in a superior position) while the other becomes **unprivileged** (inferior). In this way of thinking, the first or top elements of the pairs in the following list of binary oppositions are privileged: man/woman, human/animal, soul/body, good/bad. Key for Derrida is his assertion that Western thought has long privileged speech over writing. This privileging of speech over writing Derrida calls **phonocentrism**.

In placing speech in the privileged position, phonocentrism treats writing as inferior. We value, says Derrida, a speaker's words more than the speaker's writing, for words imply presence. Through the vehicle of spoken words, we supposedly learn directly what a speaker is trying to say. From this point of view, writing becomes a mere copy of speech, an attempt to capture the idea that was once spoken. Whereas speech implies presence, writing signifies absence, thereby placing into action another binary opposition: presence/absence.

Since phonocentrism is based on the assumption that speech conveys the meaning or direct ideas of a speaker better than writing (a mere copy of speech), phonocentrism assumes a logocentric way of thinking, that the self is the center of meaning and can best ascertain ideas directly from other selves through spoken words. Through speaking, the self declares its presence, its significance, and its being or existence.

Metaphysics of Presence

Accordingly, Derrida coins the phrase **metaphysics of presence** to encompass those ideas such as logocentrism, phonocentrism, the operation of binary oppositions, and other notions that Western thought conforms to in its conceptions of language and metaphysics. His objective is to demonstrate the shaky foundations upon which such beliefs have been established. By deconstructing the basic premises of metaphysics of presence, Derrida believes he gives us a strategy for reading that opens up a variety of new interpretations heretofore unseen by those who are bound by the restraints of Western thought.

METHODOLOGY

Acknowledging Binary Operations in Western Thought

The first stage in a deconstructive reading is to recognize the existence and the operation of binary oppositions in our thinking. According to Derrida, one of the most "violent hierarchies" derived from Platonic and Aristotelian thought is speech/writing, with speech privileged. Consequently, speech is awarded presence, and writing is equated with absence. Since it is the inferior of the two, writing becomes simply the symbols of speech, a second-hand representation of ideas.

Once the speech/writing hierarchy—or any other hierarchy—is recognized and acknowledged, Derrida proposes that we can readily reverse its elements. Such a reversal is possible because truth is ever elusive, for we can always de-center the center if any be found. By reversing the hierarchy, Derrida does not wish merely to substitute one hierarchy for another and involve himself in a negative mode. When the hierarchy is reversed, says Derrida, we can examine those values and beliefs that give rise to both the original hierarchy and the newly created one. Such an examination will reveal how the meaning of terms arises from the differences between them.

Arche-writing

In *Of Grammatology* (1967/1974), Derrida spends much time explaining why the speech/writing hierarchy can and must be reversed. In short, he argues for a redefinition of the term *writing* that will allow him to assert that writing is actually a precondition for and prior to speech. According to Derrida's metaphysical reasoning, language then becomes a special kind of writing which he calls **arche-writing** or **archi-écriture**.

Using traditional Western metaphysics that is grounded in phonocentricism, Derrida begins his reversal of the speech/writing hierarchy by noting that both language and writing share common characteristics. Both, for example, involve an encoding or inscription. In writing, this coding is obvious, for the written symbols represent various phonemes. In language or speech, a similar encoding exists. As Saussure has already shown, there exists an arbitrary relationship between the signifier and the signified (between the spoken word *cat* and the concept of cat itself). There is, then, no innate relationship between the spoken word and the concept, object, or idea it represents. Nevertheless, once a signifier and a signified join to form a sign, some kind of relationship then exists between these components of the sign. For example, some kind of inscription or encoding has taken place between the spoken word *cat* (the signifier) and its concept (the signified).

For Derrida, both writing and language are means of signification, and each can be considered a signifying system. Traditional Western metaphysics and Saussurean linguistics equate speech (language) with presence, for speech is accompanied by the presence of a living speaker. The presence of the speaker necessarily links sound and sense and therefore leads to understanding—one usually comprehends rather perfectly the spoken word. Writing, on the other hand, assumes an absence of a speaker. Such absence can produce misunderstanding, for writing is a depersonalized medium that separates the actual utterance of the speaker and his or her audience. It is this absence that can lead to misunderstanding of the signifying system.

All the more reason, Derrida asserts, that we broaden our understanding of writing. Writing, he declares, cannot be reduced to letters or other symbols inscribed on a page. Rather, it is directly related to what Saussure believed to be the basic element of language: difference. We know one phoneme or one word because each is different from another; and we know that there is no innate relationship between a signifier and its signified. The phoneme /b/, for example, could have easily become the symbol for the phoneme /d/, just as the coined word *bodt* could have become the English word *ball*. It is this free play or "undecidability" in any system of communication that Derrida calls writing. The quality of play with the various elements of signification in any system of communication totally eludes a speaker's awareness when using language, for the speaker falsely assumes a position of supposed master of his or her speech.

By equating writing with the free play or the element of undecidability at the center of all systems of communication, Derrida declares that writing actually governs language, thereby negating the speech/writing hierarchy of Western metaphysics. Writing now becomes privileged and speech unprivileged, for speech is a kind of writing called arche-writing.

This being so, Derrida then challenges Western philosophy's concept that human consciousness gives birth to language. Without language (or arche-writing), argues Derrida, there can be no consciousness, for consciousness presupposes language. Through arche-writing, we impose human consciousness upon the world.

Supplementation

The relationship between any binary hierarchy, however, is always unstable and problematic. It is not Derrida's purpose simply to reverse all binary oppositions that exist in Western thought, but rather it is to show the fragile basis for the establishment of such hierarchies and the possibility of inverting these hierarchies to gain new insights into language and life. Derrida uses the term **supplement** to refer to the unstable relationship between elements in a binary operation. For example, in the speech/writing opposition, writing supplements speech and in actuality takes the place of speech (arche-writing). **Supplementation** exists in all binary oppositions. In the truth/deception hierarchy, for example, Western thought would assert the supremacy of truth over deception, attributing to deception a mere supplementary role. The logocentric way of thinking asserts the purity of truth over deception. Upon examination, deception more frequently than not contains at least some truth; and who is to say, asks Derrida, when truth has been spoken, achieved, or even conceived. The purity of truth may simply not exist. In all human activity, then, supplementation operates.

Différance

By realizing that supplementation operates in all binary operations of Western metaphysics and by inverting the privileged and unprivileged elements, Derrida begins to develop his reading strategy of deconstruction. Once he "turns Western metaphysics on its head," he asserts his answer to logocentrism and other Western elements by coining a new word and concept: *différance*. The word itself is derived from the French word *différer*, meaning "to defer, postpone, or delay," and "to differ, to be different from." Derrida deliberately coins his word to be ambiguous, taking on both meanings simultaneously. And in French, the word is a pun, for it exists only in writing. In speech there is no way to tell the difference between the French word *différence* and Derrida's coined word *différance*.

Understanding what Derrida means by **différance** is one of the basic keys to understanding deconstruction. Basically, *différance* is Derrida's "What if?" question. What if no transcendental signified exists? What if there is no presence in whom we can find ultimate truth? What if all our knowledge does not arise from self-identity? What if there is no essence, being, or inherently unifying element in the universe? What then?

The presence of such a transcendental signified would immediately establish the binary operation presence/absence. Since Western metaphysics holds that presence is supreme or privileged and absence unprivileged, Derrida suggests that we temporarily reverse this hierarchy, making it now absence/presence. With such a reversal, we can no longer posit a transcendental signified. No longer is there an absolute standard or coherent unity from which knowledge proceeds and develops. All human knowledge and all self-identity must now spring from difference, not sameness, from absence, not presence.

When a reversal of this pivotal binary operation occurs, two dramatic results follow: First, human knowledge becomes referential; that is, we can only know something because it differs from some other bit of knowledge, not because we can compare this knowledge to any absolute or coherent unity (a transcendental signified). Human knowledge must now be based on difference. We know something because it differs from something else to which it is related. By the reversal, nothing can be studied or learned in isolation, for all knowledge becomes context-related. Second, we must also forgo closure; that is, since no transcendental signified exists, all interpretations concerning life, self-identity, and knowledge are possible, probable, and legitimate.

But what is the significance of *différance* when reading texts? If we, like Derrida, assert that *différance* operates in language and therefore also in writing (Derrida sometimes equates *différance* and arche-writing), what are the implications for textual analysis? The most obvious answer is that texts lack presence. Once we do away with the transcendental signified and reverse the presence/absence binary operation, texts can no longer have presence: in isolation, texts cannot possess meaning. Since all meaning and knowledge is now based on differences, no text can simply mean one thing. Texts become intertextual. The meaning of a text cannot be ascertained by examining only that particular text; a text's meaning *evolves* from that derived from the interrelatedness of one text to an interrelatedness of many texts. Like language itself, texts are caught in a dynamic, context-related interchange. Never can we state a text's definitive meaning; for it has no one correct or definitive interpretation. No longer can we declare one interpretation to be right and another wrong, for meaning in a text is always illusive, always dynamic, also transitory.

The search, then, for the text's "correct" meaning or the author's so-called intentions become meaningless. Since meaning is derived from differences in a dynamic, context-related, ongoing process, all texts have multiple meanings or interpretations. If we assert, as does Derrida, that no transcendental signified exists, then there can exist no absolute or pure meaning conveyed supposedly by authorial intent or professorial dictates. Meaning evolves as we, the readers, interact with the text, with both the readers and the text providing social and cultural context.

Deconstructive Suppositions for Textual Analysis

A deconstructor begins textual analysis by assuming that a text has multiple interpretations and that it allows itself to be reread and thus reinterpreted countless times. Denying the New Critical stance that a text possesses a special ontological status and has one and only one correct interpretation, deconstructors assert that the great joy of textual analysis resides in discovering new interpretations each time a text is read and reread. Ultimately, a text's meaning is undecidable, for each reading or rereading can elicit different interpretations.

When beginning the interpretative process, deconstructors seek to override their own logocentric and inherited ways of viewing a text. Such revolutionary thinking decrees that they find the binary oppositions at work in the text itself. These binary oppositions, they believe, represent established and accepted ideologies that more frequently than not posit the existence of transcendental signifieds. These binary operations, then, restrict meaning, for they already assume a fixed interpretation of reality. They assume, for instance, the existence of truth and falsehood, reason and insanity, good and bad. Realizing that these hierarchies presuppose a fixed and a biased way of viewing the world, deconstructors search for the binary oppositions operating in the text and reverse them. By reviewing these hierarchies, deconstructors wish to challenge the fixed views assumed by such hierarchies and the values associated with such rigid beliefs.

The technique of identifying the binary operations that exist in a text allows deconstructors to expose the preconceived assumptions upon which most of us base our interpretations. We all, for example, declare some activity, being, or object to be good or bad, valuable or worthless, significant or insignificant. These kinds of values or ideas automatically operate when we write or read any text. In the reversal of hierarchies that form the basis of our interpretations, deconstructors wish to free us from the constraints of our prejudiced beliefs. Such freedom, they hope, will allow us to see a text from exciting new perspectives that we have never before recognized.

These various perspectives cannot be simultaneously perceived by the reader or even the writer of a text. In Nathaniel Hawthorne's "Young Goodman Brown," for example, many readers believe that the fifty-year-old character who shepherds Goodman Brown through his night's visit in the forest is Satan and therefore necessarily an evil character. Brown's own interpretation of this character seems to support this view. According to deconstructionist ideas, at least two binary operations are at work here: good/evil and God/Satan. But what if we reverse these hierarchies? Then the scepteral figure may not be Satan and therefore may not be evil! Such a new perspective will dramatically change our interpretation of the text.

Deconstructors say that we cannot simultaneously see both of these perspectives in the story. To discover where the new hierarchy Satan/God or evil/good will lead us in our interpretation, we must suspend our first interpretation. We do not, however, forget it, for it is locked in our minds. We simply shift our allegiance to another perspective.

The process of oscillating between interpretations, levels, or perspectives allows us to see the impossibility of ever choosing a correct interpretation, for meaning is an ongoing activity that is always in progress, always based upon *différance*. By asking what will happen if we reverse the hierarchies that frame our preconceived ways of thinking, we open ourselves to a never-ending process of interpretation, one that decrees that no hierarchy or binary operation is right and no other is wrong.

Deconstruction: A New Reading Strategy

Deconstructors do not want, then, to set up a new philosophy, a new literary theory of analysis, or a new school of literary criticism. They present instead a new reading strategy, one that allows us to make choices concerning the various levels of interpretation we see operating in a text. All levels, they maintain, have validity. Deconstructors also believe that their approach to reading frees the reader from ideological allegiances that restrict the comprehension of meaning in a text.

Since meaning, they believe, emerges through interpretation, even the author does not control a text's interpretation. Although writers may have clearly stated intentions concerning their texts, such statements should and must be given little credence. Like language itself, texts have no outside referents or transcendental signifieds. What an author thinks he or she says or means in a text may be quite different from what is actually written. Deconstructors therefore look for places in the text where the author **misspeaks** or loses control of language and says what was supposedly not meant to be said. These slips of language often occur in questions, figurative language, and strong declarations. For example, suppose we read the following words: "Important Seniors Meeting." Although the author thinks that readers will interpret these words to mean that it is important that all seniors be present at this particular meeting, the author may have misspoken, for these words can actually mean that only important seniors should attend this meeting. By examining such slips and the binary operations that govern them, deconstructors are able to demonstrate the **undecidability** of a text's meaning.

At first glance, a deconstructionist reading strategy may appear to be linear—that is, having a clearly delineated beginning, middle, and end. If this is so, then to apply this strategy to a text, we must do the following:

- Discover the binary operations that govern a text
- Comment on the values, concepts, and ideas beyond these operations
- Reverse these present binary operations
- Dismantle previously held worldviews
- Accept the possibility of various perspectives or levels of meaning in a text based on the new binary inversions
- Allow meaning of the text to be undecidable

Although all these elements do operate in a deconstructionist reading, they may not operate in this exact sequence. Since we all tend toward logocentrism when reading, we may not note some logocentric binary operations functioning in the text until we have reversed some obvious binary oppositions and are interpreting the text on several levels. In addition, we must never declare such a reading to be completed or finished, for the process of meaning is ongoing, never allowing us to pledge allegiance to any one view.

Such a reading strategy disturbs most readers and critics, for it is not a neat, completed package, whereby if we follow step A through to step Z we arrive at *the* reading of the text. Since texts have no external referents, their meanings depend on the close interaction of the text, the reader, and social and cultural elements, as does every reading or interpretative process. Denying the organic unity of a text, deconstructors declare the free play of language in a text. Since language itself is reflexive, not mimetic, we can never stop finding meaning in a text, whether we have read it once or a hundred times.

Overall, deconstruction solicits an ongoing relationship between the interpreter (the critic) and the text. By examining the text alone, deconstructors hope to ask a set of questions which will continually challenge the ideological positions of power and authority that dominate literary criticism. Further, in the process of discovering meaning in a text, deconstructors declare that criticism of a text is just as valuable as the creative writing being read, thus inverting the creative writing/criticism hierarchy.

AMERICAN DECONSTRUCTORS

After Derrida's introduction of deconstruction to his American audience in 1966, the philosopher found several sympathetic listeners who soon became loyal adherents and defenders of his new reading strategy: notably, the Romantic scholar Paul de Man (*Blindness and Insight*, 1971), the rhetorical deconstructor Hayden White (*Tropics of Discourse*, 1978), the sometimes terse metaphysical deconstructor Geoffrey Hartman (*Criticism in the Wilderness*, 1980), the strong voice of Barbara Johnson (*The Critical Difference*, 1980), and the phenomenological critic turned deconstructor J. Hillis Miller (*Fiction and Repetition: Seven English Novels*, 1982). These critics assured that deconstruction would have a voice and an established place in American literary theory. Although the voices of other poststructural theories, such as New Historicism and Postcolonial theory, now clamor to be heard, deconstruction's philosophical assumptions and practical reading strategies form the basis of many postmodern literary practices.

QUESTIONS FOR ANALYSIS

- Interpret one of the aesthetic texts located at the back of this text. After you have completed your interpretation, cite the binary operations that function both within your chosen text and within your thinking to allow you to arrive at your perspective.
- Using the same text and interpretation you used for question one, reverse one of the binary operations and reinterpret the text. When you are finished, reverse two additional binaries and reinterpret the story. What differences exist between the two interpretations?
- Using a poem of your choice, demonstrate either how the author misspeaks or where the text involves itself in paradox, sometimes called **aporia.** Be specific. Be able to point to lines, figurative speech, or imaginative language to support your statements.
- Using the poem you read for the above exercise, cite at least four dramatically different interpretations, all based on a deconstructive reading.
- Reread the student-generated essay found at the end of Chapter 4, "Reader Response." What elements of the story does the author simply ignore or dismiss? Consider how Derrida's concept of supplementation is operating in this critic's analysis.
- Using the student essay found at the end of Chapter 5, "Structuralism," state the binary operations that control the critic's interpretation of the text. From these binaries, cite the ideological positions of the critic, and note what elements in the story he must ignore to arrive at his conclusions.
- Read the student essay located at the end of this chapter. Since this essay approaches textual analysis from a deconstructive point of view, the author must assume that all essays can be so analyzed. On this assumption, deconstruct the student essay, noting where the author of the essay misspeaks and how the essay dismantles itself.

SAMPLE ESSAY

In the student essay that follows, note how the author employs the various binary operations she discovers in the text to show how the text misspeaks and dismantles itself. Also note and be able to explain how the binaries used by the author of the story banquet involves the text in paradoxes. Based on the binary oppositions at work in the text, be able to explain at least four different interpretations. In addition, note how the critic tries to divorce herself from logocentric thinking and the metaphysics of presence as she seeks to analyze the story.

FURTHER READING

Atkins, G. Douglas. *Reading Deconstruction*: *Deconstructive Reading*. Lexington: University Press of Kentucky, 1983.

Bloom, Harold. *A Map of Misreading*. New York: Oxford University Press, 1975.

Caputo, John D. "The Good News about Alterity: Derrida and Theology." *Faith and Philosophy* 10.4 (Oct. 1993): 453–70.

Culler, Jonathan. *On Deconstruction*: *Theory and Criticism after Structuralism*. Ithaca, NY: Cornell University Press, 1982.

de Man, Paul. *Blindness and Insight*: *Essays in the Rhetoric of Contemporary Criticism*. New York: Oxford University Press, 1971.

———. *The Rhetoric of Romanticism*. New York: Columbia University Press, 1984.

Derrida, Jacques. "Structure, Sign, and Play in the Discourse of the Human Sciences." *Writing and Différence*. Trans. Alan Bass. Chicago: University of Chicago Press, 1978.

Ellis, John M. *Against Deconstruction*. Princeton: Princeton University Press, 1989.

Hartman, Geoffrey. *Saving the Text*: *Literature/Derrida/Philosophy*. Baltimore: Johns Hopkins University Press, 1981.

Johnson, Barbara. *The Critical Difference*: *Essays in the Contemporary Rhetoric of Reading*. Baltimore: Johns Hopkins University Press, 1980.

Gasche, Rodolphe. "Deconstruction as Criticism." *Glyph Textual Studies* 6 (1979): 177–215.

Miller, J. Hillis. *Tropes, Parables, and Performatives*: *Essays on Twentieth-Century Literature*. Hemel Hempstead: Harvester Wheatsheaf, 1990.

Norris, Christopher. *Deconstruction*: *Theory and Practice*. London: Meuthen, 1982.

Rajnath, ed. *Deconstruction*: *A Critique*. London: Macmillan, 1989.

Saussure, Ferdinand de. *Course in General Linguistics*. Ed. Charles Baly and Albert Reidlinger. Trans. Wade Baskin. New York: Philosophical Library, 1959.

WEB SITES FOR EXPLORATION

www.unisa.ac.za/dept/press/dearte/54/stevens.html
An excellent overview of postmodernism, structuralism, poststructuralism, and deconstruction terminology and criticism

www.brookes.ac.uk/schools/humanities/English/POSTRUCT.htm
An excellent review of structuralism and poststructuralism

http://s131.math.aca.mmu.ac.uk/Chreods/Issue_10/Olwen.html
Reviews Saussure's and Derrida's concepts of meaning

http://mural.uv.es/envimar/page2.html
Another excellent review of structuralism versus poststructuralist theories

www.poetrymagic.co.uk/advanced/poststructuralistapproaches.html
    Poststructuralist approaches to literary criticism
www.anglicanmediasydney.asn.au/cul/Deconstruction.htm
    An excellent overview of deconstruction

ꙅ Student Essay ꙅ

Deconstructing a "Real" House

In the short story "The House on Mango Street," Sandra Cisneros depicts a child's reaction to the living conditions she endures as her family struggles against poverty. Upon a first reading, the story seems to deal primarily with economic hardship. Cisneros's descriptions of the narrator's living conditions, however, reveal binary oppositions that often contradict one another. Rather than leading to organic unity, the ambiguity present in this story reveals a play of signification that infinitely opens the realm of possible interpretations.

Most prominently, the narrator alternates between privileging reality and dream by first acknowledging the positive aspects of the house on Mango Street and then complaining that her new conditions do not conform to her hopes. Cisneros's use of the term "real" in reference to the house leads to a questioning of what constitutes a "real" house and how the narrator accepts or rejects her own explanation. In the second paragraph, for example, the narrator privileges ownership over renting and sole possession over sharing, and her description of a "real" house continues in paragraph four with additional emphasis on "real" stairs. Other conditions include several washrooms, a big yard without a fence, and a white exterior, showing that dreaming of this house remains privileged in the fourth paragraph over the reality of the flat on Loomis.

Stated differently, the text's major dismantling reveals itself in the contradiction between the narrator's initial privileging of the reality of the house on Mango Street and her later rejection of that reality with its subsequent overturning of binary oppositions. Speaking of the flat on Loomis, the narrator privileges temporary over permanent because of the haste of the family's departure. She also lists her complaints about the water pipes breaking, the lack of a washroom, and the age of the house. As paragraph two indicates, the house on Mango Street reverses the major complaints of the flat because of the family's ownership, the washroom, and their own stairs.

These improvements, however, do not prevent the narrator from complaining that the reality of the house does not conform to the dream she had envisioned, thus re-privileging dream after a brief acknowledgment of reality. Even though the living conditions improve from the previous situation, the narrator complains several times that the house, the yard, and the washroom are smaller than expected. She rejects reality by complaining that the "tight red" bricks, the "swollen" door, the "ordinary" stairs, and "very small" washroom do not measure up to her preconceived idea even though the house belongs to the family and does not have to be shared. From a yearning for permanence, the narrator makes an abrupt shift to the temporary by asserting that the family should find a better house. Ironically, the narrator also asserts, "I know how these things go," indicating the uncertainty of finding better living conditions. Already in the story, supposed "knowledge" of the house has turned into disappointment and uncertainty, but in her last comment the narrator expresses knowledge and confidence, albeit cynical, about the certainty of uncertainty. This remark confirms a change from faith in knowledge to an undecidability in knowing what the future contains.

In her experience with the nun, the narrator delves into the binary opposition of presence and absence in relation to her house. Normally, the presence of a shelter takes precedence because of the physical needs it meets, but the stigma placed on the narrator by the condescending nun causes her to privilege the absence of the flat in favor of a "real" house. When the family obtains the house on Mango Street, the narrator reverses that privilege because of the house's perceived shortcomings and begins to favor absence again.

Different interpretations of the story emerge through the reversal of other binary oppositions in the text and re-examination of the content. In reacting to the house on Mango Street, for example, if the narrator had regarded small size as better than large, the entire description of the situation would change. Instead of moving, the family might have stayed in one location despite the addition of several children. Even the flat in Loomis would have been acceptable because it probably did not afford much room. From this perspective, the house on Mango Street would be ideal because of its one bedroom, tiny yard, minute washroom, and overall petiteness. Rather than demeaning the house, the narrator's description now seems to revel in the glory of its four little elms and the coziness of an entire family sharing one room. Decentering the American tendency to place bigger as better thus completely alters the reading of the story.

Another reading results from placing renting (nonownership) over owning. Western tradition and American culture place emphasis on possession and the individual's right to have sole possession of resources to fulfill the American dream. In this story ownership tops the list of qualities for a "real" house, but if renting received privilege, then the flat on Loomis might have seemed preferable. Even if the family made the move to Mango Street, the narrator's blunt declaration of ownership would be considered selfish, materialistic, and socially unacceptable.

"The House on Mango Street" provides an active reader with abundant opportunity to play in the signification of the text. By closely examining the language of the text and noting the author's contradictory use of binary oppositions, particularly in reality versus dream, we can formulate many unique renderings of the text.

JENNIFER DOUGLAS

✨ 7 ✨

Psychoanalytic Criticism

It is a striking truth that literary analysis, like Freud's dream analysis, does no more and no less than disclose a life in images or words that has its own momentum.

Geoffrey Hartman, *Easy Pieces*,
1985

INTRODUCTION

Our dreams fascinate, perplex, and often disturb us. Filled with bizarre twists of fate, wild exploits, and highly sexual images, our dreams can bring us pleasure or terrorize us. Sometimes they cause us to question our feelings, to contemplate our unspoken desires, and even to doubt the nature of reality itself. Do dreams, we wonder, contain any degree of truth? Do they serve any useful function?

The chemist Friedrich August Kekule answers in the affirmative. For years, Kekule investigated the molecular structure of benzene. One night he saw in a dream a string of atoms shaped like a snake swallowing its tale. Upon awakening, he drew this serpentine figure in his notebook and realized it was the graphic structure of the benzene ring he had been struggling to decipher. When reporting his findings at a scientific meeting in 1890, he stated, "Let us learn to dream, gentlemen, and then we may perhaps find the truth."

Giuseppe Tartini, an Italian violinist of the eighteenth century, similarly discovered the value of dreams. One night he dreamed the devil came to his bedside and offered to help him finish a rather difficult sonata in exchange for his soul. Tartini agreed, whereupon the devil picked up Tartini's violin and completed the unfinished work. On awakening, Tartini jotted down from memory what he had just heard. Known as *The Devil's Trill Sonata*, this piece is Tartini's best known composition.

Like numerous scientists and composers, many writers have claimed that they too have received some of their best ideas from their dreams.

Robert Louis Stevenson, for example, maintained that many of his ideas for *Dr. Jekyll and Mr. Hyde* came directly from his nightmares. Similarly, Dante, Goethe, Blake, Bunyan, and a host of others owed much of their writings, they claimed, to their world of dreams. Still others, such as Poe, DeQuincey, and Coleridge, borrowed from their drug-induced dreams the content of some of their most famous works.

That our dreams and those of others fascinate us cannot be denied. Whether it is their bizarre and often erotic content or their seemingly prophetic powers, dreams cause us to question and explore that part of our minds over which we have ostensibly little control, the unconscious.

Without question, the foremost investigator of the unconscious and its activities is the Vienna neurologist and psychologist Sigmund Freud. Beginning with the publication of *The Interpretation of Dreams* in 1900, Freud lays the foundation for a model of how our minds operate. Hidden from the workings of the conscious mind, the unconscious, he believes, plays a large part in how we act, think, and feel. According to Freud, the best avenue for discovering the content and the activity of the unconscious is through our dreams. It is in the interaction of the conscious and unconscious working together, argues Freud, that we shape both ourselves and our world.

Developing both a body of theory and a practical methodology for his science of the mind, Freud became the leading pioneer of **psychoanalysis**, a method of treating emotional and psychological disorders. During psychoanalysis, Freud would have his patients talk freely in a patient-analyst setting about their early childhood experiences and dreams. When we apply these same methods to our interpretations of works of literature, we engage in **psychoanalytic criticism**.

Unlike some other schools of criticism, psychoanalytic criticism can exist side by side with any other critical method of interpretation. Because this approach attempts to explain the how and why of human actions without developing an **aesthetic theory**—a systematic, philosophical body of beliefs about how meaning occurs in literature and other art forms—Marxists, Feminists, and New Historicists, for example, can utilize psychoanalytic methods in their interpretations without violating their own **hermeneutics**. Psychoanalytic criticism may then best be called an approach to literary interpretation rather than a particular school of criticism.

Although Freud is unquestionably the founder of this approach to literary analysis, psychoanalytic criticism has continued to develop throughout the twentieth century. Carl Jung, Freud's rebellious student, borrowed some of Freud's ideas but rejected many others. Jung branched out into new theories and concerns and established **analytical psychology**. Utilizing some of Jung's ideas, Northrop Frye, an English professor and literary theorist, developed symbolic or archetypal criticism in the mid 1950s that changed the direction of twentieth-century literary analysis. In the 1960s, the French Neo-Freudian psychoanalyst Jacques Lacan revised and expanded Freud's theories in light of new linguistic and literary principles, thereby revitalizing psychoanalytic criticism and ensuring its continued influence on literary criticism today. Many present-day feminist critics turn to psychoanalytic criticism as well, utilizing the ideas of Lacan as the basis of their critical methodology.

HISTORICAL DEVELOPMENT

Sigmund Freud

The theories and practice of Sigmund Freud (1856–1939) provide the foundation for psychoanalytic criticism. While working with patients whom he diagnosed as hysterics, Freud theorized that the root of their problems was psychological, not physical. His patients, he believed, had suppressed incestuous desires that they had unconsciously refused to confront. Suffering from his own neurotic crisis in 1887, Freud underwent self-analysis. Results from his self-analysis, together with his research and analyses of patients, led Freud to posit that fantasies and wishful thinking, not actual experiences, play a large part in the onset of neuroses.

Models of the Human Psyche: Dynamic Model   Throughout his lifetime, Freud developed various models of the human psyche, which became the changing bases of his psychoanalytic theory and his practice. Early in his career, he posited the **dynamic model,** asserting that our minds are a dichotomy consisting of the **conscious** (the rational) and the **unconscious** (the irrational). The conscious, Freud argued, perceives and records external reality and is the reasoning part of the mind. Unaware of the presence of the unconscious, we operate consciously, believing that our reasoning and analytical skills are solely responsible for our behavior. Nevertheless, Freud is the first to suggest that it is the unconscious, not the conscious, that governs a large part of our actions.

This irrational part of our psyche, the unconscious, receives and stores our hidden desires, ambitions, fears, passions, and irrational thoughts. Freud, however, did not coin this term; this honor goes to C. G. Carus. Carus and many of Freud's other contemporaries viewed the unconscious as a static system that simply collects and maintains our memories. Freud dramatically redefined the unconscious, believing it to be a dynamic system that not only contains our biographical memories but also stores our suppressed and unresolved conflicts. For Freud, the unconscious is the storehouse of disguised truths and desires that want to be revealed in and through the conscious. These disguised truths and desires will inevitably make themselves known through our so-called mistakes of speech or actions. Freud calls such mistakes **parapraxes** or **Freudian slips**. Through seemingly innocuous actions, such as accidental slips of the tongue, failures of memory, the misplacing of objects, or the misreading of texts, Freud believes we will consciously bring to our conscious minds our unconscious wishes and intentions. It is especially in our dreams, our art, our literature, and our play that these parapraxes reveal our true intentions or desires.

Economic Model   Freud's second model of the human psyche enlarges upon but retains most of the ideas he had posited in the dynamic model. In both models, the conscious and the unconscious battle for control of a person's actions; and in both models, a person's unconscious desires will force their way to the conscious state. However, in the **economic model**, Freud introduces two new concepts that describe and help govern the human psyche: the pleasure principle and the reality principle. According to Freud, the **pleasure principle** craves only pleasures, and it desires instantaneous satisfaction of instinctual drives, ignoring moral and sexual boundaries established by society. Immediate relief from all pain or suffering is its goal. The pleasure principle is held in check, however, by the **reality principle**, that part of the psyche that recognizes the need for societal standards and regulations on pleasure. Freud believed that both these principles are at war within the human psyche.

Typographical Models   Over his long career, Freud developed yet another model of the human psyche known as the **typographical model**. In an earlier version of this model, Freud separated the human psyche into three parts: the conscious, the **preconscious**, and the unconscious. The *conscious* is the mind's direct link to external reality, for it perceives and reacts with the external environment, allowing the mind to order its outside world. The *preconscious* is the storehouse of memories that the conscious part of the mind allows to be brought to consciousness without disguising these memories in some form or another. As in his previously devised models, Freud contends that the third part of the psyche, the *unconscious*, holds the repressed hungers, images, thoughts, and desires of human nature. Because these desires are not housed in the preconscious, they cannot be directly summoned into the conscious state. These repressed impulses must therefore travel in disguised forms to the conscious part of the psyche and will surface in their respective disguises in our dreams, our art, and in other unsuspecting ways in our lives.

The most famous model of the human psyche, however, is Freud's revised version of the typographical model, the **tripartite model**. This model divides the psyche into three parts: the id, the ego, and the superego. The irrational, instinctual, unknown, and unconscious part of the psyche Freud calls the **id**. Containing our secret desires, our darkest wishes, and our most intense fears, the id wishes only to fulfill the urges of the pleasure principle. In addition, it houses the **libido**, the source of all our psychosexual desires and all our psychic energy. Unchecked by any controlling will, the id operates on impulse, wanting immediate satisfaction for all its instinctual desires.

The second part of the psyche Freud names the **ego**, the rational, logical, waking part of the mind, although many of its activities remain in the unconscious. Whereas the id operates according to the pleasure principle, the ego operates in harmony with the reality principle. It is the ego's job to regulate the instinctual desires of the id and to allow these desires to be released in some nondestructive way.

The third part of the psyche, the **superego**, acts like an internal censor, causing us to make moral judgments in light of social pressures. In contrast to the id, the superego operates according to the morality principle and serves primarily to protect society and us from the id. Representing all of society's moral restrictions, the superego serves as a filtering agent, suppressing the desires and instincts forbidden by society and thrusting them back into the unconscious. Overall, the superego manifests itself through punishment. If allowed to operate at its own discretion, the superego will create an unconscious sense of guilt and fear.

It is left to the ego to mediate between the instinctual (especially sexual) desires of the id and the demands of social pressure issued by the superego. What the ego deems unacceptable it suppresses and deposits in the unconscious, and what it has most frequently repressed in all of us is our sexual desires of early childhood.

Freud's Pre-Oedipal Developmental Phases   In addition to his various models of the human psyche, Freud proposed several stages of human development that he believed are important to the healthy growth of one's psyche. According to Freud, in our early childhood all of us go through three overlapping phases: the oral, anal, and phallic stages. As infants, we experience the **oral phase**: When we suck our mother's breast to be fed, our sexuality (or libido) is activated. Through this activity our mouths develop into an erotogenic zone that will later cause us to enjoy sucking our thumbs and, still later in life, kissing. In the second or **anal stage**, the anus becomes an object of pleasure when children learn the delights of defecation and, simultaneously, realize that they are independent persons who are separate from their mothers. During this stage, the anus becomes an erotogenic zone, for children become sadistic, expelling and destroying through defecation as a means of expressing both their anger and their excitement in discovering their independence from their mothers. By withholding feces, children also learn that they can control others. In the final phase, the **phallic stage**, a child's sexual desires or libido is directed toward the genitals when the child learns the pleasure that results from stimulating one's sexual organs.

At this point in a child's development, Freud asserts that the pleasure principle basically controls the child. Being self-centered, sadistic, and assertive, the child cares for nothing but his or her own pleasure. If a child, however, is to grow up as a normal adult, he or she must develop a sense of sexuality, a sense of his maleness or her femaleness. Freud maintains that this awareness can be achieved by a successful handling of either the Oedipus or the Electra Complex.

The Oedipus, Castration, and Electra Complexes   The formulation of the **Oedipus complex** is one of Freud's most significant contributions not only to psychoanalytic criticism but also to all literary criticism in general. Freud borrows the name from the play *Oedipus Rex*, written by the Greek dramatist Sophocles. In this play, Oedipus, the protagonist, is prophesied to kill his father and marry his mother. His attempts to abort the prophecy fail, and the once-foretold events occur as predicted. According to Freud, the essence of Oedipus' story becomes universal human experience.

Using Sophocles' plot as the basis for his Oedipus complex, Freud asserts that during the late infantile stage (somewhere between ages 3 and 6), all infant males possess an erotic attachment to their mother. Unconsciously, the infant desires to engage in sexual union with his mother. He recognizes, however, a rival for his mother's affection: the father. Already in the phallic stage and therefore sexually aware of his own erogenous organs, the child perceives the father's attention to the mother as sexual.

If a child's sexual development is to proceed normally, Freud maintains, each must then pass through the **castration complex**. From observing themselves, their mothers, and perhaps their sisters, little boys know they have a penis like their fathers, while their mothers and sisters do not. What prevents the male child from continuing to have incestuous desires for his mother is fear of castration by his father. The child therefore represses his sexual desire, identifies with his father, and hopes someday to possess a woman as his father now possesses his mother. Unconsciously, the boy has thus successfully made the transition to manhood.

Whereas a boy must successfully negotiate the Oedipus complex in order to become a normal man, a girl must successfully negotiate the **Electra complex** if she is to make the transition from a girl to a normal woman. Like a boy, a young girl is also erotically attracted to her mother, and like the boy, she too recognizes a rival for her mother's affection: the father. Unconsciously, however, the girl realizes that she is already castrated like her mother. Since she knows her father possesses that which she desires, a penis, she turns her desires to him and away from her mother. After the seduction of her father fails, she turns back toward the mother and identifies with her. Her transition into womanhood being complete, the girl realizes that one day she, too, like her mother, will possess a man. Through her relationships with a man, her unfulfilled desire for a penis (**penis envy**) will be mitigated, and her sense of lack will be somewhat appeased.

The process of becoming a man or a woman, Freud maintained, may be long and difficult, but necessary. For within this process, the child passes from basing his or her life on the pleasure principle, under which all decisions are grounded in the immediate gratification of pleasure, to the reality principle, under which societal needs and the operation of the superego guide decisions. During this stage, Freud believed that a child's moral sensibility and conscience appear for the first time.

The Significance of Dreams   According to Freud, even though the passage into manhood or womanhood may be successful, the child has stored many painful memories of repressed sexual desires, anger, rage, and guilt in his or her unconscious. Since the conscious and the unconscious are part of the same psyche, the unconscious with its hidden desires and repressed wishes continues to affect the conscious in the form of inferiority feelings, guilt, irrational thoughts and feelings, and dreams and nightmares.

In his magnum opus, *The Interpretation of Dreams* (1950), Freud asserts that the unconscious will express its suppressed wishes and desires. Even though the conscious mind has repressed these desires and has forced them into the unconscious, such wishes may be too hard for the conscious psyche to handle without producing feelings of self-hatred or rage. The unconscious will then redirect and reshape these concealed wishes into acceptable social activities, presenting them in the form of images or symbols in our dreams and/or our writings. In the process, the psyche creates a window to the id by allowing these softened and socially acceptable desires to seep into the conscious state.

The psyche may create this window to the id in a variety of ways. Through the process of **displacement**, for example, the unconscious may switch a person's hatred for someone named Mr. Appleby onto a rotting apple in a dream. Or through **condensation**, the psyche may consolidate one's anger toward a variety of people and objects into a simple sentence. Whatever the case, through symbols and images, but not directly, the unconscious continually asserts its influence over our motives and behavior.

When certain repressed feelings or ideas cannot be adequately released through dreams, jokes, or other methods, the ego must act and block any outward response. In so doing, the ego and id become involved in an internal battle Freud calls **neurosis**. From a fear of heights to a pounding headache, neurosis can assume many physical and psychological abnormalities. Freud says it is the job of the psychoanalyst to identify these unresolved conflicts that give rise to a patient's neurosis. Through psychoanalytic therapy and dream analysis, the psychotherapist attempts to return the patient to a state of well-being or normalcy.

Literature and Psychoanalysis   For Freud, the unresolved conflicts that give rise to any neurosis constitute the stuff of literature. A work of literature, he believes, is the external expression of the author's unconscious mind. Accordingly, the literary work must then be treated like a dream, applying psychoanalytic techniques to the text to uncover the author's hidden motivations, repressed desires, and wishes.

Carl G. Jung

Freud's most famous pupil is Carl Gustav Jung (1875–1961), a Swiss physician, psychiatrist, philosopher, and psychologist. Selecting Jung as his favorite "son," Freud appointed him his successor. However, toward the end of their seven-year, teacher-disciple relationship (1912), Jung prophetically wrote to Freud, quoting from Nietzsche's *Thus Spake Zarathustra*, "One repays a teacher badly if one remains only a pupil." A year later, the pupil broke away from his master and eventually became one of the leading forces in the psychoanalytic movement.

Jung's dissatisfaction with some elements of Freudian psychoanalysis arose from theoretical differences with Freud concerning the interpretation of dreams and the model of the human psyche. According to Freud, all human behavior, including dreams, is fundamentally sexual since it is driven by an individual's sexual energy or libido. Freud interpreted dreams almost exclusively in sexual terms, linking most of them to the Oedipus or Electra complexes. Jung disagreed with Freud's basic premise that all human behavior is sexually driven; more than sexual imagery, Jung argued, appears in dreams. In 1912, Jung published his seminal work *Symbols of Transformation*, which ultimately led to his separation from Freud. In this work, Jung asserts that dreams include mythological images as well as sexual ones. Jung's new ideas caused him to be banished from the psychoanalytic community for the next five years. During this time, however, he formulated his own model of the human psyche, which would become his most important contribution to psychology and literary criticism.

In forming his model of the human psyche, Jung accepts Freud's assumption that the unconscious exists and that it plays a major role in our conscious decisions; he rejects, however, Freud's analysis of the contents of the unconscious. For Jung, the human psyche consists of these three parts: the personal conscious, the personal unconscious, and the collective unconscious. The **personal conscious** or waking state is that image or thought of which we are aware at any given moment. Like a slide show, every moment of our lives provides us with a new slide. As we view one slide, the previous slide vanishes from our personal consciousness, for nothing can remain in the personal conscious. Although these vanished slides are forgotten by the personal consciousness, they are stored and remembered by the **personal unconscious**. Jung asserts that all conscious thoughts begin in the personal unconscious. Since each person's moment-by-moment slide show is different, everyone's personal unconscious is unique.

In the depths of the psyche and blocked off from human consciousness lies the third part of Jung's model of the psyche: the **collective unconscious.** This part of the psyche houses the cumulative knowledge, experiences, and images of the entire human species. According to Jung, people from all over the world respond to certain myths or stories in the same way, not because everyone knows and appreciates the same story but because lying deep in our collective unconscious are the species memories of humanity's past. These memories exist in the form of **archetypes**: patterns or images of repeated human experiences—such as birth, death, rebirth, the four seasons, and motherhood, to name a few—that express themselves in our stories, our dreams, our religions, and our fantasies. Archetypes are not ready-made ideas but are predispositions, causing us to respond to stimuli in certain ways. Furthermore, they are inherited genetically (a psychic, not a biological, inheritance), making up an identical collective unconsciousness for all humankind. Jung states that the archetypes "give form to countless typical experiences of our ancestors [and are] the psychic residue of innumerable experiences of the same type, of joys and sorrows that have been repeated countless times in our ancestral history." Occurring in literature in the form of recurrent plot patterns, images, or character types, the archetypes stir profound emotions in the reader because they awaken images stored in the collective unconscious and thereby produce feelings or emotions over which the reader initially has little control.

Jung was the first to suggest that such archetypes directly effect the way we respond to external elements. For example, when we see or read about an infant in diapers surrounded by a litter of puppies licking a child's face, feelings of contentment, warmth, and love seemingly pop up in most of us. These somewhat uncontrollable emotions, Jung would claim, are the results of the stirring of an archetype.

Many anthropologists would argue that archetypes are inherited cultural responses, which are passed down from one generation to another in a particular social group. Eventually, such social phenomena become myths or stories that help give meaning and significance to people's lives. Jung would strongly disagree, asserting that myths are "symbolic expressions of the inner, unconscious drama of the psyche." For Jung, myths are the means by which archetypes evidence themselves not only in our dreams but also in the personal conscious.

Throughout the 1920s and until his death in 1961, Jung continued developing his methods of **analytical psychology**. When we apply his theories and methods to literature, we engage in **archetypal criticism**. Unquestionably, the foremost archetypal critic of the twentieth century is Northrop Frye.

Northrop Frye

With the publication of his work *Anatomy of Criticism* in 1957, Northrop Frye (1912–1991) became the primary advocate of the principles of archetypal criticism. Although he never declares allegiance to Jung's concept of the collective unconscious, Frye borrows Jung's ideas about myths and archetypes and develops a systematic approach to archetypal or **mythic criticism**. Divorcing a text from its social history, Frye maintains that there exists an overall structure or mythic development that can explain the structure and significance of all texts.

Frye believes that all of literature comprises one complete and whole story called the **monomyth**. This monomyth can best be diagramed as a circle containing four separate phases, with each phase corresponding to a season of the year and to peculiar cycles of human experiences. The Romance phase, located at the top of the circle, is our summer story. In this story, all our wishes are fulfilled, and we can achieve total happiness. At the bottom of the circle is winter or the Anti-romance phase. The opposite of summer, this phase tells the story of bondage, imprisonment, frustration, and fear. Midway between Romance and Anti-romance and to the right of the middle of the circle is spring or Comedy. This phase relates the story of our rise from Anti-romance and frustration to freedom and happiness. Correspondingly, across the circle is Tragedy or fall, narrating our fall from the Romance phase and from happiness and freedom to disaster. According to Frye, all stories can be placed somewhere on this diagram.

What Frye provides for us is a schematic of all possible kinds of stories. Such a structural framework furnishes the context whereby we can identify stories based on their particular genre, kinds of symbolization, themes, points of view, and other literary elements. In addition, Frye's schematic supplies the background and context for his form of literary criticism and allows us to compare and contrast stories on the basis of their relationship among themselves.

With the advent of archetypal criticism and Frye's schematics in the 1950s, few critics utilized Freudian analysis in their practical criticism. But in the 1960s, the French psychoanalyst, neo-Freudian, and poststructuralist critic Jacques Lacan (1901–1981) helped revive Freudian criticism and by his work rescued it from its overwhelmingly **phallocentric** or a male-dominated position.

Jacques Lacan

Like Freud, Lacan believes that the unconscious greatly affects our conscious behavior. Unlike Freud, who pictures the unconscious as a chaotic, unstructured, bubbling cauldron of dark passions, hidden desires, and suppressed wishes, Lacan asserts that the unconscious is structured, much like the structure of language. Further, like language, this highly structured part of the human psyche can be systematically analyzed. What we will learn from such an analysis, claims Lacan, is that all individuals are fragmented: No one is whole. The ideal concept of a wholly unified and psychologically complete individual is just that, an abstraction that is simply not attainable.

Lacan's Model of the Human Psyche   Like Freud, Lacan devises a three-part model of the human psyche. In Freud's model, the interactions of the id, the ego, and the superego greatly determine our behavior. Underlying Lacan's model, however, is the basic assumption that language shapes and ultimately structures our unconscious and conscious minds and thus shapes our self-identity.

For Lacan, the human psyche consists of three parts or, as Lacan names them, orders: the **Imaginary**, the **Symbolic**, and the **Real**. As in Freud's tripartite model, each of the orders interacts with the others. From our birth until somewhere around six months, we function primarily in the Imaginary Order, that is, in the part of the psyche that contains our wishes, our fantasies, and most importantly, our images. In this phase of our psychic development, we are joyfully united as one with our mother, receiving our food, our care, and all our comfort from her. In this preverbal state, we rely on images as a means of perceiving and interpreting the world. Consequently, our image of ourselves is always in flux, for we are not able to differentiate where one image stops and another begins.

Somewhere between the age of six and eighteen months, we enter what Lacan calls the looking-glass or mirror stage. In this stage, we literally see ourselves in a mirror while metaphorically seeing ourselves in our mother's image. Observing this mirror image permits us to perceive images that have discrete boundaries, allowing us to become aware of ourselves as independent beings who are separate from our mothers. This mirror image of ourselves as a whole and complete being is an ideal, an illusion, for unlike the actual mirror image, we are not in full control of ourselves. We cannot, for example, move our bodies as we want or eat when we so desire.

During the mirror stage, we come to recognize certain objects—what Lacan calls *objet petit a*—as being separate images from ourselves. These include eliminating bodily wastes, our mother's voice and breasts, and our own speech sounds. When these objects or sounds are not present, we yearn for them. Lacan says such objects become for us symbols of lack, and this sense of lack will continue to plague us for the rest of our lives.

While we are passing through the Imaginary Order, one great consuming passion dominates our existence: the desire for our mother. Mother, we believe, can fulfill all our wishes just as we can fulfill all of hers. But we, like our mothers before us, must learn that we are separate entities who can never be totally unified with our mothers. Lacan says that such total unity and wholeness is in itself an illusion.

Once we learn that we are individual beings who are separate from our mothers, we are ready to enter Lacan's second developmental phase, the Symbolic Order. Whereas the Mother dominates the Imaginary Order, the Father dominates the Symbolic Order. In this phase, we learn language. Lacan, however, would argue that language masters us, for Lacan believes that it is language that shapes our identity as separate beings and molds our psyches. Using linguistic principles formulated by Ferdinand de Saussure, Lacan declares that we differentiate between individual sounds and words on the basis of difference. We know the word *might*, for example, because it is different from *sight*, and we know *hill* because it differs from *bill*. Knowing and mastering this concept of difference enables us to enter and to pass through the Symbolic Order successfully.

Lacan contends that in the Symbolic Order we learn to differentiate between male and female. This process of learning gender identity is based on difference and loss. Whereas in the Imaginary Order we delighted in the presence of our mother, in the Symbolic Order we learn that our father comes to represent cultural norms and laws. It is he who stands between us and our mother, and it is he who enforces cultural rules by threatening to castrate us if we do not obey. Since the Castration complex is obviously different for boys and girls, the process of completing the Symbolic Order successfully is different for each sex.

For Lacan, what sex we are is biologically determined, but our gender or our sexuality is culturally created. Society decrees, for example, that a little boy should play with cars and a little girl with dolls. It is the father, the power symbol, who enforces these cultural rules and ensures we follow them. Both sexes, then, come to understand their own sexuality by observing what they are not, a boy noting that he does not do the things a young girl does and vice versa. Each must recognize that he or she will forever be a splintered self, never again being able to experience the wholeness and joy of being one with his or her mother in the Imaginary Order.

For the boy, entry into the Symbolic Order dictates that he identifies and acknowledges the father as the symbol of society's power and as the object that blocks his desire for sexual union with his mother. For the girl, entry into the Symbolic Order decrees that she too acknowledge the father or the male as the symbol of power in society and as her personal superior. Like the boy, she too wishes to return to the happy state of union with her mother in the Imaginary Order. Unlike the boy, however, she maintains more access than he to this pre-Oedipal stage as she grows up.

Lacan maintains that entering the Symbolic Order is a form of castration for both sexes. In Lacan's view, castration is symbolic, not literal, and represents each person's loss of wholeness and his or her acceptance of society's rules. For the male, it means accepting the father, the power symbol who possesses a **phallus** or penis. Likewise, the female must not only accept the father figure as dominant but also accept her lack of a phallus. Similar to his differentiation between sex and gender, Lacan distinguishes between the penis, the actual biological organ, and the phallus, what becomes for Lacan, in poststructural terms, the **transcendental signified**—that object that gives meaning to all other objects. In other words, for Lacan, the phallus is the ultimate symbol of power. Although neither males or females can ever possess the phallus, and therefore can never be complete nor whole, males do have a penis, giving them a slight claim to such power.

Lacan and Textual Analysis   At the heart of Lacan's theory and his understanding of the human psyche is lack and fragmentation. All of us have longings for love, for physical pleasure, and for countless objects, but nothing can fulfill our desire to return to the Imaginary Order and be at one with our mother. It is this fragmentation, this divided self, that concerns Lacan when he examines a literary text. For Lacan, literary texts hold the possibility of capturing, at least for a moment, our desire to return to the Imaginary Order and to regain that sense of pure joy when we were once whole and united with our mothers.

In examining a text, Lacan also looks for elements of the third and most remote and unreachable part of the human psyche, the Real Order. On the one hand, the Real Order consists of the physical world, including the material universe and everything in it; on the other hand, the Real Order also symbolizes all that a person is not. Or as Lacan would say, the Real Order contains countless *object petit a*, objects that continually function for us as symbols of primordial lack. Because these objects and, indeed, the entire physical universe are and can never be parts of ourselves, we can never experience or really know them except through language. In addition, as Lacan contends, it is language that causes our fragmentation in the first place. In Lacan's thought, literature has the particular ability to capture **jouissance**, that is, to call up a brief moment of joy or terror or desire that somehow arises from deep within our unconscious psyche and reminds us of a time of perfect wholeness when we were incapable of differentiating among images from the Real Order. More frequently than not, these experiences are sexual, although other images and experiences such as birth or death can serve this function. Such moments of joy Lacan frequently finds in the writings of Poe, Shakespeare, and Joyce.

The Present State of Psychoanalytic Criticism

Thanks primarily to Lacan, psychoanalytic criticism has enjoyed new popularity. In particular, feminist critics such as Sandra Gilbert and Susan Gubar (*Madwoman in the Attic*, 1979) and a host of others continue to adapt both Freud's and Lacan's theoretical models to show the psychological conflicts and concerns encountered by female writers in a male-dominated world. Other critics such as Felix Guattari continue to challenge both Freud's and Lacan's ideas, devising their own models of the human psyche. Without question, however, Freud and his models of the human psyche remain at the core of psychoanalytic criticism.

ASSUMPTIONS

The foundation for all forms of psychoanalytic criticism irrefutably belongs to Freud and his theories and techniques developed during his psychiatric practice. Whether any practicing psychoanalytic critic utilizes the ideas of Jung, Frye, Lacan, or any other psychoanalyst, all must acknowledge Freud as the intellectual center of this form of criticism.

Central to psychoanalytic criticism is Freud's assumption that all artists, including authors, are neurotic. Unlike most other neurotics, however, the artist escapes many of the outward manifestations and end results of neurosis, such as madness or self-destruction, by finding a pathway back to saneness and wholeness in the act of creating his or her art.

Freud says that an author's chief motivation for writing any story is to gratify some secret desire, some forbidden wish that probably developed during the author's infancy and was immediately suppressed and dumped in the unconscious. The outward manifestation of this suppressed wish becomes the literary work itself. Freud declares that the literary work is therefore the author's dream or fantasy. By employing Freud's psychoanalytic techniques developed for dream therapy, psychoanalytic critics believe we can "unlock" the hidden meanings contained within the story and housed in symbols. It is only then that we can arrive at an accurate interpretation of the text.

Since Freud believes that the literary text is really an artist's dream or fantasy, the text can and must be analyzed like a dream. For Freud, this means that we must assume that the dream is a disguised wish. All of our present wishes, Freud believed, originated in some way during infancy. As an infant, we longed to be both sensually and emotionally satisfied. It is the memory of these satisfied infantile desires that provide the fertile ground for our present wishes to occur. All present wishes are therefore re-creations of a past infantile memory—especially elements of the Oedipal phase—

brought to the surface of our unconscious and conscious states through sensations, emotions, and other present-day situations.

But the actual wish is often too strong and too forbidden to be acknowledged by the mind's censor, the ego. Accordingly, the ego distorts and hides the wish or **latent content** of the dream, thereby allowing the dreamer to remember a somewhat changed and oftentimes radically different dream. It is this changed dream or **manifest content** of the dream that the dreamer tells the dream analyst. In turn, the dream analyst must strip back the various layers of the patient's conversation and carefully analyze the multiple layers of the dream. The analyst's job is much like that of an archaeologist who painstakingly uncovers a valued historical site layer by layer. Like the archaeologist, the analyst must peal back the various layers of a dream until the true wish is uncovered.

Thus, like the dream analyst, the psychoanalytic critic believes that any author's story is a dream that on the surface reveals only the manifest content of the true tale. Hidden and censored throughout the story on various levels lies the latent content of the story, its real meaning or interpretation. More frequently than not, this latent content directly relates to some element and memory of the Oedipal phase of our development. By directly applying the techniques employed in Freudian dream analysis, the psychoanalytic critic believes the actual, uncensored wish can be brought to the surface, thereby revealing the story's true meaning.

Psychoanalysts do not all agree with Freud's basic assumptions, as noted earlier in this chapter. For example, Jung believes that mythological as well as sexual images appear in our dreams. Frye borrows this assumption from Jung and develops a schematic for interpreting all dreams and stories. Lacan, on the other hand, disavows Freud's assumption that the unconscious is a cauldron of boiling passions and announces that the unconscious is as highly structured as language itself. By analyzing this structure, Lacan declares that no one can achieve wholeness, for we are all and will always remain fragmented individuals who are seeking completeness. Nevertheless, all of these theorists and their theories relate in some way to Freud's presuppositions.

METHODOLOGIES

First introduced to literary studies in the 1920s and 1930s, Freud's psychoanalytic criticism still survives today. Although its methods have been challenged, revised, and supplemented, psychoanalytic criticism provides a stimulating approach to literary analysis that decrees that we humans are complex yet somewhat understandable creatures who often fail to note the influence of the unconscious on both our motivations and our everyday actions.

For several decades after its introduction, psychoanalytic criticism focused mainly on the author. Known as **psychobiography**, this method of analysis begins by amassing biographical information about an author through biographies, personal letters, lectures, and any other document related in some way to the author. Using these data and the author's **canon** (the collected works), psychoanalytic critics believed they could theoretically construct the author's personality, with all its idiosyncrasies, internal and external conflicts, and more importantly, neuroses. In turn, such a devised theory, they believed, could illuminate an author's individual works, giving rise to the latent content in the author's texts. By gaining an in-depth understanding of the author, these critics assumed they would be better able to interpret an author's canon. Of particular interest to them were the lives and works of Edgar Allan Poe, William Blake, and Leonardo da Vinci.

In the 1950s, psychoanalytic critics turned their attention away from psychobiography to character analysis, studying the various aspects of characters' minds found in an author's canon. Such a view gave rise to a more complex understanding of a literary work. Individual characters within a text now became the focus. Believing that the author had in mind a particular personality for his or her characters, critics also noted that readers develop their own conceptions of each character's personality. A character's motivations and actions, then, became more complex than simply attributing them to the author's ideas. How readers interpreted characters now became an integral part of the text's interpretation. Whereas the author creates a character, a reader re-creates the same character, bringing to the text and to an individual character all the reader's past experiences and knowledge. The character simultaneously, then, becomes the creation of the author and of the reader. In order to interpret the story, a psychoanalytic analysis of the author and the reader were therefore necessary.

Today, many psychoanalytic critics realize that the reader plays a major role in interpreting a work. Understanding ourselves from a Freudian point of view as well as the context in which we live is considered essential if we are to interpret a text.

One of the most controversial psychoanalytic techniques used today involves applying Freud's key assumption—that all human behavior is sexually driven—directly to a text. In the hands of novice critics, who are often ill- or misinformed about Freud's psychoanalytic techniques, everything in a text more frequently than not becomes a sexual image. For these critics, every concave image, such as a flower, a cup, a cave, or a vase, is a **yonic symbol** (female), and any image whose length exceeds its diameter, such as a tower, a sword, a knife, or a pen, becomes a **phallic symbol** (male). Consequently, a text containing a dance, a boat floating into a cave, or a pen being placed within a cup is interpreted as a symbol of sexual intercourse. From this perspective, all images and actions within a text must be traced to the author's id, for everything in a text is ultimately the hidden wishes of the author's libido.

Another psychoanalytic approach is archetypal criticism, first developed by Jung and then later by Frye. In this form of analysis, critics examine a text to discover the various archetypes that they claim appear in it. In Jung's view, these archetypes have the same meaning for all readers. The color red, for example, signifies danger just as water symbolizes life. By showing where and how these archetypes appear in the text, and whether or not they form recognizable patterns, the archetypal critic believes that he or she will be able to discover the text's meaning. To apply this method accurately, a critic must have a complete grasp of Jung's rather complex theories and terminology.

The most recent type of psychoanalytic criticism is based in ideas developed by Lacan. A Lacanian critic would attempt to uncover how a text symbolically represents elements of the Real, the Imaginary, and the Symbolic orders. By identifying the symbolic representations of these orders within the text, the critic would then examine how each of these symbols demonstrates the fragmentary nature of the self. Such a demonstration would show the reader that all individuals are in actuality splintered selves. The overall purpose of a Lacanian analysis, then, is to teach us that a fully integrated and psychologically whole person does not exist and that we must all accept fragmentation.

Whichever psychoanalytic method a critic may choose to use, he or she must master the psychoanalytic theories and practices of Freud and some of his pupils in order to devise an interpretation that is credible and clear. Although mastering the theory and its appropriate applications may be difficult, the result could be a rewarding discovery of the truth that lies within each of us.

QUESTIONS FOR ANALYSIS

- Since psychoanalytic criticism is based on various models of the mind rather than on an aesthetic theory, this critical approach to textual analysis can utilize the methodology of a variety of schools of criticism. Explain, then, how the critical methods of New Criticism, reader-response, and deconstruction can be used in a psychoanalytic reading of a text.

- Using Hawthorne's "Ethan Brand," analyze the protagonist from each of the following perspectives: Freudian, Jungian, and, Lacanian.

- Apply Freud's theories to John Keats's "To Autumn," and articulate a psychoanalytic interpretation of this poem.

- Using a short story or poem of your choice, identify the different images and structural patterns that occur in the text. Then, using your understanding of psychoanalytic criticism, explain the presence of these images and patterns and analyze how each relates to an overall psychoanalytic interpretation of the text itself.

- Investigate the life of John Keats and apply the principles of psychobiography to his poem "Ode on a Grecian Urn." When your psychobiographical analysis is completed, then apply the theories of Freud to this same poem, pointing out and explaining any phallic and/or yonic symbols that appear in the text.

SAMPLE ESSAY

In the student essay that follows, note carefully how the author, David Johnson, applies Freudian psychoanalytic terminology and methodology to arrive at his interpretation. After briefly reviewing basic elements of Freudian psychology, what primary psychoanalytic approach does he use in his analysis? Is the author concentrating his psychoanalysis more on the poet or on the poem? Can you find any evidence that Johnson interacts with the text and imposes his own personality traits upon his interpretation of the text? In your opinion, is this psychoanalytic essay a valid and legitimate interpretation of the text? Be able to defend your response.

FURTHER READING

Benvenuto, Bice, and Roger Kennedy. *The Works of Jacques Lacan: An Introduction.* New York: St. Martin's, 1986.

Crews, Frederick C. *Out of My System.* New York: Oxford University Press, 1975.

Felman, Shoshana. *Jacques Lacan and the Adventure of Insight: Psychoanalysis in Contemporary Culture.* Cambridge: Harvard University Press, 1987.

Freud, Sigmund. *The Complete Introductory Lectures on Psychoanalysis.* Trans. James Strachey. New York: Norton, 1966.

Frye, Northrop. *Anatomy of Criticism.* Princeton: Princeton University Press, 1957.

Hoffman, Frederick J. *Freudianism and the Literary Mind.* 2nd ed. Baton Rouge: Louisiana State University Press, 1957.

Holland, Norman N. *The Dynamics of Literary Response.* New York: Oxford University Press, 1968.

———. "The 'Unconscious' of Literature." *Contemporary Criticism.* Ed. Norman Bradbury and David Palmer. Stratford-upon-Avon Ser. 12. New York: St. Martin's, 1970.

Jung, Carl. *The Archetypes and the Collective Unconscious.* Vol. 9, Part I of *Collected Works,* 2nd ed. Trans. R. F. C. Hull. Princeton: Princeton University Press, 1968.

Meisel, Perry, ed. *Freud: Twentieth Century Views.* Englewood Cliffs: Prentice Hall, 1981.

Wright, Elizabeth. *Psychoanalytic Criticism: Theory and Practice.* New York: Methuen, 1984.

WEB SITES FOR EXPLORATION

www.brocku.ca/english/courses/4F70/terms.html
   Provides an excellent overview of psychoanalytic theory, terms, and concepts

www.psywww.com/books/interp/toc.htm
   Provides the complete text of Sigmund Freud's *The Interpretation of Dreams*

www.cnr.edu/home/bmcmanus/psychcrit.html
   Provides an overview of a variety of psychoanalytic approaches, including Freud, Jung, and Lacan

www.brocku.ca/english/courses/4F70/psychthry.html
   Provides links to the contributions of psychoanalytic thought to the study of literature, especially recent articles concerning Freud

www.colorado.edu/English/ENG201Klages/lacan.html
   Provides an overview of the differences between Sigmund Freud and Jacques Lacan

ঌ Student Essay ঌ

A Psychoanalytic Approach to Poe's "The City in the Sea"

Unlike many other schools of criticism, psychoanalytic theory with its accompanying practical applications is unique, for it can be used with a variety of other literary theories when analyzing a text. Although this particular approach to textual analysis has been criticized for its lack of attention toward the aesthetic elements of a work, a psychoanalytic approach can reveal intriguing details not only about the text but also about the author and the reader, elements of the interpretative process that other literary techniques often overlook.

Psychoanalytic theory finds its roots in psychoanalysis, a medical technique developed by Sigmund Freud (1856–1939). Freud bases his psychoanalytic theories on his tripartite model of the human mind. This model represents the unconscious part of the human psyche as housing three parts: the id, the ego, and the superego. According to Freud, the id is the reservoir of the primal instincts of sexuality and aggression. Being dominated by the "pleasure principle" that knows only desire, the id is lawless and amoral, striving only to gratify the dark desires it houses. Freud believes that if the id is left unchecked, it can result in a person's self-destruction. To counterbalance this dangerous part of the unconscious, the mind possesses two regulating agencies: the ego and the superego. The superego is the exact opposite of the id, working to protect society and to allow a person to abide by certain moral restrictions. Dominated by the "morality principle," an overactive superego will result in an unconscious and often overwhelming sense of guilt. But it is the ego that regulates between these two psychic forces (the id and the superego), acting as the rational governing agency of the mind. Though it may lack the vitality of the id, the ego more frequently than not succeeds in redirecting the strong and potentially dangerous urges housed in the unconscious mind into nondestructive activities.

When Freud first developed psychoanalysis, he did not intend it to be a school of literary criticism. He did believe, however, that literature contains elements relevant to his psychological theories, taking, for example, the name of his "Oedipus Complex" from Sophocles' Greek tragedy. A major component of psychoanalysis is dream interpretation, in which the analyst probes the patient's dreams for hidden symbols. In this probing, the analyst must distinguish among four key elements of a dream: repression, sublimation, displacement, and condensation. Repression represents the powerful urges of the id that have been forced into the unconscious by the ego. These repressed desires resurface in dreams through the other three processes. For example, in sublimation the unconscious mind redirects unacceptable desires into acceptable activities. In actuality, the mind leaks these forbidden desires into the acceptable activity of dreaming, thereby providing a pathway for and a view into the previously inaccessible id. Through displacement, the id disguises a repressed urge to sneak this forbidden desire past the mind's censor, often making the most interesting element of the dream the most trivial detail. All of these forces working together constitute what Freud calls a "condensed dream"—that is, in a person's dream the dream images become a highly compressed array of the dreamer's psychic expressions, offering an extensive assortment of meanings. According to Freud, a literary work is similar to a dream in that such a text is deemed an acceptable activity by society and the mind, making a work of fiction a virtual playground for the author's repressed instincts.

In her comprehensive, psychoanalytic study of Edgar Allan Poe, Marie Bonaparte, a follower of Sigmund Freud, analyzes Poe's canon, utilizing psychobiography, one of the first literary applications of psychoanalytic criticism. Rarely used today, psychobiography is the study of an author's life and events and includes the excavation of the residue of these events in the author's work. Bonaparte extensively studied Poe's life, and through the application of Freud's dream analysis techniques, she linked characters and events from Poe's writing to actual characters and events in his life.

From her study of Poe's life, Bonaparte deduced that Poe's existence was one of loneliness, poverty, and despair. Before Poe turned three, his father had already deserted the family. Shortly thereafter, his mother died of consumption, leaving Poe in the hands of a somewhat uncaring but financially successful foster father, John Allan. Poe spent the next five years in England, for the Allans' profitable business ventures had taken them abroad. Returning a lonely and introverted child, Poe lacked the self-motivation of a disciplined student, but nonetheless was an outstanding classical scholar. At age seventeen, Poe matriculated at the University of Virginia, where his excessive drinking, gambling, and aristocratic aires eventually led him to leave the university and join the United States Army.

Poe's lack of discipline once again surfaced, and about two years later—thanks, in part, to the intervention of his foster father—Poe left the army. A short time later, however, he gained entrance to West Point, remaining only eight months. Receiving little or no support from his foster father and loathing the discipline of military life, Poe deliberately violated the academy's rules and was thereby dismissed.

In 1831, after his second military stint, Poe moved to Baltimore, Maryland, where he lived with his aunt. A few years later, he married his thirteen-year-old cousin, Virginia Clemm. Many scholars believe the marriage, however, was never consummated. Throughout the remainder of Poe's brief life, bouts of depression, bursts of creativity, periods of extreme poverty, the death of his wife, and difficulties maintaining stable employment haunted him until his death in 1849.

By applying Freud's psychoanalytic principles to Poe's life and his canon, Bonaparte believes that Poe was still erotically attached to his mother at the time of her death, leaving a void in his libido. Through his marriage to his cousin and then by avoiding the sexual consummation of the marriage, Poe preserved his sexuality. According to Bonaparte, Poe's self-imposed abstinence forced the powerful urges of his libido back into his unconscious. Through the process of sublimation, his repressed sexual forces then made themselves apparent in his fiction. The unacceptable activities of his sex drive thus became sublimated to the acceptable activity of writing.

Such sublimation evidences itself in Poe's poem "The City in the Sea" (1845). In this text, Poe paints a dark image of an ancient Gothic city that is abandoned and desolate. Throughout the poem, Poe describes this solemn city with its once magnificent buildings and monuments as the remnants of a once-seething metropolis. A psychoanalytic approach to this text reveals explicit sexual imagery, signifying the emergence of Poe's repressed libido. Three types of such sexual imagery abound in the poem: phallic symbols (any object whose length exceeds its diameter and which represents the penis); yonic symbols (round, hollow objects that symbolize the vagina);

and symbols of the actual sex act. The presence of this sexual imagery combined with an understanding and the utilization of Freud's theories of displacement, repression, and sublimation reveals the resurfacing of Poe's forgotten and suppressed sexual desires in this poem.

Interestingly, "The City in the Sea" was not the poem's original title. Before the present title, Poe opted for "The Doomed City" (1831) and the "City of Sin" (1836). Both of these former titles illustrate the concept of displacement. Poe's ego probably deemed these earlier titles unacceptable; his id then developed a title that seems trivial enough, but one that still contains a highly but more repressed image. For the "City" with its buildings and pulsating activities symbolizes the penis, and the "Sea," a frequent yonic symbol, represents the vagina. "The City in the Sea," Poe's final title, then represents the sex act itself.

The poem begins with a brief description of the city, with phallic symbols immediately becoming apparent. As early as line 6 we find evidence of the phallus: "There shrines and palaces and towers/ (Time-eaten towers that tremble not!)." These shrines, palaces, and towers we quickly recognize as symbolic of the penis, but a penis that "tremble[s] not"! For in lines 8–11, Poe reveals his repressed sexual desires: "Resemble nothing that is ours. round by lifting winds forgot,/ Resignedly beneath the sky/ The melancholy waters lie." Poe now describes the phallic symbols he previously addressed—the shrines, palaces, and towers—as "forgotten" and as surrounded, "by melancholy waters" that stand unlifted (still) "resignedly beneath the sky." The use of this description illustrates Poe's forced but self-imposed sexual abstinence. The penis, as any kind of pleasure center, Poe has completely neglected.

Phallic symbols continue to abound in the second stanza of the poem. Lines 14–18 reveal these symbols and Poe's repressed sexuality:

But light from out the lurid sea
Streams up the turrets silently—
Gleams up the pinnacles far and free
Up domes—up spires—up kingly halls—
Up fanes—up Babylon-like walls—

Apparently Poe's ego sees the quickening of the penis as unacceptable, and his repressed feelings of sexuality become sublimated into poetry.

In stanzas three and four, the imagery changes to include not only phallic but also yonic symbols. In stanza three, for example, "The melancholy waters lie" (an obvious yonic symbol) and "a proud tower [. . .] looks gigantically down" (an obvious phallic symbol). But it is in stanza four that such imagery becomes most apparent. In lines 30–31, Poe writes: "There open fanes and gaping graves/ Yawn level with the luminous waves." These gaping graves represent the vagina. Poe's use of the adjective "gaping" is particularly indicative of sexual activity and possesses many sexual connotations. In addition, the "ripples" and "swellings" that follow in the rest of the stanza represent breastlike images and the curves of a woman's body.

Whereas phallic and yonic symbolism abound in the first three stanzas of the poem, the fifth and last stanza contains a symbolic representation of the actual sex act. The first two lines of the stanza (l. 42–43) imply the activity that is to come: "But lo, a stir is in the air!/ the wave—there is a movement there!" The sexual imagery becomes more explicit in the next four lines:

As if the towers had thrust aside,
In slightly sinking, the dull tide—
As if their tops had feebly given
A void within the filmy Heaven.

In these lines where the "thrusting towers" give a "void within the filmy heaven," the sex act becomes apparent. The phallic symbol, the towers, couples with the yonic symbol, the void, signifying sexual intercourse. Such imagery represents sexual climax, with the lines that follow containing images of the postclimactic sexual state:

The waves have now a redder glow—
The hours are breathing faith and low—
And when, amid no earthly moans,
Down, down that town shall settle hence.

Overall, the poem "The City in the Sea" is incredibly rich with sexual imagery and shows Poe's id at work, striving to convey the deep passions and desires of his unconscious mind. And thanks to Freud's psychoanalytic methods of dream analysis applied to this text, we can uncover such a rich and varied interpretation.

DAVID JOHNSON

8

Feminism

> *What enrages me is the way women are used as extensions of men, mirrors of men, devices for showing men off, devices for helping men get what they want. They are never there in their own right, or rarely. The world of the Western contains no women.*
> *Sometimes I think the world contains no women.*
>
> Jane Tompkins, "Me and My Shadow"

INTRODUCTION

In 1972, Judith Viorst, a well-known author of children's literature, published her short, poetic, revised version of the fairy tale "Cinderella." In her version, entitled ". . . And Then the Prince Knelt Down and Tried to Put the Glass Slipper on Cinderella's Foot," Viorst writes:

> I really didn't notice that he had a funny nose.
> And he certainly looked better all dressed up in fancy clothes.
> He's not nearly as attractive as he seemed the other night.
> So I think I'll just pretend that this glass slipper feels too tight.

Viorst's recasting of Cinderella may make us smile, or laugh, or simply wonder what has happened to our childhood version of this story that was read to us countless times by our parents, our teachers, and our friends. Viorst's Cinderella is, after all, certainly not the Cinderella we remember. The Cinderella we have been taught would never think or act the way Viorst's re-creation does. Our Cinderella is beautiful, but poor. Treated cruelly by her ugly stepsisters and her arrogant, scheming, self-assertive stepmother, our Cinderella dutifully cleans the family home while she quietly weeps, lamenting that she will not be able to attend the upcoming ball to be held at the castle. Bearing with great patience her trials, our Cinderella will triumphantly get her wish, for her fairy godmother comes to her rescue. Now clothed in a magnificent gown, the lovely Cinderella is driven to the ball in a coach fit for a princess. At the ball, she meets her handsome prince, who is immediately overwhelmed by her beauty, grace, and charm. But at the stroke of midnight, the Cinderella we remember must return home, losing her glass slipper in her haste to her carriage.

Dressed in rags, our childhood Cinderella finds herself once again cooking and cleaning for her ugly stepsisters and her wicked stepmother. Bearing her lot in life with unspeakable patience, she is scorned and rebuked time and time again by her older siblings. And then one day, the prince and his attendants come to her home, seeking the owner of the glass slipper accidently left on the steps of the castle. After her ugly stepsisters try unsuccessfully to squeeze their big feet into the small slipper, the Cinderella we remember comes face to face with her handsome prince and successfully puts her petite foot into the magical shoe. Immediately, the prince recognizes her as the woman of his dreams and proposes marriage. And after their marriage, they live happily ever after.

Viorst's version of this fairy tale characterizes Cinderella a bit differently. In this re-creation, Cinderella now has opinions of her own. In the light of day, she observes that the prince does not seem to be as attractive as he was the other night at the ball. Asserting her own independence, she pretends the glass slipper does not fit. Accordingly, there will be no marriage, for Cinderella herself has decided she does not want to marry the prince.

This new Cinderella refuses to be defined as a "nonsignificant Other." Unlike the old Cinderella, she will not allow herself to be shaped by her society. She realizes that her culture has all too often presented her with stereotypes, which she and many others like her have blindly accepted. Beautiful women, her society decrees, are often oppressed and belittled. If, however, these beautiful people will only bear with patience their lot in life, they will be rewarded. Like the traditional Cinderella, society says that they must accept that, in addition to their beauty, they must also be good-natured and meek. After all, ugly women like Cinderella's stepsisters are cruel and heartless. Beautiful women like Cinderella must bear patiently their suffering and accept that they are victims of the circumstances of life. If they accept their lot in life, they will, in time, be rewarded. According to their society's decrees, they will meet some handsome, wealthy prince who will marry them, care for them, and dote over them the rest of their lives.

Viorst's re-created Cinderella wishes to debunk the false standards and beliefs about women, both in their lives and in their portrayal in literature, that have been carefully perpetuated by the traditional Cinderella story. Women, says this new Cinderella, should not mindlessly wait for a handsome prince to come to the rescue. Women need not nor must not be like the traditional Cinderella: dependent creatures who without question or doubt accept the commands of their patriarchal society. Unlike the traditional Cinderella, women must not weep about their lot in life but take an active part in creating and determining their own lives and their own futures. They must therefore reject many of the cultural stereotypes of women such as "the wicked stepmother" syndrome, which asserts that only ugly women are aggressive and self-motivated. They must also reject the notion that marriage is a woman's ultimate goal, one that can assure her of financial security.

In sum, they must reject the idea that women (like the traditional Cinderella) are mindless, weepy, passive, helpless creatures who must wait for a man to come and make their lives meaningful. Success in life, these new Cinderellas assert, is not dependent on physical beauty, as it is for the traditional Cinderella. Above all, then, they must realize that they are not limited by their sex; like any man, they too can shape their personhood and assert their resourcefulness, their wit, and their personal drive to become what they desire to be. For the re-created Cinderella knows something the old Cinderella never knew: Whereas sex is biologically determined, gender is culturally determined. Like the revised Cinderella, all women must therefore reject the patriarchal standards of society and become persons in their own right. What they must become is a "Significant Person, " not the Other. In essence, this new version of the Cinderella fairy tale crystallizes the central issues of feminism, namely:

- That men, either unconsciously or consciously, have oppressed women, allowing them little or no voice in the political, social, or economic issues of their society;
- That by not giving voice and value to women's opinions, responses, and writings, men have therefore suppressed the female, defined what it means to be feminine, and thereby de-voiced, devalued, and trivialized what it means to be a woman; and
- That, in effect, men have made women the "nonsignificant Other."

Feminism's goal is to change this degrading view of women so that all women will realize that they are not a nonsignificant Other, but that each woman is a valuable person possessing the same privileges and rights as every man. Women, feminists declare, must define themselves and assert their own voices in the arenas of politics, society, education, and the arts. By personally committing themselves to fostering such change, feminists hope to create a society in which not only the male but also the female voice is equally valued.

HISTORICAL DEVELOPMENT

According to feminist criticism, the roots of prejudice against women have long been embedded in Western culture. Such gender discrimination may have begun, say some feminists, with the biblical narrative that places the blame for the fall of humanity on Eve, not Adam. In similar fashion, the ancient Greeks abetted such gender discrimination when Aristotle, a leading philosopher and teacher, asserted, "The male is by nature superior, and the female inferior; and the one rules and the other is ruled." Following Aristotle, religious leaders and philosophers such as Thomas Aquinas and St. Augustine declared that women are really "imperfect men." These imperfect and spiritually weak creatures, they maintained, possess a sensual nature that lures men away from spiritual truths, thereby preventing males from attaining their spiritual potential. In the centuries that follow, other theologians, philosophers, and scientists continue such gender discrimination. For example, in *The Descent of Man* (1871), Darwin announces that women are of a "characteristic of [. . .] a past and lower state of civilization." Such beings, he noted, are inferior to men, who are physically, intellectually, and artistically superior.

Century after century, men's voices continued to articulate and determine the social role and cultural and personal significance of women. In the late 1700s, a faint voice crying in the wilderness in opposition to such patriarchal and defaming opinions against women arose and began to be heard. Believing that women along with men should have a voice in the public arena, Mary Wollstonecraft authored *A Vindication of the Rights of Women* (1792). Women, she maintained, must stand up for their rights and not allow their male-dominated society to define what it means to be a woman. Women themselves must take the lead and articulate who they are and what role they will play in society. More importantly, they must reject the patriarchal assumption that women are inferior to men.

It was not until the Progressive Era of the early 1900s, however, that the major roots of feminist criticism began to grow. During this time, women gained the right to vote and became prominent activists in the social issues of the day, such as health care, education, politics, and literature, but equality with men in these arenas remained outside their grasp.

Virginia Woolf

In 1919, the British scholar and teacher Virginia Woolf (1882–1941) laid the foundation for present-day feminist criticism in her seminal work *A Room of One's Own*. In this text, Woolf declares that men have and continue to treat women as inferiors. It is the male, she asserts, who defines what it means to be female and who controls the political, economic, social, and literary structures. Agreeing with Samuel T. Coleridge, one of the foremost nineteenth-century literary critics, that great minds possess both male and female characteristics, she hypothesizes in her text the existence of Shakespeare's sister, one who is equally as gifted as a writer as Shakespeare himself. Her gender, however, prevents her from having "a room of her own." Because she is a woman, she cannot obtain an education or find profitable employment. Her innate artistic talents will therefore never flourish, for she cannot afford her own room, Woolf's symbol of the solitude and autonomy needed to seclude one's self from the world and its social constraints in order to find time to think and write. Ultimately, Shakespeare's sister dies alone without any acknowledgment of her personal genius. Even her grave bears not her name, for she is buried in a unmarked grave simply because she is female.

This kind of loss of artistic talent and personal worthiness, says Woolf, is the direct result of society's opinion of women: to wit, that they are intellectually inferior to men. Women, Woolf argues, must reject this social construct and establish their own identity. Women must challenge the prevailing, false cultural notions about their gender identity and develop a female discourse that will accurately portray their relationship "to the world of reality and not to the world of men." If women accept this challenge, Woolf believes that Shakespeare's sister can be resurrected in and through women living today, even those who may be "washing up the dishes and putting the children to bed" right now. Regrettably, the Great Depression of the 1930s and World War II in the 1940s focused humankind's attention on other matters and delayed the development of such feminist ideals.

Simone de Beauvoir

With the 1949 publication of *The Second Sex* by the French writer Simone de Beauvoir (1908–1986), however, feminist interests were once again surfacing. Heralded as the foundational work of twentieth-century feminism, Beauvoir's text declares that French society (and Western societies in general) are **patriarchal**, controlled by males. Like Woolf before her, Beauvoir believed that the male in these societies defines what it means to be human, including, therefore, what it means to be female. Since the female is not male, Beauvoir asserted, she becomes the Other, an object whose existence is defined and interpreted by the male, the dominant being in society. Always subordinate to the male, the female finds herself a secondary or nonexistent player in the major social institutions of her culture, such as the church, government, and educational systems. Beauvoir asserts that a woman must break the bonds of her patriarchal society and define herself if she wishes to become a significant human being in her own right and defy male classification as the Other. She must ask herself, "What is a woman?" Beauvoir insists that a woman's answer must not be "mankind," for such a term once again allows men to define women. This generic label must be rejected, for it assumes that "humanity is male and man defines woman not in herself but as relative to him."

Beauvoir insists that women see themselves as autonomous beings. Women, she maintains, must reject the societal construct that men are the subject or the absolute and that women are the Other. Embedded in this false assumption is the supposition that males have power and define cultural terms and roles. Accordingly, women must define themselves outside the present social construct and reject being labeled as the Other.

Kate Millett

With the advent of the 1960s and its political activism and social concerns, feminist issues found new voices, and prominent among them is Kate Millett. With her publication of *Sexual Politics* in 1969, a new wave of feminism begins. Millett is one of the first feminists to challenge the social ideological characteristics of both the male and the female. Millett argues that a female is born and a woman is created. In other words, one's sex, be that male or female, is determined at birth. One's gender, however, is a social construct created by cultural ideals and norms. Consciously or unconsciously, women and men conform to the cultural ideas established for them by society. Little boys, for example, must be aggressive, self-assertive, and domineering, whereas little girls must be passive, meek, and humble. These cultural norms and expectations are transmitted through media: television, movies, songs, and literature. Conforming to these prescribed sex roles dictated by society is what Millett calls **sexual politics**. Women, Millett maintains, must revolt against the power center of their culture: male dominance. In order to do so, women must establish female social conventions for themselves by establishing and articulating female discourse, literary studies, and feminist theory.

Feminism in the 1960s and 1970s

Moving from the political to the literary arena throughout the 1960s and 1970s, feminist critics began to examine the traditional literary canon and discovered example after example of male dominance and prejudice that supported Beauvoir's and Millett's assertion that males considered the female "the Other," an unnatural or deviant being. First, stereotypes of women abounded in the canon: Women were sex maniacs, goddesses of beauty, mindless entities, or old spinsters. Second, while Dickens, Wordsworth, Hawthorne, Thoreau, Twain, and a host of other male authors found their way into the established literary canon, few female authors achieved such status. Third, for the most part, the roles of female, fictionalized characters were limited to secondary positions, more frequently than not occupying minor parts within the stories or simply reverting to the male's stereotypical images of women. Fourth, female scholars such as Virginia Woolf and Simone de Beauvoir were ignored, their writings seldom, if ever, referred to by the male crafters of the literary canon.

Feminist critics of this era asserted that these males and their male counterparts who created and enjoyed a place of prominence within the canon assumed that all readers were males. Women reading such works could unconsciously, then, be duped into reading as a male. In addition, since most of the university professors were males, more frequently than not female students were trained to read literature as if they were males. The feminists of the 1960s and 1970s now postulated the existence of a female reader who was affronted by the male prejudices abounding in the canon. Questions concerning the male or female qualities of literary form, style, voice, and theme became the rallying points for feminist criticism, and throughout the late 1970s books that defined women's writings in feminine terms flourished.

Having highlighted the importance of gender, feminist critics then began to uncover and rediscover a body of literary works authored by females that their male counterparts had decreed inferior and therefore unworthy to be part of the canon. In America, for example, Kate Chopin's late nineteenth-century novel *The Awakening* (1899) served as the archetypal, rediscovered feminist text of this period, whereas in England Doris Lessing's *The Golden Notebook* (1962) and in France Monique Wittig's *Les Guérillères* (1969) fulfilled these roles. Throughout the universities and in the reading populace, readers turned their attention to historical and current works authored by women. Simultaneously, works that attempted to define the feminine imagination, to categorize and explain female literary history, and to attempt to define the female aesthetic or concept of beauty became the focus of feminist critics.

The ongoing debate over definitive answers to these key feminist interests continued throughout the decades of the 1980s and 1990s, as it does today.

Elaine Showalter

The dominating voice of feminist criticism throughout the 1980s is that of Elaine Showalter. In her text *A Literature of Their Own* (1977), Showalter chronicles what she believes to be the three historical phases of evolution in female writing. The "feminine" phase (1840–1880), the "feminist" phase (1880–1920), and the "female" phase (1970–present). During the "feminine" phase, writers such as Charlotte Brontë, George Eliot, and George Sand accepted the prevailing social constructs of their day on the role and therefore the definition of women. Accordingly, these female authors wrote under male pseudonyms, hoping to equal the intellectual and artistic achievements of their male counterparts. During the "feminist" phase, female authors dramatized the plight of the "slighted" woman. More often than not, these authors depicted the harsh and often cruel treatment of female characters at the hands of their more powerful male creations. At present, in the "female" phase, women reject the imitation prominent during the "feminine" phase and the protest that dominated the "feminist" phase. Showalter points out that feminist critics now concern themselves with developing a peculiarly female understanding of the female experience in art, including a feminine analysis of literary forms and techniques. Such a task necessarily includes the uncovering of **misogyny** in male texts, a term Showalter uses to describe the male hatred of women.

Showalter asserts that female authors were consciously and therefore deliberately excluded from the literary canon by those male professors who first established the canon itself. Authors like Susan Warner, E. D. N. Southworth, and Mary E. Wilkins Freeman, by far the most popular authors of the second half of the nineteenth century in American fiction, were not deemed worthy to be included in the canon. Showalter urges that such exclusion of the female voice must stop. She thus coins the term **gynocritics** to refer to the process of "construct[ing] a female framework for analysis of women's literature to develop new models based on the study of female experience, rather than to adapt to male models and theories." Through gynocritics, Showalter hopes to expose the false cultural assumptions of women as depicted in literature. By exposing inaccurate pictures of women, she hopes to establish women as both readers and writers in their own right.

Showalter's term **gynocriticism** has now become synonymous with the study of women as writers and provides critics with four models that address the nature of women's writing and help answer some of the chief concerns of feminist criticism: the biological, the linguistic, the psychoanalytic, and the cultural. Each of Showalter's models are sequential, subsuming and developing the preceding model(s). The *biological model* emphasizes how the female body marks itself upon a text by providing a host of literary images and a personal, intimate tone. The *linguistic model* concerns itself with the need for a female discourse. This model investigates the differences between how women and men use language. It asserts that women can and do create a language peculiar to their gender and addresses the way in which this language can be utilized in their writings. The *psychoanalytic model*, based on an analysis of the female psyche and how such an analysis affects the writing process, emphasizes the flux and fluidity of female writing as opposed to male rigidity and structure. The *cultural model* investigates how the society in which female authors work and function shapes women's goals, responses, and points of view.

Geographical Strains of Feminism

Since no one critical theory of writing dominates feminist criticism, and few theorists agree upon a unifying feminist approach to textual analysis, physical geography plays a great part in determining the major interests of various voices of feminist criticism. Three somewhat distinct, geographical strains of feminism have emerged: American, British, and French. According to Elaine Showalter, American feminism is essentially textual, stressing repression; British feminism is essentially Marxist, stressing oppression; and French feminism is essentially psychoanalytic, stressing repression. All groups, however, attempt to rescue women from being considered "the Other."

American Feminism   The American feminist critic Annette Kolodny helps set the major concern of American feminism: the restoration of the writings of female authors to the literary canon. Believing that literary history is itself a fiction, Kolodny wishes to restore the history of women so that they themselves can tell "herstory." In order to tell and write "herstory," however, women must first find a means to gain their voice in the midst of numerous voices—particularly male voices—clamoring for attention in society.

Like Kolodny, Sandra M. Gilbert and Susan Gubar, authors of *The Madwoman in the Attic: The Woman Writer and the Nineteenth-Century Literary Imagination* (1979), assert that the male voice has for too long been dominant. Because males have also had the power of the pen and therefore the press, they have been able to define and create images of women as they so choose in their male texts. Gilbert and Gubar argue that the coercion of this male power has caused "anxiety of authorship" in women, causing them to fear the act of literary creation itself and the act of writing. Literary creation, they believe, will isolate them from society and may even destroy them. Gilbert and Gubar's solution is that women develop a "woman's sentence" that would encourage literary autonomy. By inventing such a sentence, a woman can sentence a man to isolation, to fear, and to literary banishment from the canon, just as for centuries men have been sentencing women. In effect, by formulating a woman's sentence, women writers can finally free themselves from being defined by men.

A woman's sentence, argue Gilbert and Gubar, could also free women from being reduced to the stereotypical images that all too often appear in literature. They identify the two principal stereotyped images as "the angel in the house" and the "madwoman in the attic." If a woman is depicted as the angel in the house, she supposedly realizes that her physical and material comforts are gifts from her husband. Knowing this fact, her goal in life is to please her husband, to attend to his every comfort, and to obey him.

Through these selfless acts, she finds the utmost contentment by serving both her husband and her children. If, perchance, a female character should reject this role, the male critics quickly dub her a "monster," a freakish anomaly who is obviously sexually fallen.

Gilbert and Gubar assert that either of these images—the angel or the madwoman—are unrealistic representations of woman in society. One canonizes and places the woman above the world, while the other denigrates and places her below the world. Further, the message is clear to all women: If you are not an angel, then you are a monster. Such stereotypical, male-created images of women in literature must be uncovered, examined, and transcended if women are to achieve literary autonomy.

British Feminism   Whereas American feminism emphasizes repression, British feminism stresses oppression. Essentially Marxist, British feminism refuses to separate art, literature, and life. Denying the existence of any spiritual reality, some British feminists view reading, writing, and publishing as facets of material reality. As part of material reality, literature, like one's job and one's social activities, is part of a great whole, with each part affecting the other. How women are depicted in life, then, directly affects how they are treated in real life. Particularly in the West, women are exploited not only in literature but also in economic and social conditions. From this perspective, the traditional Western family structure helps to subordinate women, causing them to be economically dependent. Such dependency will then be reflected in literature, and it is the job of feminist critics, British feminism maintains, to change this unfair social status of women economically and socially and also in texts. For these feminist critics, the goal of criticism is to change society, not simply critique it.

French Feminism   Believing that women are oppressed both in life and art, French feminism, the third geographical division of feminism, typically stresses the repression of women. As a whole, French feminism is closely associated with the theoretical and practical applications of psychoanalysis. At first, the association with psychoanalysis may be a bit puzzling, for Sigmund Freud and his patriarchal theories seemingly dominate psychoanalysis. Believing that penis is power, Freud viewed women as incomplete males. All women, he thought, were envious of a male's power, as symbolized by the penis. Wanting this power, all women possess **penis envy**, desiring to gain the male **phallus** and thereby obtain power. Fortunately for feminist criticism, the French psychoanalytic critic Jacques Lacan rescues psychoanalysis from some of Freud's mysognistic theories (for a detailed explanation of Lacan's theories, see "Jacques Lacan," Chapter 7). Lacan, argues that language ultimately shapes and structures our conscious and unconscious minds and thus shapes our self identity, not the phallus.

Indeed, he maintains that it is language that ultimately denies women the power of language and therefore the power of literature and writing.

Lacan believes that the human psyche consists of three parts, or what he calls orders: the Imaginary, the Symbolic, and the Real. Each of these orders interacts with the others. From birth to six months or so, we primarily function in the Imaginary Order, a preverbal state that contains our wishes, our fantasies, and our physical images. In this state, we are basically sexless, for we are not yet capable of differentiating ourselves from our mothers. Once we successfully pass through the Oedipal crisis, we pass from a biological language to a socialized language and thus into the second of the Lacanian orders: the Symbolic Order. Unfortunately for the female, in this order the male is socialized to the dominant position of discourse, whereas the female is socialized to a subordinated language. On entering this order, the father becomes the dominant image (the Law). At this stage of psychic development, both the male and the female fear castration by the father. For the male, fear of castration means obeying and becoming like the father, while simultaneously repressing the Imaginary Order that is most closely associated with the female body. The Imaginary Order with its pre-Oedipal male desires becomes a direct threat for the male in the third Lacanian order, the Real Order, or the actual world as perceived by the individual. Similarly for the female, entrance into the Symbolic Order means submission to law of the father. Such submission unfortunately means subservience to the male. Being socialized to a subordinated language, the female becomes a second-class citizen. Since language, for Lacan, is a psychological, not a biological construct, women can learn the dominant discourse of both the Symbolic and the Real Orders and become tools of social change.

Other French feminists, such as Julia Kristeva and Hélène Cixous, further develop and apply Lacan's theories to their own form of feminist criticism. Kristeva, for example, posits that the Imaginary Order is characterized by a continuous flow of fluidity or rhythm, which she calls **chora**. On entering the Symbolic Order, both males and females are separated from the chora and repress the feelings of fluidity and rhythm. Similar to a **Freudian slip** in which an unconscious thought breaks through the conscious mind, the chora can, at times, break through into the Real Order and disturb the male-dominant discourse. On the other hand, Hélène Cixous chooses to explore an entirely different mode of discourse that arises from the Symbolic, not the Imaginary Order. Cixous maintains that there exists a particular kind of female writing that she calls *l'écriture féminine*. Characterized by fluidity, this particularly feminine discourse will, when fully explored, transform the social and cultural structures within literature.

In addition to the three geographical strains of feminism, other significant feminist strains,—for example, black and lesbian feminists—transcend geographical boundaries. Some of these strains have an individual stamp. Alice Walker, a spokesperson for Black feminism, refuses to be associated with traditional feminist criticism and with the term *feminist* itself. She prefers to be called a "womanist." On the other hand, the French lesbian feminist Monique Wittig rejects the label of "woman," asserting that this term does not include a lesbian. She prefers to be called a lesbian, believing that this nomenclature will allow women "to name and redefine themselves."

No matter what they emphasize in theory, however, all feminist critics assert that they are on a journey of self-discovery that will lead them to a better understanding of themselves. Once they understand and then define themselves as women, they believe they will be able to change their world.

ASSUMPTIONS

To the onlooker, feminist theory and practice may appear to be a diffuse, loosely connected body of criticism that is more divided than unified, more prone to internal disagreements than to unity among its adherents than perhaps any other approach to literary analysis. Since it claims no ultimate spokesperson but many different voices, there exists not one but a variety of feminist theories. Behind all these seemingly contradictory voices and theories, however, is a set of principles that unites this criticism.

Although feminist critics' ideas concerning the directions of their criticism vary, feminists possess a collective identity: they are women (and some men) who are struggling to discover who they are, how they arrived at their present situation, and where they are going. In their search, they value differing opinions, thereby giving significance to the personal as opposed to a group of people or a codified and authoritative collection of texts. Their search, they assert, is political, for their aim is to change the world in which they live, a world that they maintain needs to and must be changed if all individuals, all cultures, all subcultures, and both sexes are to be valued as creative, rational people who can all contribute to their societies and their world. Such a revisionist, revolutionary, and ideological stance seeks to understand the place of women in society and to analyze all aspects that affect women as writers and their writings in what feminists believe is a male-dominated world. In this masculine world, the feminists declare that it is man who defines what it means to be human, not woman. Because a woman is not a man, she has become the Other, the "not-male." Man is the subject, the one who defines meaning; woman is the object, having her existence defined and determined by the male. The man is therefore the significant (or privileged using Derrida's term) figure in the male/female relationship, while the female is subordinate (or unprivileged).

Female subordination did not make its first appearance in the twentieth century, declare feminists such as Jane Tompkins and others. Long before the existence of our present-day, male-dominated world, societies have been governed, for the most part, by males. These patriarchal societies, say the feminists, have simply passed down their erroneous beliefs from generation to generation, culminating with the predominant Western assumption that women are less than, not equal to, men. Arbitrarily using the male as the standard, these societies apparently agree with Aristotle's assertion that "The female is female by virtue of a certain lack of qualities." Or they quote and support St. Thomas Aquinas's conviction that all women are simply imperfect men. Indeed, some still believe that Freud is correct when he argues that female sexuality is based upon a lack of the male sexual organ, a penis.

For feminist critics, by defining the female in relation to the male and claiming simultaneously the superiority of the male, Western and other cultures have decreed that the female, by nature, is inferior. Once Western culture consciously or unconsciously assimilated this belief into its social structures and allowed it to permeate all levels of society, females became an oppressed people, inferiors who must be suppressed least humankind fail to reach its maximum potential.

Feminist critics want to show humankind the errors in this way of thinking. Women, they pronounce, are people in their own right; they are not incomplete or inferior men. Despite how frequently literature and society have fictionalized and stereotyped women as angels, bar maids, bitches, whores, brainless housewives, or old maids, women must break free from this oppression and define themselves. No longer, assert these critics, can women permit male-dominated society to define and articulate their roles, their values, and their opinions.

To free themselves from definitional oppression, say feminist critics, women must analyze and challenge the established literary canon that has helped shape the images of female inferiority and subordination ingrained in our culture. Women themselves must create an atmosphere that is less oppressive by contesting the long-held patriarchal assumptions about their sex. Since no Aristotle has articulated a philosophy for women, all women must muster a variety of resources to clarify, assert, and implement their beliefs. Through a re-examination of the established literature in all fields, by validating what it means to be a woman, and by involving themselves in literary theory and its multiapproaches, women can legitimatize their responses to texts written by both males and females, their own writings, and their political, economic, and social positions in their culture.

METHODOLOGY

As there is no single feminist theory but many theories, so there exists not one but a variety of feminist approaches to a text. Wanting to challenge and change Western culture's assumption that males are superior to females and are therefore better thinkers, more rational, more serious, and more reflective than women, some feminist critics begin their debunking of male superiority by exposing stereotypes of women in every literary period. Women, they argue, cannot be simply depicted and classified as either angels or demons, saints or whores, or brainless housewives or eccentric spinsters. Such characterizations must be identified and challenged, and this kind of abuse/diminishment of women by male authors must be acknowledged as a way that men have consciously or unconsciously demeaned, devalued, and demoralized women.

Having identified the antifeminist characterization that occurs in many texts, the feminist critic turns to either the American, English, or a non-Western literary canon, seeking to discover works written by women. This is a difficult task, since males have published the majority of texts. American literature, for example, is decidedly male. With the works of Hawthorne, Melville, Poe, and other male notables filling the pages of the canon, little or no room is allowed for the writings of Susan Warner, E. D. N. Southworth, and Mary E. Wilkins Freeman, three of the most widely read authors in nineteenth-century America. Feminists assert that these female authors must be rediscovered by having their works republished and re-evaluated. When completed, this rediscovery will necessarily surface a valuable body of female authors who share common themes, histories, and often writing styles.

Other feminist critics suggest that we reread the canonized works of male authors from a woman's point of view. Such an analysis is possible, they maintain, by developing a uniquely female consciousness based on female experience rather than relying on the traditional male theories of reading, writing, and critiquing. Known as gynocriticism (see Historical Development section of this chapter and the Glossary for additional information), this female model of literary analysis offers four areas of investigation:

1. Images of the female body as presented in a text: Such an anatomical study, for example, would highlight how various parts of the female body such as the uterus and breasts often become significant images in works authored by women.
2. Female language: Such a concern centers on the differences between male and female language. Since we live in patriarchal societies, is it not fair to assume, wonder feminists, that our language is also male-dominated? Do women speak or write differently from men? Although there is little consensus to the answers to these questions, critics interested in this kind of investigation analyze grammatical constructions, recurring themes, and other linguistic elements.
3. The female psyche and its relationship to the writing process: Such an analysis applies the psychological works of Freud and Lacan to a text and shows how the physical and psychological development of the female evidences itself in

the writing process through penis envy, the Oedipus complex, and other psychological stages.

4. Culture: By analyzing cultural forces (such as the importance and value of women's roles in a given society), critics who emphasize this area of study investigate how society shapes a woman's understanding of herself, her society, and her world.

QUESTIONS FOR ANALYSIS

Whatever method of feminist criticism we choose to apply to a text, we can begin textual analysis by asking some general questions, such as these:

- Is the author male or female?
- Is the text narrated by a male or female?
- What types of roles do women have in the text?
- Are the female characters the protagonists or secondary and minor characters?
- Do any stereotypical characterizations of women appear?
- What are the attitudes toward women held by the male characters?
- What is the author's attitude toward women in society?
- How does the author's culture influence her or his attitude?
- Is feminine imagery used? If so, what is the significance of such imagery?
- Do the female characters speak differently than do the male characters? In your investigation, compare the frequency of speech for the male characters to the frequency of speech for the female characters.

By applying any or all of these questions to a text, we can begin our journey in feminist criticism and simultaneously help ourselves to understand better the world in which we live.

SAMPLE ESSAY

In Lori Huth's student essay, "Throwing Off the Yoke: 'Rip Van Winkle' and Women," what principles of feminist literary theory does the author utilize in her interpretation? What feminist issues does she highlight? What feminist issues does she ignore? Is the author's use of quotations from the short story accurate and fair; that is, are any quotations taken out of context to help the author prove her point? Finally, what is the overall tone of the essay? How is this tone established?

FURTHER READING

Beauvoir, Simone de. *The Second Sex*. 1949. Ed. and trans. H. M. Parshley. New York: Modern Library, 1952.

Cohen, Ralph, ed. "Feminist Directions." *New Literary History: A Journal of Theory and Interpretation* 19 (Autumn 1987): 1–208.

Eagleton, Mary, ed. *Feminist Literary Theory: A Reader*. 2nd ed. Oxford: Blackwell, 1996.

Gates, Henry Louis, Jr., ed. *Reading Black, Reading Feminist: A Critical Anthology*. New York: Meridian, 1990.

Gilbert, Sandra M., and Susan Gubar. *The Madwoman in the Attic: The Woman Writer and the Nineteenth-Century Literary Imagination*. New Haven, CT: Yale UP, 1979.

Humm, Maggie, ed. *Feminism: A Reader*. Hemel Hempstead, Eng.: Harvester Wheatsheaf, 1992.

Kolodny, Annette. "Some Notes on Defining a 'Feminist Literary Criticism.'" *Critical Inquiry* 2 (1975): 75–92.

Meese, Elizabeth. *Crossing the Double-Cross: The Practice of Feminist Criticism*. Chapel Hill: U of North Carolina P, 1986.

Mohanty, Chandra Talpade, Ann Russo, and Lourdes Torres, eds. *Third World Women and the Politics of Feminism*. Bloomington: Indiana UP, 1991.

Moi, Toril. *Sexual/Textual Politics: Feminist Literary Theory*. London: Methuen, 1985.

Showalter, Elaine. *A Literature of Their Own: British Women Novelists from Brontë to Lessing*. Princeton: Princeton UP, 1977.

——, ed. *The New Feminist Criticism*. New York: Pantheon Books, 1985.

Todd, Janet. *Feminist Literary History*. New York: Routledge, 1988.

Warhol, Robin, and Diane Price Herndl, eds. *Feminisms: An Anthology of Literary Theory and Criticism*. 2nd ed. New Brunswick: Rutgers UP, 1997.

WEB SITES FOR EXPLORATION

http://eserver.org/feminism/discourse/discourse.html
    Offers a variety of topics from feminisms to literary theory

www.ualberta.ca/~cguertin/gesture.htm
    An excellent essay discussing feminist theory and the visual arts

http://eserver.org/cultronix.smith
    Discusses "Men in Feminism"

www.cddc.vt.edu/feminism/lit.html
    A solid discussion of feminist literary criticism and theory

www.sou.edu/English/IDTC/Issues/Gender/Resources/femtax1.htm
    Provides an excellent review in chart form of the various kinds of feminism

www.drizzle.com/~tmercer/Fem/psyan.html
   Provides a bibliography of feminist theory and psychoanalysis

✐ Student Essay ✐

Throwing Off the Yoke: "Rip Van Winkle" and Women

As the author of the first American short story, and as an intentional cre-
ator of an early American archetype, what kind of images of American men
and women did Washington Irving develop and perpetuate in the American psyche? As the "first Ambassador whom the New World of Letters sent
to the Old," what kind of messages did Irving send across the ocean with
his stories? Long ago escorted into the canon of so-called great American literature, and still found in anthologies such as *The World's 50 Best Short Stories*, Irving's "Rip Van Winkle" blatantly promotes negative stereotypes of
women. Revolving around the antics of its male protagonist, Rip, the story
uses sexist, demeaning diction to describe women and presents static female characters whose identity is defined in relationship to men. Addition-
ally, as a parable for America's revolt and subsequent freedom from England, Dame Van Winkle represents an overbearing mother country from
which Rip, the hero and archetypal American man, is happy to be free.

Irving uses blatantly sexist and insulting language to describe Dame
Van Winkle. She is a "shrew" and a "termagant"; she is a henpecking wife
with "a tart temper [. . .] and a sharp tongue" that only grows sharper with
use. *Shrew* and *termagant* are words meaning "an ill-tempered or nagging
woman," having no equivalent terms for men. By using words that are
inherently sexist, Irving singles women out as objects of negative biases.
By highlighting Dame Van Winkle's shrill tongue, which is "incessantly
going," as her primary characteristic, Irving relegates her and all women to
a negative stereotype. With her "shrill voice" she disrupts the "tranquility"
of the village's old boys' club. With the comment "what courage can withstand the ever-during and all-besetting terror of a woman's tongue," the
narrator extrapolates the Dame's characteristic and applies it to all women.
The story implicitly says not only that Rip is afraid of the Dame's tongue,
but also that everyone is afraid of "a woman's tongue" (all of which can be
assumed to be shrill like the Dame's). Irving also stereotypes Dame Van
Winkle as a witch, saying she gives Rip's dog the "evil eye."

Rip Van Winkle, on the other hand, is a "simple good-natured fellow."
Using positive language and diction to describe Rip, Irving contrasts Rip to
the Dame. Although Rip has an "aversion to [. . .] profitable labour," the
root causes of this supposed "great error" are positive rather than negative.
They are not due to "the want of assiduity or perseverance," but rather to

his fear of his witchy, shrewish wife and to his love of activities such as fishing and philosophizing with his buddies.

Always willing to help a neighbor in need or sit patiently for hours waiting for a fish to bite, Rip is obviously favored and forgiven (by Irving and by the narrator) for his minor shortcomings. Despite the Dame's "dinning" and "terror," Rip remains obedient, developing a meek spirit and becoming universally popular in his village. His "great error" is thus nullified and almost made to seem a virtue or, at least, a logical and reasonable reaction to the terrors of his wife. Whereas children shout for joy to see him and dogs refrain from barking at him, not even the other village women support or defend Dame Van Winkle. All the "good wives" favor Rip and take his side in family squabbles. Gossiping among themselves, they place all the blame on Dame Van Winkle and exemplify yet another negative stereotype of women: women as cat-fighters who compete with each other for men's favor and attention.

As this stereotype suggests, the story relegates women to minor, limited roles compared to men and defines women only according to their relationships to men. Significantly, no woman in the story is named besides Rip's daughter, Judith Gardiner, who cares for him in his old age. The only named woman, then, is the "comely and fresh" one who nurtures a man and keeps a "snug, well-furnished house" for him. Because the story names Dame Van Winkle as such, it may seem that she is named, but the essence of this name is that it identifies her as Rip's wife. Like the HandMaid's "Ofrred" and "Ofwarren" in Margaret Atwood's *The HandMaid's Tale*, she is the dame *of* Van Winkle, but she has no name or identity of her own.

In contrast to women's namelessness, the story names a great number of men, including minor characters who are mentioned only once. These names include Nicholas Vedder, the village patriarch and innkeeper, Derrick van Bummel, a schoolmaster and a "dapper learned man," Peter Vanderdonk, a "well-versed writer," and Brom Dutcher, an old friend of Rip's. The descriptions of these men and others also reveal the variety and dignity of roles that the men in this story hold. They are philosophers and "sage[s]" who conduct "profound" and "solemn" discussions about politics and news. They are congressmen, soldiers, and generals. They are writers, philosophers, teachers, landlords, leaders, and kings. Women's roles, on the other hand, include "gossipers," housekeepers, "good wives" and termagant wives. They care for babies, old men, and their husbands. Like their names, women's roles are limited to their relationship to men. Dame Van Winkle's one good quality, although the narrator is reluctant to admit even this, is that she always keeps her house in order.

If we view Rip as an early example of the archetypal American who has recently freed himself from England, the story serves as a parable with Dame Van Winkle representing the overbearing British government, and

Rip representing the hero who has happily freed himself from that government. Irving found value in the past and the traditions of the Old World and did not share the hopeful vision of America as New Eden. His construction of what it means to be an American, however, as seen in the person of Rip Van Winkle, privileges a man's escape from society and government, both of which Dame Van Winkle embodies. The archetypal American woman, ruling at home through "petticoat government," gossips, cares for babies, fights with other women, and nags her husband incessantly.

Irving's archetypal American would be a bachelor, who, with a dog by his side, escapes the offensive behavior of his wife by sitting around with his buddies by the village tavern, pontificating on his freedom. His overbearing wife drives him to adopt mildly negative qualities as a defense mechanism against domination by an oppressive force. During his twenty years of sleep, Rip threw of the "yoke of matrimony" just as his country "[threw] off the yoke of Old England." Perhaps it is time we throw off the yoke of negative stereotypes and biases against women with which canonical stories such as "Rip Van Winkle" have falsely defined what it means to be a woman.

LORI HUTH

ᴐ 9 ᴕ

Marxism

*For Marxism is as inseparable from modern civilization as Darwinism or Freu-
dianism, as much part of our "historical unconscious" as Newton was for the
Enlightenment.*

Terry Eagleton, *Marxist Literary Theory*,
1996

INTRODUCTION

With the collapse of communism and the Soviet Union in the late 1980s,
many thought they heard the dead knell pronouncing loudly the
demise of **Marxism**, with its accompanying political and ideological structures. Down came the Berlin Wall, down came the Iron Curtain, and supposedly down came Marxism as an acceptable alternative form of government to
capitalism and as an acceptable worldview. Many capitalists rejoiced. Marxism had fallen. Seemingly, individual Marxists only had the glorious memories of the earlier decades of the twentieth century in which to rejoice—a time
when Stalin ruled Russia, when Marxist theory dominated both English and
American writings, and when college campuses both in the East and the West
were led and taught by intellectuals who pledged alliance to Marxist ideology. Many now believed that such ideology was finally dead!

But is it? Performing only a limited Internet search under the keyword
"Marxism" results in a listing of over 19,500 sites, with titles such as "Marxism and Utopian Vision: El Salvador," "Marxism and the National Question," "Marxism and Problems of Linguistics," "Rethinking Marxism,"
"Marxism, Psychoanalysis, and Labor Competition," "Baha's Future and
Marxism," to name a few. In addition, announcements for newly published
texts advocating sympathy for and support of Marxist ideology in all academic disciplines appear regularly. College courses in Marxist political theory, sociological concerns, literature, and literary theory abound. Perhaps
the death knell for Marxism was struck prematurely.

What is it that apparently fascinates intellectuals, politicians, and others about Marxism? Why did it not die out with the death of communism in the East? Perhaps the answer lies in some of the core principles of Marxist thought: that reality itself can be defined and understood, that society shapes our consciousness, that social and economic conditions directly influence how and what we believe and value, and that Marxism details a plan for changing the world from a place of bigotry, hatred, and conflict due to class struggle to a classless society in which wealth, opportunity, and education are actually accessible for all people. By claiming it furnishes us with a coherent, clear, and comprehensive worldview and plan of action, Marxism asserts that it provides answers to many of the complex questions about how life is and ought to be experienced while challenging other ideologies to provide their answers for these same concerns.

The self-same problems that gave rise to Marxism still exist today. Despite its glory decades of the 1900s and its present-day embattled position, Marxism declares that it provides a comprehensive, positive view of human life and history and attempts to show how humanity can save itself from a meaningless life of alienation and despair. A worldview that seemingly affords a bright promise for the future and a transformation of present-day society will not die quietly, and in the words of Mark Twain, "Announcements of Marxism's death have certainly been exaggerated."

HISTORICAL DEVELOPMENT

Karl Marx and Friedrich Engels

Unlike other schools of literary criticism, Marxism did not begin as an alternative, theoretical approach to literary analysis. Before many twentieth-century writers and critics embraced the principles of Marxism and employed these ideas in their criticism, Marxism had already flourished in the nineteenth century as a pragmatic view of history that offered the working classes of society an opportunity to change their world and their lives. By providing both a philosophical system and a plan of action to initiate change in society, Marxism offered to humanity a social, political, economic, and cultural understanding of the nature of reality, society, and the individual, not a literary theory. These and other similar ideas have become the basis of what we know today as socialism and communism.

Without question, Marxist literary theory has its roots in the nineteenth-century writings of the German social critic and philosopher Karl Heinrich Marx (1818–1883). Marx himself, however, said little about the relationship of his ideas to literature. Marxist literary theory and criticism is a twentieth-century phenomenon. Utilizing Marx's philosophical assumptions, twenti-eth-century critics developed a variety of Marxist approaches to textual analysis that focus on the study of the relationship between a text and the society that reads it. At the core of all these diverse approaches are Marx and his philosophical assumptions about the nature of reality itself.

Marx articulates his views on the nature of reality in two works: *The German Ideology* (1845) and *The Communist Manifesto* (1848), a work Marx coauthored with Friedrich Engels (1820–1895). In *The German Ideology*, Marx develops what has become known as **dialectical materialism**, the core be-liefs of Marxism. Marx declares that "consciousness does not determine life: life determines consciousness." In other words, for Marx, a person's con-sciousness is not shaped by any spiritual entity or means; through daily liv-ing and interacting with each other, humans define themselves. To Marx, then, our ideas and concepts about ourselves are fashioned in everyday in-teractions, in the language of real life, and are not derived from some Pla-tonic essence or any other spiritual reality. In addition, Marx argues that the economic means of production within a society—what he calls the **base**—both engenders and controls all human institutions and ideologies—what Marx calls the **superstructure**—including all social and legal institutions, all political and educational systems, all religions, and all art. These ideologies and institutions develop as a direct result of the economic means of produc-tion, not the other way around.

Marx also claims that all societies are progressing toward communism. Believing progress is reactionary or revolutionary, Marx asserts that as a so-ciety progresses in its economic mode of production from a feudal system to a more market-based economy, the actual process for producing, distribut-ing, and consuming goods becomes more complex. Accordingly, people's functions within the economic system become differentiated. It is this differ-entiation that inevitably divides people into different social classes. Eventu-ally, the desires and expectations of the various social classes will clash. Marx believes that such a clash or class conflict leads to a radical change in the economic base of society from a feudal system of power, based on inher-ited wealth and status, to a capitalist system, based on the ownership of pri-vate property. This shift entails innumerable changes in the laws, customs, and religion of society. Overall, Marx cites four historical periods that were developed by these forces: feudalism, capitalism, socialism, and commu-nism. For Marx, socialism is not a true historical period but a transitional stage between capitalism and society's ultimate goal, communism. When society reaches this goal—what Marx called "the worker's paradise"—then benevolent self-rule will finally reign.

In their coauthored text *The Communist Manifesto*, Marx and Engels fur-ther develop Marx's ideas. In this work, they maintain that the capitalists, or the **bourgeoisie**, have successfully enslaved the working class, or the

proletariat, through economic policies and production of goods. The proletariat must now revolt and strip the bourgeoisie of their economic and political power and place the ownership of all property in the hands of the government who will then fairly distribute the people's wealth.

In a later work, *Das Kapital* (1867), authored by Marx himself, Marx enunciates the view of history that has become the basis for twentieth-century Marxism, socialism, and communism. Marx argues that history and an understanding of people and their actions and beliefs are determined by economic conditions. He maintains that an intricate web of social relationships emerges when any group of people engage in the production of goods. A few, for example, will be the employers, but many more will be the employees. It is the employers (the bourgeoisie) who have the economic power and who will readily gain social and political control of their society. Eventually, this upper class will articulate their beliefs, their values, and even their art. Consciously and unconsciously, they will then force these ideas, or what Marx calls their **ideology**, on the working class, otherwise known as the proletariat or the "wage slaves." In effect, the bourgeoisie will develop and control the superstructure. In such a system, the rich become richer, while the poor become poorer and more and more oppressed; the bourgeoisie's ideology effectively works to perpetuate the system upon which it was founded. Referred to as **false consciousness**, this ideology also describes the way in which the dominant social class shapes and controls an individual's self-definition or class consciousness.

In a capitalist society, Marx believes that such an ideology leads to fragmentation and alienation of individuals, particularly those of the proletariat. As a direct result of division of labor within the capitalist society, workers no longer have contact with the entire process of producing, distributing, and consuming material goods. Individuals are cut off from the full value of their work as well as from each other, each performing discrete functional roles assigned to them by the bourgeoisie. To rid society of this situation, Marx believes that the government must own all industries and control the economic production of a country to protect the people from the oppression of the bourgeoisie.

Taken together, *The Communist Manifesto* and *Das Kapital* provide us with a theory of history, economics, politics, sociology, and even metaphysics. In these writings, little or no mention of literature, literary theory, or practical analysis of how to arrive at an interpretation of a text emerges. The link between the Marxism of its founders and literary theory resides in Marx's concept of history and the sociological leanings of Marxism itself. Marx believed that the history of a people is directly based on the production of goods and the social relationships that develop from this situation. He also assumed that the totality of a people's experience—social interactions, employment, and other day-to-day activities—is directly responsible for the shaping and the development of an individual's personal consciousness. The idea that our place in society and our social interaction determine our consciousness or who we really are is a theme Marx highlighted throughout his writings.

Since the literary approach to a text that was common during Marx's time was based in similar sociological assumptions as did his own theories of society and the individual, Marx had no difficulty accepting his literary peers' methodology (hermeneutics) for interpreting a text. Known today as the "traditional historical approach," this critical position declares that a critic must place a work in its historical setting, paying attention to the author's life, the time period in which the work was written, and the cultural milieu of both the text and the author, all of these concerns being related to sociological issues. To these criteria, however, Marx and Engels add another: the economic means of production. This fourth factor addresses, for example, who decides what texts should be published, when a text should be published, or how a text is to be distributed. These questions require an understanding of the social forces at work at the time a text is written or at the time it is being interpreted. In addition, this added criterion forces the critic to investigate the scheme of social relationships not only within the text itself but also outside the text and within the world of the author. In adding this sociological dimension, Marxism expands the traditional, historical approach to literary analysis by dealing with sociological issues that concern both the characters in a work of fiction as well as the authors and the readers. This added dimension, Marx believed, links literature and society and shows how literature reflects society and how literary texts can reveal truths about our social interactions.

Russia and Marxism

Thanks to G. K. Plehanov's Russian translation of *The Communist Manifesto*, Marx's theories soon gained wide exposure and prominence. Interestingly, Russia's fascination with Marxism's political ideas carried over into the aesthetic realm as well, for the Russian leadership at the beginning of the twentieth century insisted that writers should also play a political role. Russia thus became the first country to promote Marxist principles as both aesthetic and literary guidelines.

Even before the Russian Revolution of 1919, Communist Party leaders insisted that literature promote the standards set forth by the Party. For example, in 1905 Vladimir Ilyitch Lenin wrote *The Organization and Party Literature*, in which he directly links good literature with the working-class movement. Lenin's text defends all kinds of literature, believing that something can be gleaned from any kind of writing. After the Bolshevik Revolution of 1917, however, Lenin amended his literary theory and argued that the Party could not accept or support literary works that blatantly defied established Party policies.

Soon after the Russian Revolution, the revolutionary Leon Trotsky authored *Literature and Revolution* (1925) and in the process becomes the founder of Marxist literary criticism. Advocating a tolerance for open, critical dialogue, Trotsky contends that the content of a literary work need not be revolutionary. To force all poets to write about nothing but factory chimneys or revolts against capitalism, he believed, was simply absurd.

Unfortunately, the Soviet Union's next political leader, Joseph Stalin (1879–1953), was not as liberal as Lenin or Trotsky in his aesthetic judgments. In 1927, Stalin established the RAPP, the Russian Association of Proletarian Writers, a group formed to guard against liberal cultural tendencies. However, this group proved to be too tolerant for Stalin. In 1932, he abolished all artists' unions and associations, and established the Soviet Writers' Union, a group which he himself headed. The Union decreed that all literature must glorify Party actions and decisions. In addition, literature should exhibit revolutionary progress and teach about the spirit of socialism, revolving around Soviet heroes. Such aesthetic commandments quickly stifled many Russian writers, for the Union allowed only "politically correct" works to be published. Not surprisingly, Stalin soon banished Trotsky, with the result that increasingly most Russian critics and writers succumbed to Stalin's guidelines rather than follow Trotsky's public (and dangerous) example. It was left to critics outside Russia to explore and develop other Marxist approaches to literary criticism.

Georg Lukács

The first major branch of Marxist theory to appear outside Russia was developed by the Hungarian Georg Lukács. Lukács and his followers adapted and applied the techniques of **formalism**, believing that a detailed analysis of symbols, images, and other literary devices would ultimately reveal class conflict and effectively expose the direct relationship between the economic base and the superstructure reflected in art. Known as **reflection theory**, this approach to literary analysis declares that texts directly reflect a society's consciousness. Reflection theorists such as Lukács are didactic, emphasizing the negative effects of capitalism such as alienation. Known today as **vulgar Marxism**, reflectionists persist in supporting a form of Marxism in which there is a one-way relationship between the base and the superstructure; for instance, literature, as part of the superstructure, directly reflects the economic base. By giving a text a close reading, these critics believe they can reveal the reality of the text and the author's **Weltanschauung**, or worldview. It is the critic's job to show how the characters within the text are typical of their historical, socioeconomic setting and the author's worldview.

The Frankfurt School

Closely allied to Lukács and reflection theory, another group of theorists emerged in Germany known as the **Frankfurt school**, a neo-Marxist group devoted to developing Western Marxist principles. Included in this group are Theodor Adorno, Walter Benjamin, and Max Horkheimer. Agreeing with Lukács that literature reveals a culture's alienation and fragmentation, the Frankfurt school critics such as Benjamin assert that a text is like any other commodity produced by capitalism. The market—that is, how well a commodity sells—ultimately determines what texts and when texts are published. Hence there exists no purely aesthetic activity that seeks to relate to human consciousness. That a text reveals a culture's fragmentation and not its wholeness is for Benjamin a useful bit of knowledge for promoting socialist ideals. Having stripped literature of what he calls its "quasi-religious aura," the enlightened reader will be able to resist the bourgeois ideology embedded within the text and will not mindlessly acquiesce to the inane images, thinking, and desires depicted in some works.

Bertolt Brecht, a close friend of Benjamin, applies this new way of thinking directly to the theater. According to Brecht, dramatists believe they use the theater to express their ideas, but, in fact, the theater controls them. Instead of blindly accepting bourgeois conventionality as established through dramatic conventions, dramatists should revolt and seize the modes of production. Applying this principle to what became known as the **epic theater**, Brecht advocated an abandonment of the Aristotelian premise of unity of time, place, and action, including the assumption that the audience should be made to believe that what they are seeing is real. Accordingly, Brecht sought to create alienation effects by, for instance, frequently interrupting the drama with a direct appeal to the audience via a song or speech to keep the audience constantly aware of the moral and social issues they were being exposed to in a drama. In the hands of Brecht, the epic theatre became a tool for exposing the bourgeois ideology that had pervasively permeated the arts.

Antonio Gramsci

Unlike Georg Lukács and his followers, who assert that the superstructure reflects the economic base, the Italian Antonio Gramsci takes Marxism in another direction. Gramsci declares that there exists a complex relationship between the base and the superstructure. How, Gramsci asks, is the bourgeoisie able to control and to maintain its dominance over the proletariat? According to Gramsci, the bourgeoisie establish and maintain what he calls **hegemony**. Because the bourgeoisie actually control the economic base and thereby establish all the elements that comprise the superstructure—music, literature, art, and so forth—they gain the spontaneous accolades of the working class. It is the working people themselves who give their consent to the bourgeoisie and who adopt bourgeois values and beliefs. As sustainers of the economic base, the dominant class thus enjoy the prestige of the masses and control the ideology—a term often used synonymously with hegemony—that shapes individual consciousness.

If literature, however, is only a part of the superstructure, then all literature actually concerns itself with the bourgeoisie. In effect, literature becomes a tool of the privileged class, and it cannot be used to further Marxist revolutions. Why write and study literature if it is only a reflection of the superstructure which is, in itself, the reflection of bourgeois ideas established in the economic base? Although Gramsci concerned himself with this question, it is one of his followers who provides the answer.

Louis Althusser

In seeking an answer to the question of why write and study literature, Louis Althusser rejects a basic assumption of reflection theory: namely, that the superstructure directly reflects the base. His answer, known today as **production theory**, asserts that literature should not be strictly relegated to the superstructure. According to Althusser, the superstructure can and does influence the base. Art, then, can and does inspire revolution.

Althusser believes that the dominant hegemony, or prevailing ideology, forms the attitudes of people in society through a process he calls **interpellation** or "hailing the subject." The people's worldview is craftily shaped by a complex network of messages sent to them through the elements contained in the superstructure, including the arts. Although the dominant class can use military and police force to repress the working class in order to maintain its dominant position and to achieve interpellation, it chooses to utilize the "Ideological State Apparatus," or the hegemony. In effect, it is the dominant class's hegemony that prevents the insurrection of the working class.

The dominant class's hegemony, however, is never complete. Such incompleteness suggests that alternative hegemonies exist and are competing with the dominant hegemony for supremacy. If the dominant class's interpellation or hailing the subject fails, then another hegemony can come to dominate, and revolution can occur. Such a revolution can begin if working-class people write their own literature (dramas, poems, and novels), their own music, and their own paintings, thereby establishing an alternate hegemony to challenge the bourgeoisie's hegemony. It is not through guns or battles or the shedding of blood, but through artistic expression of their own cultural activities that the working classes can successfully revolt and usurp the hegemony of the dominant class.

Since Althusser, a number of post-Althusserian critics have continued to develop such Marxist thinking, including Pierre Macherey and Raymond Williams.

Marxist Theorists Today

Since the 1960s, Fredric Jameson in the United States and Terry Eagleton in Great Britain have dominated Marxist criticism. As a critic, Jameson merges psychoanalytic and Marxist theories. Borrowing Freud's idea of a repressed unconscious, Jameson discovers a **political unconscious**, the repressed conditions of exploitation and oppression. The function of literary analysis, Jameson believes, is to uncover the political unconscious present in a text.

Prior to his discovery of the political unconscious, Jameson developed **dialectical criticism**. In *Marxism and Form* (1971), a text which has become almost sacred for American Marxists, Jameson asserts that all critics must be aware of their own ideology when analyzing a text and must therefore possess **dialectial self-awareness**.

Perhaps the most influential Marxist critic today is the British scholar Terry Eagleton, author of numerous works, including *Literary Theory* (1983), a pivotal introductory text surveying literary criticism. Believing that literature is neither a product of pure inspiration nor the product of the author's feelings, Eagleton holds that, in actuality, literature is a product of an ideology which is itself a product of history. This ideology is a result of the actual social interactions that occur between people in definite times and locations. One of the critic's tasks, then, is to reconstruct an author's ideology or the author's ideological milieu.

Throughout his long and prestigious career, Eagleton, like most critics, develops, changes, and redirects his own literary theory. At times, he employs a variety of approaches to a text: the scientific approach of Louis Althusser, the psychoanalytic ideas of Lacan, and the poststructuralism of Jacques Derrida. All his diverse approaches, however, attack the bourgeois dominance of the hegemony and advocate revolution against such values.

From the mid-1970s to the present, Marxism has continued to challenge what it deems the bourgeois concerns of its literary counterparts through the voices of a variety of Marxist critics. Critical movements and theories like structuralism, deconstruction, feminism, and New Historicism have all examined Marxism's basic tenets and share some of its social, political, and revolutionary nature. Like Marxism, these contemporary schools of criticism desire to change the way we think about literature and life. Likewise, from these various schools of thought, present-day Marxism has borrowed many ideas and has evolved into an array of differing theories, so much so that there no longer exists a single school of Marxist thought but a variety of Marxist critical positions. Common to all these theoretical positions, however, is the assumption that Marx, no matter how he is interpreted by any of his followers, believed that change for the good in a society is possible if we will but stop and examine our culture through the eyes of its methods of economic production.

ASSUMPTIONS

Marxism is not primarily a literary theory that can be used to interpret a text. Unlike other schools of criticism, it is first a set of social, economic, and political ideas that its followers believe will enable them to interpret and, more importantly, change their world. Although a variety of Marxist positions exist, most Marxists adhere to a similar understanding of the world.

Ultimate reality, declares Marxism, is material, not spiritual. What we know beyond any doubt is that human beings exist and live in social groups. All of our actions and responses to such activities as eating, working, and even playing are related in some way to our culture and society. In order to understand ourselves and our world, we must first acknowledge the interrelatedness of all our actions within society. If, for example, we want to know who we are and how we should live, we must stop trying to find answers by looking solely to religion or philosophy and begin by examining all aspects of our daily activities within our own culture. Upon examining our daily routines, including our beliefs and values, we will discover that it is our cultural and our social circumstances that determine who we are. What we believe, what we value, and, in many ways, what we think are a direct result of our culture and our society, not our religion or our supposed philosophy of life.

When we examine our society, declares Marxism, we will discover that its structure is built upon a series of ongoing conflicts between social classes. The chief reason for these conflicts is the varying ways the members of society work and utilize their economic resources. According to Marx, the methods of economic production and the social relationships they engender form the economic structure of society called the base. In America, for example, the capitalists exploit the working classes, determining for them their salaries and their working conditions, among a host of other elements of their lives. From this base, maintains Marx, arises the superstructure, or a multitude of social and legal institutions, political and educational systems, religious beliefs, values, and a body of art and literature that one dominant, social class (the capitalists in America, for instance) uses to keep in check members of the working classes.

The exact relationship between the base and the superstructure, however, is not easily defined. Some early Marxists posited what is known today as vulgar Marxism or reflection theory, believing that the base directly affects the superstructure and, in essence, determines its existence. Other Marxists assert that even Marx and Engels changed their opinions about this relationship and attest that the elements contained in the superstructure have a reality of their own, with each element affecting the other elements of the superstructure while simultaneously affecting the base. Whatever the position held by Marxists today, most would agree that the relationship between the base and the superstructure is a complex one and will continue to remain a contentious point in Marxist theories.

The relationship between the base and the superstructure becomes clearer when we consider capitalistic America. Marxism declares that in America the capitalists hold the economic purse strings, and because they do, they control the base, making the capitalists the center of power. It is the capitalists who decree what beliefs are acceptable, what values are to be held, and what laws are to be formed. In other words, the capitalists, not the working classes, control society's ideology or its hegemony: its social consciousness. It is they who, in effect, determine the acceptable standards of behavior and thoughts in their society.

Consciously and unconsciously, this social elite inevitably forces its ideas on the working classes. Almost without their knowing it, the working classes have become trapped in an economic system that decrees how much money they will earn, when they will take vacations, how they will spend their leisure time, what entertainment they will enjoy, and even what they believe concerning the nature of humanity itself.

It is to the working classes that Marxism addresses its rallying cry. All working peoples can free themselves from the chains of social, economic, and political oppression if they will recognize that they are presently not free agents, but individuals controlled by an intricate social web dominated by a self-declared, self-empowered, and self-perpetuating social elite.

Since this social elite or the bourgeoisie shape a society's superstructure and its ideology, this social class necessarily controls its literature, for literature is one of many elements contained within the superstructure. From this perspective, literature, like any other element of the superstructure, becomes involved in a social process whereby the bourgeoisie indoctrinate the working classes with their elite and acceptable ideology as reflected in bourgeois literature. What becomes natural and acceptable behavior in that society is now pictured in its literature and, in essence, controlled by the bourgeoisie, who also control the economic means of production.

Because literature is part of a society's superstructure, its relationship to other elements of the superstructure and to the base becomes the central focus in varying Marxist literary theories. If, for example, a Marxist holds to the reflection theory on the relationship of the base to the superstructure, then such a theorist posits that the economic base directly determines the literature. For this critic, literature will mirror the economic base. On the other hand, if a Marxist theorist believes that elements of the superstructure have realities of their own and affect each other and also affect the base, a text may be responsible for altering not only other elements within the superstructure but also the base. Further, even the critics who give allegiance to this position hold differing opinions concerning the definition of a text and its relationship to other elements of the superstructure and to the base.

Although all Marxists assert that a text must be interpreted in light of its culture, how they define the text and its social relationships provides us with an array of Marxist literary theories and differing methods of analyses. There exists, then, not one Marxist theory of literature, but many, each hoping to change society.

METHODOLOGY

Since there exists no absolute voice of authority who expounds pure Marxist principles, there can exist no single Marxist approach to literary analysis. Like other methods of interpretation, Marxism includes an array of differing voices with each articulating particular interests. These differing voices all agree that Marxism, with its concerns for the working classes and the individual, provides the most workable and satisfying framework for understanding our world. Recognizing the interrelatedness of all human activities, Marxism, they believe, enables us to understand ourselves and how we as individuals relate to and are affected by our society. And these voices assert that we must help direct and change our society, our culture, our nation, and our world by leading humanity toward an understanding and an acceptance of socialism.

As an approach to literary analysis, Marxism's methodology is a dynamic process which maintains that a proper critique (*proper* defined as that which agrees with socialistic or Marxist beliefs) of a text cannot exist in isolation from the cultural situation in which the text evolved. Necessarily, Marxists argue, the study of literature and the study of society are intricately bound. Such a relationship demands that a Marxist approach to a text must deal with more than the conventional literary themes, matters of style, plot, or characterization, and the usual emphasis on figures of speech and other literary devices utilized by other approaches to literary analysis. Marxist theory must move beyond these literary elements and must uncover the author's world and his or her worldview. By placing the text in its historical context and by analyzing the author's view of life, Marxist critics arrive at one of their chief concerns: ideology. It is the ideology expressed by the author, as evidenced through his or her fictional world, and how this ideology interacts with the reader's personal ideology that interests these critics.

This kind of an ideological and obviously political investigation will necessarily expose class conflict, showing the dominant class and its accompanying ideology being imposed either consciously or unconsciously upon the proletariat. The task of the critic, then, is to uncover and denounce this antiproletariat ideology and show how such a destructive ideology entraps the working classes and oppresses them in every area of their lives. Most importantly, through such an analysis the Marxist critic wishes to reveal to the working classes how they may end their oppression by the bourgeoisie through a commitment to socialism.

A Marxist critic may begin such an analysis by elucidating how an author's text reflects the writer's ideology through an examination of the fictional world's characters, settings, society, or any other aspect of the text. From this starting point, the critic may then launch an investigation into that particular author's social class and its effects on the author's society. Or the critic may choose to begin textual analysis by examining the history and the culture of the times reflected in the text and then investigate how the author either correctly or incorrectly pictures this historical period.

Whatever method the critic chooses to use, a Marxist approach seeks to expose the dominant class, to demonstrate how the bourgeoisie's ideology controls and oppresses the working class, and to highlight those elements of society most affected by such oppression. Such an analysis, hopes the Marxist critic, will lead to action, to social change, to revolution, and to the rise of socialism.

QUESTIONS FOR ANALYSIS

To gain a working understanding of a Marxist approach to literary analysis, Ira Shor, a Marxist critic and writer, suggests that we ask certain questions of any text, questions that will enable us to see the Marxist concerns that are evidenced or ignored in the text by its author. The following questions, Shor believes, will provide the framework for a close analysis of a text and demonstrate Marxism's concern for the direct relationship between literature and society. (These and other questions can be found in Shor's article "Questions Marxists Ask About Literature," found in the journal *College English*, volume 34, number 2, 1974.)

- Is there an outright rejection of socialism in the work?
- Does the text raise fundamental criticism about the emptiness of life in bourgeois society?

- In portraying society, what approximation of totality does the author achieve? What is emphasized, what is ignored?
- How well is the fate of the individual linked organically to the nature of societal forces? What are the work's conflicting forces?
- At what points are actions or solutions to problems forced or unreal?
- Are characters from all social levels equally well sketched?
- What are the values of each class in the work?
- What is valued most? Sacrifice? Assent? Resistance?
- How clearly do narratives of disillusionment and defeat indicate that bourgeois values—competition, acquisitiveness, chauvinism—are incompatible with human happiness?
- Does the protagonist defend or defect from the dominant values of society? Are those values in ascendancy or decay?

SAMPLE ESSAY

In the student essay that follows at the end of the chapter, note how the critic applies Marxist principles in her interpretation of Tony Harrison's poem "Marked with D." What is her main interest—class struggle? Economics? Social behavior? Or is it something else? Does she use any of Shor's questions in her analysis? If so, which ones? Does she successfully show the dynamic relationship between society and literature? Where in her analysis may she strengthen her interpretation?

FURTHER READING

Adorno, Theodor W., Walter Benjamin, Ernst Block, Bertolt Brecht, and Georg Lukács. *Aesthetics and Politics*. London: New Left Books, 1977.

Ahern, Edward J. *Marx and Modern Fiction*. New Haven: Yale University Press, 1989.

Eagleton, Terry. *Criticism and Ideology*. New York: Schocken, 1978.

———. *Literary Theory: An Introduction*. Minneapolis: University of Minnesota Press, 1983; 1996.

———. *Marxism and Literary Theory*. Berkeley: University of California Press, 1976.

Eagleton, Terry, and Drew Milne, eds. *Marxist Literary Theory*. Oxford, Eng.: Blackwell, 1996.

Gottlieb, Roger S., ed. *An Anthology of Western Marxism: From Lukács and Gramsci to Socialist-Feminism*. New York: Oxford University Press, 1989.

Hicks, Granville. *The Great Tradition*. Rev. ed. New York: Macmillan, 1935.

Jay, Martin. *Marxism and Totality*. Berkeley: University of California Press, 1990.

Jameson, Fredric. *Marxism and Form: Twentieth-Century Dialectical Theories of Litera ture*. Princeton: University Press, 1971.

———. *Postmodernism, or, the Cultural Logic of Late Capitalism*. Durham, NC: Duke University Press, 1991.

McMurtry, John. *The Structure of Marx's World-View*. Princeton: Princeton University Press, 1978.

Mulhern, Francis, ed. *Contemporary Marxist Literary Criticism*. New York: Longman, 1992.

Nelson, Cary, and Lawrence Grossberg, eds. *Marxism and the Interpretation of Culture*. London: Macmillan, 1988.

Williams, Raymond. *Marxism and Literature*. Oxford: Oxford University Press, 1977.

WEB SITES FOR EXPLORATION

www.shebeen.com/marx.htm
  Provides links to a variety of Marxist sites on the Web
http://csf.colorado.edu/psn/marx/index.html
  Provides an excellent overview of the theories of Marx and Engles, plus a picture gallery of the two men
www.westga.edu/~dnewton/engl2300/marxism.html
  Provides a good overview of Marxist criticism
www.mcauley.acu.edu.au/staff/simonr/marxist_lit.htm
  Provides an excellent overview of Marxist theory and criticism
www.uow.edu.au/arts/joscci/boer.html
  A solid discussion of "Marxism and the Bible"
www.wbenjamin.org/links1.html
  Presents a discussion of the Marxist theories of Walter Benjamin
www.othervoices.org/parkerj/benj.html
  A good review of historical materialism

৵ Student Essay ৵

Baking Bread for the Bourgeoisie

In Tony Harrison's poem "Marked with D." (1981), the persona records not only the thoughts and passions once voiced by a now-deceased baker but also the persona's own evaluation of the baker's life. The speaker indicates that the baker had led a life of servanthood, always fulfilling the demands of others, while simultaneously contemplating his supposed serene and glorious reward awaiting him in Heaven, a place the persona is sure does not exist. After meditating on the baker's life, the persona concludes that revolution, not subservience to the will of others, is the goal toward which one should strive. A close reading of the poem quickly uncovers the speaker's references to such sentiments and to the oppression inherent in society that must necessarily lead to revolt.

The capitalist society portrayed in this poem is divided into "the haves," the bourgeoisie, and "the have-nots," the proletariat. "The haves" press "the have-nots" into serving them to increase the amount of capital and goods they possess. Through the enforcement of their values and interests, or their hegemony, the bourgeoisie deliberately oppress the proletariat.

Expressions of such oppression are present in the children's rhyming game "Pat-a-cake," alluded to by the title:

> Pat-a-cake, pat-a-cake, baker's man.
> So I do, master, as fast as I can.
> Pat it and prick it, and *mark it with a B,*
> And then it will serve for baby and me.

The words to this popular game reflect the ideology of the bourgeoisie, for the bourgeoisie believe that anyone in the proletariat should necessarily serve "as fast as [they] can." In the case of the baker, the bourgeoisie believe that he should bake goods for them to eliminate the inconvenience of baking goods for themselves. Unfortunately, the baker, a typical member of the "working class," faithfully serves the bourgeoisie all his life.

Daily the baker took "chilled dough" from his refrigerator and put it in the oven, dutifully performing his function in society. Like Marx himself, the baker believed that one's function in society comprises one's class—either proletariat or bourgeoisie—and subsequently one's identity. For him, as for Marx, "Life is not determined by consciousness, but consciousness by life." Life exists within the functions of eating, sleeping, obtaining shelter, and clothing one's self. And the "first historical act" is the manufacture of these goods needed for survival. People like the baker must therefore produce these goods through the modes of production, or the base. As a member of the proletariat, the baker dutifully carried out his appointed mode of production, making baked goods. He thus existed within the base of baking dough, and his essence became equivalent to his existence. Just as the baker daily placed unbaked loaves into a stoked oven, so his body is now placed within "an oven/ Not unlike those he fueled all his life." In actuality, he is now not a dead man being cremated, but dough being baked.

The metaphor comparing the baker's chilled, stiff flesh to dough further enhances the relevance of the title, "Marked with D." When the baker baked his dough, he kneaded it, formed it, and marked it with a "B," for baby or perhaps bourgeoisie. In the ideological bakery, the bourgeoisie treat the baker like a baked good. They mix all the ingredients together in their recipe to make ideal proletariat "dough," the baker himself. Then they "prick" him

and "pat" him down, oppressing his true freedom by conforming and forming him to their mold. In the end, they mark him with a "D" for dead and
place him in the crematory oven to bake his "doughy" flesh.

In contemplating the "baking process" of cremation, the persona imag-
ines that the "diseased" eyes of the baker burn. Their burning, however, is
not only the result of the literal fire within the crematory oven but also a result of a metaphorical fire—the desire to see the paradise of Heaven
preached to him so often. His mouth opens, and "light [streams]" forth from
his soul, yearning for a reunion with his wife "Florrie" on Heaven's celestial
shore. Although in a formal bourgeoisie setting, "Florence and Flo" would
have been the proper names used for addressing one's wife, the baker man
called her Florrie. Being completely inappropriate for the seriousness of
sophisticated bourgeoisie affairs, this pet name used by a member of the
"lower class" further emphasizes the baker's place in society as an enslaved
member of the proletariat.

As his mouth opens to alert Florrie to his coming, "his cold tongue
[bursts] into flame." Unfortunately, the tongue is enflamed "only literally"
in the cremation oven. As a member of the proletariat, he never spoke out
about his oppression, nor did he ever vocalize a plan for revolution. One
sadly wonders whether the baker man even realized that he was oppressed!

Once again bourgeoisie ideology has successfully prevented a member
of the proletariat from realizing his oppression. Craftily, the ideology of the
bourgeoisie promotes the idea of a literal Heaven to keep the proletariat like
the baker in their service. By convincing them that Heaven exists, the proletariat will keep "pressing forward" in their earthly toil. Even if they believe
they are oppressed, they will still labor on, trusting that someday they will
reach the "pearly gates," behind which no one weeps, suffers, toils, or cries,
and no one is oppressed. The idea of "Heaven" also implies a bourgeois ideology encompassing Christianity. Many philosophers view Christianity as a
"slave religion." "Good" Christians submit themselves to God and to
earthly "authority," and they even turn the other cheek if anyone abuses
them in any way. What clever bourgeoisie would fail to utilize the full
power of such an effective ideological state apparatus?

The persona, however, identifies the interpellation occurring in society,
and he is "sorry for [the baker's] sake there's no Heaven to reach." He thus
adopts a Marxist materialist philosophy. In this present moment, material
possessions are all that exist. The persona's statement, "I get it all from
earth, my daily bread," implies that a providential being and a transcendental signified do not reside in another "world." Meaning resides in the daily
bread produced in the economic base of society itself.

The baker "hungered," however, for the ideological "bread of Heaven"
that would "release [him] from mortal speech." The bourgeoisie utter their
dictates and commands, and the proletariat obeys, whether in the production of goods or the adoption of values and beliefs in their personal lives.

The word "mortal" (line 11) not only signifies that the speech is human but also suggests its "deadliness" and "fatality." This fatal "speech" killed the baker's vision, his "sight" for "reality." Because of the bourgeois hegemony, he developed a metaphorical blindness as signified by his physical cataracts. Instead of seeing the physical state of society with his own eyes, he depended on the "speech" of the bourgeoisie. Their "speech" dictated "reality" as viewed through their lenses, resulting eventually in his inability to see anything not "described" by the bourgeoisie. In addition, the "deadly" speech of the bourgeoisie also murdered his revolutionary spirit. The "tongue" pressing on him, "weighed like lead" upon his weary frame, "kept him down," working him to the grave.

The baker will not therefore "rise" from his grave to Heaven. Nor will he "rise" like the dough he baked, for he resembles a lump of dough without yeast. What he lacks is the "yeast" of revolution, an ingredient deliberately omitted from the recipe by the bourgeoisie ideology. He will never "rise"—dead or alive.

In the poem, Harrison uses the word "England" (line 14) to symbolize the bourgeois culture whose ideology controlled the baker's life and being. "England" labeled the baker a "dull oaf," meaning an "unintelligent, uninteresting, and clumsy person"; she never labeled him a threat, so he never thought of himself as one. As a "model member" of the proletariat, he embodied the bourgeois ideology. Yet the effects of his death and cremation could incite a revolution!

Reminiscent of the insignificance of his life, the smoke lingering from the burnt loaf of the baker's body could irritate someone's eyes. The baker died after a life of servility. He awaited the false hope of heaven instead of "uprising." He never took control of his life on earth to create the only option of paradise open for him and for all humanity. Only revolution can achieve paradise and can prevent such a tragic end to the "dough" of the entire proletariat body. The proletariat must therefore revolt and seize the modes of production in the bourgeois bakery. While so doing, they will form "one small loaf" with the "flour" of the baker man's ashes to symbolize a *former* life of servitude and oppression. This small loaf of revolution will never be marked with a "D" because it will not die under the oppression of the bourgeoisie.

JUANITA WOLFE

﹋ *10* ﹌

Cultural Poetics
or New Historicism

I had dreamed of speaking with the dead, and even now I do not abandon this dream. But the mistake was to imagine that I would hear a single voice, the voice of the other. If I wanted to hear one, I had to hear the many voices of the dead. And if I wanted to hear the voice of the other, I had to hear my own voice. The speech of the dead, like my own speech, is not private property.

Stephen Greenblatt, *Shakespearean Negotiations*, p. 20

INTRODUCTION

During the 1940s, 1950s, and 1960s, **New Criticism** (see Chapter 3 and the Glossary) was the dominant approach to literary analysis. At this time, René Wellek and Austin Warren's text *Theory of Literature (1942)* became the bible of hermeneutics, focusing the interpretive process on the text itself rather than on historical, authorial, or reader concerns.

A New-Critical Lecture

During this high tide of New Criticism, it would have been common to hear a college lecture like the following in a literature classroom.

> Today, class, we will quickly review what we learned about Elizabethan beliefs from our last lecture so that we can apply this knowledge to our understanding of Act I of Shakespeare's *King Lear*. As you remember, the Elizabethans believed in the interconnectedness of all life. Having created everything, God imposed on creation a cosmic order. At all costs, this cosmic order was not to be upset. Any element of the created universe that portended change, such as a violent storm, eclipses of the sun or moon, or even disobedient children within the family structure, suggested chaos that could possibly lead to anarchy and the destruction of the earth itself. Nothing, believed the Elizabethans, should break any link in this Great Chain of Being, the name given to this created cosmic order. With God and the angels in their place, with the King governing his obedient people in their places, and the

animals being subdued and utilized by humankind in theirs, all would be right in the world and operate as ordained by God.

Having gained an understanding of the Elizabethan worldview, let's turn to Act I, Scene ii, lines 101–12 of Shakespeare's *King Lear*. You will recall that in this scene Edmund, the illegitimate son of the Duke of Gloucester, has persuaded the Duke that Edgar, the Duke's legitimate son and heir to the dukedom, wants his father dead so that he may inherit the Duke's title, lands, and wealth. Believing his natural son has betrayed both him and Edmund, Edgar's half-brother, the Duke, says, "These late eclipses in the sun and moon portend no good to us. Though the wisdom of nature can reason it thus and thus, yet nature finds itself scourged by the sequent effects. Love cools, friendship falls off, brothers divide.[. . .]"

What we see in these lines, class, is the Elizabethan worldview in operation. The Duke obviously believes in the interrelatedness of the created cosmic order and the concept of the Great Chain of Being. The significance of the eclipses of the sun and moon rests in their representing change and chaos. Because the Duke believes that the macrocosm (the universe) directly affects the microcosm (the world of humanity on earth), he blames these natural occurrences (the eclipses) for interfering in familial relationships and destroying love between brothers, between father and daughters, (King Lear having already banished his most beloved daughter, Cordelia), and between King and servant (Kent, King Lear's loyal courtier also having being expelled from the kingdom).

Old Historicism

In the typical formalist lecture above, the professor's method of literary analysis represents an example of both New Criticism and what is known today as the "old historicism." In this methodology, history serves as a background to literature. Of primary importance is the text, the art object itself. The historical background of the text is only secondarily important, for it is the aesthetic object, the text, that mirrors the history of its times. The historical context serves only to shed light on the object of primary concern, the text.

Underlying this methodology is a view of history that declares that history, as written, is an accurate view of what really occurred. Such a view assumes that historians are able to write objectively about any given historical time period and, therefore, are able to state definitively the truth about that era. Through various means of historical analyses, historians are seemingly capable of discovering the mind-set, the worldview, or the beliefs of any group of people. For example, when the professor in our hypothetical lecture states the beliefs of the Elizabethans at the beginning of the lecture, he or she is articulating the Elizabethan worldview—the unified set of presuppositions or assumptions that all Elizabethans supposedly held concerning their world. By applying these assertions to the Elizabethan text *King Lear*, the professor believes he or she can formulate a more accurate interpretation of the play than if the teacher did not know the play's historical context.

The New Historicism

That historians can articulate a unified and internally consistent worldview of any given people, country, or time period and can reconstruct an accurate and objective picture of any historical event are key assumptions that **Cultural Poetics** challenges. Appearing as an alternate approach to textual interpretation in the 1970s and early 1980s, Cultural Poetics—often called *New Historicism* in America and *Cultural Materialism* in Great Britain—declares that all history is subjective, written by people whose personal biases affect their interpretation of the past. History, asserts Cultural Poetics, can never provide us with the truth or give us a totally accurate picture of past events nor the worldview of a group of people. Disavowing the old historicism's autonomous view of history, Cultural Poetics declares that history is one of many **discourses,** or ways of seeing and thinking about the world. By highlighting and viewing history as one of many equally important discourses, such as sociology and politics, and by closely examining how all discourses (including that of textual analysis itself) effect a text's interpretation, Cultural Poetics or New Historicism proclaims it provides its adherents with a practice of literary analysis that highlights the interrelatedness of all human activities, admits its own prejudices, and gives a more complete understanding of a text than does the old historicism and other interpretative approaches.

HISTORICAL DEVELOPMENT

Although the assumptions of Cultural Poetics and its accompanying practices have been employed by critics for several decades, the beginning of New Historicism, the distinctively American form of this analysis, begins in the span 1979–1980 with the publication of several essays and texts, such as "Improvisation and Power" and *Renaissance Self-Fashioning* (1980) by the Renaissance scholar Stephen Greenblatt and a variety of works by Louis Montrose, Jonathan Dollimore, and others. Wishing to remain open to differing politics, theories, and ideologies, these critics share a similar set of concerns, not a codified theory or school of criticism. Of chief interest is their shared view that from the mid-1800s to the middle of the twentieth century, historical methods of literary analysis were erroneous. During this time, many scholars believed that history served as background information for textual analysis and that historians were able to objectively reproduce a given historical period and state "how it really was." In disclaiming these assumptions of "old historicism" and formulating its own theories of history and interpretative analysis, Cultural Poetics was first and aptly named New Historicism by one of its chief proponents, Stephen Greenblatt, in the introduction to a collection of Renaissance essays in a 1982 volume of the journal *Genre*. Because of its broader concerns with culture, history, literature, and a host of other factors that help determine a text's meaning, Greenblatt and his followers have come to believe that the term *Cultural Poetics* more aptly describes their approach to textual analysis than does New Historicism.

According to Stephen Greenblatt, Cultural Poetics was mostly shaped by the institutional character of American literary criticism during the 1960s and 1970s. During this time, one of the dominating influences in literary criticism was **New Criticism**, with its accompanying theoretical assumptions and practical methodology. For example, during Greenblatt's graduate studies at Yale—a place he has since called the cathedral of High Church New Criticism—Greenblatt himself mastered New Critical principles. New Critical scholars, writers, and critics like T. S. Eliot, Allen Tate, John Crowe Ranson, Cleanth Brooks, and Robert Penn Warren were revered, and their methodology widely practiced throughout the country.

Aided early on in its development by the publication and wide use of Cleanth Brooks and Robert Penn Warren's textbook *Understanding Poetry* (1939), New Criticism presented scholars and teachers a workable and teachable methodology for interpreting texts. From a theoretical perspective, New Criticism regards a literary text as an artifact or object with an existence of its own, independent of and not necessarily related to its author, its readers, the historical time it depicts, or the historical period in which it was written. From this viewpoint, a text's meaning emerges when readers scrutinize it and it alone. Such a close scrutiny will result, the New Critics maintain, in perceiving a text as an organic whole, wherein all of its parts fit together and support one overarching theme. A literary text is highly structured and contains its meaning in itself; it will reveal that meaning to a critic-reader who examines it on its own terms by applying a rigorous and systematic methodology. Such an analysis, say the New Critics, is particularly rewarding, for literature offers us a unique kind of knowledge that presents us with the deepest truths related to humanity, truths that science is unable to disclose.

What New Criticism did not provide for Greenblatt and other critics was an attempt to understand literature from a historical perspective. In a New Critical analysis, the text was what mattered, not its historical context. Considerations that any given text may be the result of historical phenomena were devalued or silenced. In addition, Greenblatt felt that questions about the nature and definition of literature were not encouraged. He and other critics wanted to discuss how literature was formed, whose interest it serves, and what the term *literature* really means. Do contemporary issues and the cultural milieu of the times operate together to create literature, they wondered, or is literature simply an art form that will always be with us?

Cultural Poetics, then, began to develop as a direct result of New Criticism's dominance of literary criticism and its response or lack thereof to questions concerning the nature, the definition, and the function of literature itself. At the same time that Greenblatt was asking a different set of literary questions, a variety of new critical theories and theorists appeared on the literary scene. Deconstruction, Marxism, feminism, and Lacanian psychoanalysis also began to challenge the assumptions of New Criticism. Rejecting New Criticism's claim that the meaning of a text can be found, for the most part, in the text alone, these poststructural theories had been developing a variety of theoretical positions about the nature of the reading process, the part the reader plays in that process, and the definition of a text or the actual work of art. It is among this cacophony of voices that Cultural Poetics arose.

After reading sociological and cultural studies authored by Michel Foucault, Greenblatt and other critics admired and emulated Foucault's tireless questioning of the nature of literature, history, culture, and society. Like Foucault, they refused to accept the traditional, well-worn answers. From the Marxist scholars—Georg Lukács, Walter Benjamin, Raymond Williams, and others—they learned that history is shaped by the people who live it, and they accepted the Marxist idea of the interconnectedness of all life. What we do with our hands and how we make our money does indeed, they believed, affect how and what we think.

But unlike many of the poststructuralist theories—especially deconstruction—Cultural Poetics struggled to find a way out of **undecidability**, or **aporia**, about the nature of reality and the interpretation of a text. While not denying that many factors affect the writing, the production, and the publication of texts, New Historicists sought to move beyond undecidability rather than simply assert that a text has many possible meanings. In so doing, they challenged the assumptions of the old historicism, which presupposed historians could actually write an objective history of any situation; they redefined the meaning of a text; and they asserted that all critics must acknowledge and openly declare their own biases.

Throughout the 1980s and 1990s, critics such as Catherine Gallagher, Jonathan Dollimore, Jerome McGann, Stephen Greenblatt, and others have voiced their concerns that the study of literature and its relationship to history has been too narrow. Viewing a text as culture in action, these critics blur the distinction between an artistic production and any other kind of social production or event. They want us to see that the publication of Swift's "A Modest Proposal" is a political act, while noting that the ceremonies surrounding the inauguration of a United States president is an aesthetic event, with all the trappings of symbolism and structure found in any poem. Many similar examples that highlight their critical practices can be found in their chief public voice, the journal *Representations*.

It would be an invalid assumption, however, to think that consensus can be found among those who espouse the theory and practice of Cultural Poetics about theories of art, terminology, and practical methods of interpretation. Cultural Poetics, like all other approaches to literary analysis, is best understood as a practice of literary interpretation that is still in process, one that is continually redefining and fine-tuning its purposes, its philosophy, and its practices while, at the same time, gaining new followers. Presently, its followers can be divided into two main branches: Cultural Materialism and New Historicism. Members of either group continue to call for a reawakening of our historical consciousness, declare that history and literature must be seen as disciplines to be analyzed together, place all texts in their appropriate contexts, and believe that while we are researching and learning about different societies that provide the historical context for various texts, we are simultaneously learning about ourselves, our own habits, and our own beliefs.

Cultural Materialism

Cultural Materialism, the British branch of Cultural Poetics, is openly Marxist in its theories and overtly political and cultural in its aims. It finds its ideological roots in the writings of the Marxist critics Louis Althusser and Raymond Williams. Believing that literature can serve as an agent of change in today's world, cultural materialists declare that any culture's hegemony is basically unstable. For literature to produce change, a critic must read the works of the established canon "against the grain." By so doing, the critic will expose the political unconscious of the text and help debunk the social and political myths created by the bourgeoisie.

New Historicism

The American branch of Cultural Poetics is frequently called **New Historicism,** as discussed in the "Historical Development" section. Its founder, Stephen Greenblatt, along with a host of other scholars holds that one's culture permeates both texts and critics. As all of society is intricately interwoven, so are critics and texts, both to each other and in the culture in which the critics live and the texts are produced. Since all critics are influenced by the culture in which they live, New Historicists believe that they cannot escape public and private cultural influences. Each critic will therefore arrive at a unique interpretation of a text. Less overtly political than its British counterpart, New Historicism continues to be refined and redefined by its many practitioners.

ASSUMPTIONS

Like other poststructuralist practices, Cultural Poetics begins by challenging the long-held belief that a text is an autonomous work of art that contains all elements necessary to arrive at a supposedly correct interpretation. Disavowing the "old historical" assumption that a text simply reflects its historical context—the **mimetic** view of art and history—and that such historical information provides an interesting and sometimes useful backdrop for literary analysis, Cultural Poetics redirects our attention to a series of philosophical and practical concerns that it believes will highlight the complex interconnectedness of all human activities. It redefines both a text and history while simultaneously redefining the relationship between a text and history. Unlike the old historicism, New Historicism asserts that an intricate connection exists between an aesthetic object—a text or any work of art—and society, while denying that a text can be evaluated in isolation from its cultural context. We must know, it declares, the societal concerns of the author, of the historical times evidenced in the work, and of other cultural elements exhibited in the text before we can devise a valid interpretation. This new approach to textual analysis questions the very act of how we can arrive at meaning for any human activity, whether it is a text, a social event, a long-held tradition, or a political act.

Michel Foucault

Cultural Poetics finds the basis for its concerns as well as a coherent body of assumptions in the writings of the twentieth-century French archaeologist, historian, and philosopher Michel Foucault (1926–1984). Foucault begins his rather complex and sometimes paradoxical theoretical structure by redefining the concept of history. Unlike many past historians, Foucault declares that history is not **linear**—it does not have a definite beginning, a middle, and an end—nor is it necessarily **teleological**, that is, purposefully going forward toward some known end. Nor can history be explained as a series of causes and effects controlled by some mysterious destiny or an all-powerful deity. For Foucault, history is the complex interrelationship of a variety of discourses, the various ways—artistic, social, political, and so on—that people think and talk about their world. How these discourses interact in any given historical period is not random. Rather, the interaction is dependent on a unifying principle or pattern Foucault calls the **episteme**: Through language and thought, each period in history develops its own perceptions concerning the nature of reality (or what it defines as truth), sets up its own acceptable and unacceptable standards of behavior, establishes its criteria for judging what it deems good or bad, and certifies what group of people articulate, protect, and defend the yardstick whereby all established truths, values, and actions will be deemed acceptable.

To unearth the episteme of any given historical period, Foucault borrows techniques and terminology from archaeology. Just as an archaeologist must slowly and meticulously dig through various layers of earth to uncover the symbolic treasures of the past, historians must expose each layer of discourse that comes together to shape a people's episteme. And just as an archaeologist must date each finding and then piece together the artifacts that define and help explain that culture, so must the historian piece together the various discourses and their interconnections among themselves and with nondiscursive practices—any cultural institution such as a form of government, for example—that will assist in articulating the episteme under investigation.

Seen from this point of view, history is a form of power. Since each era or people develop their own episteme, it is, in actuality, the episteme that controls how that era or group of people will view reality. History becomes the study and unearthing of a vast, complex web of interconnecting forces that ultimately determines what takes place in each culture or society.

Why or how epistemes change from one historical period to another is basically unclear. That they change seemingly without warning is certain. Such a change occurred at the beginning of the nineteenth century—the shift from the Age of Reason to romanticism, for example—and initiated a new episteme. In this new historical era, different relationships develop among discourses that had not previously evolved or had existed and were deemed unacceptable in the previous historical period. Foucault asserts that the abrupt and often radical changes that cause breaks from one episteme to another are neither good nor bad, valid nor invalid. Like the discourses that help produce them, different epistemes exist in their own right; they are neither moral or immoral, but amoral.

Historians must realize, according to Foucault, that they are influenced and prejudiced by the episteme(s) in which they live. Since their thoughts, customs, habits, and other actions are colored by their epistemes, historians must realize that they can never be totally objective about their own or any other historical period. To be a historian, Foucault asserts, means one must be able to confront and articulate one's own set of biases before examining the various discourses or the material evidence of past events that comprise an episteme of any given period. Such an archaeological examination of the various discourses, Foucault believes, will not unearth a monological view of an episteme (that is, one that presupposes a single, overarching, political vision or design), but a set of inconsistent, irregular, and often contradictory discourses that will explain the development of that episteme, including which elements were accepted, changed, or rejected to form the "truth" and set the acceptable standards for that era.

Clifford Geertz

In addition to borrowing many of its ideas from Foucault, Cultural Poetics also utilizes theories and methodologies from the cultural anthropologist Clifford Geertz. Geertz believes that there exists "no human nature independent of culture," culture being defined by Geertz as "a set of control mechanisms—plans, recipes, rules, instructions," for governing behavior. Each person must be viewed as a cultural artifact. How each person views society is always unique, for there exists what Geertz call an "information gap" between what our body tells us and what we have to know in order to function in society. This gap also exists in society because society cannot know everything that happens among all its people. Like individuals, society simply fills in the gaps with what it assumes to have taken place. And it is this information gap, both within people and society, that results in the subjectivity of history.

Cultural Poetics also borrows and adapts Geertz's anthropological methodology for describing culture as **thick description**. Coined by Geertz, Geertz uses this term to describe the seemingly insignificant details present in any cultural practice. By focusing on these details, one can then reveal the inherent contradictory forces at work within a culture. Borrowing this idea from Geertz, Cultural Poetics theorists declare that each separate discourse of a culture must be uncovered and analyzed in hopes of showing how all discourses interact with each other and with institutions, peoples, and other elements of culture. It is the interaction among the many different discourses which shapes a culture and interconnects all human activities, including the writing, reading, and interpretation of a text that the Cultural Poetics critic wishes to emphasize.

Texts, History, and Interpretation

Since texts are simply one of many elements that help shape a culture, Cultural Poetics critics believe that all texts are really social documents that reflect but also, and more importantly, respond to their historical situation. Also, since any historical situation is an intricate web of oftentimes competing discourses, Cultural Poetics scholars necessarily center history and declare that any interpretation of a text would be incomplete if we do not consider the text's relationship to the discourses that helped fashion it and to which the text is a response. From this point of view, a text becomes a battleground of competing ideas among the author, society, customs, institutions, and social practices that are all eventually negotiated by the author and the reader and influenced by each contributor's episteme. By allowing history a prominent place in the interpretative process, and by examining the various convoluted webs that interconnect the discourses found within a text and in its historical setting, we can negotiate a text's meaning.

Overall, Cultural Poetics posits the interconnectedness of all our actions. For a Cultural Poetics critic, everything we do is interrelated to and within a network of practices embedded in our culture. No act is insignificant; everything is important. In our search to attach meaning to our actions, Cultural Poetics critics believe that we can never be fully objective, for we are all biased by cultural forces. Only by examining the complex latticework of these interlocking forces or discourses that empower and shape culture, and by realizing that no single discourse reveals the pathway to absolute truth about ourselves or our world, can we begin to interpret either our world or a text.

In Cultural Poetics theory, the goal of interpretative analysis is really the formation and an understanding of a "poetics of culture," a process that sees life and its sundry activities as something more like art than we think, certainly a more metaphorical interpretation of reality than an analytic one. Through the practice of their analysis, Cultural Poetics critics maintain that we will discover not only the social world of the text but also the present-day social forces working upon us as we negotiate meaning with printed material. Like history itself, our interaction with any text is a dynamic, ongoing process that will always be somewhat incomplete.

METHODOLOGY

Like other approaches to literary analysis, Cultural Poetics includes an array of techniques and strategies in its interpretative inquiries with no one method being dubbed the correct form of investigation. No matter what the technique, Cultural Poetics scholars begin by assuming that language shapes and is shaped by the culture that uses it. By language, Cultural Poetics critics mean much more than spoken words. For them, language includes discourse, writing, literature, social actions, and any social relationship whereby a person or a group impose their ideas or actions upon another.

Included in this definition of language is history. Like literature, writing, or other relationships that involve either a transfer or some other relationship of power, history now becomes a narrative discourse. As in literature or any other narrative discourse, history must now be viewed as a language that can never be fully articulated or completely explained. From this perspective, history and literature are nearly synonymous terms, both being narrative discourses that interact with their historical situations, their authors, their readers, and their present-day cultures. Neither can claim a complete or an objective understanding of its content or historical situation, for, in fact, both are ongoing conversations with their creators, readers, and cultures.

Since Cultural Poetics critics view history, literature, and other social activities as forms of discourse, they strongly reject the old historicism, which sees history as necessary background material for the study of literature. Cultural Poetics critics view a work of art, a text, as they would any other social discourse that interacts with its culture to produce meaning. No longer is one discourse superior to another, but all are necessary components that shape and are shaped by society. No longer do clear lines of distinction exist among literature, history, literary criticism, anthropology, art, the sciences, and other disciplines. Blurring the boundaries between disciplines, Cultural Poetics scholars investigate all discourses that effect any social production. Since they believe that meaning evolves from the interaction of the variously interwoven social discourses, no hierarchy of discourses can exist; all discourses are necessary and must be investigated in the process of textual analysis. The interpretative process, then, must also include questions about the methodological assumptions for discerning meaning for each discourse and for every practitioner, for no one discourse or method or critic can reveal the truth about any social production in isolation from other discourses.

Since Cultural Poetics critics view an aesthetic work as a social production, for them a text's meaning resides in the cultural system composed of the interlocking discourses of its author, the text, and its reader. To unlock textual meaning, a Cultural Poetics critic investigates three areas of concern: the life of the author, the social rules and dictates found within a text, and a reflection of a work's historical situation as evidenced in the text. Since an actual person authors a text, his or her actions and beliefs reflect both individual concerns and those of the author's society and are essential elements of the text itself. In addition, the standard of behavior as reflected in a society's rules of decorum must also be investigated because these behavioral codes simultaneously helped shape and were shaped by the text. The text must also be viewed as an artistic work that reflects on these behavioral social codes. To begin to understand a text's significance and to realize the complex social structure of which it is a part, Cultural Poetics critics declare that all three areas of concern must be investigated. If one area is ignored, the risk of returning to the old historicism, with its lack of understanding about a text as a social production, is great. During the process of textual analysis, critics must not forget to question their individual assumptions and methods as well, for they too are products of and act as shaping influences upon their culture.

To avoid the old historicism's error of thinking that each historical period evidences a single, political worldview, Cultural Poetics avoids sweep-

ing generalizations and seeks the seemingly insignificant details and manifestations of culture frequently ignored by most historians or literary critics.
Because Cultural Poetics views history and literature as social discourses
and therefore battlegrounds for conflicting beliefs, actions, and customs, a
text becomes "culture in action." By highlighting seemingly insignificant
happenings, such as a note written by Thomas Jefferson to one of his slaves
or a sentence etched on a window pane by Hawthorne, these critics hope to
bring to the surface those competing social codes and forces that mold a
given society. Emphasizing a particular moment or incident rather than an
overarching vision of society, a Cultural Poetics critic will often point out
nonconventional connections: for example, between Sophia Hawthorne's
having a headache after reading *The Scarlet Letter* and the ending of
Nathaniel Hawthorne's next romance, *The House of the Seven Gables*, or between the climate and environs of Elmira, New York, and some locations,
descriptions, and actions in Mark Twain's *Huckleberry Finn*. Cultural Poetics
scholars believe that an investigation into these and similar happenings will
demonstrate the complex relationship that exists among all discourses and
show how narrative discourses such as history, literature, and other social
productions interact with, define, and are in turn shaped by their culture.
What we will learn by applying these principles and methodologies, say the
Cultural Poetics critics, is that there is not one voice but many voices to be
heard interpreting texts and our culture: our own, the voices of others, the
voices of the past, the voices of the present, and the voices that will be in the
future.

QUESTIONS FOR TEXTUAL ANALYSIS

When analyzing any text from a Cultural Poetics point of view, Stephen
Greenblatt suggests we ask and investigate the following questions:

- What kinds of behavior, what models of practice, does this work seem to rein-
  force?
- Why might readers at a particular time and place find this work compelling?
- Are there differences between my values and the values implicit in the work I
  am reading?
- Upon what social understanding does the work depend?
- Whose freedom of thought or movement might be constrained implicitly or ex-
  plicitly by this work?
- What are the larger social structures with which these particular acts of praise
  or blame might be connected?

QUESTIONS FOR ANALYSIS

- Read the Tony Harrison poem "Marked with a D." and ask yourself what voices you hear in the poem. What is the text saying about its culture? About its readers? About itself?
- After reading Hawthorne's "Ethan Brand," see if you can discover any propaganda in the story. What was Hawthorne's position concerning the nature of sin? Of Puritan theology? Of the concept of forgiveness?
- Does Cultural Poetics ask us to make any connections between the 1840s and the 1640s? If so, what are these connections?
- How does Hawthorne's "The Maypole of Merry Mount" question dominant cultural values of Hawthorne's day? Of the 1640s?
- What is a working definition of the word *sin* as used in our present culture? In Hawthorne's day? In the 1640s? Why would Cultural Poetics be interested in this definition?
- How is our reading of both "Marked with a D." and "Ethan Brand" shaped by our history? Our understanding of our history?
- Identify four discourses operating in "The Maypole of Merry Mount" and "Marked with a D." Show how these discourses interconnect to enable the reader to arrive at an interpretation of each of the works.
- Examine the student essay written at the end of Chapter 9, "Marxism." Describe the student's hegemony on the basis of this essay. Provide evidence to support your answer.

SAMPLE ESSAY

In the student essay that ends this chapter, entitled "Hawthorne's Understanding of History in 'The Maypole of Merry Mount,'" be able to show how or whether the critic investigates the three major areas of concern for Cultural Poetics. Is one area emphasized more than another? Does the author highlight a historical moment or a culture's single vision of reality? Does the critic admit his own prejudices and methodology? Is history used as background or brought to the center of the literary analysis? What would be different about this essay if it were written from the old historicism's point of view?

FURTHER READING

Collier, Peter, and Helga Geyer-Ryan, eds. *Literary Theory Today*. Ithaca: Cornell University Press, 1990.

Cox, Jeffrey N., and Larry J. Reynolds, eds. *New Historical Literary Study: Essays on Reproducing Texts, Representing History*. Princeton: Princeton University Press, 1993.

Dollimore, Jonathan. *Radical Tragedy: Religion, Ideology, and Power in the Drama of Shakespeare and His Contemporaries*. 2nd ed. Durham, NC: Duke University Press, 1993.

During, Simon. "New Historicism." *Text and Performance Quarterly* 11 (July 1991): 171–89.

Foucault, Michel. *The Foucault Reader*. Ed. Paul Rabinow. New York: Pantheon, 1984.

Geertz, Clifford. *The Interpretation of Cultures: Selected Essays*. New York: Basic, 1973.

———. *Local Knowledge: Further Essays in Interpretive Anthropology*. New York: Routledge, 1991.

Greenblatt, Stephen. Introduction. "The Forms of Power and the Power of Forms in the Renaissance." *Genre* 15 (Summer 1982): 3–6.

———. *Renaissance Self-Fashioning: From More to Shakespeare*. Chicago: University of Chicago Press, 1980.

———. *Shakespearean Negotiations: The Circulation of Social Energy in Renaissance England*. Berkeley: University of California Press, 1988.

Howard, Jean E. "The New Historicism in Renaissance Studies." *English Literary Renaissance* 16 (Winter 1986): 13–43.

Montrose, Louis. "Renaissance Literary Studies and the Subject of History." *English Literary Renaissance* 16 (Winter 1986): 5–12.

Robertson, D. W., Jr. "Historical Criticism." *English Institute Essays: 1950*. Ed. Alan S. Downer. New York: Columbia University Press, 1951. 3–31.

Thomas, Brook. "The Historical Necessity for—and Difficulties With—New Historical Analysis in Introductory Literature Courses." *College English* 49 (September 1987): 509–22.

Vesser, H. Aram, ed. *The New Historicism*. New York: Routledge, 1989.

WEB SITES FOR EXPLORATION

www.sou.edu/English/Hedges/Sodashop/RCenter/Theory/Explaind/nhistexp.htm
    A good review of the principles and theories of New Historicism

www.chosun.ac.kr/~mgoh/crit/structuralism/newhistoricism.htm
    Another good review of New Historicism's basic principles

ww.cnr.edu/home/bmcmanus/newhistoricism.html
    Provides links for new sites and includes a discussion of the theory of Michel Foucault

www.nyu.edu/classes/stephesn/Greenblat%20page.htm
    A discussion of Stephen Greenblatt and his relationship to New Historicism

www.sou.edu/English/IDTC/issues/history/nwhist2.htm
Provides links to New Historicists—Steven Greenblatt, W. B. Michaels, and Michel Foucault—plus a discussion of related literary terms

↭ Student Essay ↭

Hawthorne's Understanding of History in "The Maypole of Merry Mount"

Synonymous with the flowering of American literature during the 1840s and 1850s is the name Nathaniel Hawthorne. Known particularly for his four romances—*The Scarlet Letter*, *The House of the Seven Gables*, *The Blithedale Romance*, and *The Marble Faun*—Hawthorne also penned over sixty short stories, including "The Maypole of Merry Mount" (c. 1829). Based upon an actual event occurring at Mount Wollaston or Merry Mount between the fun-loving, anti-Puritan Thomas Morton and the Puritan leader William Bradford, this tale presents a mirthful scene suddenly brought to a close by the arrival of the staunch Puritans.

More frequently than not scholars, such as Richard Harter Fogle, Randall Stewart, John T. Frederick, and many others, note that Hawthorne paints the revelers of Merry Mount as "immitigable zealot[s]," whereas the Puritans are "most dismal wretches." Put another way, Hawthorne embodies in the conflict between Merry Mount and Plymouth two distinct personality types: the jolly colonists versus the gloomy Puritans. That his sympathies reside with the Lord and Lady of the May are undoubtable, but if he were forced to choose between the rivaling parties, Hawthorne would have sided with Endicott, for life, after all, is not a party but a rather serious affair. His story, assert Hawthorian scholars, demonstrates that the Puritan worldview, with its accompanying assumptions about the nature of reality, triumphs over the colonists because the Puritans, not the fun-loving revelers, are in tune with the nature of reality itself.

Such an interpretation rests upon the standards set by the old historicism. Yes, Hawthorne was a historian, and he did understand Puritan theology and history. But the history Hawthorne understood was itself a narrative written by historians who can at best only present their own personal and biased understanding of the past. From a New Historicist's point of view, there exists no definitive view of the Puritans, no definitive view of Hawthorne, and no definitive understanding of "The Maypole of Merry Mount." What we can gain from rereading this tale from a New Historicist viewpoint is a glimpse of how Hawthorne saw life in early America and how he himself was shaped by his own historical era. Such an understanding will reveal how seemingly insignificant events in Hawthorne's life and what appears as arbitrary information within the text of the short story reveal insights into our understanding and enjoyment of this tale.

Hawthorne sets "The Maypole of Merry Mount" in Salem, Massachusetts. Once a thriving seaport during the Puritan era, the Salem of Hawthorne's time is now relatively quiet and in decay. Gone are the boisterous sailors, the many schooners unloading their goods at Derby's Wharf, and the crowded streets. In their place Hawthorne saw gabled housetops, decaying docks, and old maids scurrying from the crumbling mansions of Chestnut Street and Federal Street to buy books at the once-profitable bookstores of downtown Salem. From Hawthorne's point of view, Salem must have resembled the ancient cities of mediaeval Europe that were, like Salem, displaced by modern towns and trades. And like these all but forgotten cities, the spirit of the Gothic hung over Salem.

In Hawthorne's Salem there was no need to invent tales of horror, of witchcraft, or any other kind of legend, for wherever Hawthorne went—on Charter Street near the town's cemetery, nearby Crystal Hills once populated by the Indians, or on the fringes of Salem society known for their superstitious ways—Hawthorne heard tales of sea adventures, wizards, witches, and of the "Maypole's" Endicott and a time when the Puritan punishment for even small sins or mistakes was harsh and swift.

Hawthorne's Salem, a center of legends and Gothic tales, was a city where reality and symbols blended into each other. Where the supernatural began and physical reality ended was often confused, ignored, or avoided. Hawthorne himself was not immune to his town's Gothic tales and horrors. Van Wyck Brooks notes in *The Flowering of New England* that Hawthorne saw apparitions in his family yard located on Herbert Street. At least in Hawthorne's mind, a ghost or apparition haunted the yard, peering into the windows, passing through the house's gate, or simply staring at family members as they entered the house. And Hawthorne knew the identity of this ghost and why it haunted his family: Hawthorne's first American ancestor, William Hathorne, settled in Puritan Salem and quickly became known for his persecution of Quakers. William's son, John Hathorne, followed in his father's footsteps and became one of the judges and interrogators during the Salem witch trials of the 1690s. According to Nathaniel Hawthorne, his family's land was cursed because of the enormous sins committed by his Puritan ancestors upon many undeserving people who were accused, tried, and convicted of witchcraft. It is his personal shame of such unspeakable deeds that causes Hawthorne to question Puritanism, to ask why such supposedly God-fearing people could be filled with so much hate, so much destruction. How could their God be so harsh, Hawthorne wondered. How could they not see the joy in life: a dance, a party, bright and colorful clothing? How could they be so spiritually minded and of so little earthly good?

It was thus the Gothic nature of his Salem, the ubiquitous telling of old wives' tales of ghosts and wizards, and the reappearing apparition in the yard outside his family's home that helped shaped Hawthorne's opinion of his Puritan ancestors. Although he had studied Puritan history, it was his town's milieu, his personal experience with ghosts, and his personal identification with the horrors of the Salem witch trials that ultimately formed his understanding of Puritan theology, the supernatural, and his own guilt of the past. It is these factors that directly contribute to his writing of "The Maypole of Merry Mount."

Like all historians, Hawthorne's view of his Puritan ancestors is tainted by his own historical era and its existing cultural milieu. Hawthorne knew, of course, that his Puritan ancestors came to America to escape the oppression that faced them in England. Seeking religious freedom, Hawthorne's ancestors immigrated to the New World and established their own culture. As a result, the social boundaries and restrictions of their past changed. Now they were in the dominant social position. Now they were the ruling class rather than the oppressed. Such a change is affirmed by Hawthorne in "The Maypole of Merry Mount." Knowing his history, Hawthorne knew the mistakes of his ancestors and their prejudices. But the Puritans he knew were not the actual Puritans, but concoctions created by his own mind and the stories and tales of his contemporary Salem.

Puritans, said Hawthorne and his contemporary historians, hated gaiety, parties, beautiful clothes, and alcoholic beverages. Although present-day historians have proved all these assumptions to be in error—the Puritans loved to throw parties, drink brandy, engage in wrestling matches, and wear brightly colored clothing—Hawthorne writes that the revelers of Merry Mount were "gaily decked." Indeed, he notes that "Bright were the days at Merry Mount, when the Maypole was the banner staff of that gay colony!" The leaders of the colony, the Lord and Lady of the May, were a "youth in glistening apparel" and "a fair maiden," each holding the other's hand while dancing together. Waiting to marry this fair couple was the English priest, who, Hawthorne notes, waited "decked with flowers, in heathen fashion." Although this priest is actually of English descent, he is apparently shaking off his loyalty and giving in to his wild nature.

When the Puritans arrive, John Endicott, the Puritan leader, cuts down the Maypole and contemplates the penalties the worshipers are to receive. After some time, Endicott decides that part of the punishment of the Lord and Lady of the Maypole is that their hair must be cut. "Crop it forthwith, and in the true pumpkin-shell fashion." Such a punishment may appear slight or even trifling, but in actuality it is not. According to Hawthorne's understanding of Puritan theology with its accompanying rules and punishments, all youths must have shortly cropped hair, a symbol of acceptance by and of Puritan customs, laws, and theology. In addition to having their hair cut, the revelers must also don "garments of a more decent fashion." Once again, we observe the Puritans oppressing those who disagree with them and wielding their newfound power over the New Englanders. Lastly, Endicott commands his lieutenant to "bestow on them a small matter of stripes apiece," a punishment that was common during the late 1690s for those who went against Puritan standards.

When writing his romances and short stories like "The Maypole of Merry Mount," Hawthorne was unable to escape his own history. In his stories we catch small glimpses of his life as it was shaped by his culture and his own readings and how his Puritan ancestors and his contemporary Salem contribute to the ideas and questions he had concerning the theology and beliefs of his Puritan forefathers. Throughout his writings, he continually questions the Puritans' so-called perfection while emphasizing their sinfulness. Although his historical facts are sometimes inaccurate, he reveals in "The Maypole of Merry Mount" the power struggle existing in the Puritan society of the late 1690s while examining Puritan religion and its newly-developing culture. In writing this tale, Hawthorne really gives us two contrasting views of American society, the first being his personal understanding of Puritan theology and the second our glimpse of American society in the mid-1840s through the eyes of Hawthorne.

KRISTA ADLHOCK

ℬ *11* ℛ

Cultural Studies

The post-colonial desire is the desire of decolonized communities for an identity.

Simon During, *Textual Practice*,
1987

INTRODUCTION

The 1960s saw a revolutionary change in literary theory. Until this decade, New Criticism dominated literary theory and practice, with its insistence that one, fundamentally correct interpretation of a text could be discovered if the critical reader followed the prescribed methodology given by the New Critics. Positing an autonomous text, New Critics paid little attention to a text's historical context or to the feelings, beliefs, and ideas of a text's reader. For New Critics, a text's meaning was inextricably bound to ambiguity, irony, and paradox found within the structure of the text itself. By analyzing the text alone, New Critics believed that an astute critic would be able to identify a text's central paradox and be able to explain how the text ultimately resolved that paradox while also supporting the text's overarching theme.

Into this seemingly self-assured system of hermeneutics marched Jacques Derrida and his friends in the 1960s. Unlike the New Critics, Derrida, the chief spokesperson for deconstruction, disputes a text's objective existence. Denying that a text is an **autotelic artifact**, Derrida and other poststructural critics also challenge the accepted definitions and assumptions of both the reading and writing processes. Joined by reader-response critics, these postmodern thinkers insist on questioning what part not only the text but also the reader and the author plays in the interpretive process.

Joined by a host of authors and scholars—Stanley Fish, J. Hillis Miller, Michel Foucault, and many others—these philosopher-critics also question the language of texts and of literary analysis. Unlike the New Critics, who believed that the language of literature was somehow different from the language of science and everyday conversation, these postmodernists insist that the language of texts is not distinct from the language used to analyze such writings. For these critics, all language is **discourse**. In other words, the discourse or culturally bound language of ideas used in literary analysis helps shape and form the text being analyzed. We cannot separate, they maintain, the text and the language used to critique it. For these critics, language helps create what we call "objective reality."

Believing that objective reality can be created by language, many postmodernists posit that all reality is a social construct. From this point of view, no single or primary objective reality exists, but many realities. Thus, in disavowing a universal, objective reality, these critics assert that reality is perspectival, with each individual creating his or her subjective understanding of the nature of reality itself. How, then, do we come to agree upon public and social concerns, such as values, ethics, and the common good, if reality is different for each individual? The answer for many postmodern thinkers is that each society or culture contains within itself a dominant cultural group who determines that culture's ideology or, using the Marxist term, its **hegemony**: its dominant values, its sense of right and wrong, and its sense of personal self-worth. All people in a given culture are consciously and unconsciously asked to conform to the prescribed hegemony.

What happens, however, when one's ideas, one's thinking, or one's personal background does not conform? What happens, for example, when the dominant culture consists of white, Anglo-Saxon males and one is a black female? Or how does one respond to a culture dominated by these same white males when one is a Native American? For people of color living in Africa or the Americas, for Native Americans, for females, and for a host of others, the traditional answer has been articulated by the dominant class and its accompanying hegemony: *silence*. Live quietly, work quietly, think quietly. The message sent to these "Others" by the dominant culture has been clear and consistent—conform and be quiet; deny yourself and all will be well.

Many have not been quiet. Writers and thinkers, such as Toni Morrison, Alice Walker, Gabriel García Márquez, Carlos Fuentes, Gayatri Spivak, Edward Said, and Frantz Fanon, to name a few, have dared to speak out and challenge the dominant cultures and the dictates these cultures decree. They continue to refuse silence and choose defiance, if necessary. They believe that an individual's view of life, of values, and of ethics matters. They assert a different perspective, a vantage point not of the dominant culture, but one from which to view the world and its peoples: They speak for not one culture, but many; not one cultural perspective, but a host; not one interpretation of life, but countless numbers.

Joined by postmodern literary theorists and philosophers, these new voices—African, Australian, Native American, women, and others—are letting their voices be heard among the cacophony of the insistent, dominant, and generally overpowering cultural voices. Believing that they can affect cultural change, these writers and thinkers refuse to conform to their culture's hegemony. Becoming empowered, these newly heard but long-existent voices are now being listened to in the discussions taking place at the literary table, where these authors are presenting their understanding of reality, of society, and of personal self-worth.

Known overall as **cultural studies**, an analysis of the new voices allows us at present to group them into three approaches to literary theory and practice: postcolonialism, African American criticism, and gender studies. Although each group has its personal concerns, all seek to be heard and understood as valuable and contributing members of their society. Their individual and public histories, they assert, do matter. They believe that their past and their present are intricately interwoven. They declare that by denying and suppressing their past, they will be denying who they are themselves. Their desire is to be able to articulate their feelings, their concerns, and their assumptions about the nature of reality in their particular cultures without being treated as marginal or minor voices. Often referred to as **subaltern writers**, a term used by the Marxist critic Antonio Gramsci to refer to those classes who are not in control of a culture's ideology (hegemony), these writers provide new ways to see and understand the cultural forces at work in society, in literature, and in ourselves. Although the literary theory and accompanying methodology of each cultural studies approach is still developing, an overview of the central tenets of the three approaches will enable us to understand their distinctive visions of literature's purposes in today's ever-changing world.

POSTCOLONIALISM: "THE EMPIRE WRITES BACK"

Postcolonialism (or post-colonialism—either spelling is acceptable, but each represents slightly different theoretical assumptions) can be defined as an approach to literary analysis that particularly concerns itself with literature written in English in formerly colonized countries. It usually excludes literature that represents either British or American viewpoints and concentrates on writings from colonized or formerly colonized cultures in Australia, New Zealand, Africa, South America, and other places that were once dominated by, but remained outside of, the white, male, European cultural, political, and philosophical tradition. Often referred to as "third world literature" by Marxist critics—a term many other critics think pejorative—postcolonial literature and its theorists investigate what happens when two cultures clash and, more specifically, what happens when one of them, with its accessory ideology, empowers and deems itself superior to the other.

HISTORICAL DEVELOPMENT OF POSTCOLONIALISM

Rooted deeply in colonial power and prejudice, postcolonialism develops from a four-thousand-year history of strained cultural relations between colonies in Africa and Asia and the Western world. Throughout this long history, the West became the colonizers, while many African and Asian countries and their peoples became the colonized. During the nineteenth century, Great Britain emerged as the largest colonizer and imperial power, quickly gaining control of almost one quarter of the earth's landmass. By the middle of the nineteenth century, terms such as *colonial interests* and the *British Empire* were widely used both in the media and in government polices and international politics. Many English people believed that Great Britain was destined to rule the world. Accompanying the belief in this supposed destiny grew the assumption that Western Europeans, and, in particular, the British people, were biologically superior to any other "race," a term for a class of people based on physical and/or cultural distinctions that was unquestioned at the time.

Such beliefs directly affected the ways in which the colonizers treated the colonized. Using its political and economic muscles, Great Britain, the chief imperalist power of the day, dominated her colonies, making them produce and then give up their countries' raw materials in exchange for what material goods the colonized desired or, more likely, the few they could afford to purchase. Forced labor of the colonized became the rule of the day, and thus the institution of slavery was commercialized. It was common for the colonizers to justify their oftentimes cruel treatment of the colonized by invoking European religious beliefs. From the perspective of many white Westerners, the peoples of Africa, the Americas, and Asia (as the Irish before them) were "heathens," possessing heathen ways that therefore, at whatever cost, must be Christianized. How one treats peoples thus defined does not really matter, for many Westerners subscribed to the colonialist ideology that all races other than the white were inferior or subhuman. These subhumans or "savages" quickly became the inferior and equally "evil" Others.

By the early twentieth century, however, England's political, social, economic, and ideological domination of its many colonies began to disappear. By mid-century, for example, India had gained her independence. Many scholars believe that this event marks the beginning of "third world studies" or postcolonialism, for India's independence seemingly ignites the social, moral, and political consciousness and considerable outrage of a vast array of scholars, writers, and critics about social, political, and economic conditions of what was once called third world countries.

The beginnings of postcolonialism's theoretical and social concerns can be traced to the 1950s. During this decade, France ended its long involvement in Indochina, Jean-Paul Sartre and Albert Camus parted ways over their differing views about Algeria, Fidel Castro delivered his now-famous speech "History Shall Absolve Me," and Alfred Sauvy coined the term *third world* to represent those countries that philosophically, politically, and culturally were not defined by Western metaphysics. During the 1960s, Frantz Fanon, Albert Memmi, George Lamming, and other authors, philosophers, and critics began publishing texts which would become the cornerstone of postcolonial writings.

The terms *post-colonial* and *postcolonialism* first appear in scholarly journals in the late 1980s and as a subtitle in Bill Ashcroft, Gareth Griffiths, and Helen Tiffin's text *The Empire Writes Back: Theory and Practice in Post-Colonial Literatures* (1989) and again, in 1990, in Ian Adam and Helen Tiffin's *Past the Last Post: Theorizing Post-Colonialism and Post-Modernism*. By the early and mid-1990s, the terms had become firmly established in scholarly writing, and now, more frequently than not, the word *postcolonialism* refers to literature of colonized cultures by the British Empire.

Like deconstruction and other postmodern approaches to textual analysis, postcolonialism refers to a heterogenous field of study, in which even its spelling provides several alternatives. Some argue that it should be spelled *postcolonialism* with no hyphen between *post* and *colonialism*, while others insist on using the hyphen, as in *post-colonialism*. Many of its adherents suggest there are two branches, one that views postcolonialism as a set of diverse methodologies that possess no unitary quality, as suggested by Homi Bhabha and Arun P. Murkerjee, and those who see postcolonialism as a set of cultural strategies "centered in history." Even this latter group, however, can be subdivided into two branches: those who believe postcolonialism refers to that period after the colonized societies or countries have become independent as opposed to those who regard postcolonialism as referring to all the characteristics of a society or culture from the time of colonization to the present moment.

However postcolonialism may be defined, that it concerns itself with diverse and numerous issues becomes evident when we examine the various topics discussed in one of its most prominent texts, Ashcroft, Griffiths, and Tiffin's *The Post-Colonial Studies Reader* (1995). Its subjects include universality, difference, nationalism, postmodernism, representation and resistance, ethnicity, feminism, language, education, history, place, and production. As diverse as these topics appear to be, all of them draw attention to one of postcolonialism's major concerns: highlighting the struggle that occurs when one culture is dominated by another. As postcolonial critics are ever ready to point out, to be colonized is "to be removed from history." In its interaction with the conquering culture, the colonized or indigenous culture is forced to go underground or to be obliterated.

Only after colonization occurs, and the colonized people have had time to think and then to write about their oppression and loss of cultural identity, does postcolonial theory come into existence. Born out of the colonized peoples' frustrations, their direct and personal cultural clashes with the conquering culture, and their fears, hopes, and dreams about the future and their own identities, postcolonial theory slowly emerges. How the colonized respond to changes in language, curricular matters in education, race differences, and a host of other discourses, including the act of writing itself, becomes the context and the theories of postcolonialism.

ASSUMPTIONS OF POSTCOLONIALIST THEORY

Since different cultures that have been subverted, conquered, and often removed from history will necessarily respond to the conquering culture in a variety of ways, no single approach to postcolonial theory, practice, or concerns is possible or even preferable. What all postcolonialist critics emphatically state, however, is that European colonialism did occur, that the British Empire was at the center of this colonialism, that the conquerors not only dominated the physical land but also the hegemony or ideology of the colonized people, and that the effects of these colonizations are many and are still being felt today.

An inherent tension, however, exists at the center of postcolonial theory, for those who practice this theory and provide and develop its discourse are themselves a heterogeneous group of critics. On the one hand, critics like Fredric Jameson and Georg Gugelberger come from a European and American cultural, literary, and scholarly background. Another group that includes Gayatri Spiva, Edward Said, Homi K. Bhabha, and many others were raised in third world cultures but now reside, study, and write in the West. And still another group includes writers such as Aijaz Ahmad who live and work in the third world. A theoretical and a practical gap occurs between the theory and practice of those trained and living in the West and those third world, subaltern writers living and writing in non-Western cultures. Out of such tension, postcolonial theorists have and will continue to discover problematic topics for exploration and debate.

Although a number of postcolonial theorists and critics, such as Frantz Fanon, Homi K. Bhadba, and Gayatri Chakravorty Spivak, have contributed to postcolonialism's ever-growing body of theory and its practical methodology, the key text in the establishment of postcolonial theory is Edward W. Said's *Orientalism* (1978). In this text, Said, who grew up in Egypt and Lebanon, chastises the literary world for not investigating and taking seriously the study of colonization or imperialism. He then establishes several terms and concepts that are central to postcolonial theory. According to Said, nineteenth-century Europeans tried to justify their territorial conquests by propagating a manufactured belief called **Orientalism**: the creation of non-European stereotypes that suggested so-called Orientals were indolent, thoughtless, sexually immoral, unreliable, and demented. The European conquerors, Said notes, believed that they were accurately describing the inhabitants of their newly-acquired lands in "the East." What they failed to realize, maintains Said, is that all human knowledge can be viewed only through one's political, cultural, and ideological framework. No theory, either political or literary, can be totally objective. In effect, what the colonizers were revealing was their unconscious desires for power, wealth, and domination, not the nature of the colonized subjects. In *Culture and Imperialism* (1994), Said captures the basic thought behind colonization and imperialism: " 'They're not like us,' and for that reason deserve to be ruled."

Building on Said's concept of the *other* and the *Oriental*, Homi K. Bhabha, one of the leading voices in postcolonial studies, raises the concerns of the colonized. What of the individual who has been colonized? On the one hand, the colonized observes two somewhat distinct views of the world: that of the colonizer (the conqueror) and that of himself or herself, the colonized (he or she who has been conquered). To what culture does this person belong? Seemingly, neither culture feels like home. This feeling of homelessness, of being caught between two clashing cultures, Bhabha calls **unhomeliness**, a concept referred to as **double consciousness** by other postcolonial theorists. This feeling or perception of abandonment by both cultures causes the colonial subject (the colonized) to become a psychological refugee. Further, because each psychological refugee uniquely blends his or her two cultures, no two writers who have been colonial subjects will interpret their culture(s) exactly alike. Hence, Bhabha argues against the tendency to essentialize third world countries into a homogenous identity. One of Bhabha's major contributions to postcolonial studies is his belief that there is always ambivalence at the site of colonial dominance.

In his pivotal text *The Empire Writes Back* (1989), Bhabha proposes an answer to the colonial subject's sense of unhomeliness. The colonized writer must create a new **discourse** by rejecting all the established **transcendental signifieds** created by the colonizers. Such a writer must also embrace pluralism, believing that no single truth and no metatheory of history exist. To accomplish such goals, Bhabha consistently uses the tools of deconstruction theory to expose cultural metaphors and discourse.

Although Said and Bhabha lay the theoretical foundations of postcolonialism, many other voices have joined them in continuing the dialogue between what Bhabha calls "the Occident" and "the Orient" and a host of other concerns. Concentrating on what some critics call the "flows of culture," postcolonialism subdivides into smaller theoretical schools, identified through their African American, structuralist, poststructuralist, and feminist concerns. For example, Gayatri Spivak, the publisher of the English translation of Jacques Derrida's *Of Grammatology* (1974), is a feminist, postcolonial critic who applies deconstructive interpretations of imperalism while simultaneously questioning the premises of the Marxism, feminism, and Derridean deconstruction which she espouses.

METHODOLOGY

Like many schools of criticism, postcolonialism utilizes a variety of approaches to textual analysis. Deconstruction, feminism, Marxism, reader-response, and African American cultural studies all can lend a hand in interpreting a text from a postcolonial perspective. Of course, it also matters whether or not the one performing the act of literary criticism has been a colonial subject. For those who have been the subjects of colonization must necessarily ask themselves a somewhat different set of questions than those postcolonialists who have not.

The person living and writing in a colonized culture must ask three questions: Who am I? How did I develop into the person I am? and To what country or countries or to what cultures am I forever linked? In asking the first question, the colonized author is connecting himself or herself to historical roots. By asking the second question, the author is admitting a tension between these historical roots and the new culture or hegemony imposed on the writer by the conquerors. By asking the third question, the writer confronts the fact that he or she is both an individual and a social construct created and shaped primarily by the dominant culture. The written works penned by these authors will necessarily be personal and always political and ideological. Furthermore, both the creation of a text and its reading may be painful and disturbing, but also enlightening. Whatever the result, the story will certainly be a message sent back to the Empire, telling the imperialists what they did wrong and how their Western hegemony damaged and suppressed the ideologies of those who were conquered.

Postcolonialists are quick to point out that they do not claim that they make no value judgments. They ask us, their readers and critics, to examine carefully the standards against which we are making our value judgments. Edward Said cautions us that "It is not necessary to regard every reading or interpretation of a text as the moral equivalent of war, but whatever else they are, works of literature are not merely texts" (1994). The postcolonial aim is to read a text in its fullest context, not to remain caught within academic dissection. When reading and analyzing postcolonial texts, we must remember that this diverse and oftentimes psychologically laden and complex theory centers around the "writing back," as Bill Ashcroft notes (1995), of those who have experienced colonial oppression in a variety of circumstances. We must therefore give such texts a close reading, noting particularly the language of the text. Second, we must question the taken-for-granted positions held by the Western mind-set. We must also become more interested in how truth is constructed rather than in exposing errors. Because different prejudices and attitudes may be present from text to text, we must necessarily vary our approach for each text, letting the text itself establish our critical agenda. And we must be forever on guard against ascribing our own cultural ideas into postcolonial works, realizing that any attempt to completely understand a subaltern group will be impossible and can lead to another form of repression.

QUESTIONS FOR ANALYSIS

When applying postcolonialist theory to a text, consider these kinds of questions.

- What happens in the text when the two cultures clash, when one sees itself as superior to another?
- Describe the two cultures exhibited in the text. What does each value? What does each reject?
- Describe the worldviews of each of the cultures exhibited in the text.
- Demonstrate how the superior or privileged culture's hegemony affects the colonized culture.
- How do the colonized people view themselves? Is there any change in this view by the end of of the text?
- Describe the language of the two cultures. How are they alike? Different?
- Cite the various ways in which the colonized culture is silenced.

POSTCOLONIALISM AND AFRICAN AMERICAN CRITICISM

The growing interest in postcolonialism in American literary theory during the late 1970s to the present propelled a renewed interest in African American writers and their works. To say that postcolonialism and/or other postmodern theories initiated African American criticism and theory, however, would be incorrect. For the first seven decades of the twentieth century, **African American criticism** was alive and well, its chief concern being the relationship between the arts—writing, music, theater, poetry, and so forth—and a developing understanding of the nature of African American culture. During this time, writers like Langston Hughes (*The Weary Blues*, 1926; *Not Without Laughter*, 1930), Richard Wright (*Native Son*, 1940; *Black Boy*, 1945), Zora Neale Hurston (*Their Eyes were Watching God*, 1937; *Dust Tracks on a Road*, 1942), James Baldwin (*Go Tell It on the Mountain*, 1953; *The Fire Next Time*, 1963), Ralph Ellison (*The Invisible Man*, 1953), and others wrote texts depicting African Americans interacting with their culture. In this body of literature, these American subaltern writers concerned themselves mainly with issues of nationalism and the exposure of the unjust treatment of African Americans—a suppressed, repressed, and colonized subculture—at the hands of their white conquerors. Presenting a variety of themes in their fiction, essays, and autobiographical writings—the African American's search for personal identity; the bitterness of the struggle of black men and women in America to achieve political, economic, and social success; and both mild and militant pictures of racial protest and hatred— these authors gave to America personal portraits of what it meant to be a black writer struggling with personal, cultural, and national identity.

While literature authored by black writers was gaining in popularity, it was being interpreted through the lens of the dominant culture, a lens that, for the most part, was focused based only on one color—white, the dominant element in the binary opposition white/black as Derrida would state it. A black aesthetics had not yet been established, and critics and theorists alike applied the principles of Western metaphysics and Western hermeneutics to this ever-evolving and steadily increasing body of literature. Although theoretical and critical essays authored by W. E. B. DuBois, Langston Hughes, Richard Wright, and Ralph Ellison had begun to announce to America and the literary world that black literature was a distinctive literary practice with its own aesthetics and should not be dubbed a subcategory or a footnote of American literature, it was not until the late 1970s and into 1980s that black theorists began to articulate the distinctive characteristics of African American literature. In this increasingly important group of literary critics, two stand out: Abdul R. JanMohamed and Henry Louis Gates Jr.

The founding editor of *Cultural Critique*, Abdul JanMohamed is presently one of the most influential postcolonial theorists. A professor of English at the University of California at Berkeley, JanMohamed has authored a variety of scholarly articles and texts that stress the interdisciplinary nature of literary criticism. Raised in Kenya (and therefore not considered by some to be an African American), JanMohamed witnessed firsthand British imperialism and colonial methods that attempt to dominate, to quell, and otherwise eliminate the vital elements of the colonized culture. He has spent his life studying the effects of colonization and the intertwined economic and social dynamics of both the conqueror and the conquered. Of particular importance is his text *Manichean Aesthetics: The Politics of Literature in Colonial Africa* (1983), in which JanMohamed argues that literature authored by the colonized (Africans in Kenya and African Americans in America, for example) is more interesting for its **noematic** value—the complexities of the world it reveals—than for its **noetic** or subjective qualities concerning what it perceives. Consequently, JanMohamed delineates the antagonistic relationship that develops between a hegemonic and a non-hegemonic literature. In African American literature, for example, he notes that black writers like Richard Wright and Frederick Douglass were shaped by their personal socioeconomic conditions. At some point in their development as writers and as persons who were on the archetypal journey of self-realization, these writers became "agents of resistance" and were no longer willing to "consent" to the hegemonic culture. According to JanMohamed, at some time, subaltern writers will resist being shaped by their oppressors and become literary agents of change. It is this process of change from passive observers to resistors that forms the basis of JanMohamed's aesthetics.

Perhaps the most important and leading African American theorist, however, is Henry Louis Gates Jr. Unlike many African American writers and critics, Gates directs much of his attention to other African American critics, declaring that they and he "must redefine 'theory' itself from within [their] own black cultures, refusing to grant the premise that theory is something that white people do. . . . We are all heirs to critical theory, but we black critics are heir to the black vernacular as well" ("Authority, [White] Power, and the [Black] Critic" 344). Accordingly, Gates attempts to provide a theoretical framework for developing a peculiarly African American literary canon. In this new framework, he insists that African American literature be viewed as a form of language, not a representation of social practices or culture. For black literary criticism to develop, he contends that its principles must be derived from the black tradition itself and must include what he calls "the language of blackness, the signifying difference which makes the black tradition our very own." In his texts *The Signifying Monkey* (1988) and *Figures in Black: Words, Signs, and the "Radical" Self* (1987), Gates develops these ideas and announces the "double-voicedness" of African American literature—that is, African American literature draws upon two voices and cultures, the white and the black. It is the joining of these two discourses, Gates declares, that produces the uniqueness of African American literature.

Along with other theorists such as Houston Baker and a host of African American feminist critics, present-day African American critics believe that they must develop a culture-specific theory of African American literature. Theirs, they believe, is a significant discourse that has for too long been neglected. The study of this body of literature, they insist, needs to be re-formed. The beginnings of this reformation has also brought to the foreground another body of literature that has also been ignored or at least relegated to second-class citizenship: the writings of females with its accompanying literary theory, gender studies.

GENDER STUDIES: NEW DIRECTIONS IN FEMINISM

What do Toni Morrison, Alice Walker, and Gloria Naylor have in common? All are African American women writers who have successfully bridged the gap between subaltern authors and the dominant culture. Each has achieved a place of prominence in American culture, with Toni Morrison winning the Nobel Prize in literature in 1993. Thanks, at least in part, to an increasing interest in postcolonial literature, these female authors have not only bridged the cultural but also the gender gap. These writers, who are now models for other women, have found their voice in a society dominated by males and Western metaphysics, and their works have become seminal texts in feminist and gender studies.

Concerned primarily with feminist theories of literature and criticism and sometimes used synonymously with feminism and/or feminist theories (see Chapter 8 for an explanation of feminist theories and practice), **gender studies** broadens traditional feminist criticism to include an investigation not only of "femaleness" but also of "maleness." What does it mean, it asks, to be a "woman" and a "man"? Like traditional feminist theory, gender studies continues to investigate how women and men view such concepts as *ethics*, *definitions of truth*, *personal identity*, and *society*. Is it possible, gender specialists question, that women view each of these differently than men?

Into the multivoiced feminist theories, gender studies adds the ever-growing and increasingly diverse voices of black feminists, the ongoing concerns of French feminism, and the impact of poststructural theories on customary feminist issues. Its authors include those with almost canonical status—writers such as Adrienne Rich, Bonnie Zimmerman, and Barbara Smith—along with oft-cited writers such as Elaine Showalter, Sandra Gilbert, Susan Gubar, Gayatri Chakravorty Spivak, and Toril Moi. New authors and critics such as Yvvonne Vera, Anne McClintlock, Sara Suleri, Dorothea Drummond Mbalia, and Sara Mills also appear, asking and adding their own unique set of questions to feminist theory.

Striving to develop a philosophical bases of feminist literary theory, gender studies re-examines the canon and questions traditional definitions of the family, sexuality, and female reproduction. In addition, it continues to articulate and investigate the nature of feminine writing itself. And it joins feminist scholarship with postcolonial discourses, noting that postcolonial literature and feminist writings share many characteristics, chief among them that both are examples of oppressed peoples.

Like feminist theory, the goal of gender studies is to analyze and challenge the established literary canon. Women themselves, gender specialists assert, must challenge the hegemony and free themselves from the false assumptions and the long-held prejudices that have prevented them from defining themselves. By involving themselves in literary theory and its accompanying practices, gender specialists show their understanding that women and men alike can redefine who they are, what they want to be, and where they wish to go.

SAMPLE ESSAY

The student essay "'The Gentlemen of the Jungle': Or Are They Beasts?" follows at the end of the chapter. How is the colonized culture it describes being oppressed? State the worldviews of the two clashing cultures, as defined by the author, citing elements from the text to support your ideas. How does she characterize the way in which the colonized characters evaluate themselves? What do they think about the colonizers? Do their opinions change? If so, why? Explain how the author suggests the dominant culture's hegemony directly affects the colonial subjects. Does the text reveal anything about the political, social, and economic resistance of the colonized people against the dominant culture? What part does "Othering" play in both the story and in the sample essay? Can you discover any elements of colonial repression within the essay? If so, be able to support your answer.

FURTHER READING

Ashcroft, Bill, Gareth Griffiths, and Helen Tiffin. *The Empire Writes Back: Theory and Practice in Post-Colonial Literatures*. London: Routledge, 1989.

————, eds. *The Post-Colonial Studies Reader*. New York: Routledge, 1995.

Bhabha, Homi K., ed. *Nation and Narration*. New York: Routledge and Keegan Paul, 1990.

————. *The Location of Culture*. New York: Routledge, 1994.

Boehmer, Elleke. *Colonial and Postcolonial Literature: Migrant Metaphors*. New York: Oxford University Press, 1995.

Fanon, Frantz. *The Wretched of the Earth*. Trans. Constance Farrington. New York: Grove, 1968.

Gates, Henry Louis, Jr. *The Signifying Monkey: A Theory of African-American Literary Criticism*. New York: Oxford University Press, 1988.

————. *Loose Canons: Notes on the Culture Wars*. New York: Oxford University Press, 1992.

JanMohamed, Abdul R. *Manichean Aesthetics: The Politics of Literature in Colonial Africa*. Amherst: University of Massachusetts Press, 1983.

Lacapra, Dominick, ed. *The Bounds of Race: Perspectives on Hegemony and Resistance*. Ithaca: Cornell University Press, 1991.

Mohanty, Chandra Talpade, Anne Russo, and Lourdes Torres, eds. *Third World Women and the Politics of Feminism*. Bloomington: Indiana University Press, 1991.

Niranjana, Tejaswine. *Sitting Translation: History, Post-Structuralism, and the Colonial Context*. Berkeley: University of California Press, 1990.

Rushdie, Salman. *Imaginary Homelands: Essays and Criticism, 1981–91*. London: Penguin, 1991.

Said, Edward W. *Culture and Imperialism*. New York: Knopf, 1994.

———. "Figures, Configurations, Transfigurations." *Race & Class* 32.1 (July–September 1990): 1–16.

———. *Orientalism*. New York: Vintage, 1979.

Spivak, Gayatri Chakavorty. "The Making of Americans, the Teaching of English, and the Future of Culture Studies." *New Literary History* 21 (1990): 781–98.

———. *In Other Worlds: Essays in Cultural Politics*. New York: Routledge, 1987.

Suleri, Sara. "Woman Skin Deep: Feminism and the Postcolonial Condition." *Critical Inquiry*, 18 (Summer, 1992): 756–69.

———. *The Rhetoric of English India*. Chicago: University of Chicago Press, 1992.

Tiffin, Helen. "Post-Colonial Literatures and Counter-Discourse." *Kunapipi* 9.3 (1987): 17–34.

Williams, Patrick, and Laura Chrisman, eds. *Colonial Discourse and Post-colonial Theory: A Reader*. New York: Columbia University Press, 1994.

WEB SITES FOR EXPLORATION

www.wsu.edu/~amerstu/tm/poco.html
Provides a discussion of postcolonial theory and practice in American cultural studies

www.library.upenn.edu/special/gallery/kislak/index/biblio.html
Provides a bibliography and links

http://65.107.211.208/poldiscourse/discourseov.html
Provides an overview of theories of colonialism and postcolonialism

www.eng.fju.edu.tw/Literary_Criticism/postcolonism/postcolonial_link.htm
Provides a discussion and relevant links of postcolonial theories in world literature in English

www.emory.edu/ENGLISH/Bahri/AfricanAmerican.html
An introduction to African American postcolonialism

✧ Student Essay ✧

"The Gentlemen of the Jungle": Or Are They Beasts?

Postcolonial critics concern themselves with literature written in the "third world." Specifically, they focus on texts written after colonization ends, and many critics consider anything written after colonization begins to be postcolonial as well. Jomo Kenyatta, an East African writer, vividly portrays the events of colonization and its end in his short story "The Gentlemen of the Jungle."

In Kenyatta's allegorical story, the colonizer and the native of the land start out on friendly terms. Mr. Elephant (Britain) befriends a man (inhabitant of land) and, one day during a thunderstorm, asks the man if he can stick his trunk in the man's hut (land) to keep it dry. The man willingly helps his friend in need, not knowing that soon Mr. Elephant would take over the whole hut (country) and force the man out. Hearing the man begin to protest, the other forest animals (British colonizers) come to see what the problem is between them. Then the lion (ruler) sets up a Commission (British officials) to investigate. Despite the man's concerns, no one from his side is included on the council (due to the inferiority and stupidity of the "savage"). Eventually, the council meets and decides that Mr. Elephant is only fulfilling his God-given right to occupy the hut and put it to the best economic use possible since the man is not able to fill it adequately (because the inhabitants are backward and underdeveloped people). The commission also gives the man permission to rebuild the hut somewhere else (displacement from original culture), but this situation only leads to the same incident recurring (continual oppression) with Mr. Buffalo, Mr. Leopard, and so on. Finally, the man decides that he must defend himself (awakening to the oppression around him) and builds a bigger and newer hut than the ones the animals are currently occupying. The new hut attracts all the jungle animals, and they end up fighting among themselves inside the hut. His plan effectively in place, the man lights the hut on fire (taking steps to end oppression), and everyone burns down with the house (oppression ends). Declaring that "Peace is costly, but it's worth the expense," the man lives happily ever after (free from colonization).

This explanation of the allegory demonstrates how the events of colonization in East Africa as well as other nations came to be, and it touches on life after colonization. Evident throughout this work is an anticolonist attitude. Kenyatta chooses animals to represent the members of the colonizing nation and gentlemen to represent the native inhabitants of the land. Suggesting that the colonizers are beasts conveys the attitude that they are not behaving humanely. Similarly, use of the word *gentlemen* shows that the colonizer's view is wrong and that people of third-world countries are not savages after all.

Kenyatta's text leads us to a central concept of postcolonial theory: *othering*, the division of the world between "us," the "civilized," and "them," the *others* or the "savages." Colonizers repeatedly view themselves as superior to those living in the area they are trying to colonize. Early on, Mr. Elephant tells his "friend," the man, to remain outside during the thunderstorm because his "skin is harder," and he can survive the elements better than he. After this episode, still trusting of these animals, the gentleman innocently believes that the lion is looking out for his best interests. When the Commission is formed, it becomes evident that the man is in an inferior position in the investigation. No one from his side is "well enough educated" to understand how law works. Besides, the council members have divine authority to rule and thus will look after "the interests of race less adequately endowed with teeth and claws." The people of the land are backward and not far enough developed as a nation to rightly use what they own. Clearly, the man is the *other*, unfit to function on his own without the help from superior and divinely appointed rulers. Realizing that something is amiss in these jungle proceedings, the gentleman slowly awakens to the colonization around him. Although the man and Mr. Elephant started out as friends, Mr. Elephant's forceful behavior makes the man realize that perhaps he is not as friendly as he appears. The man "starts to grumble," but these early protests are squelched by the soothing King of the Jungle. Again, the man tries to protest when he has no one from his side on the council, but these words prove futile too. After the council meets, the man wants to tell his version of the story, but this telling cannot occur either. Afraid that violence may ensue, the man acquiesces to the council and relocates to a new hut. After the other jungle inhabitants have taken over this hut and others as well, the man decides that he has had enough and must finally protect himself. Taking steps to end his oppression, he builds a new hut, in the hopes that it will attract all the animals. Successfully, all the animals pile inside and argue among themselves about ownership rights. With dissension among the ruling class, the man takes the final step to end domination: He burns down the hut, and thus all the ruling animals die. Free at last, the man decides that "Peace is costly, but it's worth the expense." Life ends happily ever after, for this man now knows that the colonizers are out of his way. The text suggests, then, through these examples, that freedom from oppressors only occurs when people awaken to the injustices around them and take matters into their own hands.

The statement that the man lives "happily ever after" may seem too simple an ending, but it is reflective of the exuberance and disillusionment that often follows independence from a colonizer. Although Kenyatta's tale is short and simple on the surface, the allegorical undertones refer to a problem that is more serious than a simple tale of an animal living in a man's hut. The saga of colonization, with its detrimental and incrementally aggressive oppression, is indeed a complex tale and would lead most to believe that postcolonial life will now end happily after such forces have been exterminated!

WENDY RADER

Literary Selections

John Keats, "To Autumn" (1820) (Short poem)

Nathaniel Hawthorne, "Ethan Brand" (1850) (Short story)

James Thurber, "The Secret Life of Walter Mitty" (1941) (Short story)

Sandra Cisneros, "The House on Mango Street" (1983)
(Short story from the collection of short stories with the same title)

Edgar Allan Poe, "The City in the Sea" (1831–1845) (short poem)

Washington Irving, "Rip Van Winkle" (1820) (Short story)

Tony Harrison, "Marked with D." (1981) (Short poem)

Nathaniel Hawthorne, "The Maypole of Merry Mount" (1836) (Short story)

Jomo Kenyatta, "The Gentlemen of the Jungle" (ca. 1950) (Short story)

To Autumn (1820)

by John Keats

1

Season of mists and mellow fruitfulness,
   Close bosom-friend of the maturing sun;
Conspiring with him how to load and bless
   With fruit the vines that round the thatch-eaves run;
To bend with apples the mossed cottage-trees,   5
   And fill all fruit with ripeness to the core;
     To swell the gourd, and plump the hazel shells

With a sweet kernel; to set budding more,
And still more, later flowers for the bees,
Until they think warm days will never cease,   10
    For Summer has o'er-brimmed their clammy cells.

2

Who hath not seen thee oft amid thy store?
  Sometimes whoever seeks abroad may find
Thee sitting careless on a granary floor,
  Thy hair soft-lifted by the winnowing wind;   15
Or on a half-reaped furrow sound asleep,
  Drowsed with the fume of poppies, while thy hook
    Spares the next swath and all its twinèd flowers:
And sometimes like a gleaner thou dost keep
  Steady thy laden head across a brook;   20
  Or by a cider-press, with patient look,
    Thou watchest the last oozings hours by hours.

3

Where are the songs of Spring? Aye, where are they?
  Think not of them, thou hast thy music too—
While barrèd clouds bloom the soft-dying day,   25
  And touch the stubble-plains with rosy hue;
Then in a wailful choir the small gnats mourn
  Among the river sallows, borne aloft
    Or sinking as the light wind lives or dies;
And full-grown lambs loud bleat from hilly bourn;   30
  Hedge crickets sing; and now with treble soft
  The redbreast whistles from a garden croft;
    And gathering swallows twitter in the skies.

Ethan Brand (1850)

A Chapter from an Abortive Romance

by Nathaniel Hawthorne

Bartram the lime-burner, a rough, heavy-looking man, begrimed with char-coal, sat watching his kiln at nightfall, while his little son played at building houses with the scattered fragments of marble, when, on the hill-side below them, they heard a roar of laughter, not mirthful, but slow, and even solemn, like a wind shaking the boughs of the forest.

"Father, what is that?" asked the little boy, leaving his play, and pressing betwixt his father's knees.

"Oh, some drunken man, I suppose," answered the lime-burner; "some merry fellow from the bar-room in the village, who dared not laugh loud enough within doors lest he should blow the roof of the house off. So here he is, shaking his jolly sides at the foot of Graylock."

"But, father," said the child, more sensitive than the obtuse, middle-aged clown, "he does not laugh like a man that is glad. So the noise frightens me!"

"Don't be a fool, child!" cried his father, gruffly. "You will never make a man, I do believe; there is too much of your mother in you. I have known the rustling of a leaf startle you. Hark! Here comes the merry fellow now. You shall see that there is no harm in him."

Bartram and his little son, while they were talking thus, sat watching the same lime-kiln that had been the scene of Ethan Brand's solitary and meditative life, before he began his search for the Unpardonable Sin. Many years, as we have seen, had now elapsed, since that portentous night when the IDEA was first developed. The kiln, however, on the mountain-side, stood unimpaired, and was in nothing changed since he had thrown his dark thoughts into the intense glow of its furnace, and melted them, as it were, into the one thought that took possession of his life. It was a rude, round, tower-like structure about twenty feet high, heavily built of rough stones, and with a hillock of earth heaped about the larger part of its circumference; so that the blocks and fragments of marble might be drawn by cart-loads, and thrown in at the top. There was an opening at the bottom of the tower, like an oven-mouth, but large enough to admit a man in a stooping posture, and provided with a massive iron door. With the smoke and jets of flame issuing from the chinks and crevices of this door, which seemed to give admittance into the hill-side, it resembled nothing so much as the private entrance to the infernal regions, which the shepherds of the Delectable Mountains were accustomed to show to pilgrims.

There are many such lime-kilns in that tract of country, for the purpose of burning the white marble which composes a large part of the substance of the hills. Some of them, built years ago, and long deserted, with weeds growing in the vacant round of the interior, which is open to the sky, and grass and wildflowers rooting themselves into the chinks of the stones, look already like relics of antiquity, and may yet be overspread with the lichens of centuries to come. Others, where the lime-burner still feeds his daily and night-long fire, afford points of interest to the wanderer among the hills, who seats himself on a log of wood or a fragment of marble, to hold a chat with the solitary man. It is a lonesome, and, when the character is inclined to thought, may be an intensely thoughtful occupation; as it proved in the case of Ethan Brand, who had mused to such strange purpose, in days gone by, while the fire in this very kiln was burning.

The man who now watched the fire was of a different order, and troubled himself with no thoughts save the very few that were requisite to his business. At frequent intervals, he flung back the clashing weight of the iron door, and, turning his face from the insufferable glare, thrust in huge logs of oak, or stirred the immense brands with a long pole. Within the furnace were seen the curling and riotous flames, and the burning marble, almost molten with the intensity of heat; while without, the reflection of the fire quivered on the dark intricacy of the surrounding forest, and showed in the foreground a bright and ruddy little picture of the hut, the spring beside its door, the athletic and coal-begrimed figure of the lime-burner, and the half-frightened child, shrinking into the protection of his father's shadow. And when, again, the iron door was closed, then reappeared the tender light of the half-full moon, which vainly strove to trace out the indistinct shapes of the neighboring mountains; and, in the upper sky, there was a flitting congregation of clouds, still faintly tinged with the rosy sunset, though thus far down into the valley the sunshine had vanished long and long ago.

The little boy now crept still closer to his father, as footsteps were heard ascending the hill-side, and a human form thrust aside the bushes that clustered beneath the trees.

"Halloo! who is it?" cried the lime-burner, vexed at his son's timidity, yet half infected by it. "Come forward, and show yourself, like a man, or I'll fling this chunk of marble at your head!"

"You offer me a rough welcome," said a gloomy voice, as the unknown man drew nigh. "Yet I neither claim nor desire a kinder one, even at my own fireside."

To obtain a distincter view, Bartram threw open the iron door of the kiln, whence immediately issued a gush of fierce light, that smote full upon the stranger's face and figure. To a careless eye there appeared nothing very remarkable in his aspect, which was that of a man in a coarse, brown, country-made suit of clothes, tall and thin, with the staff and heavy shoes of a wayfarer. As he advanced, he fixed his eyes—which were very bright—intently upon the brightness of the furnace, as if he beheld, or expected to behold, some object worthy of note within it.

"Good evening, stranger," said the lime-burner; "whence come you, so late in the day?"

"I come from my search," answered the wayfarer; "for, at last, it is finished."

"Drunk!—or crazy!" muttered Bartram to himself. "I shall have trouble with the fellow. The sooner I drive him away, the better."

The little boy, all in a tremble, whispered to his father, and begged him to shut the door of the kiln, so that there might not be so much light; for that there was something in the man's face which he was afraid to look at, yet could not look away from. And, indeed, even the lime-burner's dull and torpid sense began to be impressed by an indescribable something in that thin, rugged, thoughtful visage, with the grizzled hair hanging wildly about it, and those deeply sunken eyes, which gleamed like fires within the entrance of a mysterious cavern. But, as he closed the door, the stranger turned towards him, and spoke in a quiet, familiar way, that made Bartram feel as if he were a sane and sensible man, after all.

"Your task draws to an end, I see," said he. "This marble has already been burning three days. A few hours more will convert the stone to lime."

"Why, who are you?" exclaimed the lime-burner. "You seem as well acquainted with my business as I am myself."

"And well I may be," said the stranger; "for I followed the same craft many a long year, and here, too, on this very spot. But you are a new-comer in these parts. Did you never hear of Ethan Brand?"

"The man that went in search of the Unpardonable Sin?" asked Bartram, with a laugh.

"The same," answered the stranger. "He has found what he sought, and therefore he comes back again."

"What! then you are Ethan Brand himself?" cried the lime-burner, in amazement. "I am a new-comer here, as you say, and they call it eighteen years since you left the foot of Graylock. But, I can tell you, the good folks still talk about Ethan Brand, in the village yonder, and what a strange errand took him away from his lime-kiln. Well, and so you have found the Unpardonable Sin?"

"Even so!" said the stranger, calmly.

"If the question is a fair one," proceeded Bartram, "where might it be?"

Ethan Brand laid his finger on his own heart.

"Here!" replied he.

And then, without mirth in his countenance, but as if moved by an involuntary recognition of the infinite absurdity of seeking throughout the world for what was the closest of all things to himself, and looking into every heart, save his own, for what was hidden in no other breast, he broke into a laugh of scorn. It was the same slow, heavy laugh, that had almost appalled the lime-burner when it heralded the wayfarer's approach.

The solitary mountain-side was made dismal by it. Laughter, when out of place, mistimed, or bursting forth from a disordered state of feeling, may be the most terrible modulation of the human voice. The laughter of one asleep, even if it be a little child,—the madman's laugh,—the wild, screaming laugh of a born idiot,—are sounds that we sometimes tremble to hear, and would always willingly forget. Poets have imagined no utterance of fiends or hobgoblins so fearfully appropriate as a laugh. And even the obtuse lime-burner felt his nerves shaken, as this strange man looked inward at his own heart, and burst into laughter that rolled away into the night, and was indistinctly reverberated among the hills.

"Joe," said he to his little son, "scamper down to the tavern in the village, and tell the jolly fellows there that Ethan Brand has come back, and that he has found the Unpardonable Sin!"

The boy darted away on his errand, to which Ethan Brand made no objection, nor seemed hardly to notice it. He sat on a log of wood, looking steadfastly at the iron door of the kiln. When the child was out of sight, and his swift and light footsteps ceased to be heard treading first on the fallen leaves and then on the rocky mountain-path, the lime-burner began to regret his departure. He felt that the little fellow's presence had been a barrier between his guest and himself, and that he must now deal, heart to heart, with a man who, on his own confession, had committed the one only crime for which Heaven could afford no mercy. That crime, in its indistinct blackness, seemed to overshadow him. The lime-burner's own sins rose up within him, and made his memory riotous with a throng of evil shapes that asserted their kindred with the Master Sin, whatever it might be, which it was within the scope of man's corrupted nature to conceive and cherish. They were all of one family; they went to and fro between his breast and Ethan Brand's, and carried dark greetings from one to the other.

Then Bartram remembered the stories which had grown traditionary in reference to this strange man, who had come upon him like a shadow of the night, and was making himself at home in his old place, after so long absence, that the dead people, dead and buried for years, would have had more right to be at home, in any familiar spot, than he. Ethan Brand, it was said, had conversed with Satan himself in the lurid blaze of this very kiln. The legend had been matter of mirth heretofore, but looked grisly now. According to this tale, before Ethan Brand departed on his search, he had been accustomed to evoke a fiend from the hot furnace of the lime-kiln, night after night, in order to confer with him about the Unpardonable Sin; the man and the fiend each laboring to frame the image of some mode of guilt which could neither be atoned for nor forgiven. And, with the first gleam of light upon the mountain-top, the fiend crept in at the iron door, there to abide the intensest element of fire until again summoned forth to share in the dreadful task of extending man's possible guilt beyond the scope of Heaven's else infinite mercy.

While the lime-burner was struggling with the horror of these thoughts, Ethan Brand rose from the log, and flung open the door of the kiln. The action was in such accordance with the idea in Bartram's mind, that he almost expected to see the Evil One issue forth, red-hot, from the raging furnace.

"Hold! hold!" cried he, with a tremulous attempt to laugh; for he was ashamed of his fears, although they overmastered him. "Don't, for mercy's sake, bring out your Devil now!"

"Man!" sternly replied Ethan Brand, "what need have I of the Devil? I have left him behind me, on my track. It is with such half-way sinners as you that he busies himself. Fear not, because I open the door. I do but act by old custom, and am going to trim your fire, like a lime-burner, as I was once."

He stirred the vast coals, thrust in more wood, and bent forward to gaze into the hollow prison-house of the fire, regardless of the fierce glow that reddened upon his face. The lime-burner sat watching him, and half suspected this strange guest of a purpose, if not to evoke a fiend, at least to plunge bodily into the flames, and thus vanish from the sight of man. Ethan Brand, however, drew quietly back, and closed the door of the kiln.

"I have looked," said he, "into many a human heart that was seven times hotter with sinful passions than yonder furnace is with fire. But I found not there what I sought. No, not the Unpardonable Sin!"

"What is the Unpardonable Sin?" asked the lime-burner; and then he shrank farther from his companion, trembling lest his question should be answered.

"It is a sin that grew within my own breast," replied Ethan Brand, standing erect, with a pride that distinguishes all enthusiasts of his stamp. "A sin that grew nowhere else! The sin of an intellect that triumphed over the sense of brotherhood with man and reverence for God, and sacrificed everything to its own mighty claims! The only sin that deserves a recompense of immortal agony! Freely, were it to do again, would I incur the guilt. Unshrinkingly I accept the retribution!"

"The man's head is turned," muttered the lime-burner to himself. "He may be a sinner like the rest of us,—nothing more likely,—but, I'll be sworn, he is a madman too."

Nevertheless, he felt uncomfortable at his situation, alone with Ethan Brand on the wild mountain-side, and was right glad to hear the rough murmur of tongues, and the footsteps of what seemed a pretty numerous party, stumbling over the stones and rustling through the underbrush. Soon appeared the whole lazy regiment that was wont to infest the village tavern, comprehending three or four individuals who had drunk flip beside the bar-room fire through all the winters, and smoked their pipes beneath the stoop through all the summers, since Ethan Brand's departure. Laughing boisterously, and mingling all their voices together in unceremonious talk, they now burst into the moonshine and narrow streaks of firelight that illuminated the open space before the lime-kiln. Bartram set the door ajar again, flooding the spot with light, that the whole company might get a fair view of Ethan Brand, and he of them.

There, among other old acquaintances, was a once ubiquitous man, now almost extinct, but whom we were formerly sure to encounter at the hotel of every thriving village throughout the country. It was the stage-agent. The present specimen of the genus was a wilted and smoke-dried man, wrinkled and red-nosed, in a smartly cut, brown, bobtailed coat, with brass buttons, who, for a length of time unknown, had kept his desk and corner in the bar-room, and was still puffing what seemed to be the same cigar that he had lighted twenty years before. He had great fame as a dry joker, though, perhaps, less on account of any intrinsic humor than from a certain flavor of brandy-toddy and tobacco-smoke, which impregnated all his ideas and expressions, as well as his person. Another well-remembered, though strangely altered, face was that of Lawyer Giles, as people still called him in courtesy; an elderly ragamuffin, in his soiled shirt-sleeves and tow-cloth trousers. This poor fellow had been an attorney, in what he called his better days, a sharp practitioner, and in great vogue among the village litigants; but flip, and sling, and toddy, and cocktails, imbibed at all hours, morning, noon, and night, had caused him to slide from intellectual to various kinds and degrees of bodily labor, till at last, to adopt his own phrase, he slid into a soap-vat. In other words, Giles was now a soap-boiler, in a small way. He had come to be but the fragment of a human being, a part of one foot having been chopped off by an axe, and an entire hand torn away by the devilish grip of a steam-engine. Yet, though the corporeal hand was gone, a spiritual member remained; for, stretching forth the stump, Giles steadfastly averred that he felt an invisible thumb and fingers with as vivid a sensation as before the real ones were amputated. A maimed and miserable wretch he was; but one, nevertheless, whom the world could not trample on, and had no right to scorn, either in this or any previous stage of his misfortunes, since he had still kept up the courage and spirit of a man, asked nothing in charity, and with his one hand—and that the left one—fought a stern battle against want and hostile circumstances.

Among the throng, too, came another personage, who, with certain points of similarity to Lawyer Giles, had many more of difference. It was the village doctor; a man of some fifty years, whom, at an earlier period of his life, we introduced as paying a professional visit to Ethan Brand during the latter's supposed insanity. He was now a purple-visaged, rude, and brutal, yet half-gentlemanly figure, with something wild, ruined, and desperate in his talk, and in all the details of his gesture and manners. Brandy possessed this man like an evil spirit, and made him as surly and savage as a wild beast, and as miserable as a lost soul; but there was supposed to be in him such wonderful skill, such native gifts of healing, beyond any which medical science could impart, that society caught hold of him, and would not let him sink out of its reach. So, swaying to and fro upon his horse, and grumbling thick accents at the bedside, he visited all the sick-chambers for miles about among the mountain towns, and sometimes raised a dying man, as it were; by miracle, or quite as often, no doubt, sent his patient to a grave that was dug many a year too soon. The doctor had an everlasting pipe in his mouth, and, as somebody said, in allusion to his habit of swearing, it was always alight with hell-fire.

These three worthies pressed forward, and greeted Ethan Brand each after his own fashion, earnestly inviting him to partake of the contents of a certain black bottle, in which, as they averred, he would find something far better worth seeking for than the Unpardonable Sin. No mind, which has wrought itself by intense and solitary meditation into a high state of enthusiasm, can endure the kind of contact with low and vulgar modes of thought and feeling to which Ethan Brand was now subjected. It made him doubt—and, strange to say, it was a painful doubt—whether he had indeed found the Unpardonable Sin, and found it within himself. The whole question on which he had exhausted life, and more than life, looked like a delusion.

"Leave me," he said bitterly, "ye brute beasts, that have made yourselves so, shrivelling up your souls with fiery liquors! I have done with you. Years and years ago, I groped into your hearts and found nothing there for my purpose. Get ye gone!"

"Why, you uncivil scoundrel," cried the fierce doctor, "is that the way you respond to the kindness of your best friends? Then let me tell you the truth. You have no more found the Unpardonable Sin than yonder boy Joe has. You are but a crazy fellow,—I told you so twenty years ago,—neither better nor worse than a crazy fellow, and the fit companion of old Humphrey, here!"

He pointed to an old man, shabbily dressed, with long white hair, thin visage, and unsteady eyes. For some years past this aged person had been wandering about among the hills, inquiring of all travellers whom he met for his daughter. The girl, it seemed, had gone off with a company of circus-performers, and occasionally tidings of her came to the village, and fine stories were told of her glittering appearance as she rode on horseback in the ring, or performed marvellous feats on the tight-rope.

The white-haired father now approached Ethan Brand, and gazed unsteadily into his face.

"They tell me you have been all over the earth," said he, wringing his hands with earnestness. "You must have seen my daughter, for she makes a grand figure in the world, and everybody goes to see her. Did she send any word to her old father, or say when she was coming back?"

Ethan Brand's eye quailed beneath the old man's. That daughter, from whom he so earnestly desired a word of greeting, was the Esther of our tale, the very girl whom, with such cold and remorseless purpose, Ethan Brand had made the subject of a psychological experiment, and wasted, absorbed, and perhaps annihilated her soul, in the process.

"Yes," murmured he, turning away from the hoary wanderer, "it is no delusion. There is an Unpardonable Sin!"

While these things were passing, a merry scene was going forward in the area of cheerful light, beside the spring and before the door of the hut. A number of the youth of the village, young men and girls, had hurried up the hill-side, impelled by curiosity to see Ethan Brand, the hero of so many a legend familiar to their childhood. Finding nothing, however, very remarkable in his aspect,—nothing but a sunburnt wayfarer, in plain garb and dusty shoes, who sat looking into the fire as if he fancied pictures among the coals,—these young people speedily grew tired of observing him. As it happened, there was other amusement at hand. An old German Jew travelling with a diorama on his back, was passing down the mountain-road towards the village just as the party turned aside from it, and, in hopes of eking out the profits of the day, the showman had kept them company to the lime-kiln.

"Come, old Dutchman," cried one of the young men, "let us see your pictures, if you can swear they are worth looking at!"

"Oh yes, Captain," answered the Jew,—whether as a matter of courtesy or craft, he styled everybody Captain,—"I shall show you, indeed, some very superb pictures!"

So, placing his box in a proper position, he invited the young men and girls to look through the glass orifices of the machine, and proceeded to exhibit a series of the most outrageous scratchings and daubings, as specimens of the fine arts, that ever an itinerant showman had the face to impose upon his circle of spectators. The pictures were worn out, moreover, tattered, full of cracks and wrinkles, dingy with tobacco-smoke, and otherwise in a most pitiable condition. Some purported to be cities, public edifices, and ruined castles in Europe; others represented Napoleon's battles and Nelson's sea-fights; and in the midst of these would be seen a gigantic, brown, hairy hand,—which might have been mistaken for the Hand of Destiny, though, in truth, it was only the showman's,—pointing its forefinger to various scenes of the conflict, while its owner gave historical illustrations. When, with much merriment at its abominable deficiency of merit, the exhibition was concluded, the German bade little Joe put his head into the box. Viewed through the magnifying-glasses, the boy's round, rosy visage assumed the strangest imaginable aspect of an immense Titanic child, the mouth grinning broadly, and the eyes and every other feature overflowing with fun at the joke. Suddenly, however, that merry face turned pale, and its expression changed to horror, for this easily impressed and excitable child had become sensible that the eye of Ethan Brand was fixed upon him through the glass.

"You make the little man to be afraid, Captain," said the German Jew, turning up the dark and strong outline of his visage from his stooping posture. "But look again, and, by chance, I shall cause you to see somewhat that is very fine, upon my word!"

Ethan Brand gazed into the box for an instant, and then starting back, looked fixedly at the German. What had he seen? Nothing, apparently; for a curious youth, who had peeped in almost at the same moment, beheld only a vacant space of canvas.

"I remember you now," muttered Ethan Brand to the showman.

"Ah, Captain," whispered the Jew of Nuremburg, with a dark smile, "I find it to be a heavy matter in my show-box,—this Unpardonable Sin! By my faith, Captain, it has wearied my shoulders, this long day, to carry it over the mountain."

"Peace," answered Ethan Brand, sternly, "or get thee into the furnace yonder!"

The Jew's exhibition had scarcely concluded, when a great, elderly dog—who seemed to be his own master, as no person in the company laid claim to him—saw fit to render himself the object of public notice. Hitherto, he had shown himself a very quiet, well-disposed old dog, going round from one to another, and, by way of being sociable, offering his rough head to be patted by any kindly hand that would take so much trouble. But now, all of a sudden, this grave and venerable quadruped, of his own mere motion, and without the slightest suggestion from anybody else, began to run round after his tail, which, to heighten the absurdity of the proceeding, was a great deal shorter than it should have been. Never was seen such headlong eagerness in pursuit of an object that could not possibly be attained; never was heard such a tremendous outbreak of growling, snarling, barking, and snapping,—as if one end of the ridiculous brute's body were at deadly and most unforgivable enmity with the other. Faster and faster, round about went the cur; and faster and still faster fled the unapproachable brevity of his tail; and louder and fiercer grew his yells of rage and animosity; until, utterly exhausted, and as far from the goal as ever, the foolish old dog ceased his performance as suddenly as he had begun it. The next moment he was as mild, quiet, sensible, and respectable in his deportment, as when he first scraped acquaintance with the company.

As may be supposed, the exhibition was greeted with universal laughter, clapping of hands, and shouts of encore, to which the canine performer responded by wagging all that there was to wag of his tail, but appeared totally unable to repeat his very successful effort to amuse the spectators.

Meanwhile, Ethan Brand had resumed his seat upon the log, and moved, it might be, by a perception of some remote analogy between his own case and that of this self-pursuing cur, he broke into the awful laugh, which, more than any other token, expressed the condition of his inward being. From that moment, the merriment of the party was at an end; they stood aghast, dreading lest the inauspicious sound should be reverberated around the horizon, and that mountain would thunder it to mountain, and so the horror be prolonged upon their ears. Then, whispering one to another that it was late,—that the moon was almost down,—that the August night was growing chill,—they hurried homewards, leaving the lime-burner and little Joe to deal as they might with their unwelcome guest. Save for these three human beings, the open space on the hill-side was a solitude, set in a vast gloom of forest. Beyond that darksome verge, the firelight glimmered on the stately trunks and almost black foliage of pines, intermixed with the lighter verdure of sapling oaks, maples, and poplars, while here and there lay the gigantic corpses of dead trees, decaying on the leaf-strewn soil. And it seemed to little Joe—a timorous and imaginative child—that the silent forest was holding its breath until some fearful thing should happen.

Ethan Brand thrust more wood into the fire, and closed the door of the kiln; then looking over his shoulder at the lime-burner and his son, he bade, rather than advised, them to retire to rest.

"For myself, I cannot sleep," said he. "I have matters that it concerns me to meditate upon. I will watch the fire, as I used to do in the old time."

"And call the Devil out of the furnace to keep you company, I suppose," muttered Bartram, who had been making intimate acquaintance with the black bottle above mentioned. "But watch, if you like, and call as many devils as you like! For my part, I shall be all the better for a snooze. Come, Joe!"

As the boy followed his father into the hut, he looked back at the wayfarer, and the tears came into his eyes, for his tender spirit had an intuition of the bleak and terrible loneliness in which this man had enveloped himself.

When they had gone, Ethan Brand sat listening to the crackling of the kindled wood, and looking at the little spirts of fire that issued through the chinks of the door. These trifles, however, once so familiar, had but the slightest hold of his attention, while deep within his mind he was reviewing the gradual but marvelous change that had been wrought upon him by the search to which he had devoted himself. He remembered how the night dew had fallen upon him,—how the dark forest had whispered to him,—how the stars had gleamed upon him,—a simple and loving man, watching his fire in the years gone by, and ever musing as it burned. He remembered with what tenderness, with what love and sympathy for mankind, and what pity for human guilt and woe, he had first begun to contemplate those ideas which afterwards became the inspiration of his life; with what reverence he had then looked into the heart of man, viewing it as a temple originally divine, and, however desecrated, still to be held sacred by a brother; with what awful fear he had deprecated the success of his pursuit, and prayed that the Unpardonable Sin might never be revealed to him. Then ensued that vast intellectual development, which, in its progress, disturbed the counterpoise between his mind and heart. The Idea that possessed his life had operated as a means of education; it had gone on cultivating his powers to the highest point of which they were susceptible; it had raised him from the level of an unlettered laborer to stand on a star-lit eminence, whither the philosophers of the earth, laden with the lore of universities, might vainly strive to clamber after him. So much for the intellect! But where was the heart? That, indeed, had withered,—had contracted,—had hardened,—had perished! It had ceased to partake of the universal throb.

He had lost his hold of the magnetic chain of humanity. He was no longer a brother-man, opening the chambers or the dungeons of our common nature by the key of holy sympathy, which gave him a right to share in all its secrets; he was now a cold observer, looking on mankind as the subject of his experiment, and, at length, converting man and woman to be his puppets, and pulling the wires that moved them to such degrees of crime as were demanded for his study.

Thus Ethan Brand became a fiend. He began to be so from the moment that his moral nature had ceased to keep the pace of improvement with his intellect. And now, as his highest effort and inevitable development,—as the bright and gorgeous flower; and rich, delicious fruit of his life's labor,—he had produced the Unpardonable Sin!

"What more have I to seek? what more to achieve?" said Ethan Brand to himself. "My task is done, and well done!"

Starting from the log with a certain alacrity in his gait and ascending the hillock of earth that was raised against the stone circumference of the lime-kiln, he thus reached the top of the structure. It was a space of perhaps ten feet across, from edge to edge, presenting a view of the upper surface of the immense mass of broken marble with which the kiln was heaped. All these innumerable blocks and fragments of marble were red-hot and vividly on fire, sending up great spouts of blue flame, which quivered aloft and danced madly, as within a magic circle, and sank and rose again, with continual and multitudinous activity. As the lonely man bent forward over this terrible body of fire, the blasting heat smote up against his person with a breath that, it might be supposed, would have scorched and shrivelled him up in a moment.

Ethan Brand stood erect, and raised his arms on high. The blue flames played upon his face, and imparted the wild and ghastly light which alone could have suited its expression; it was that of a fiend on the verge of plunging into his gulf of intensest torment.

"O Mother Earth," cried he, "who art no more my Mother, and into whose bosom this frame shall never be resolved! O mankind, whose brotherhood I have cast off, and trampled thy great heart beneath my feet! O stars of heaven, that shone on me of old, as if to light me onward and upward!—farewell all, and forever. Come, deadly element of Fire,—henceforth my familiar friend! Embrace me, as I do thee!"

That night the sound of a fearful peal of laughter rolled heavily through the sleep of the lime-burner and his little son; dim shapes of horror and anguish haunted their dreams, and seemed still present in the rude hovel, when they opened their eyes to the day-light.

"Up, boy, up!" cried the lime-burner, staring about him. "Thank Heaven, the night is gone, at last; and rather than pass such another, I would watch my lime-kiln, wide awake, for a twelvemonth. This Ethan Brand, with his humbug of an Unpardonable Sin, has done me no such mighty favor, in taking my place!"

He issued from the hut, followed by little Joe, who kept fast hold of his father's hand. The early sunshine was already pouring its gold upon the mountaintops, and though the valleys were still in shadow, they smiled cheerfully in the promise of the bright day that was hastening onward. The village, completely shut in by hills, which swelled away gently about it, looked as if it had rested peacefully in the hollow of the great hand of Providence. Every dwelling was distinctly visible; the little spires of the two churches pointed upwards, and caught a fore-glimmering of brightness from the sun-gilt skies upon their gilded weather-cocks. The tavern was astir, and the figure of the old, smoke-dried stage-agent, cigar in mouth, was seen beneath the stoop. Old Graylock was glorified with a golden cloud upon his head. Scattered likewise over the breasts of the surrounding mountains, there were heaps of hoary mist, in fantastic shapes, some of them far down into the valley, others high up towards the summits, and still others, of the same family of mist or cloud, hovering in the gold radiance of the upper atmosphere. Stepping from one to another of the clouds that rested on the hills, and thence to the loftier brotherhood that sailed in air, it seemed almost as if a mortal man might thus ascend into the heavenly regions. Earth was so mingled with sky that it was a day-dream to look at it.

To supply that charm of the familiar and homely, which Nature so readily adopts into a scene like this, the stage-coach was rattling down the mountain-road, and the driver sounded his horn, while Echo caught up the notes, and intertwined them into a rich and varied and elaborate harmony, of which the original performer could lay claim to little share. The great hills played a concert among themselves, each contributing a strain of airy sweetness.

Little Joe's face brightened at once.

"Dear father," cried he, skipping cheerily to and fro, "that strange man is gone, and the sky and the mountains all seem glad of it!"

"Yes," growled the lime-burner, with an oath, "but he has let the fire go down, and no thanks to him if five hundred bushels of lime are not spoiled. If I catch the fellow hereabouts again, I shall feel like tossing him into the furnace!"

With his long pole in his hand, he ascended to the top of the kiln. After a moment's pause, he called to his son.

"Come up here, Joe!" said he.

So little Joe ran up the hillock, and stood by his father's side. The marble was all burnt into perfect, snow-white lime. But on its surface, in the midst of the circle,—snow-white too, and thoroughly converted into lime,—lay a human skeleton, in the attitude of a person who, after long toil, lies down to long repose. Within the ribs—strange to say—was the shape of a human heart.

"Was the fellow's heart made of marble?" cried Bartram, in some perplexity at this phenomenon. "At any rate, it is burnt into what looks like special good lime; and, taking all the bones together, my kiln is half a bushel the richer for him."

So saying, the rude lime-burner lifted his pole, and, letting it fall upon the skeleton, the relics of Ethan Brand were crumbled into fragments.

The Secret Life of Walter Mitty (1941)

by James Thurber

"We're going through!" The Commander's voice was like thin ice breaking. He wore his full-dress uniform, with the heavily braided white cap pulled down rakishly over one cold gray eye. "We can't make it, sir. It's spoiling for a hurricane, if you ask me." "I'm not asking you, Lieutenant Berg," said the Commander. "Throw on the power lights! Rev her up to 8,500! We're going through!" The pounding of the cylinders increased: ta-pocketa-pocketa-pocketa-*pocketa-pocketa*. The Commander stared at the ice forming on the pilot window. He walked over and twisted a row of complicated dials. "Switch on No. 8 auxiliary!" he shouted. "Switch on No. 8 auxiliary!" repeated Lieutenant Berg. "Full strength in No. 3 turret!" shouted the Commander. "Full strength in No. 3 turret!" The crew, bending to their various tasks in the huge, hurtling eight-engined Navy hydroplane, looked at each other and grinned. "The Old Man'll get us through," they said to one another. "The Old Man ain't afraid of Hell!" . . .

"Not so fast! You're driving too fast!" said Mrs. Mitty. "What are you driving so fast for?"

"Hmm?" said Walter Mitty. He looked at his wife, in the seat beside him, with shocked astonishment. She seemed grossly unfamiliar, like a strange woman who had yelled at him in a crowd. "You were up to fifty-five," she said. "You know I don't like to go more than forty. You were up to fifty-five." Walter Mitty drove on toward Waterbury in silence, the roaring of the SN202 through the worst storm in twenty years of Navy flying fading in the remote, intimate airways of his mind. "You're tensed up again," said Mrs. Mitty. "It's one of your days. I wish you'd let Dr. Renshaw look you over."

Walter Mitty stopped the car in front of the building where his wife went to have her hair done. "Remember to get those overshoes while I'm having my hair done," she said. "I don't need overshoes," said Mitty. She put her mirror back into her bag. "We've been all through that," she said, getting out of the car. "You're not a young man any longer." He raced the engine a little. "Why don't you wear your gloves? Have you lost your gloves?" Walter Mitty reached in a pocket and brought out the gloves. He put them on, but after she had turned and gone into the building and he had driven on to a red light, he took them off again. "Pick it up, brother!" snapped a cop as the light changed, and Mitty hastily pulled on his gloves and lurched ahead. He drove around the streets aimlessly for a time, and then he drove past the hospital on his way to the parking lot.

. . . "It's the millionaire banker, Wellington McMillan," said the pretty nurse. "Yes?" said Walter Mitty, removing his gloves slowly. "Who has the case?" "Dr. Renshaw and Dr. Benbow, but there are two specialists here, Dr. Remington from New York and Mr. Pritchard-Mitford from London. He flew over." A door opened down a long, cool corridor and Dr. Renshaw came out. He looked distraught and haggard. "Hello, Mitty," he said. "We're having the devil's own time with McMillan, the millionaire banker and close personal friend of Roosevelt. Obstreosis of the ductal tract. Tertiary. Wish you'd take a look at him." "Glad to," said Mitty.

In the operating room there were whispered introductions: "Dr. Remington, Dr. Mitty. Mr. Pritchard-Mitford, Dr. Mitty." "I've read your book on streptothricosis," said Pritchard-Mitford, shaking hands. "A brilliant performance, sir." "Thank you," said Walter Mitty. "Didn't know you were in the States, Mitty," grumbled Remington. "Coals to Newcastle, bringing Mitford and me up here for a tertiary." "You are very kind," said Mitty. A huge, complicated machine, connected to the operating table, with many tubes and wires, began at this moment to go pocketa-pocketa-pocketa. "The new anesthetizer is giving way!" shouted an interne. "There is no one in the East who knows how to fix it!" "Quiet, man!" said Mitty, in a low, cool voice. He sprang to the machine, which was now going pocketa-pocketa-queep-pocketa-queep. He began fingering delicately a row of glistening dials. "Give me a fountain pen!" he snapped. Someone handed him a fountain pen. He pulled a faulty piston out of the machine and inserted the pen in its place. "That will hold for ten minutes," he said. "Get on with the operation." A nurse hurried over and whispered to Renshaw, and Mitty saw the man turn pale. "Coreopsis has set in," said Renshaw nervously. "If you would take over, Mitty?" Mitty looked at him and at the craven figure of Benbow, who drank, and at the grave, uncertain faces of the two great specialists. "If you wish," he said. They slipped a white gown on him; he adjusted a mask and drew on thin gloves; nurses handed him shining . . .

"Back it up, Mac! Look out for that Buick!" Walter Mitty jammed on the brakes. "Wrong lane, Mac," said the parking-lot attendant, looking at Mitty closely. "Gee. Yeh," muttered Mitty. He began cautiously to back out of the lane marked "Exit Only." "Leave her sit there," said the attendant. "I'll put her away." Mitty got out of the car. "Hey, better leave the key." "Oh," said Mitty, handing the man the ignition key. The attendant vaulted into the car, backed it up with insolent skill, and put it where it belonged.

They're so damn cocky, thought Walter Mitty, walking along Main Street; they think they know everything. Once he had tried to take his chains off, outside New Milford, and he had got them wound around the axles. A man had had to come out in a wrecking car and unwind them, a young, grinning garageman. Since then Mrs. Mitty always made him drive to a garage to have the chains taken off. The next time, he thought, I'll wear my right arm in a sling; they won't grin at me then. I'll have my right arm in a sling and they'll see I couldn't possibly take the chains off myself. He kicked at the slush on the sidewalk. "Overshoes," he said to himself, and he began look- ing for a shoe store.

When he came out into the street again, with the overshoes in a box under his arm, Walter Mitty began to wonder what the other thing was his wife had told him to get. She had told him, twice, before they set out from their house for Waterbury. In a way he hated these weekly trips to town—he was always getting something wrong. Kleenex, he thought, Squibb's, razor blades? No. Toothpaste, toothbrush, bicarbonate, carborundum, initiative and referendum? He gave it up. But she would remember it. "Where's the what's-its-name?" she would ask. "Don't tell me you forgot the what's-its- name." A newsboy went by shouting something about the Waterbury trial.

. . . "Perhaps this will refresh your memory." The District Attorney sud- denly thrust a heavy automatic at the quiet figure on the witness stand. "Have you ever seen this before?" Walter Mitty took the gun and examined it expertly. "This is my Webley-Vickers 50.80," he said calmly. An excited buzz ran around the courtroom. The Judge rapped for order. "You are a crack shot with any sort of firearms, I believe?" said the District Attorney, insinuatingly. "Objection!" shouted Mitty's attorney. "We have shown that the defendant could not have fired the shot. We have shown that he wore his right arm in a sling on the night of the fourteenth of July." Walter Mitty raised his hand briefly and the bickering attorneys were stilled. "With any known make of gun," he said evenly, "I could have killed Gregory Fitzhurst at three hundred feet *with my left hand*." Pandemonium broke loose in the courtroom. A woman's scream rose above the bedlam and suddenly a lovely, dark-haired girl was in Walter Mitty's arms. The District Attorney struck at her savagely. Without rising from his chair, Mitty let the man have it on the point of the chin. "You miserable cur!" . . .

"Puppy biscuit," said Walter Mitty. He stopped walking and the build- ings of Waterbury rose up out of the misty courtroom and surrounded him again. A woman who was passing laughed. "He said 'Puppy biscuit,'" she said to her companion. "That man said 'Puppy biscuit' to himself." Walter Mitty hurried on. He went into an A. & P., not the first one he came to but a smaller one farther up the street. "I want some biscuit for small, young dogs," he said to the clerk. "Any special brand, sir?" The greatest pistol shot in the world thought a moment. "It says 'Puppies Bark for It' on the box," said Walter Mitty.

His wife would be through at the hairdresser's in fifteen minutes, Mitty saw in looking at his watch, unless they had trouble drying it; sometimes they had trouble drying it. She didn't like to get to the hotel first; she would want him to be there waiting for her as usual. He found a big leather chair in the lobby, facing a window, and he put the overshoes and the puppy biscuit on the floor beside it. He picked up an old copy of *Liberty* and sank down into the chair. "Can Germany Conquer the World Through the Air?" Walter Mitty looked at the pictures of bombing planes and of ruined streets.
. . . "The cannonading has got the wind up in young Raleigh, sir," said the sergeant. Captain Mitty looked up at him through touseled hair. "Get him to bed," he said wearily. "With the others. I'll fly alone." "But you can't, sir," said the sergeant anxiously. "It takes two men to handle that bomber and the Archies are pounding hell out of the air. Von Richtman's circus is between here and Saulier." "Somebody's got to get that ammunition dump," said Mitty. "I'm going over. Spot of brandy?" He poured a drink for the sergeant and one for himself. War thundered and whined around the dugout and battered at the door. There was a rending of wood and splinters flew through the room. "A bit of a near thing," said Captain Mitty carelessly. "The box barrage is closing in," said the sergeant. "We only live once, Sergeant," said Mitty, with his faint, fleeting smile. "Or do we?" He poured another brandy and tossed it off. "I never see a man could hold his brandy like you, sir," said the sergeant. "Begging your pardon, sir." Captain Mitty stood up and strapped on his huge Webley-Vickers automatic. "It's forty kilometers through hell, sir," said the sergeant. Mitty finished one last brandy. "After all," he said softly, "what isn't?" The pounding of the cannon increased; there was the rat-tat-tatting of machine guns, and from somewhere came the menacing pocketa-pocketa-pocketa of the new flamethrowers. Walter Mitty walked to the door of the dugout humming "Auprès de Ma Blonde." He turned and waved to the sergeant. "Cheerio!" he said. . . .
Something struck his shoulder. "I've been looking all over this hotel for you," said Mrs. Mitty. "Why do you have to hide in this old chair? How did you expect me to find you?" "Things close in," said Walter Mitty vaguely. "What?" Mrs. Mitty said. "Did you get the what's-its-name? The puppy biscuit? What's in that box?" "Overshoes," said Mitty. "Couldn't you have put them on in the store?" "I was thinking," said Walter Mitty. "Does it ever

occur to you that I am sometimes thinking?" She looked at him. "I'm going to take your temperature when I get you home," she said.

They went out through the revolving doors that made a faintly derisive whistling sound when you pushed them. It was two blocks to the parking lot. At the drugstore on the corner she said, "Wait here for me. I forgot something. I won't be a minute." She was more than a minute. Walter Mitty lighted a cigarette. It began to rain, rain with sleet in it. He stood up against the wall of the drugstore, smoking. . . . He put his shoulders back and his heels together. "To hell with the handkerchief," said Walter Mitty scornfully. He took one last drag on his cigarette and snapped it away. Then, with that faint, fleeting smile playing about his lips, he faced the firing squad; erect and motionless, proud and disdainful, Walter Mitty the Undefeated, in-scrutable to the last.

The House on Mango Street (1983)

by Sandra Cisneros

We didn't always live on Mango Street. Before that we lived on Loomis on the third floor, and before that we lived on Keeler. Before Keeler it was Paulina, and before that I can't remember. But what I remember most is moving a lot. Each time it seemed there'd be one more of us. By the time we got to Mango Street we were six—Mama, Papa, Carlos, Kiki, my sister Nenny and me.

The house on Mango Street is ours and we don't have to pay rent to any-body or share the yard with the people downstairs or be careful not to make too much noise and there isn't a landlord banging on the ceiling with a broom. But even so, it's not the house we'd thought we'd get.

We had to leave the flat on Loomis quick. The water pipes broke and the landlord wouldn't fix them because the house was too old. We had to leave fast. We were using the washroom next door and carrying water over in empty milk gallons. That's why Mama and Papa looked for a house, and that's why we moved into the house on Mango Street, far away, on the other side of town.

They always told us that one day we would move into a house, a real house that would be ours for always so we wouldn't have to move each year. And our house would have running water and pipes that worked. And inside it would have real stairs, not hallway stairs, but stairs inside like the houses on T.V. And we'd have a basement and at least three washrooms so when we took a bath we didn't have to tell everybody. Our house would be white with trees around it, a great big yard and grass growing without a fence. This was the house Papa talked about when he held a lottery ticket and this was the house Mama dreamed up in the stories she told us before we went to bed.

But the house on Mango Street is not the way they told it at all. It's small and red with tight little steps in front and windows so small you'd think they were holding their breath. Bricks are crumbling in places, and the front door is so swollen you have to push hard to get in. There is no front yard, only four little elms the city planted by the curb. Out back is a small garage for the car we don't own yet and a small yard that looks smaller between the two buildings on either side. There are stairs in our house, but they're ordinary hallway stairs, and the house has only one washroom, very small. Everybody has to share a bedroom—Mama and Papa, Carlos and Kiki, me and Nenny.

Once when we were living on Loomis, a nun from my school passed by and saw me playing out front. The laundromat downstairs had been boarded up because it had been robbed two days before and the owner had painted on the wood YES WE'RE OPEN so as not to lose business.

> Where do you live? she asked.
> There, I said pointing up to the third floor.
> You live *there*?

There. I had to look to where she pointed—the third floor, the paint peeling, wooden bars Papa had nailed on the windows so we wouldn't fall out. You live *there*? The way she said it made me feel like nothing. *There.* I lived *there.* I nodded.

I knew then I had to have a house. A real house. One I could point to. But this isn't it. The house on Mango Street isn't it. For the time being, Mama says. Temporary, says Papa. But I know how those things go.

The City in the Sea (1831–1845)

by Edgar Allan Poe

Lo! Death has reared himself a throne
In a strange city lying alone
Far down within the dim West,
Where the good and the bad and the worst and the best
Have gone to their eternal rest.   5
There shrines and palaces and towers
(Time-eaten towers that tremble not!)

Resemble nothing that is ours.
Around, by lifting winds forgot,
Resignedly beneath the sky   10
The melancholy waters lie.

No rays from the holy heaven come down
On the long night-time of that town;
But light from out the lurid sea
Streams up the turrets silently—   15
Gleams up the pinnacles far and free
Up domes—up spires—up kingly halls—
Up fanes—up Babylon-like walls—
Up shadowy long-forgotten bowers
Of sculptured ivy and stone flowers—   20
Up many and many a marvellous shrine
Whose wreathéd friezes intertwine
The viol, the violet, and the vine.
Resignedly beneath the sky
The melancholy waters lie.   25
So blend the turrets and shadows there
That all seem pendulous in air,
While from a proud tower in the town
Death looks gigantically down.

There open fanes and gaping graves   30
Yawn level with the luminous waves;
But not the riches there that lie
In each idol's diamond eye—
Not the gaily-jewelled dead
Tempt the waters from their bed;   35
For no ripples curl, alas!
Along that wilderness of glass—
No swellings tell that winds may be
Upon some far-off happier sea—
No heavings hint that winds have been   40
On seas less hideously serene.

But lo, a stir is in the air!
The wave—there is a movement there!
As if the towers had thrust aside,
In slightly sinking, the dull tide—   45
As if their tops had feebly given
A void within the filmy Heaven.
The waves have now a redder glow—
The hours are breathing faint and low—
And when, amid no earthly moans,   50
Down, down that town shall settle hence,
Hell, rising from a thousand thrones,
Shall do it reverence.

Rip Van Winkle (1820)

A posthumous writing of Diedrich Knickerbocker

by Washington Irving

By Woden, God of Sacons,
From whence comes Wensday, that is Wodensday.
Truth is a thing that ever I will keep
Unto thylke day in which I creep into
My sepulchre—
  Cartwright

[The following Tale was found among the papers of the late Diedrich Knickerbocker, an old gentleman of New York, who was very curious in the Dutch history of the province, and the manners of the descendants from its primitive settlers. His historical researches, however, did not lie so much among books as among men; for the former are lamentably scanty on his favorite topics; whereas he found the old burghers, and still more their wives, rich in that legendary lore, so invaluable to true history. Whenever, therefore, he happened upon a genuine Dutch family, snugly shut up in its low-roofed farmhouse, under a spreading sycamore, he looked upon it as a little clasped volume of black-letter, and studied it with the zeal of a book-worm.

The result of all these researches was a history of the province during the reign of the Dutch governors, which he published some years since. There have been various opinions as to the literary character of his work, and, to tell the truth, it is not a whit better than it should be. Its chief merit is its scrupulous accuracy, which indeed was a little questioned on its first appearance, but has since been completely established; and it is now admitted into all historical collections, as a book of unquestionable authority.

The old gentleman died shortly after the publication of his work, and now that he is dead and gone, it cannot do much harm to his memory to say that his time might have been much better employed in weightier labors. He, however, was apt to ride his hobby his own way; and though it did now and then kick up the dust a little in the eyes of his neighbors, and grieve the spirit of some friends, for whom he felt the truest deference and affection; yet his errors and follies are remembered "more in sorrow than in anger," and it begins to be suspected, that he never intended to injure or offend. But however his memory may be appreciated by critics, it is still held dear by many folk, whose good opinion is well worth having; particularly by certain biscuit-bakers, who have gone so far as to imprint his likeness on their new-year cakes; and have thus given him a chance for immortality, almost equal to the being stamped on a Waterloo Medal, or a Queen Anne's Farthing.]

Whoever has made a voyage up the Hudson must remember the Kaatskill mountains. They are a dismembered branch of the great Appalachian family, and are seen away to the west of the river, swelling up to a noble height, and lording it over the surrounding country. Every change of season, every change of weather, indeed, every hour of the day, produces some change in the magical hues and shapes of these mountains, and they are regarded by all the good wives, far and near, as perfect barometers. When the weather is fair and settled, they are clothed in blue and purple, and print their bold outlines on the clear evening sky; but, sometimes, when the rest of the landscape is cloudless, they will gather a hood of gray vapors about their summits, which, in the last rays of the setting sun, will glow and light up like a crown of glory.

At the foot of these fairy mountains, the voyager may have descried the light smoke curling up from a village, whose shingle-roofs gleam among the trees, just where the blue tints of the upland melt away into the fresh green of the nearer landscape. It is a little village, of great antiquity, having been founded by some of the Dutch colonists, in the early times of the province, just about the beginning of the government of the good Peter Stuyvesant, (may he rest in peace!) and there were some of the houses of the original settlers standing within a few years, built of small yellow bricks brought from Holland, having latticed windows and gable fronts, surmounted with weather-cocks.

In that same village, and in one of these very houses (which, to tell the precise truth, was sadly time-worn and weather-beaten), there lived many years since, while the country was yet a province of Great Britain, a simple good-natured fellow, of the name of Rip Van Winkle. He was a descendant of the Van Winkles who figured so gallantly in the chivalrous days of Peter Stuyvesant, and accompanied him to the siege of Fort Christina. He inherited, however, but little of the martial character of his ancestors. I have observed that he was a simple good-natured man; he was, moreover, a kind neighbor, and an obedient hen-pecked husband. Indeed, to the latter circumstance might be owing that meekness of spirit which gained him such universal popularity; for those men are most apt to be obsequious and conciliating abroad, who are under the discipline of shrews at home. Their tempers, doubtless, are rendered pliant and malleable in the fiery furnace of domestic tribulation; and a curtain lecture is worth all the sermons in the world for teaching the virtues of patience and long-suffering. A termagant wife may, therefore, in some respects, be considered a tolerable blessing; and if so, Rip Van Winkle was thrice blessed.

Certain it is, that he was a great favorite among all the good wives of the village, who, as usual, with the amiable sex, took his part in all family squabbles; and never failed, whenever they talked those matters over in their evening gossipings, to lay all the blame on Dame Van Winkle. The children of the village, too, would shout with joy whenever he approached. He assisted at their sports, made their playthings, taught them to fly kites and shoot marbles, and told them long stories of ghosts, witches, and Indians. Whenever he went dodging about the village, he was surrounded by a troop of them, hanging on his skirts, clambering on his back, and playing a thousand tricks on him with impunity; and not a dog would bark at him throughout the neighborhood.

The great error in Rip's composition was an insuperable aversion to all kinds of profitable labor. It could not be from the want of assiduity or perseverance; for he would sit on a wet rock, with a rod as long and heavy as a Tartar's lance, and fish all day without a murmur, even though he should not be encouraged by a single nibble. He would carry a fowling-piece on his shoulder for hours together, trudging through woods and swamps, and up hill and down dale, to shoot a few squirrels or wild pigeons. He would never refuse to assist a neighbor even in the roughest toil, and was a foremost man at all country frolics for husking Indian corn, or building stone-fences; the women of the village, too, used to employ him to run their errands, and to do such little odd jobs as their less obliging husbands would not do for them. In a word Rip was ready to attend to anybody's business but his own; but as to doing family duty, and keeping his farm in order, he found it impossible.

In fact, he declared it was of no use to work on his farm; it was the most pestilent little piece of ground in the whole country; every thing about it went wrong, and would go wrong, in spite of him. His fences were continually falling to pieces; his cow would either go astray, or get among the cabbages; weeds were sure to grow quicker in his fields than anywhere else; the rain always made a point of setting in just as he had some out-door work to do; so that though his patrimonial estate had dwindled away under his management, acre by acre, until there was little more left than a mere patch of Indian corn and potatoes, yet it was the worst conditioned farm in the neighborhood.

His children, too, were as ragged and wild as if they belonged to nobody. His son Rip, an urchin begotten in his own likeness, promised to inherit the habits, with the old clothes of his father. He was generally seen trooping like a colt at his mother's heels, equipped in a pair of his father's cast-off galligaskins, which he had much ado to hold up with one hand, as a fine lady does her train in bad weather.

Rip Van Winkle, however, was one of those happy mortals, of foolish, well-oiled dispositions, who take the world easy, eat white bread or brown, whichever can be got with least thought or trouble, and would rather starve on a penny than work for a pound. If left to himself, he would have whistled life away in perfect contentment; but his wife kept continually dinning in his ears about his idleness, his carelessness, and the ruin he was bringing on his family. Morning, noon, and night, her tongue was incessantly going, and every thing he said or did was sure to produce a torrent of household eloquence. Rip had but one way of replying to all lectures of the kind, and that, by frequent use, had grown into a habit. He shrugged his shoulders, shook his head, cast up his eyes, but said nothing. This, however, always provoked a fresh volley from his wife; so that he was fain to draw off his forces, and take to the outside of the house—the only side which, in truth, belongs to a hen-pecked husband.

Rip's sole domestic adherent was his dog Wolf, who was as much hen-pecked as his master; for Dame Van Winkle regarded them as companions in idleness, and even looked upon Wolf with an evil eye, as the cause of his master's going so often astray. True it is, in all points of spirit befitting an honorable dog, he was as courageous an animal as ever scoured the woods—but what courage can withstand the everduring and all-besetting terrors of a woman's tongue? The moment Wolf entered the house his crest fell, his tail drooped to the ground, or curled between his legs, he sneaked about with a gallows air, casting many a sidelong glance at Dame Van Winkle, and at the least flourish of a broomstick or ladle, he would fly to the door with yelping precipitation.

Times grew worse and worse with Rip Van Winkle as years of matrimony rolled on; a tart temper never mellows with age, and a sharp tongue is the only edged tool that grows keener with constant use. For a long while he used to console himself, when driven from home, by frequenting a kind of perpetual club of the sages, philosophers, and other idle personages of the village; which held its sessions on a bench before a small inn, designated by a rubicund portrait of His Majesty George the Third. Here they used to sit in the shade through a long lazy summer's day, talking listlessly over village gossip, or telling endless sleepy stories about nothing. But it would have been worth any statesman's money to have heard the profound discussions that sometimes took place, when by chance an old newspaper fell into their hands from some passing traveller. How solemnly they would listen to the contents, as drawled out by Derrick Van Bummel, the schoolmaster, a dapper learned little man, who was not to be daunted by the most gigantic word in the dictionary; and how sagely they would deliberate upon public events some months after they had taken place.

The opinions of this junto were completely controlled by Nicholas Vedder, a patriarch of the village, and landlord of the inn, at the door of which he took his seat from morning till night, just moving sufficiently to avoid the sun and keep in the shade of a large tree; so that the neighbors could tell the hour by his movements as accurately as by a sun-dial. It is true he was rarely heard to speak, but smoked his pipe incessantly. His adherents, however (for every great man has his adherents), perfectly understood him, and knew how to gather his opinions. When any thing that was read or related displeased him, he was observed to smoke his pipe vehemently and to send forth short, frequent and angry puffs; but when pleased, he would inhale the smoke slowly and tranquilly, and emit it in light and placid clouds; and sometimes, taking the pipe from his mouth, and letting the fragrant vapor curl about his nose, would gravely nod his head in token of perfect approbation.

From even this stronghold the unlucky Rip was at length routed by his termagant wife, who would suddenly break in upon the tranquillity of the assemblage and call the members all to naught; nor was that august personage, Nicholas Vedder himself, sacred from the daring tongue of this terrible virago, who charged him outright with encouraging her husband in habits of idleness.

Poor Rip was at last reduced almost to despair; and his only alternative, to escape from the labor of the farm and clamor of his wife, was to take gun in hand and stroll away into the woods. Here he would sometimes seat himself at the foot of a tree, and share the contents of his wallet with Wolf, with whom he sympathized as a fellow-sufferer in persecution. "Poor Wolf," he would say, "thy mistress leads thee a dog's life of it; but never mind, my lad, whilst I live thou shalt never want a friend to stand by thee!" Wolf would wag his tail, look wistfully in his master's face, and if dogs can feel pity I verily believe he reciprocated the sentiment with all his heart.

In a long ramble of the kind on a fine autumnal day, Rip had unconsciously scrambled to one of the highest parts of the Kaatskill mountains. He was after his favorite sport of squirrel shooting, and the still solitudes had echoed and reechoed with the reports of his gun. Panting and fatigued, he threw himself, late in the afternoon, on a green knoll, covered with mountain herbage, that crowned the brow of a precipice. From an opening between the trees he could overlook all the lower country for many a mile of rich woodland. He saw at a distance the lordly Hudson, far, far below him, moving on its silent but majestic course, with the reflection of a purple cloud, or the sail of a lagging bark, here and there sleeping on its glassy bosom, and at last losing itself in the blue highlands.

On the other side he looked down into a deep mountain glen, wild, lonely, and shagged, the bottom filled with fragments from the impending cliffs, and scarcely lighted by the reflected rays of the setting sun. For some time Rip lay musing on this scene; evening was gradually advancing; the mountains began to throw their long blue shadows over the valleys; he saw that it would be dark long before he could reach the village, and he heaved a heavy sigh when he thought of encountering the terrors of Dame Van Winkle.

As he was about to descend, he heard a voice from a distance, hallooing, "Rip Van Winkle! Rip Van Winkle!" He looked round, but could see nothing but a crow winging its solitary flight across the mountain. He thought his fancy must have deceived him, and turned again to descend, when he heard the same cry ring through the still evening air; "Rip Van Winkle! Rip Van Winkle!"—at the same time Wolf bristled up his back, and giving a low growl, skulked to his master's side, looking fearfully down into the glen. Rip now felt a vague apprehension stealing over him; he looked anxiously in the same direction, and perceived a strange figure slowly toiling up the rocks, and bending under the weight of something he carried on his back. He was surprised to see any human being in this lonely and unfrequented place, but supposing it to be some one of the neighborhood in need of his assistance, he hastened down to yield it.

On nearer approach he was still more surprised at the singularity of the stranger's appearance. He was a short square-built old fellow, with thick bushy hair, and a grizzled beard. His dress was of the antique Dutch fashion—a cloth jerkin strapped round the waist—several pair of breeches, the outer one of ample volume, decorated with rows of buttons down the sides, and bunches at the knees. He bore on his shoulder a stout keg, that seemed full of liquor, and made signs for Rip to approach and assist him with the load. Though rather shy and distrustful of this new acquaintance, Rip complied with his usual alacrity; and mutually relieving one another, they clambered up a narrow gully, apparently the dry bed of a mountain torrent. As they ascended, Rip every now and then heard long rolling peals, like distant thunder, that seemed to issue out of a deep ravine, or rather cleft, between lofty rocks, toward which their rugged path conducted. He paused for an instant, but supposing it to be the muttering of one of those transient thunder-showers which often take place in mountain heights, he proceeded. Passing through the ravine, they came to a hollow, like a small amphitheatre, surrounded by perpendicular precipices, over the brinks of which impending trees shot their branches, so that you only caught glimpses of the azure sky and the bright evening cloud. During the whole time Rip and his companion had labored on in silence; for though the former marvelled greatly what could be the object of carrying a keg of liquor up this wild mountain, yet there was something strange and incomprehensible about the unknown, that inspired awe and checked familiarity.

On entering the amphitheatre, new objects of wonder presented themselves. On a level spot in the centre was a company of odd-looking personages playing at nine-pins. They were dressed in a quaint outlandish fashion; some wore short doublets, others jerkins, with long knives in their belts, and most of them had enormous breeches, of similar style with that of the guide's. Their visages, too, were peculiar: one had a large beard, broad face, and small piggish eyes: the face of another seemed to consist entirely of nose, and was surmounted by a white sugar-loaf hat, set off with a little red cock's tail. They all had beards, of various shapes and colors. There was one who seemed to be the commander. He was a stout old gentleman, with a weather-beaten countenance; he wore a laced doublet, broad belt and hanger, high crowned hat and feather, red stockings, and high-heeled shoes, with roses in them. The whole group reminded Rip of the figures in an old Flemish painting, in the parlor of Dominic Van Shaick, the village parson, and which had been brought over from Holland at the time of the settlement.

What seemed particularly odd to Rip was, that though these folks were evidently amusing themselves, yet they maintained the gravest faces, the most mysterious silence, and were, withal, the most melancholy party of pleasure he had ever witnessed. Nothing interrupted the stillness of the scene but the noise of the balls, which, whenever they were rolled, echoed along the mountains like rumbling peals of thunder.

As Rip and his companion approached them, they suddenly desisted from their play, and stared at him with such fixed statue-like gaze, and such strange, uncouth, lack-lustre countenances, that his heart turned within him; and his knees smote together. His companion now emptied the contents of the keg into large flagons, and made signs to him to wait upon the company. He obeyed with fear and trembling; they quaffed the liquor in profound silence, and then returned to their game.

By degrees Rip's awe and apprehension subsided. He even ventured, when no eye was fixed upon him, to taste the beverage, which he found had much of the flavor of excellent Hollands. He was naturally a thirsty soul, and was soon tempted to repeat the draught. One taste provoked another; and he reiterated his visits to the flagon so often that at length his senses were overpowered, his eyes swam in his head, his head gradually declined, and he fell into a deep sleep.

On waking, he found himself on the green knoll whence he had first seen the old man of the glen. He rubbed his eyes—it was a bright sunny morning. The birds were hopping and twittering among the bushes, and the eagle was wheeling aloft, and breasting the pure mountain breeze. "Surely," thought Rip, "I have not slept here all night." He recalled the occurrences before he fell asleep. The strange man with a keg of liquor—the mountain ravine—the wild retreat among the rocks—the wobegone party at nine-pins—the flagon—"Oh! that flagon! that wicked flagon!" thought Rip— "what excuse shall I make to Dame Van Winkle!"

He looked round for his gun, but in place of the clean well-oiled fowling-piece, he found an old firelock lying by him, the barrel incrusted with rust, the lock falling off, and the stock worm-eaten. He now suspected that the grave roysters of the mountain had put a trick upon him, and, having dosed him with liquor, had robbed him of his gun. Wolf, too, had disappeared, but he might have strayed away after a squirrel or partridge. He whistled after him and shouted his name, but all in vain; the echoes repeated his whistle and shout, but no dog was to be seen.

He determined to revisit the scene of the last evening's gambol, and if he met with any of the party, to demand his dog and gun. As he rose to walk, he found himself stiff in the joints, and wanting in his usual activity. "These mountain beds do not agree with me," thought Rip, "and if this frolic should lay me up with a fit of the rheumatism, I shall have a blessed time with Dame Van Winkle." With some difficulty he got down into the glen: he found the gully up which he and his companion had ascended the preceding evening; but to his astonishment a mountain stream was now foaming down it, leaping from rock to rock, and filling the glen with babbling murmurs. He, however, made shift to scramble up its sides, working his toilsome way through thickets of birch, sassafras, and witch-hazel, and sometimes tripped up or entangled by the wild grapevines that twisted their coils or tendrils from tree to tree, and spread a kind of network in his path.

At length he reached to where the ravine had opened through the cliffs to the amphitheatre; but no traces of such opening remained. The rocks presented a high impenetrable wall over which the torrent came tumbling in a sheet of feathery foam, and fell into a broad deep basin, black from the shadows of the surrounding forest. Here, then, poor Rip was brought to a stand. He again called and whistled after his dog; he was only answered by the cawing of a flock of idle crows, sporting high in air about a dry tree that overhung a sunny precipice; and who, secure in their elevation, seemed to look down and scoff at the poor man's perplexities. What was to be done? The morning was passing away, and Rip felt famished for want of his breakfast. He grieved to give up his dog and gun; he dreaded to meet his wife; but it would not do to starve among the mountains. He shook his head, shouldered the rusty firelock, and, with a heart full of trouble and anxiety, turned his steps homeward.

As he approached the village he met a number of people, but none whom he knew, which somewhat surprised him, for he had thought himself acquainted with every one in the country round. Their dress, too, was of a different fashion from that to which he was accustomed. They all stared at him with equal marks of surprise, and whenever they cast their eyes upon him, invariably stroked their chins. The constant recurrence of this gesture induced Rip, involuntarily, to do the same, when, to his astonishment, he found his beard had grown a foot long!

He had now entered the skirts of the village. A troop of strange children ran at his heels, hooting after him, and pointing at his gray beard. The dogs, too, not one of which he recognized for an old acquaintance, barked at him as he passed. The very village was altered; it was larger and more populous. There were rows of houses which he had never seen before, and those which had been his familiar haunts had disappeared. Strange names were over the doors—strange faces at the windows—every thing was strange. His mind now misgave him; he began to doubt whether both he and the world around him were not bewitched. Surely this was his native village, which he had left but the day before. There stood the Kaatskill mountains—there ran the silver Hudson at a distance—there was every hill and dale precisely as it had always been—Rip was sorely perplexed—"That flagon last night," thought he, "has addled my poor head sadly!"

It was with some difficulty that he found the way to his own house, which he approached with silent awe, expecting every moment to hear the shrill voice of Dame Van Winkle. He found the house gone to decay—the roof fallen in, the windows shattered, and the doors off the hinges. A half-starved dog that looked like Wolf was sulking about it. Rip called him by name, but the cur snarled, showed his teeth, and passed on. This was an unkind cut indeed—"My very dog," sighed poor Rip, "has forgotten me!"

He entered the house, which, to tell the truth, Dame Van Winkle had always kept in neat order. It was empty, forlorn, and apparently abandoned. This desolateness overcame all his connubial fears—he called loudly for his wife and children—the lonely chambers rang for a moment with his voice, and then all again was silence.

He now hurried forth, and hastened to his old resort, the village inn—but it too was gone. A large rickety wooden building stood in its place, with great gaping windows, some of them broken and mended with old hats and petticoats, and over the door was painted, "the Union Hotel, by Jonathan Doolittle." Instead of the great tree that used to shelter the quiet little Dutch inn of yore, there now was reared a tall naked pole, with something on the top that looked like a red night-cap, and from it was fluttering a flag, on which was a singular assemblage of stars and stripes—all this was strange and incomprehensible. He recognized on the sign, however, the ruby face of King George, under which he had smoked so many a peaceful pipe; but even this was singularly metamorphosed. The red coat was changed for one of blue and buff, a sword was held in the hand instead of a sceptre, the head was decorated with a cocked hat, and underneath was painted in large characters, GENERAL WASHINGTON.

There was, as usual, a crowd of folk about the door, but none that Rip recollected. The very character of the people seemed changed. There was a busy, bustling, disputatious tone about it, instead of the accustomed phlegm and drowsy tranquillity. He looked in vain for the sage Nicholas Vedder, with his broad face, double chin, and fair long pipe, uttering clouds of tobacco-smoke instead of idle speeches; or Van Bummel, the schoolmaster, doling forth the contents of an ancient newspaper. In place of these, a lean, bilious-looking fellow, with his pockets full of handbills, was haranguing vehemently about rights of citizens—elections—members of congress—liberty—Bunker's Hill—heroes of seventy-six—and other words, which were a perfect Babylonish jargon to the bewildered Van Winkle.

The appearance of Rip, with his long grizzled beard, his rusty fowling-piece, his uncouth dress, and an army of women and children at his heels, soon attracted the attention of the tavern politicians. They crowded around him, eyeing him from head to foot with great curiosity. The orator bustled up to him, and, drawing him partly aside, inquired "on which side he voted?" Rip stared in vacant stupidity. Another short but busy little fellow pulled him by the arm, and, rising on tiptoe, inquired in his ear, "Whether he was Federal or Democrat?" Rip was equally at a loss to comprehend the question; when a knowing, self-important old gentleman, in a sharp cocked hat, made his way through the crowd, putting them to the right and left with his elbows as he passed, and planting himself before Van Winkle, with one arm akimbo, the other resting on his cane, his keen eyes and sharp hat penetrating, as it were, into his very soul, demanded in an austere tone, "what brought him to the election with a gun on his shoulder, and a mob at his heels, and whether he meant to breed a riot in the village?"—"Alas! gentlemen," cried Rip, somewhat dismayed, "I am a poor quiet man, a native of the place, and a loyal subject of the king, God bless him!"

Here a general shout burst from the by-standers—"A tory! a tory! a spy! a refugee! hustle him! away with him!" It was with great difficulty that the self-important man in the cocked hat restored order; and, having assumed a tenfold austerity of brow, demanded again of the unknown culprit, what he came there for, and whom he was seeking? The poor man humbly assured him that he meant no harm, but merely came there in search of some of his neighbors, who used to keep about the tavern.

"Well—who are they?—name them."

Rip bethought himself a moment, and inquired, "Where's Nicholas Vedder?"

There was a silence for a little while, when an old man replied, in a thin piping voice, "Nicholas Vedder! why, he is dead and gone these eighteen years! There was a wooden tombstone in the church-yard that used to tell all about him, but that's rotten and gone too."

"Where's Brom Dutcher?"

"Oh, he went off to the army in the beginning of the war; some say he was killed at the storming of Stony Point—others say he was drowned in a squall at the foot of Antony's Nose. I don't know—he never came back again."

"Where's Van Bummel, the schoolmaster?"

"He went off to the wars too, was a great militia general, and is now in congress."

Rip's heart died away at hearing of these sad changes in his home and friends, and finding himself thus alone in the world. Every answer puzzled him too, by treating of such enormous lapses of time, and of matters which he could not understand: war—congress—Stony Point:—he had no courage to ask after any more friends, but cried out in despair, "Does nobody here know Rip Van Winkle?"

"Oh, Rip Van Winkle!" exclaimed two or three, "Oh, to be sure! that's Rip Van Winkle yonder, leaning against the tree."

Rip looked, and beheld a precise counterpart of himself, as he went up to the mountain: apparently as lazy, and certainly as ragged. The poor fellow was now completely confounded. He doubted his own identity, and whether he was himself or another man. In the midst of his bewilderment, the man in the cocked hat demanded who he was, and what was his name?

"God knows," exclaimed he, at his wit's end; "I'm not myself—I'm somebody else—that's me yonder—no—that's somebody else got into my shoes—I was myself last night, but I fell asleep on the mountain, and they've changed my gun, and every thing's changed, and I'm changed, and I can't tell what's my name, or who I am!"

The by-standers began now to look at each other, nod, wink significantly, and tap their fingers against their foreheads. There was a whisper, also, about securing the gun, and keeping the old fellow from doing mischief, at the very suggestion of which the self-important man in the cocked hat retired with some precipitation. At this critical moment a fresh comely woman pressed through the throng to get a peep at the gray-bearded man. She had a chubby child in her arms, which, frightened at his looks, began to cry. "Hush, Rip," cried she, "hush, you little fool; the old man won't hurt you." The name of the child; the air of the mother, the tone of her voice, all awakened a train of recollections in his mind. "What is your name, my good woman?" asked he.

"Judith Gardenier."

"And your father's name?"

"Ah, poor man, Rip Van Winkle was his name, but it's twenty years since he went away from home with his gun, and never has been heard of since—his dog came home without him; but whether he shot himself, or was carried away by the Indians, nobody can tell. I was then but a little girl."

Rip had but one question more to ask; but he put it with a faltering voice: "Where's your mother?"

"Oh, she too had died but a short time since; she broke a blood-vessel in a fit of passion at a New-England peddler."

There was a drop of comfort, at least, in this intelligence. The honest man could contain himself no longer. He caught his daughter and her child in his arms. "I am your father!" cried he—"Young Rip Van Winkle once—old Rip Van Winkle now!—Does nobody know poor Rip Van Winkle?"

All stood amazed, until an old woman, tottering out from among the crowd, put her hand to her brow, and peering under it in his face for a moment, exclaimed, "Sure enough! it is Rip Van Winkle—it is himself! Welcome home again, old neighbor—Why, where have you been these twenty long years?"

Rip's story was soon told, for the whole twenty years had been to him but as one night. The neighbors stared when they heard it; some were seen to wink at each other, and put their tongues in their cheeks: and the self-important man in the cocked hat, who, when the alarm was over, had returned to the field, screwed down the corners of his mouth, and shook his head—upon which there was a general shaking of the head throughout the assemblage.

It was determined, however, to take the opinion of old Peter Vanderdonk, who was seen slowly advancing up the road. He was a descendant of the historian of that name, who wrote one of the earliest accounts of the province. Peter was the most ancient inhabitant of the village, and well versed in all the wonderful events and traditions of the neighborhood. He recollected Rip at once, and corroborated his story in the most satisfactory manner. He assured the company that it was a fact, handed down from his ancestor the historian, that the Kaatskill mountains had always been haunted by strange beings. That it was affirmed that the great Hendrick Hudson, the first discoverer of the river and country, kept a kind of vigil there every twenty years, with his crew of the Half-moon; being permitted in this way to revisit the scenes of his enterprise, and keep a guardian eye upon the river, and the great city called by his name. That his father had once seen them in their old Dutch dresses playing at nine-pins in a hollow of the mountain; and that he himself had heard, one summer afternoon, the sound of their balls, like distant peals of thunder.

To make a long story short, the company broke up, and returned to the more important concerns of the election. Rip's daughter took him home to live with her; she had a snug, well-furnished house, and a stout cheery farmer for a husband, whom Rip recollected for one of the urchins that used to climb upon his back. As to Rip's son and heir, who was the ditto of himself, seen leaning against the tree, he was employed to work on the farm; but evinced an hereditary disposition to attend to any thing else but his business.

Rip now resumed his old walks and habits; he soon found many of his former cronies, though all rather the worse for the wear and tear of time; and preferred making friends among the rising generation, with whom he soon grew into great favor.

Having nothing to do at home, and being arrived at that happy age when a man can be idle with impunity, he took his place once more on the bench at the inn door, and was reverenced as one of the patriarchs of the village, and a chronicle of the old times "before the war." It was some time before he could get into the regular track of gossip, or could be made to comprehend the strange events that had taken place during his torpor. How that there had been a revolutionary war—that the country had thrown off the yoke of old England—and that, instead of being a subject of his Majesty George the Third, he was now a free citizen of the United States. Rip, in fact, was no politician; the changes of states and empires made but little impression on him; but there was one species of despotism under which he had long groaned, and that was—petticoat government. Happily that was at an end; he had got his neck out of the yoke of matrimony, and could go in and out whenever he pleased, without dreading the tyranny of Dame Van Winkle. Whenever her name was mentioned, however, he shook his head, shrugged his shoulders, and cast up his eyes; which might pass either for an expression of resignation to his fate, or joy at his deliverance.

He used to tell his story to every stranger that arrived at Mr. Doolittle's hotel. He was observed, at first, to vary on some points every time he told it, which was, doubtless, owing to his having so recently awaked. It at last settled down precisely to the tale I have related, and not a man, woman, or child in the neighborhood, but knew it by heart. Some always pretended to doubt the reality of it, and insisted that Rip had been out of his head, and that this was one point on which he always remained flighty. The old Dutch inhabitants, however, almost universally gave it full credit. Even to this day they never hear a thunderstorm of a summer afternoon about the Kaatskill, but they say Hendrick Hudson and his crew are at their game of nine-pins; and it is a common wish of all henpecked husbands in the neighborhood, when life hangs heavy on their hands, that they might have a quieting draught out of Rip Van Winkle's flagon.

Note

The foregoing Tale, one would suspect, had been suggested to Mr. Knickerbocker by a little German superstition about the Emperor Frederick *der Rothbart*, and the Kypphaüser mountain: the subjoined note, however, which he had appended to the tale, shows that it is an absolute fact, narrated with his usual fidelity:

> "The story of Rip Van Winkle may seem incredible to many, but nevertheless I give it my full belief, for I know the vicinity of our old Dutch settlements to have been very subject to marvellous events and appearances. Indeed, I have heard many stranger stories than this, in the villages along the Hudson; all of which were too well authenticated to admit of a doubt. I have even talked with Rip Van Winkle myself, who, when last I saw him, was a very venerable old man, and so perfectly rational and consistent on every other point, that I think no conscientious person could refuse to take this into the bargain; may, I have seen a certificate on the subject taken before a country justice and signed with a cross, in the justice's own handwriting. The story, therefore, is beyond the possibility of doubt.
>
> D.K."

Marked with D. (1981)

by Tony Harrison

When the chilled dough of his flesh went in an oven
not unlike those he fuelled all his life,
I thought of his cataracts ablaze with Heaven
and radiant with the sight of his dead wife,
light streaming from his mouth to shape her name,   5
"not Florence and not Flo but always Florrie."
I thought how his cold tongue burst into flame
but only literally, which makes me sorry,
sorry for his sake there's no Heaven to reach.
I get it all from Earth my daily bread   10
but he hungered for release from mortal speech
that kept him down, the tongue that weighed like lead.

The baker's man that no-one will see rise
and England made to feel like some dull oaf
is smoke, enough to sting one person's eyes   15
and ash (not unlike flour) for one small loaf.

The Maypole of Merry Mount (1836)

by Nathaniel Hawthorne

There is an admirable foundation for a philosophic romance in the curious history of the early settlement of Mount Wollaston, or Merry Mount. In the slight sketch here attempted, the facts, recorded on the grave pages of our New England annalists, have wrought themselves, almost spontaneously, into a sort of allegory. The masques, mummeries, and festive customs, described in the text, are in accordance with the manners of the age. Authority on these points may be found in Strutt's Book of English Sports and Pastimes.

Bright were the days at Merry Mount, when the Maypole was the banner staff of that gay colony! They who reared it, should their banner be triumphant, were to pour sunshine over New England's rugged hills, and scatter flower seeds throughout the soil. Jollity and gloom were contending for an empire. Midsummer eve had come, bringing deep verdure to the forest, and roses in her lap, of a more vivid hue than the tender buds of Spring. But May, or her mirthful spirit, dwelt all the year round at Merry Mount, sporting with the Summer months, and revelling with Autumn, and basking in the glow of Winter's fireside. Through a world of toil and care she flitted with a dreamlike smile, and came hither to find a home among the lightsome hearts of Merry Mount.

Never had the Maypole been so gayly decked as at sunset on midsummer eve. This venerated emblem was a pine-tree, which had preserved the slender grace of youth, while it equalled the loftiest height of the old wood monarchs. From its top streamed a silken banner, colored like the rainbow. Down nearly to the ground the pole was dressed with birchen boughs, and others of the liveliest green, and some with silvery leaves, fastened by ribbons that fluttered in fantastic knots of twenty different colors, but no sad ones. Garden flowers, and blossoms of the wilderness, laughed gladly forth amid the verdure, so fresh and dewy that they must have grown by magic on that happy pinetree. Where this green and flowery splendor terminated, the shaft of the Maypole was stained with the seven brilliant hues of the banner at its top. On the lowest green bough hung an abundant wreath of roses, some that had been gathered in the sunniest spots of the forest, and others, of still richer blush, which the colonists had reared from English seed. O, people of the Golden Age, the chief of your husbandry was to raise flowers!

But what was the wild throng that stood hand in hand about the May pole? It could not be that the fauns and nymphs, when driven from their classic groves and homes of ancient fable, had sought refuge, as all the persecuted did, in the fresh woods of the West. These were Gothic monsters, though perhaps of Grecian ancestry. On the shoulders of a comely youth uprose the head and branching antlers of a stag; a second, human in all other points, had the grim visage of a wolf; a third, still with the trunk and limbs of a mortal man, showed the beard and horns of a venerable he-goat. There was the likeness of a bear erect, brute in all but his hind legs, which were adorned with pink silk stockings. And here again, almost as wondrous, stood a real bear of the dark forest, lending each of his fore paws to the grasp of a human hand, and as ready for the dance as any in that circle. His inferior nature rose half way, to meet his companions as they stooped. Other faces wore the similitude of man or woman, but distorted or extravagant, with red noses pendulous before their mouths, which seemed of awful depth, and stretched from ear to ear in an eternal fit of laughter. Here might be seen the Salvage Man, well known in heraldry, hairy as a baboon, and girdled with green leaves. By his side, a noble figure, but still a counterfeit, appeared an Indian hunter, with feathery crest and wampum belt. Many of this strange company wore foolscaps, and had little bells appended to their garments, tinkling with a silvery sound, responsive to the inaudible music of their gleesome spirits. Some youths and maidens were of soberer garb, yet well maintained their places in the irregular throng by the expression of wild revelry upon their features. Such were the colonists of Merry Mount, as they stood in the broad smile of sunset round their venerated Maypole.

Had a wanderer, bewildered in the melancholy forest, heard their mirth, and stolen a half-affrighted glance, he might have fancied them the crew of Comus, some already transformed to brutes, some midway between man and beast, and the others rioting in the flow of tipsy jollity that foreran the change. But a band of Puritans, who watched the scene, invisible themselves, compared the masques to those devils and ruined souls with whom their superstition peopled the black wilderness.

Within the ring of monsters appeared the two airiest forms that had ever trodden on any more solid footing than a purple and golden cloud. One was a youth in glistening apparel, with a scarf of the rainbow pattern crosswise on his breast. His right hand held a gilded staff, the ensign of high dignity among the revellers, and his left grasped the slender fingers of a fair maiden, not less gayly decorated than himself. Bright roses glowed in contrast with the dark and glossy curls of each, and were scattered round their feet, or had sprung up spontaneously there. Behind this lightsome couple, so close to the Maypole that its boughs shaded his jovial face, stood the figure of an English priest, canonically dressed, yet decked with flowers, in heathen fashion, and wearing a chaplet of the native vine leaves. By the riot of his rolling eye, and the pagan decorations of his holy garb, he seemed the wildest monster there, and the very Comus of the crew.

"Votaries of the Maypole," cried the flower-decked priest, "merrily, all day long, have the woods echoed to your mirth. But be this your merriest hour, my hearts! Lo, here stand the Lord and Lady of the May, whom I, a clerk of Oxford, and high priest of Merry Mount, am presently to join in holy matrimony. Up with your nimble spirits, ye morris-dancers, green men, and glee maidens, bears and wolves, and horned gentlemen! Come; a chorus now, rich with the old mirth of Merry England, and the wilder glee of this fresh forest; and then a dance, to show the youthful pair what life is made of, and how airily they should go through it! All ye that love the Maypole, lend your voices to the nuptial song of the Lord and Lady of the May!"

This wedlock was more serious than most affairs of Merry Mount, where jest and delusion, trick and fantasy, kept up a continual carnival. The Lord and Lady of the May, though their titles must be laid down at sunset, were really and truly to be partners for the dance of life, beginning the measure that same bright eve. The wreath of roses, that hung from the lowest green bough of the Maypole, had been twined for them, and would be thrown over both their heads, in symbol of their flowery union. When the priest had spoken, therefore, a riotous uproar burst from the rout of monstrous figures.

"Begin you the stave, reverend Sir," cried they all; "and never did the woods ring to such a merry peal as we of the Maypole shall send up!"

Immediately a prelude of pipe, cithern, and viol, touched with practised minstrelsy, began to play from a neighboring thicket, in such a mirthful cadence that the boughs of the Maypole quivered to the sound. But the May Lord, he of the gilded staff, chancing to look into his Lady's eyes, was wonder struck at the almost pensive glance that met his own.

"Edith, sweet Lady of the May," whispered he reproachfully, "is yon wreath of roses a garland to hang above our graves, that you look so sad? O, Edith, this is our golden time! Tarnish it not by any pensive shadow of the mind; for it may be that nothing of futurity will be brighter than the mere remembrance of what is now passing."

"That was the very thought that saddened me! How came it in your mind too?" said Edith, in a still lower tone than he, for it was high treason to be sad at Merry Mount. "Therefore do I sigh amid this festive music. And besides, dear Edgar, I struggle as with a dream, and fancy that these shapes of our jovial friends are visionary, and their mirth unreal, and that we are no true Lord and Lady of the May. What is the mystery in my heart?"

Just then, as if a spell had loosened them, down came a little shower of withering rose leaves from the Maypole. Alas, for the young lovers! No sooner had their hearts glowed with real passion than they were sensible of something vague and unsubstantial in their former pleasures, and felt a dreary presentiment of inevitable change. From the moment that they truly loved, they had subjected themselves to earth's doom of care and sorrow, and troubled joy, and had no more a home at Merry Mount. That was Edith's mystery. Now leave we the priest to marry them, and the masquers to sport round the Maypole, till the last sunbeam be withdrawn from its summit, and the shadows of the forest mingle gloomily in the dance. Meanwhile, we may discover who these gay people were.

Two hundred years ago, and more, the old world and its inhabitants became mutually weary of each other. Men voyaged by thousands to the West: some to barter glass beads, and such like jewels, for the furs of the Indian hunter; some to conquer virgin empires; and one stern band to pray. But none of these motives had much weight with the colonists of Merry Mount. Their leaders were men who had sported so long with life, that when Thought and Wisdom came, even these unwelcome guests were led astray by the crowd of vanities which they should have put to flight. Erring Thought and perverted Wisdom were made to put on masques, and play the fool. The men of whom we speak, after losing the heart's fresh gayety, imagined a wild philosophy of pleasure, and came hither to act out their latest day-dream. They gathered followers from all that giddy tribe whose whole life is like the festal days of soberer men. In their train were minstrels, not unknown in London streets: wandering players, whose theatres had been the halls of noblemen; mummers, rope-dancers, and mountebanks, who would long be missed at wakes, church ales, and fairs; in a word, mirth makers of every sort, such as abounded in that age, but now began to be discountenanced by the rapid growth of Puritanism. Light had their footsteps been on land, and as lightly they came across the sea. Many had been maddened by their previous troubles into a gay despair; others were as madly gay in the flush of youth, like the May Lord and his Lady; but whatever might be the quality of their mirth, old and young were gay at Merry Mount. The young deemed themselves happy. The elder spirits, if they knew that mirth was but the counterfeit of happiness, yet followed the false shadow wilfully, because at least her garments glittered brightest. Sworn triflers of a lifetime, they would not venture among the sober truths of life not even to be truly blest.

All the hereditary pastimes of Old England were transplanted hither. The King of Christmas was duly crowned, and the Lord of Misrule bore potent sway. On the Eve of St. John, they felled whole acres of the forest to make bonfires, and danced by the blaze all night, crowned with garlands, and throwing flowers into the flame. At harvest time, though their crop was of the smallest, they made an image with the sheaves of Indian corn, and wreathed it with autumnal garlands, and bore it home triumphantly. But what chiefly characterized the colonists of Merry Mount was their veneration for the Maypole. It has made their true history a poet's tale. Spring decked the hallowed emblem with young blossoms and fresh green boughs; Summer brought roses of the deepest blush, and the perfected foliage of the forest; Autumn enriched it with that red and yellow gorgeousness which converts each wildwood leaf into a painted flower; and Winter silvered it with sleet, and hung it round with icicles, till it flashed in the cold sunshine, itself a frozen sunbeam. Thus each alternate season did homage to the Maypole, and paid it a tribute of its own richest splendor. Its votaries danced round it, once, at least, in every month; sometimes they called it their religion, or their altar; but always, it was the banner staff of Merry Mount.

Unfortunately, there were men in the new world of a sterner faith than these Maypole worshippers. Not far from Merry Mount was a settlement of Puritans, most dismal wretches, who said their prayers before daylight, and then wrought in the forest or the cornfield till evening made it prayer time again. Their weapons were always at hand to shoot down the straggling savage. When they met in conclave, it was never to keep up the old English mirth, but to hear sermons three hours long, or to proclaim bounties on the heads of wolves and the scalps of Indians. Their festivals were fast days, and their chief pastime the singing of psalms. Woe to the youth or maiden who did but dream of a dance! The selectman nodded to the constable; and there sat the light-heeled reprobate in the stocks; or if he danced, it was round the whipping-post, which might be termed the Puritan Maypole.

A party of these grim Puritans, toiling through the difficult woods, each with a horseload of iron armor to burden his footsteps, would sometimes draw near the sunny precincts of Merry Mount. There were the silken colonists, sporting round their Maypole; perhaps teaching a bear to dance, or striving to communicate their mirth to the grave Indian; or masquerading in the skins of deer and wolves, which they had hunted for that especial purpose. Often, the whole colony were playing at blindman's buff, magistrates and all, with their eyes bandaged, except a single scapegoat, whom the blinded sinners pursued by the tinkling of the bells at his garments. Once, it is said, they were seen following a flower-decked corpse, with merriment and festive music, to his grave. But did the dead man laugh? In their quietest times, they sang ballads and told tales, for the edification of their pious visitors; or perplexed them with juggling tricks; or grinned at them through horse collars; and when sport itself grew wearisome, they made game of their own stupidity, and began a yawning match. At the very least of these enormities, the men of iron shook their heads and frowned so darkly that the revellers looked up, imagining that a momentary cloud had overcast the sunshine, which was to be perpetual there. On the other hand, the Puritans affirmed that, when a psalm was pealing from their place of worship, the echo which the forest sent them back seemed often like the chorus of a jolly catch, closing with a roar of laughter. Who but the fiend, and his bond slaves, the crew of Merry Mount, had thus disturbed them? In due time, a feud arose, stern and bitter on one side, and as serious on the other as anything could be among such light spirits as had sworn allegiance to the Maypole. The future complexion of New England was involved in this important quarrel. Should the grizzly saints establish their jurisdiction over the gay sinners, then would their spirits darken all the clime, and make it a land of clouded visages, of hard toil, of sermon and psalm forever. But should the banner staff of Merry Mount be fortunate, sunshine would break upon the hills, and flowers would beautify the forest, and late posterity do homage to the Maypole.

After these authentic passages from history, we return to the nuptials of the Lord and Lady of the May. Alas! we have delayed too long, and must darken our tale too suddenly. As we glance again at the Maypole, a solitary sunbeam is fading from the summit, and leaves only a faint, golden tinge blended with the hues of the rainbow banner. Even that dim light is now withdrawn, relinquishing the whole domain of Merry Mount to the evening gloom, which has rushed so instantaneously from the black surrounding woods. But some of these black shadows have rushed forth in human shape.

Yes, with the setting sun, the last day of mirth had passed from Merry Mount. The ring of gay masquers was disordered and broken; the stag lowered his antlers in dismay; the wolf grew weaker than a lamb; the bells of the morris-dancers tinkled with tremulous affright. The Puritans had played a characteristic part in the Maypole mummeries. Their darksome figures were intermixed with the wild shapes of their foes, and made the scene a picture of the moment, when waking thoughts start up amid the scattered fantasies of a dream. The leader of the hostile party stood in the centre of the circle, while the route of monsters cowered around him, like evil spirits in the presence of a dread magician. No fantastic foolery could look him in the face. So stern was the energy of his aspect, that the whole man, visage, frame, and soul, seemed wrought of iron, gifted with life and thought, yet all of one substance with his headpiece and breastplate. It was the Puritan of Puritans; it was Endicott himself!

"Stand off, priest of Baal!" said he, with a grim frown, and laying no reverent hand upon the surplice. "I know thee, Blackstone! Thou art the man who couldst not abide the rule even of thine own corrupted church, and hast come hither to preach iniquity, and to give example of it in thy life. But now shall it be seen that the Lord hath sanctified this wilderness for his peculiar people. Woe unto them that would defile it! And first, for this flower-decked abomination, the altar of thy worship!"

And with his keen sword Endicott assaulted the hallowed Maypole. Nor long did it resist his arm. It groaned with a dismal sound; it showered leaves and rosebuds upon the remorseless enthusiast; and finally, with all its green boughs and ribbons and flowers, symbolic of departed pleasures, down fell the banner staff of Merry Mount. As it sank, tradition says, the evening sky grew darker, and the woods threw forth a more sombre shadow.

"There," cried Endicott, looking triumphantly on his work, "there lies the only Maypole in New England! The thought is strong within me that, by its fall, is shadowed forth the fate of light and idle mirth makers, amongst us and our posterity. Amen, saith John Endicott."

"Amen!" echoed his followers.

But the votaries of the Maypole gave one groan for their idol. At the sound, the Puritan leader glanced at the crew of Comus, each a figure of broad mirth, yet, at this moment, strangely expressive of sorrow and dismay.

"Valiant captain," quoth Peter Palfrey, the Ancient of the band, "what order shall be taken with the prisoners?"

"I thought not to repent me of cutting down a Maypole," replied Endicott, "yet now I could find in my heart to plant it again, and give each of these bestial pagans one other dance round their idol. It would have served rarely for a whipping-post!"

"But there are pine-trees enow," suggested the lieutenant.

"True, good Ancient," said the leader. "Wherefore, bind the heathen crew, and bestow on them a small matter of stripes apiece, as earnest of our future justice. Set some of the rogues in the stocks to rest themselves, so soon as Providence shall bring us to one of our own well-ordered settlements, where such accommodations may be found. Further penalties, such as branding and cropping of ears, shall be thought of hereafter."

"How many stripes for the priest?" inquired Ancient Palfrey.

"None as yet," answered Endicott, bending his iron frown upon the culprit. "It must be for the Great and General Court to determine, whether stripes and long imprisonment, and other grievous penalty, may atone for his transgressions. Let him look to himself! For such as violate our civil order, it may be permitted us to show mercy. But woe to the wretch that troubleth our religion!"

"And this dancing bear," resumed the officer. "Must he share the stripes of his fellows?"

"Shoot him through the head!" said the energetic Puritan. "I suspect witchcraft in the beast."

"Here be a couple of shining ones," continued Peter Palfrey, pointing his weapon at the Lord and Lady of the May. "They seem to be of high station among these misdoers. Methinks their dignity will not be fitted with less than a double share of stripes."

Endicott rested on his sword, and closely surveyed the dress and aspect of the hapless pair. There they stood, pale, downcast, and apprehensive. Yet there was an air of mutual support, and of pure affection, seeking aid and giving it, that showed them to be man and wife, with the sanction of a priest upon their love. The youth, in the peril of the moment, had dropped his gilded staff, and thrown his arm about the Lady of the May, who leaned against his breast, too lightly to burden him, but with weight enough to express that their destinies were linked together, for good or evil. They looked first at each other, and then into the grim captain's face. There they stood, in the first hour of wedlock, while the idle pleasures, of which their companions were the emblems, had given place to the sternest cares of life, personified by the dark Puritans. But never had their youthful beauty seemed so pure and high as when its glow was chastened by adversity.

"Youth," said Endicott, "ye stand in an evil case thou and thy maiden wife. Make ready presently, for I am minded that ye shall both have a token to remember your wedding day!"

"Stern man," cried the May Lord, "how can I move thee? Were the means at hand, I would resist to the death. Being powerless, I entreat! Do with me as thou wilt, but let Edith go untouched!"

"Not so," replied the immitigable zealot. "We are not wont to show an idle courtesy to that sex, which requireth the stricter discipline. What sayest thou, maid? Shall thy silken bridegroom suffer thy share of the penalty, besides his own?"

"Be it death," said Edith, "and lay it all on me!"

Truly, as Endicott had said, the poor lovers stood in a woful case. Their foes were triumphant, their friends captive and abased, their home desolate, the benighted wilderness around them, and a rigorous destiny, in the shape of the Puritan leader, their only guide. Yet the deepening twilight could not altogether conceal that the iron man was softened; he smiled at the fair spectacle of early love; he almost sighed for the inevitable blight of early hopes.

"The troubles of life have come hastily on this young couple," observed Endicott. "We will see how they comport themselves under their present trials ere we burden them with greater. If, among the spoil, there be any garments of a more decent fashion, let them be put upon this May Lord and his Lady, instead of their glistening vanities. Look to it, some of you."

"And shall not the youth's hair be cut?" asked Peter Palfrey, looking with abhorrence at the lovelock and long glossy curls of the young man.

"Crop it forthwith, and that in the true pumpkin-shell fashion," answered the captain. "Then bring them along with us, but more gently than their fellows. There be qualities in the youth, which may make him valiant to fight, and sober to toil, and pious to pray; and in the maiden, that may fit her to become a mother in our Israel, bringing up babes in better nurture than her own hath been. Nor think ye, young ones, that they are the happiest, even in our lifetime of a moment, who misspend it in dancing round a Maypole!"

And Endicott, the severest Puritan of all who laid the rock foundation of New England, lifted the wreath of roses from the ruin of the Maypole, and threw it, with his own gauntleted hand, over the heads of the Lord and Lady of the May. It was a deed of prophecy. As the moral gloom of the world overpowers all systematic gayety, even so was their home of wild mirth made desolate amid the sad forest. They returned to it no more. But as their flowery garland was wreathed of the brightest roses that had grown there, so, in the tie that united them, were intertwined all the purest and best of their early joys. They went heavenward, supporting each other along the difficult path which it was their lot to tread, and never wasted one regretful thought on the vanities of Merry Mount.

The Gentlemen of the Jungle (ca. 1950)

by Jomo Kenyatta

Once upon a time an elephant made a friendship with a man. One day a heavy thunderstorm broke out, the elephant went to his friend, who had a little hut at the edge of the forest, and said to him: "My dear good man, will you please let me put my trunk inside your hut to keep it out of this torrential rain?" The man, seeing what situation his friend was in, replied: "My dear good elephant, my hut is very small, but there is room for your trunk and myself. Please put your trunk in gently." The elephant thanked his friend, saying: "You have done me a good deed and one day I shall return your kindness." But what followed? As soon as the elephant put his trunk inside the hut, slowly he pushed his head inside, and finally flung the man out in the rain, and then lay down comfortably inside his friend's hut, saying: "My dear good friend, your skin is harder than mine, and as there is not enough room for both of us, you can afford to remain in the rain while I am protecting my delicate skin from the hailstorm."

The man, seeing what his friend had done to him, started to grumble; the animals in the nearby forest heard the noise and came to see what was the matter. All stood around listening to the heated argument between the man and his friend the elephant. In this turmoil the lion came along roaring, and said in a loud voice: "Don't you all know that I am the King of the Jungle! How dare any one disturb the peace of my kingdom?" On hearing this the elephant, who was one of the high ministers in the jungle kingdom, replied in a soothing voice, and said: "My lord, there is no disturbance of the peace in your kingdom. I have only been having a little discussion with my friend here as to the possession of this little hut which your lordship sees me occupying." The lion, who wanted to have "peace and tranquillity" in his kingdom, replied in a noble voice, saying: "I command my ministers to appoint a Commission of Enquiry to go thoroughly into this matter and report accordingly." He then turned to the man and said: "You have done well by establishing friendship with my people, especially with the elephant, who is one of my honourable ministers of state. Do not grumble any more, your hut is not lost to you. Wait until the sitting of my Imperial Commission, and there you will be given plenty of opportunity to state your case. I am sure that you will be pleased with the findings of the Commission." The man was very pleased by these sweet words from the King of the Jungle, and innocently waited for his opportunity, in the belief that naturally the hut would be returned to him.

The elephant, obeying the command of his master, got busy with other ministers to appoint the Commission of Enquiry. The following elders of the jungle were appointed to sit in the Commission: (1) Mr. Rhinoceros; (2) Mr. Buffalo; (3) Mr. Alligator; (4) The Rt. Hon. Mr. Fox to act as chairman; and (5) Mr. Leopard to act as Secretary to the Commission. On seeing the personnel, the man protested and asked if it was not necessary to include in this Commission a member from his side. But he was told that it was impossible, since no one from his side was well enough educated to understand the intricacy of jungle law. Further, that there was nothing to fear, for the members of the Commission were all men of repute for their impartiality in justice, and as they were gentlemen chosen by God to look after the interests of races less adequately endowed with teeth and claws, he might rest assured that they would investigate the matter with the greatest care and report impartially.

The Commission sat to take the evidence. The Rt. Hon. Mr. Elephant was first called. He came along with a superior air, brushing his tusks with a sapling which Mrs. Elephant had provided, and in an authoritative voice said: "Gentlemen of the Jungle, there is no need for me to waste your valuable time in relating a story which I am sure you all know. I have always regarded it as my duty to protect the interests of my friends, and this appears to have caused the misunderstanding between myself and my friend here. He invited me to save his hut from being blown away by a hurricane. As the hurricane had gained access owing to the unoccupied space in the hut, I considered it necessary, in my friend's own interests, to turn the undeveloped space to a more economic use by sitting in it myself; a duty which any of you would undoubtedly have performed with equal readiness in similar circumstances."

After hearing the Rt. Hon. Mr. Elephant's conclusive evidence, the Commission called Mr. Hyena and other elders of the jungle, who all supported what Mr. Elephant had said. They then called the man, who began to give his own account of the dispute. But the Commission cut him short, saying: "My good man, please confine yourself to relevant issues. We have already heard the circumstances from various unbiased sources; all we wish you to tell us is whether the undeveloped space in your hut was occupied by any one else before Mr. Elephant assumed his position?" The man began to say: "No, but—" But at this point the Commission declared that they had heard sufficient evidence from both sides and retired to consider their decision. After enjoying a delicious meal at the expense of the Rt. Hon. Mr. Elephant, they reached their verdict, called the man, and declared as follows: "In our opinion this dispute has arisen through a regrettable misunderstanding due to the backwardness of your ideas. We consider that Mr. Elephant has fulfilled his sacred duty of protecting your interests. As it is clearly for your good that the space should be put to its most economic use, and as you yourself have not reached the stage of expansion which would enable you to fill it, we consider it necessary to arrange a compromise to suit both parties. Mr. Elephant shall continue his occupation of your hut, but we give you permission to look for a site where you can build another hut more suited to your needs, and we will see that you are well protected."

The man, having no alternative, and fearing that his refusal might expose him to the teeth and claws of members of the Commission, did as they suggested. But no sooner had he built another hut than Mr. Rhinoceros charged in with his horn lowered and ordered the man to quit. A Royal Commission was again appointed to look into the matter, and the same finding was given. This procedure was repeated until Mr. Buffalo, Mr. Leopard, Mr. Hyena and the rest were all accommodated with new huts. Then the man decided that he must adopt an effective method of protection, since Commissions of Enquiry did not seem to be of any use to him. He sat down and said, "Ng'enda thi ndagaga motegi," which literally means "there is nothing that treads on the earth that cannot be trapped," or in other words, you can fool people for a time, but not for ever.

Early one morning, when the huts already occupied by the jungle lords were all beginning to decay and fall to pieces, he went out and built a bigger and better hut a little distance away. No sooner had Mr. Rhinoceros seen it than he came rushing in, only to find that Mr. Elephant was already inside, sound asleep. Mr. Leopard next came to the window, Mr. Lion, Mr. Fox and

Mr. Buffalo entered the doors, while Mr. Hyena howled for a place in the shade and Mr. Alligator basked on the roof. Presently they all began disputing about their rights of penetration, and from disputing they came to fighting, and while they were all embroiled together the man set the hut on fire and burnt it to the ground, jungle lords and all. Then he went home, saying: "Peace is costly, but it's worth the expense," and lived happily ever after.

Glossary

absolutist critic One who believes that there is one and only one theory or set of principles a reader may utilize when interpreting a text.

actual reader A term devised by Wolfgang Iser to distinguish between two kinds of readers: the implied and the actual reader. The actual reader is the person who physically picks up the text and reads it. According to Iser, the actual reader comes to the text shaped by cultural and personal norms and prejudices. See **implied reader**.

aesthetic experience The effects produced in and upon an individual when contemplating a work of art. See **aesthetic reading**.

aesthetic reading A term used by Louise M. Rosenblatt in The Reader, the Text, the Poem: The Transactional Theory of the Literary Work (1978) to describe the act of reading or the process whereby a reader transacts with a text. During this event, the "object of aesthetic contemplation is what perceivers or readers make of their responses to the artistic stimulus, no matter whether this be a physical object, such as a statue, or a set of verbal symbols. Readers contemplate their own shaping of their responses to the text." The term thus refers to each reader's personal response to a text and how individual readers find and create meaning when transacting with printed material. Such a process assumes an active role on the part of the reader to create meaning or individual interpretations with and from a text.

aesthetic theory A systematic, philosophical body of beliefs concerning how meaning occurs and functions in texts, especially the element of beauty and/or pleasure.

aesthetics The branch of philosophy that deals with the concept of the beautiful and strives to determine the criteria for beauty in any work of art. It asks such questions as, Where is the source of beauty? In the object? In the perceiver? What is beauty? and How is beauty recognized?

affective fallacy A term used by New Critics to explain that a reader's emotional response to a text is neither important nor equivalent to its interpretation. Believing those who evaluate a work of art on the basis of its emotional effect upon its perceiver to be incorrect, New Critics assert that the Affective Fallacy confuses what a poem is (its meaning) and what it does. The term was first introduced by W. K. Wimsatt Jr. and M. C. Beardsley.

African American criticism An approach to literary analysis that develops a black aesthetics to be applied when interpreting African American writings. Its leading advocate, Henry Louis Gates Jr., believes such an aesthetics provides a new theoretical framework for developing and analyzing the ever-growing and popular African American canon. In this new framework, Gates insists that African American literature be viewed as a form of language, not as a representation of social practices or culture. According to Gates, a black aesthetics must be derived from the black tradition itself and must include what he calls "the language of blackness, the signifying difference which makes the black tradition our very own." Gates asserts the "double-voicedness" of African American literature, declaring that this literature draws upon two voices and cultures, the white and the black. It is the joining of these two discourses, Gates declares, that produces the uniqueness of this literature. Also see **cultural studies, double consciousness,** and **postcolonialism.**

allegoric reading   A reading in which one character, place, or idea represents another. The characters, events, or places within a text represent meanings independent of the action in the surface story. These interpretations are most often religious, but may be moral, political, personal, or satiric.

allophone   The family of nearly identical speech sounds that comprise a phoneme (see **phoneme**). For example, the sound of the *p* in *pit* and the *p* in *spit* are allophones of the phoneme /p/.

ambiguity   Commonly defined as a stylistic error in everyday speech, in which a word or expression has multiple meanings. Since the publication of William Empson's *Seven Types of Ambiguity* (1930) and the specialized use of this term adopted by New Criticism, ambiguity is now synonymous with *plurisignation*, both terms implying the complexity and richness of poetic language that allows for a word or expression to simultaneously have two or more distinct meanings. New Critics believe that ambiguity becomes one of the chief tools good poets use intentionally and effectively to demonstrate the valid meanings contained in a word or expression. See **connotation** and **denotation.**

anal stage   The second stage of child development, as articulated by Sigmund Freud. In this stage, the anus becomes the object of pleasure when the child learns the delights of defecation.

analytical psychology   Founded and developed by Carl Gustav Jung, this system of psychology is akin to psychoanalysis, with its emphasis on the functions that the conscious and the unconscious play in influencing human behavior. In this branch of psychology, Jung emphasizes humankind's racial origins and adapts the use of the free association technique in studying an individual's problems.

aporia   A term referring to postmodernism's undecidability about the nature of reality and the interpretation of texts. This term is also used in deconstruction theory denoting paradoxes, contradictions, and other puzzling statements that cannot be resolved—apparent contradictions.

appetencies   A term brought into literary criticism via the writings of the formalist critic I. A. Richards. According to Richards, human beings are basically bundles of desires called *appetencies*. Richards believes that to achieve psychic health, every person must balance these desires by creating a personally acceptable vision of the world. Whereas religion once provided this vision, Richards declares that poetry can best harmonize and satisfy humankind's appetencies and thereby create a fulfilling and intellectually acceptable worldview. See **formalism.**

applied criticism Applies the theories and tenets of theoretical criticism to a particular work of art. Also known as *practical criticism*. In applied criticism, the critic defines the standards of taste and explains, evaluates, or justifies a particular text.

archetypal criticism An approach to literary analysis that applies the theories of Carl Jung, Northrop Frye, and other critics to literary analysis. An *archetypal critic* studies images or patterns of repeated human experiences (archetypes) found within a specific text and common to other works of art. See **archetype**.

archetype Refers to a recurrent plot pattern, image, descriptive detail, or character that evokes from the reader strong but illogical responses. This term was brought into literary criticism via the psychological writings of Carl Jung. Jung believed that the mind was composed of three parts: the *personal conscious*, the *personal unconscious*, and the *collective unconscious*. Lying deep within the mind in the collective unconscious is the collective knowledge of humanity, the memories of humanity's past. Formed through the repeated experiences of humankind, this knowledge can be tapped through images of birth, death, rebirth, the seasons, and so forth, within a text and can cause profound emotions to surface within a reader. See **collective unconscious**.

arche-writing (archi-écriture) A term used by the deconstructionist Jacques Derrida in *Of Grammatology* (1974) to assert that language is a kind of writing. Derrida, however, redefines the term *writing*. Derrida asserts that writing cannot be reduced to letters or other symbols inscribed on a page. Rather, it is directly related to what Saussure believed to be the basic element of language: difference. We can know a word because it differs from another word. The word *tall* could just as easily have become *sall* in American English. This free play or element of undecidability in any system of communication Derrida calls writing.

Aristotelian poetics The name given to the underlying principles of interpretation found in Aristotle's *Poetics*. In this work, Aristotle states the first definition of tragedy. The *Poetics* has now become the cornerstone of Western literary criticism.

artifacts Any product of artistic endeavor, such as a poem, a novel, a painting, a short story, and so on. The word implies that the artistic endeavor can be analyzed or studied to help ascertain its meaning, as its general meaning is "something created by humans" which implies an analyzable entity or object.

aspirated A linguistic term designating a sound such as the *p* in *pat*, in which a brief delay occurs before pronouncing the vowel sound with an accompanying release of air.

autotelic artifact A term used most often by New Critics that refers to the existence of a text. For the New Critics, a text exists in its own right as an autonomous object that can be analyzed.

bad critic A term employed by New Criticism for that kind of critic who insists on imposing extrinsic evidence such as historical or biographical information upon a text to discover its meaning.

base A term used by Karl Marx to designate the economic structure of society. According to Marx, the various methods of economic production and the social relationships they engender form the base. In America, for example, Marxism asserts that the capitalists exploit the working classes, determining for them their salaries and their working conditions, their salaries and working conditions being the base.

binary operations (binary oppositions) A term introduced into literary theory by Jacques Derrida to represent the conceptual oppositions on which he believes Western metaphysics is based, such as light/dark, good/bad, and big/small. See **metaphysics**.

bourgeoisie According to Karl Marx and Fredrich Engels in *The Communist Manifesto* (1848), this term refers to the social elite, or members of the upper class, who control and therefore define the economic base of society through economic policies and the production of goods. The bourgeoisie also defines a society's superstructure and its hegemony. See **hegemony**.

canon The collected works of an author or of a tradition.

castration complex According to Sigmund Freud, if a child's sexual development is to proceed normally, each much pass through the castration complex. Boys, for example, know they have a penis like their fathers, while their mother and/or sisters do not. What stops the male child from having incestuous desires for his mother is fear of castration by his father. The child therefore represses his sexual desire, identifies with his father, hopes to possess a woman as his father now possesses his mother, and unconsciously makes a successful transition to manhood. The female child, however, realizes that, like her mother, she is already castrated. Knowing that her father possesses what she desires (a penis), she turns her attention away from her mother and toward her father. After unsuccessfully attempting to seduce her father, she turns back toward her mother, identifies with her, and successfully makes her transition to womanhood.

catalyst An agent or element that causes but is not affected by a reaction.

catharsis A term used by Aristotle in the *Poetics* in discussing the nature and function of tragedy. Although its meaning is highly controversial and by no means clear, *catharsis* had both a medical and a religious meaning in Aristotle's day. Medically, the word referred to a body's discharge of excess elements during sickness and its subsequent return to health. In a religious sense, the word referred to the soul's method of purification, freeing itself from the body and becoming unfettered. As to its use in tragedy, Aristotle writes, "Through tragedy, then, the audience's emotions would somehow be purified." How this process actually occurs, however, is open to debate.

chora A term used by the feminist critic Julia Kristeva to refer to the continuous flow of fluidity or rhythm that characterizes the Imaginary Order of psychic development. See **imaginary order**.

close readers A term used by the New Critics for that kind of reader or critic who applies the principles of New Criticism to a text to arrive at an interpretation. Implied in the term is a close and detailed analysis of the text itself to derive its meaning without historical, authorial, or cultural input. See **New Criticism**.

close reading A term employed by the New Critics for that kind of reading or analysis of a text that applies the principles of New Criticism. Implied in the term is a close and detailed analysis of the text itself to arrive at an interpretation without referring to historical, authorial, or cultural concerns. See **New Criticism**.

collective meaning   A term employed by the reader-response, subjective critic David Bleich as a substitute for the word *interpretation*. According to Bleich, a text's meaning is developed when a reader works in cooperation with other readers to achieve the text's collective meaning or its interpretation. Bleich argues that only when each reader is able to articulate his or her individual responses within a group about the text, then and only then can the group, working together, negotiate meaning and arrive at the text's collective meaning.

collective unconscious   A term brought into literary criticism via the psychology of Carl Jung. The collective unconscious is that part of the psyche that contains the cumulative knowledge, experiences, and images of the human race. This knowledge evidences itself as "primordial images" in humankind's religions, myths, dreams, and literature and can be tapped by writers through the use of archetypes. See **archetype**.

concretized   A term used by reader-response critics to mean the phenomenological process whereby the text registers upon the reader's consciousness. See **phenomenology**.

condensation   A term used by Sigmund Freud in psychoanalysis and dream interpretation to designate the process whereby one compacts a feeling or emotion toward a person or group and objectifies it into a simple sentence, phrase, or symbol.

connotation   The implied meaning of a word, as opposed to its dictionary definition. See **denotation**.

conscious   A term brought into literary criticism via the psychoanalysis of Carl Jung that refers to one of the three parts of the human psyche, a person's waking state. The term was also used by Sigmund Freud to define the rational and waking part of the human psyche. See **personal unconscious** and **collective unconscious**.

cultural materialism   The British branch of cultural poetics. Compared to New Historicism or the American branch of cultural poetics, cultural materialism is overtly political and cultural in its aims. Accordingly, adherents to this critical methodology (mainly Marxists) believe we should read the works of the established canon "against the grain." By so doing, the critic can expose the political unconscious of the text and debunk the social and political myths created by the bourgeoisie.

cultural poetics   According to Stephen Greenblatt, one of its founders, cultural poetics is now the preferred name for New Historicism. See **New Historicism** and **cultural materialism**.

cultural studies   That body of literary theorists, philosophers, and critics who study the works of subaltern writers, those such as Africans, Australians, Native Americans, women, and a host of others who are suppressed and repressed by their dominant cultures. These newly heard but long existent voices are now taking their place at literature's table, where they can present their understanding of reality, of society, and of personal self-worth. Some scholars divide this broad group into three categories: postcolonialism, African American criticism, and gender studies. See **subaltern writers**, **postcolonialism**, **African American criticism**, and **gender studies**.

deconstruction   Introduced in America in 1966 by Jacques Derrida's speech at Johns Hopkins University, this poststructural approach to literary analysis is best considered a strategic device for interpreting a text rather than a critical theory, school of criticism, or philosophy. Such theories, schools of criticism, and philosophies, Derrida asserts, must identify with a body of knowledge that they decree to be true or, at least, to contain truth. The idea that truth or a core of metaphysical ideals can be definitely believed, articulated, and supported is exactly what Derrida and **deconstructists** wish to "deconstruct."

Considered to be the most intellectually formidable approach to literary analysis, deconstruction bases its ideas on the linguistics of Ferdinand de Saussure and his assertion that language is a system based on differences; for example, we know the difference between the sounds /b/ and /p/ because we have heard both and can note the difference. Derrida enlarges this concept of difference by declaring that how we come to know concepts is also a matter of difference.

Denying any center of truth, such as God, humanity, or self, deconstruction maintains that we can never be certain about our values, beliefs, and assumptions. If this is the case, then we can never be certain about a text's meaning, and we can therefore never declare a text to have but one meaning. The "undecidability" of a text's meaning thus becomes the cardinal rule of deconstruction.

denotation   The dictionary definition of a word, as distinct from its *connotation* or its suggestive and/or emotional meaning(s). See **connotation**.

diachronic   A term used in linguistics to designate a process of language study in which language change is traced over long expanses of time. Such study can discover, for example, how a particular phenomenon in one language has changed through several centuries and whether a similar change could be noted in other languages. (The term is also used in other fields in which cultural phenomena are studied as they occur or change overtime.)

dialectical criticism   A term coined by the Marxist postcolonialist critic Fredric Jameson that refers to his belief that all critics must be consciously aware of their own ideology when analyzing a text, what Jameson calls "dialectial self-awareness."

dialectical materialism   A term used to refer to the core beliefs of Marxism as defined by Marx and Engels in *The Communist Manifesto* (1848) and by Marx in *The German Ideology* (1846). For Marx and Engels, "Consciousness does not determine life: life determines consciousness." In other words, our ideas and concepts about ourselves are fashioned in everyday discourse in the language of real life and are not derived from any spiritual reality. The basis of reality is material; no spiritual reality exists. In addition, the economic means of production within a society—its *base*—engenders and controls all human institutions and ideologies—the *superstructure*. See **Marxism**.

dialectial self-awareness   A term brought into Marxist criticism by the American critic Fredric Jameson. Jameson posits that all readers or critics must be consciously aware of their own ideology when analyzing a text. Such self-knowledge Jameson calls dialectial self-awareness.

différance   Introduced by the French deconstructionist Jacques Derrida. *Différance* is derived from the French word *différer*, meaning (1) to defer, postpone, or delay, and (2) to differ, to be different from. Derrida deliberately coined this word to be ambiguous, taking on both meanings simultaneously. One of the keys to understanding deconstruction, *différance* is Derrida's "What if" question. What if there is no ultimate truth? What if there is no essence, being, or inherently unifying element in the universe? What then? Derrida's answer is that all meaning or interpretations of a text are *undecidable*, for a text can have innumerable meanings and interpretations.

discourse A way of seeing and thinking about the world. Bounded by ideology, culture, education, politics, and a variety of other influences, *discourse* refers not only to speech patterns but also to a particular mind-set secured by philosophical assumptions that predisposes a person to interpret the world in a particular fashion.

displacement A term used by Sigmund Freud in psychoanalysis to designate the process whereby we suppress wishes and desires that are too difficult for our psyches to handle by concealing them in symbols that take the place of the original desire. Our unconscious mind may switch, for example, a person's hatred of another onto a rotting apple in a dream.

double consciousness A postcolonial term used synonymously with unhomeliness. See **unhomeliness**.

dynamic model The earliest of Sigmund Freud's models of the human psyche; with it, Freud declared that our minds are based in a dichotomy consisting of the *conscious* (the rational) and the *unconscious* (the irrational).

economic model Sigmund Freud's later or revised model of the human psyche, after the dynamic model. In the economic model, Freud introduces two new concepts: the *pleasure principle* and the *reality principle*. See **pleasure principle** and **reality principle**.

écriture féminine A term used in feminist criticism to refer specifically to "women's writing." Modern feminist critics speculate that a style of writing peculiar to women exists, and that this *écriture féminine* is fundamentally different from the way males write and obtain meaning through the writing process.

efferent reading A term used by Louise M. Rosenblatt in *The Reader, the Text, the Poem* (1978) to refer to that type of reading "in which the primary concern of the reader is with what he or she will carry away from the reading." We read efferently, for example, when we read solely for information, as we do when we read the directions on how to heat a can of soup. During this process we are interested only in newly gained information. This is different from aesthetic reading, in which the reader "lives through" and experiences the reading process. See **aesthetic reading**.

ego A term used by Sigmund Freud to designate the rational, logical, waking part of the psyche as differentiated from the id and the superego.

Electra complex The female version of the Oedipus complex as defined by Sigmund Freud. Freud borrows the name from Greek mythology: Electra, the sister of Orestes, aids him in killing their mother, Clytemnestra, to avenge their father, Agamemnon, who Clytemnestra murdered. According to Freud, all females must successfully negotiate the Electra complex in order to make the transition from girlhood to a normal, mature woman. Like a boy, a young girl is erotically attracted to her mother and recognizes that her father is a rival for her mother's affection. Unconsciously, however, the girl realizes she is already castrated, as is her mother. Since she knows her father possesses that which she desires, a penis, she turns her desires to him and away from her mother. After the seduction of her father fails, she turns back toward the mother and identifies with her, thus successfully negotiating the Electra complex. See **Oedipus complex**.

eme A linguistic term used by Ferdinand de Saussure to designate the basic units or building blocks of language, such as phonemes, morphemes, words, and so on.

epic theater Developed by the playwright and Marxist critic Bertolt Brecht, epic theater refers to that kind of theatrical theory and production that advocates an abandonment of the Aristotelian premise of unity of time, place, and action, including the assumption that the audience should be made to believe that what they are seeing is real. Epic theater seeks to create alienation effects such as interrupting the drama by a direct appeal to the audience via a song or speech to keep the audience constantly aware of the moral and social issues to which they are being exposed in the drama itself. Brecht believed that dramatists should not blindly accept bourgeois conventionality within the drama and thus should revolt and seize the modes of production within this genre.

epiphany A sudden understanding or insight, especially concerning a divine being or the essential nature of truth. The term is often used in its Christian sense, the first Epiphany having taken place on January 6 with the manifestation of Christ to the Gentiles in the form of the Magi, and thereafter observed as a Holy Day in the Christian Church.

James Joyce is responsible for bringing this term into literary critical usage to mean a sudden, intuitive understanding of a person, a situation, or an object.

episteme A term borrowed from the French writer, philosopher, and critic Michel Foucault and used by New Historicists to define the unifying principle or pattern that develops in each historical epoch. Through language and thought, each period in history develops its own perceptions about the nature of reality (or what it defines as truth) and sets up its own standards of behavior.

epistemological Of or relating to that branch of philosophy called epistemology, which studies the nature of knowledge, especially its limits and validity.

esoteric work A text meant for private as opposed to public circulation.

etymologically The adverbial form of etymology, or the process of tracing the historical development of a word, including its various meanings and form(s), from the word's earliest recorded occurrence in a language to the present.

exoteric treatise A text meant for general publication.

expressive school Emphasizes the individuality of the artist and the reader's privilege to share in this individuality. Disavowing rhetorical or objective theories of art, expressive critics emphasize the subjective experience of sharing emotions. Wordsworth and other nineteenth-century Romantics are prime examples of this school of thought.

extrinsic analysis The process of examining elements outside the text (such as historical events and biographies) to uncover the text's meaning.

false consciousness A term used by Karl Marx to describe how the consciousness of the working class is shaped and controlled by the bourgeoisie. By defining what it means to be an individual and thereby prescribing its class consciousness, the bourgeoisie create a false consciousness for the proletariat and perpetuate the dominant class's social structure.

feminism An approach to textual analysis having its roots in the Progressive Era in the early decades of the twentieth century. Some of its earliest and major philosophical tenets are articulated by the British feminist Virginia Woolf (*A Room of One's Own*, published in 1919) and the French feminist Simone de Beauvoir (*The Second*

Sex, published in 1949). Feminists assert that Western societies are patriarchal, being controlled by men. Either consciously or unconsciously, men have oppressed women, allowing them little or no voice in the political, social, or economic issues of their society. By not giving voice, and therefore value, to women's opinions, responses, and writings, men have suppressed the female, defined what it means to be feminine, and thereby de-voiced, devalued, and trivialized what it means to be a woman. Men have made women the "nonsignificant Other."

A goal of feminism is to change this degrading view of women so that each woman will realize that she is a valuable person possessing the same privileges and rights as every man. Women must therefore define themselves and assert their own voices in politics, education, the arts, and in all other areas of society. By debunking stereotypical images of women found throughout the literary canon, by rediscovering and publishing texts written by females but suppressed by men, by rereading the canonized works of male authors from a woman's point of view, and by engaging in the discussion of literary theory, women can begin to challenge the concept of male superiority and work toward creating equality between the sexes.

Since feminism is more an approach or mind-set than a school of criticism, feminist theory and thought have been embraced by scholars belonging to a variety of critical schools, such as Marxism, deconstruction, psychoanalysis, and New Historicism. Some of the leading twentieth-century feminists are Virginia Woolf, Simone de Beauvoir, Elaine Showalter, Hélène Cixous, Sandra Gilbert, and Gayatri Chakravorty Spivak.

form A term used by the New Critics—adherents of New Criticism—to mean the overall effect a text creates. From this perspective, a text's form encompasses the actual structure of the text along with the text's overall effect on the reader. In New Critical theory, all the elements of a text work together to form a single, unified effect known as the text's form.

formalism A term used to designate those critics (**formalists**) who rely on a work's form or structure to determine its meaning. The term is often applied to the New Critics, who insist that the interpretation of a work of art must evolve from the work's structure, not from extrinsic elements such as the author's life or historical context.

formalists Literary theorists and critics who adhere to the principles of formalism. See **formalism**.

Frankfurt school Neo-Marxist critics devoted to developing Western Marxist principles. These critics assert that the superstructure reflects the economic base. They also believe that a text reveals a culture's fragmentation, not its wholeness. See **superstructure** and **base.**

Freudian slips A term used in psychoanalysis to describe accidental slips of the tongue. According to Freud, these "disguised truths" are stored in a person's unconscious until, inadvertently, they slip into our conscious minds and pop out in statements in one's speech.

gender studies A term sometimes used synonymously with *feminism;* however, the field broadens traditional feminist criticism to include an investigation of not only femaleness but also maleness. To the multivoiced feminist theories, gender studies adds the ever-growing and increasingly diverse voices of black feminists, the ongoing concerns of French feminism, and the impact of poststructural theories on customary feminist issues.

good critic A term employed by New Criticism to characterize that kind of critic who examines a poem's (or any text's) structure by scrutinizing its poetic elements, rooting out and showing its inner tensions, and demonstrating how the poem supports its overall meaning as the writer reconciles these tensions into a unified whole.

grammar The system of rules that govern the production and interpretation of language. *Prescriptive grammar* refers to matters of "correctness," such as not using the word *ain't* or saying "It is *I*," and not "It is *me*." *Descriptive grammar* refers to the process of describing how actual speakers use their language for communication.

grammatical Of or referring to the rules of grammar.

grammatical sentence See **sentence**.

grapheme The symbols of a writing system (the letters of the alphabet, for example) that represent a phoneme. See **phoneme**.

gynocriticism A term coined by the feminist scholar–critic Elaine Showalter that has become synonymous with the study of women as writers. It provides critics with four models about the nature of women's writing that help answer some of the chief concerns of feminist criticism. Each of Showalter's models are sequential, subsuming and developing the preceding model(s), to encompass the full analytical scope: (1) biological, (2) linguistic, (3) psychoanalytic, (4) cultural.

gynocritics A term coined by the feminist scholar–critic Elaine Showalter to define the process of constructing "a female framework for analysis of women's literature [in order] to develop new models [of interpretation] based on the study of female experience, rather than to adapt to male models and theories." See **gynocriticism**.

hamartia A term used by Aristotle in the *Poetics* to refer to the tragic hero's mistake or error that leads to a downfall. Literally, the word means "missing the mark" (from the Greek *hamartanein*, "to err"). Aristotle explains that the hero of a tragedy will commit some action or exhibit some frailty (*hamartia*) that will lead to a reversal of fortune.

hegemony A term used in Marxist criticism that refers to the system of beliefs, values, and meanings to which most people in a given society subscribe. Marxist critics assert that the dominant culture in a given society is under the control of the bourgeoisie, and it is therefore the bourgeoisie who control and dictate the hegemony of a culture. According to the Italian Marxist Antonio Gramsci, a given society's hegemony may be successful, but never complete. Rather than one all-encompassing ruling class, there usually exist several, interconnected yet somewhat divergent classes, each influencing the superstructure at different times and in different ways. Marxist revolutions, then, can begin within alternative hegemonies rather than direct political action.

heresy of paraphrase A term used by New Critics to suggest that a work of art is not equal to its paraphrase. A poem, for example, is not the same as its paraphrased version, for the paraphrased version will miss the poem's uniqueness, with its many connotations and various complexities of thought.

hermeneutical principles The rules governing the interpretation of a text. See **hermeneutics**.

hermeneutics First defined by religious scholars as the art and science of biblical interpretation, this term now refers to any theory and practice of interpretation. (From the Greek *hermeneutike*, meaning the "act of interpretation.")

holistic approach An approach to literary study that investigates, analyzes, and interprets all elements of the artistic situation—text, author, historical context, and so on—instead of concentrating on one or more specific aspects.

horizons of expectation A term used by reader-response critics to refer to all of a historical period's critical vocabulary and assessments of a particular text. Used especially by those who adhere to reception theory. See **reception theory**.

id A term used by Sigmund Freud to designate the irrational, instinctual, unknown, and unconscious part of the psyche as differentiated from the *ego* and *superego*.

ideal reader A term devised by the narratologist Gerard Prince to differentiate among the *real*, *virtual*, and *ideal reader*. According to Prince, the ideal reader is one who explicitly and implicitly understands all the nuances, terminology, and structure of a text. See **virtual reader** and **real reader**.

identity theme A term devised by the Freudian psychoanalyst Norman Holland, who argues that, at birth, all of us receive from our mothers a primary identity. Through each of our life's experiences, we personalize this identity, transforming it into our own individualized identity theme, which becomes the lens through which we see the world.

ideology A much debated term in Marxist criticism, the term often refers to a culture's collective or social consciousness (as opposed to the material reality on which experience is based), that is, to the culture's internal awareness of a body of laws or codes governing its politics, law, religion, philosophy, and art to which that culture's bourgeoisie and therefore its superstructure subscribes. For Marx and Engels, a culture's ideology is more frequently than not synonymous with "false consciousness," for it has been defined and established by the bourgeoisie and therefore represents a set of false assumptions or illusions used by the elite to dominate the working classes and to maintain stability. An ideology, then, may be conscious or explicit (in precepts that state and shape a society's philosophy, its laws, or its acceptable customs), or it may be a somewhat vaguer and implicit understanding of its controlling beliefs (as in ceremony, for example).

Imaginary Order According to psychoanalyst Jacques Lacan, the Imaginary Order is one of three parts of the human psyche; it contains our wishes, fantasies, and images. In this preverbal state (from birth to six months), Lacan believes humans are joyfully united with their mothers, receiving food, care, and all comforts from them, relying on images as a means of perceiving and interpreting the world. In this psychic stage of development, our image of ourselves is always in flux, for we are not able to differentiate where one image stops and another begins.

implied reader A term devised by the German phenomenologist Wolfgang Iser to differentiate between two kinds of readers: the *implied reader* and the *actual reader*. According to Iser, the implied reader is the reader who "embodies all those predispositions laid down, not by an empirical outside reality, but by the text itself. Hence, the implied reader has his or her roots firmly planted in the structure of the text." See **actual reader**.

impressionistic critics Those critics who believe that how we feel and what we personally see in a work of art are what really matters. Capturing what we see from a particular point of view and at a specific moment in time is what is important, not an objective, lengthy investigation of text or an aesthetic object. The term *impressionism* was first used by nineteenth-century French painters such as Claude Monet and Pierre-August Renoir and referred to the impressions an object makes upon the artist rather than the actual representation of an objective picture of that object.

inflection Used in linguistics to describe the various forms a word undergoes to mark changes in elements such as tense, number, gender, and mood. For example, the *-ed* in the word *worked* signals the past tense, and the *-s* in the word *dogs* signals the plural form of that word.

in medias res From the Latin, meaning "in the middle of things." This term refers to a story or narrative such as The *Iliad* that begins in the middle rather than at its chronological starting point in time.

intentional fallacy A term used by New Critics to refer to what they believe is the erroneous assumption that the interpretation of a literary work can be equated to the author's stated or implied intentions and/or private meanings. Claiming such external information to be irrelevant in ascertaining a text's meaning, New Critics base interpretation on the text itself. The term was first used by W. K. Wimsatt and Monroe C. Beardsley in "The Intentional Fallacy" (1946).

interpellation Or "hailing the subject." A term coined by the Marxist critic Louis Althusser to refer to the process whereby the dominant hegemony or prevailing ideology forms the attitudes of people in society. See **hegemony**.

interpretive community A term coined by the reader-response critic Stanley Fish to designate a group of readers who share the same interpretive strategies.

intertexuality A term denoting that any given text's meaning or interpretation is related or interrelated to the meaning of all other texts. Hence, no text can be interpreted in isolation, and all texts are **intertexual**.

irony The use of words whereby a writer or speaker suggests the opposite of what is actually stated. According to New Critics such as Cleanth Brooks, John Crowe Ransom, and I. A. Richards, irony is the key to the "dramatic structure" of poetry and unlocks the door to show how meaning is contained in and evolves from a poem's structure. New Critics believe a poem's meaning is structurally determined, created by the tension between the denotative meaning of a poem's words and their connotations, which are, in turn, determined by the context of that particular poem. Irony, then, is "an equilibrium of [these] opposing attitudes and evaluations," which ultimately determine the poem's meaning.

jouissance A term used by the psychoanalytic critic Jacques Lacan to refer to a brief moment of joy, terror, or desire that somehow arises from deep within the unconscious psyche and reminds us of a time of perfect wholeness when we were incapable of differentiating among images from the Real Order. See **Real Order**, **Imaginary Order**, and **Symbolic Order**.

language Defined by the linguist Thomas Pyles as "a systematized combination of sounds that have meaning for all people in a given cultural community." Broadly speaking, *language* may be considered any system of signs, or codes that convey meaning, such as road signs, the language of fashion (wearing different clothes in different social settings), or even the language of eating.

langue The linguistic term used by Ferdinand de Saussure to refer to the rules that comprise a language or the structure of the language that is mastered and shared by all its speakers. By the age of five or six, children have mastered their language's langue, although they have not mastered the exceptions. For example, a six-year-old may say, "I drinked a glass of milk," and "I climbed a tree." Having mastered his or her langue, the child has learned that most English verbs form their past tense by adding -d or -ed. What the child has not mastered is the many exceptions to this rule, in this case the past tense of the irregular verb *to drink*.

latent content A term used by Sigmund Freud in psychoanalytic dream interpretation. It is Freud's view that the ego (the rational part of the psyche) hides the true wish or *latent content* of our dreams, thereby allowing the dreamer to remember a somewhat changed and often radically different dream than the one that actually occurred.

L'écriture féminine See *écriture féminine*.

lexical Used in linguistics to refer to the base or root meaning of a word. For example, the word *love* is the base word in the following word model: *loves, loved, loving*.

lexicon The word stock or the entire vocabulary of a language.

libido A term used by Sigmund Freud in psychoanalysis that has become synonymous with sexual drive. Freud used this designation to refer to the emotional energy that springs from primitive biological urges and is usually directed toward some goal.

linear A term used to refer to something that has a definite beginning, middle, and end. A philosophy of life or one's worldview, for example, may be considered linear.

linguistics The science of language and human speech, including the study of sounds, inflections, structure, and modification of language.

linguistic sign A term used in linguistics in reference to words. As used by Ferdinand de Saussure, a *sign* is composed of two parts: the signifier (a written or spoken mark) and the signified (the concept it represents). See **sign**.

literacy experience An event that occurs when a reader and print interact.

literary competence An internalized set of rules that govern a reader's interpretation of a text. The critic Jonathan Culler states that all readers possess literary competence or the ability to make sense of a text.

literary critic One who interprets literature. This term often implies one who is an expert at interpreting a text. Anyone, however, who reads and offers an interpretation of a text is a practicing literary critic.

literary criticism According to the nineteenth-century English critic and writer Matthew Arnold, *literary criticism* is "a disinterested endeavor to learn and propagate the best that is known and thought in the world." It is therefore a disciplined activity that attempts to study, analyze, interpret, and evaluate a work of art.

literary theory A set of principles or assumptions on which our interpretation of a text is based. Our personal literary theory is our conscious or unconscious development of a mind-set—including values, aesthetics sense, morals, and so on—concerning our expectations when reading any type of literature. By articulating this framework and piecing together the various elements of our practical criticism into a coherent, unified body of knowledge, we create a literary theory.

literature Derived from the Latin word *littera*, meaning "letter," the word *literature* refers primarily to the written word, especially prose or verse.

logocentrism A term used by the French deconstructionist Jacques Derrida that refers to Western culture's proclivity for desiring absolute truths, or what Derrida calls "centers." *Logocentrism* is therefore the belief that there is an ultimate reality or center of truth that can serve as the basis for all our thoughts and actions.

manifest content A term used by Sigmund Freud in psychoanalytic dream interpretation. Freud argues that the ego or the rational part of the psyche hides the true wish or *latent content* of our dreams and allows the dreamer to remember a somewhat changed and often radically different dream than the one that actually occurred. This changed dream is the *manifest content* that the dreamer remembers and tells his or her dream analyst.

Marxism An approach to literary analysis founded on principles articulated by Friedrich Engels and Karl Marx. Unlike other schools of criticism, Marxism is not primarily a literary theory that can be used to interpret a text, for it is first a set of social, economic, and political ideas that its followers believe will enable them to interpret and change their world. Ultimate reality, they declare, is material, not spiritual. What we know beyond any doubt is that human beings exist and live in social groups. In order to understand ourselves and our world, we must first acknowledge the interrelatedness of all our actions within society. Once understood properly, we will note that it is our cultural and our social circumstances that determine who we are. What we believe, what we value, and how we think are a direct result of our society, and that society, says Marxism, is built upon a series of ongoing conflicts between the "haves" and the "have nots."

In *The Communist Manifesto* (1848), Engels and Marx declare that the "haves" (the capitalists or the *bourgeoisie*) have successfully enslaved the "have nots" (the working class or the *proletariat*) through economic policies and control of the production of goods. In addition, the bourgeoisie have established society's beliefs, its values, and even its art. Now the proletariat must revolt and strip the bourgeoisie of their economic and political power and place the ownership of all property in the hands of the government, which will fairly distribute the people's wealth.

Since the bourgeoisie controls a society's art and therefore its literature, **Marxist critics** believe they must move beyond the usual analysis of literary devices, themes, and style and concentrate on determining an author's worldview, the historical context of the work, and the sociological concerns of the text to see if such an analysis of the author's ideology advances either the bourgeoisie's or the proletariat's concerns.

Some of the leading Marxist critics of the twentieth century are Georg Lukács, Raymond Williams, Walter Benjamin, Fredric Jameson, and Terry Eagleton.

metalanguage A language (words) used to describe or talk about language.

metaphor A figure of speech that directly compares two unlike objects (without using *like* or *as*), in which the qualities of one object are ascribed to the other. For example, in the sentence, "My love is a rose," the qualities of the rose are directly ascribed to "my love."

metaphysics A term derived from Aristotle's treatise *Metaphysica*, denoting a division of philosophy that studies the nature of *Being*. The term implies a reality beyond what we can see and experience with our five senses.

metaphysics of presence A term coined by the French deconstructionist Jacques Derrida to encompass those ideas such as logocentrism, phonocentrism, the operation of binary oppositions, and other notions held in Western thought and culture about the nature of language and metaphysics. Derrida's objectives are to demonstrate the shaky foundations on which such beliefs have been established, and thereby "deconstruct" or take apart what Western culture values, and to show how such a deconstructive process will lead to new and exciting interpretations of a text.

metatheory An overarching or all-inclusive literary theory—that is, a theory of all theories—which can encompass all possible interpretations of a text suggested by its readers.

mimesis From the Greek, meaning "imitation." Often refers to Aristotle's theory of imitation.

mimetic theory A term used in literary criticism to refer to art as an imitation or copy of various elements of the universe. In linguistics, the *mimetic theory of language* asserts that words are symbols for things in the world; that is, each word has its own referent—the object, concept, or idea that is represented or symbolized by that word. Accordingly, a word equals its referent. See **referent**.

minimal pair Two words that differ by one significant phonological sound. For example, *pit* and *bit* differ only in their first phonemes or significant first sounds.

mirror stage A term coined by the psychoanalyst Jacques Lacan to describe what happens during the development of the human psyche sometime between 6 to 18 months of age. According to Lacan, the human psyche consists of three parts or orders: the Imaginary, the Symbolic, and the Real. During the latter part of development in the first order, the Imaginary, Lacan asserts that we literally see ourselves in a mirror, or we may metaphorically see ourselves in our mothers' image. Seeing this mirror image permits us to perceive images that have discrete boundaries, thereby allowing us to become aware of ourselves as independent beings who are separate from our mothers.

misogyny A term used in feminist criticism to refer to a hatred or distrust of women.

misspeaks According to the deconstructionist critic Jacques Derrida, at some point in all texts the author loses control of language and says what was supposedly not meant to be said and thus "misspeaks." Such slips of tongue usually occur in questions, figurative language, and strong declarations. By examining these slips and the binary operations that govern them, Derrida believes he is able to demonstrate the undecidability of a text's meaning. See **binary operations** and **undecidability**.

modernism A literary movement in both England and America considered by some to have begun with the influence of the French Symbolist poetry of Charles Baudelaire and Paul Valéry at the beginning of the twentieth century. Some assert this period begins in 1914, with the start of the First World War, and ends right after the Second World War, while still others mark its ending around 1965.

However its span is dated, modernism is marked, as T. S. Eliot notes, by an impersonal view of humanity and produced a literature that is distinctly anti-romantic and anti-expressionistic. In its ardent search for meaning through form, modernism typically employs hard, dry language which asserts that feeling or emotions are elicited by the text itself through the textual arrangement of its images. By rejecting a sheerly personal reading of a work, modernism declares that a text's meaning can be found by examining its structure, a technique that is especially true for poetry. The modernist period thus provides literary criticism with a formal explanation for how a poem or any other work of literature achieves or produces meaning through its form.

monomyth A term used in the archetypal criticism of Northrop Frye, who states that all literature comprises one complete and whole story called the "monomyth." This monomyth can best be diagramed as a circle containing four separate phases, with each phase corresponding to a season of the year and to peculiar cycles of human experiences. The phases are *romance* (the summer story of total happiness and wish fulfillment), *anti-romance* (the winter story of bondage, imprisonment, frustration, and fear), *comedy* (the spring story that tells of our rise from frustration to freedom and happiness), and *tragedy* (the fall story, narrating our fall from happiness to disaster). According to Frye, all stories fall somewhere within these categories.

morpheme Used in linguistics to describe the smallest part of a word that has lexical or grammatical significance. For example, the word *dog* contains one morpheme, *dog*, whereas the word *dogs* contains two morphemes, *dog* and *-s*.

morphology Used in linguistics to describe the process of word formation, such as compound words and inflections.

mythemes A term coined by the structuralist critic Claude Lévi-Strauss that refers to the many recurrent themes running through humankind's countless myths. These basic structures, he maintains, are similar to the individual sounds of language, the primary building blocks of language itself. Like these sounds, mythemes find meaning in and through their relationships within the mythic structure, not in their own individuality. The meaning of any individual myth, then, depends upon the interaction and order of the mythemes found within the story.

mythic criticism Criticism that examines archetypes and archetypal patterns to explain the structure and significance of texts. This type of criticism was especially emphasized by Carl Jung and Northrop Frye.

narratee A term used by the structuralist and narratologist Gerard Prince to refer to the person to whom the narrator of a text is speaking. It is Prince's view that the narratee is not the actual person reading the text but, in fact, is produced by the narrative itself.

narratologists A particular kind of structuralist who utilizes the principles of narratology to interpret texts. See **narratology**.

narratology A form of structuralism espoused by Vladimir Propp, Tzvetan Todorov, Roland Barthes, and Gerard Genette that illustrates how a story's meaning develops from its overall structure (its *langue*) rather than from each individual story's isolated theme. To ascertain a text's meaning, narratologists emphasize grammatical elements such as verb tenses and the relationships and configurations of figures of speech within the story.

naturalism A term that refers to the late nineteenth and early twentieth-century view of life that emphasizes the importance of scientific thought and determinism in literary study. A naturalistic critic views humans as animals who respond in deterministic ways to their environment and internal drives.

neo-Platonic A term used to describe any philosophical system that closely resembles that established by Plato, thus the prefix *neo*, meaning "new." The term originated in the third century in Alexandria in a philosophical system that mixed Asian, Platonic, and Christian beliefs.

neurosis A nervous disorder that has no known bodily or physical cause that can lead to a variety of physical and psychological abnormalities.

New Criticism A loosely structured school of criticism that dominated American literary criticism from the early 1930s to the 1960s. Named after John Crowe Ransom's 1941 book *The New Criticism*, the theory is based on the view that a work of art or a text is a concrete object that can, like any other concrete object, be analyzed to discover its meaning independent of its author's intention or the emotional state and/or values of either its author or reader. For the **New Critic**, a poem's meaning must reside within its own structure (in New Criticism, the word *poem* refers to any text, not only a poem). By giving a poem a "close reading," the New Critics believe they can ascertain the text's correct meaning. See **close reading**.

Often referred to as "the text and text alone" approach to literary analysis, New Criticism has found many practitioners, such as John Crowe Ransom, René Wellek, W. K. Wimsatt, R. P. Blackmur, I. A. Richards, Cleanth Brooks, and Robert Penn Warren. With the publication of Brooks and Warren's 1938 college text *Understanding Poetry*, New Criticism became the dominant approach to textual analysis until the 1960s.

New Critics Those critics who employ the doctrines, assumptions, and methodology of New Criticism in their literary analysis. See **New Criticism**.

New Historicism Refers to the American branch of cultural poetics. Appearing in the late 1970s and early 1980s, New Historicism is one of the most recent approaches to textual analysis to develop. Led by such scholars as Stephen Greenblatt and Louis Montrose, New Historicism challenges the "old historicism" founded in nineteenth-century thought which declares (1) that history serves as a background to literature, (2) that history, as written, is an accurate view of what really occurred, and (3) that historians can articulate a unified and internally consistent worldview of any people, country, or era.

New Historicism declares that all history is subjective and that historians therefore can never provide us with the truth or give us a totally accurate picture of past events or the worldview of a people. Similar to language, history is but one of many discourses or ways of viewing the world. By viewing history as one of several important discourses that directly affect the interpretation of a text, **New Historicists** assert that their approach provides its followers with a practice of literary analysis that highlights the interrelatedness of all human activities, admits its own prejudices, and gives a more complete understanding of a text than do the old historicism and other interpretative approaches.

Adherents to the multiple approaches to textual analysis inherent in New Historicism now prefer to call this approach *cultural poetics*, emphasizing and noting the multiple factors that help determine a text's meaning. Its British counterpart is known as cultural materialism. See **cultural materialism**.

New Humanists A school of twentieth-century American literary critics who value the moral qualities of art. Declaring that human experience is basically ethical, these critics demand that literary analysis be based on the moral values exhibited in a text.

noematic A term that refers to the complexities of the objective world—its cultural, social, religious, and political realities—as detailed by an individual or class of writers.

noetic A term that refers to the subjective qualities of authors as exhibited in their writings.

objective correlative A term coined by T. S. Eliot that refers to a set of objects, a situation, a chain of events, or reactions that can serve to awaken in the reader the emotional response which the author desires without being a direct statement of that emotion.

objective theory of art A term introduced by M. H. Abrams that declares that the literary work itself is an object. Every work of art must therefore be a public text that can be understood by applying the standards of public discourse, not the private experience, intentions, and vocabulary of its author or a particular audience.

objet petit a A term used by Jacques Lacan to refer to those images that we discover in our mirror stage of psychic development. These images are separate from ourselves, such as bodily wastes, our mothers' voice and breasts, and our own speech sounds, and become for us symbols of lack that will plague us for our entire lives. See **mirror stage**.

Oedipus complex According to Sigmund Freud's theory of child development, all children between the ages of three and six develop sexual or libidinal feelings toward the parent of the opposite sex and hostile feelings toward the parent of the same sex. In young boys, this is known as the *Oedipus complex*, named after the legendary Theban Oedipus, who murdered his father and married his mother. In young girls, this period is called the *Electra complex*, named after the legendary Electra, who avenged her father's death by killing her mother and her mother's lover. See **Electra complex**.

The One The term used by Plato to describe his concept of spiritual reality. Plato says The One possesses ontological status, existing whether any mind posits its existence or reflects its attributes. It is composed of three elements: absolute Beauty, Truth, and Goodness.

ontological Relating to or based on being or existence. The term is used by New Critics in recognition of their belief that a work of art is a concrete entity (one that really exists) and can therefore be analyzed and dissected like any other object to ascertain its meaning.

ontological critic A critic who utilizes the assumptions of New Criticism and believes that a text is a concrete entity—like a painting, vase or doorlock—that can be analyzed to ascertain its meaning.

oral phase The first stage of child development as postulated by Sigmund Freud. In this stage, children suck at their mothers' breasts to be fed, but simultaneously the child's sexuality or libido is activated. Our mouths become erotogenic zones that will later cause us to enjoy sucking our tongues and, still later, kissing.

organic unity A term describing the concept that a text's structure is like a living plant, with all its parts supporting each other and living in a complex interrelationship. First advanced by the nineteenth-century poet-critic Samuel Taylor Coleridge, the concept of the organic unity of a work of art declares that each part of a text reflects and helps support the text's central idea, or as the New Critics would call it, the work's chief *paradox*. No part of a text is superfluous, but like a living organism, each serves to enhance the whole. The whole is therefore greater than the sum of its parts. See **paradox**.

Orientalism   A term introduced to postcolonist theory by Edward Said and refers to the creation of non-European stereotypes that suggest "Orientals" or Asians are indolent, thoughtless, sexually immoral, unreliable, and demented.

paradox   A term used by the New Critics (especially Cleanth Brooks) to help explain the nature and essence of poetry. According to Brooks, scientific language must be precise and exact. On the other hand, poetry's chief characteristic is its many rich connotations, not the scientific denotations of words. The meaning of a poem is therefore built on paradox, a juxtaposition of connotations and meanings that all support the poem's central idea.

parapraxes   A term coined by Sigmund Freud for those slips of tongue, failures of memory, acts of misplacing an object, and a host of other so-called mistakes we make, all of which can be directly traced to our unconscious desires, wishes, or intentions.

parole   A linguistic term used by Ferdinand de Saussure and others to refer to an individual's actual speech utterances, as opposed to *langue*, the rules that comprise a language. An individual can generate countless examples of parole, but all will be governed by the language's structure, its langue. For Saussure and other linguists, the proper study of linguistics is the system—the langue—not parole. See **langue**.

patriarchal   A term used by feminist critics and others to describe a society or culture dominated by males; the adjective form of *patriarchy*, a societal or social organization in which males hold a disproportionate amount of power. In these societies, the male defines what it means to be human, including what it means to be female.

penis envy   According to Sigmund Freud, all woman have an unfulfilled desire for a penis and thus possess a sense of lack throughout their lives. See **Electra complex**.

personal conscious   A term used in psychoanalytic criticism to refer to that part of the human psyche that directly perceives and interacts with the external world. It is sometimes referred to as the *waking state*, for the personal conscious is the image or thought of which we are aware at any given moment.

personal unconscious   A term brought into literary criticism via the psychology of Carl Jung. According to Jung, the personal unconscious exists directly below the surface of the conscious and contains elements of all those private affairs that occur daily in each of our lives. The personal unconscious is therefore peculiar to one individual and not shared with any other.

personification   A figure of speech that attributes human qualities to animals, ideas, or inanimate objects.

phallic stage   The last stage of child development as theorized by Sigmund Freud. In this stage, the child's sexual desires or libido is directed toward the genitals.

phallic symbol   A term used in psychoanalytic criticism to describe the male's symbol of power as represented by any penislike image whose length exceeds its diameter, such as a tower, a sword, a knife, or a pen.

phallocentric A term used to describe any form of criticism, philosophy, or theory dominated by males and thus governed by a male way of thinking.

phallus A symbol or representation of the penis. In much psychoanalytic theory (Jacques Lacan's ideas, for example), the phallus becomes a *transcendental signified* and the ultimate symbol of power. Although neither males nor females can ever possess the phallus and therefore can never be complete or whole, males do have a penis and so have a slight claim to such power. See **transcendental signified**.

phenomenology Founded by Edmund Husserl, phenomonology is a modern philosophical tendency that emphasizes the perceiver. Objects exist and achieve meaning if and only if we register them on our consciousness. **Phenomenological critics** are therefore concerned with the ways in which our consciousness perceives works of art.

philologist The name given to a linguist prior to the mid–twentieth century. A philologist is one who describes, compares, and analyzes the languages of the world to discover their similarities and relationships.

philology The name given to the science of linguistics prior to the mid–twentieth century; used now especially to refer to historical and comparative linguistics. Typically, philology approached the study of language diachronically, whereas present-day linguistics uses both the diachronic and synchronic approaches. See **diachronic, linguistics**, and **synchronic**.

phoneme A linguistic term for the smallest distinct and significant sounds that comprise a language. Phonemes are the primary building blocks of language. American English, for example, contains approximately 45 phonemes, including /p/, /b/, /k/, and others.

phonetically The adverbial form of *phonetics*. See **phonetics**.

phonetics The study of how sounds are classified, described, and transcribed within a particular language.

phonocentrism A term coined by the French deconstructionist Jacques Derrida that asserts that Western culture *privileges* or prefers speech over writing. See **privileged**.

phonologically The adverbial form of *phonology*. See **phonology**.

phonology The study of the various sound changes in a word or a particular language, often including the study of phonetics.

pleasure principle Introduced by Sigmund Freud in his economic model of the human psyche. Freud defines the pleasure principle as that part of the human psyche that craves only pleasures and desires instantaneous satisfaction of instinctual drives; it ignores moral and sexual boundaries established by society.

poem A term used by Louise M. Rosenblatt that refers to the creation of a new interpretation each time a reader transacts with a text, be that interaction a first reading or any of countless rereadings of that same text. The interpretation thus becomes the poem, the new creation. New Critics also use this term to refer generically to any literary work.

Poetics Written by Aristotle, the *Poetics* is the earliest known work containing a definition of *literature*, particularly the genre of *tragedy*.

poetikes The Greek word meaning "things that are made or crafted." In critical theory, this word refers to Aristotle's text *Poetics*, which contains the component or "crafted parts" of a tragedy.

political unconscious A term coined by the Marxist critic Fredric Jameson. Borrowing Freud's idea of a repressed unconscious, Jameson posits the existence of a political unconscious, or repressed conditions of exploitation and oppression. The function of literary analysis, Jameson declares, is to uncover the political unconscious present in a text.

postcolonialism or **post-colonialism** One of the most recent approaches to literary analysis to appear on the literary scene. Postcolonialism concerns itself with literature written in English in formerly colonized countries and therefore excludes literature that represents either British or American viewpoints, concentrating on writings from colonized cultures such as Australia, New Zealand, Africa, and South America—to name a few—that were once dominated by, but remained outside of, the white male, European cultural, political, and philosophical tradition.

Often referred to as "third world literature" by Marxist critics—a term many other critics think pejorative—postcolonial literature and theory investigate what happens when two cultures clash and when one of them, with its accompanying ideology, empowers and deems itself superior to the other. Postcolonial theorists include Fredric Jameson, Georg Gugelberger, Edward W. Said, Bill Ashcroft, Gareth Griffiths, Helen Tiffin, Frantz Fanon, Ian Adam, Gayatri Chakravorty Spivak, Homi K. Bhabha, and a host of others.

postmodernism A term used synonymously with deconstruction and poststructuralism. First used in literary circles in the 1930s, the term gained in popularity during the late 1960s and 1970s. Presently, it connotes a group of philosophers, literary critics, and contemporary scholars who deny the existence of objective reality. For these thinkers, reality is a human construct that is shaped by each individual's dominant social group.

poststructuralism A term applied to a variety of literary theories and practical criticisms developed after structuralism. Dating from the late 1960s, poststructuralism is often used synonymously with deconstruction, although the term is much broader and includes such critical schools of thought as feminism, psychoanalysis (especially the ideas of Jacques Lacan), Marxism or any of its revisionist forms, New Historicism, and others.

Theoretically speaking, structuralism posits the objective reality of the text; that is, a structuralist believes one can examine a text using a standard and objective methodology and arrive at a conclusion. **Poststructuralists**, however, often assert the "undecidability" of a text's meaning and declare that a text may not in and of itself have any objective reality. Poststructuralists also question the long-held assumptions of the processes involved in both reading and writing and of the metaphysics of language.

practical critic One who applies the theories and tenets of theoretical criticism to a particular work of art. It is the practical critic who often defines the standards of taste and explains, evaluates, or justifies a particular text.

practical criticism See **applied criticism**.

preconscious A term used by Sigmund Freud in his typographic model of the human psyche. Freud defines the preconscious as that part of the psyche that is the storehouse of memories and which the conscious part of the mind allows to be brought to consciousness without disguise in some other form. These memories are manageable in the consciousness without "masking."

prescriptive grammar Prescriptive rules dictated by grammarians who believe educated people should speak and write in the correct way, with the correct way specifically defined by these same grammarians.

private symbol See **symbol**.

privileged A term introduced into literary criticism by the French deconstructionist Jacques Derrida. According to Derrida, Western society bases its values and its metaphysical assumptions on opposites, such as good/bad, light/dark, true/false. In each of these pairs, Derrida asserts, Western culture values or *privileges* the first element, while devaluing or *unprivileging* the second.

production theory A term developed by the Marxist critic Louis Althusser that rejects the assumption of *reflection theory* that the superstructure must directly reflect the base. Althusser asserts that literature, for example, should not be strictly relegated to the superstructure; further, he believes that the superstructure can and does influence the base. See **reflection theory** and **superstructure**.

proletariat A term used by Karl Marx and Friedrich Engels to refer to the working class of society. According to Marxist theory, the bourgeoisie (or upper class) oppresses and enslaves the proletariat by controlling the economic policies and the production of goods. It is the bourgeoisie, not the proletariat, who define and articulate a society's ideology.

prosody The mechanical or structural elements that comprise poetry, such as rhythm, meter, rhyme, stanza, diction, alliteration, and so forth. Used synonymously with *versification*.

psychoanalysis A method first employed by Sigmund Freud in treating emotional and psychological disorders. During this type of therapy, the psychoanalyst has patients talk freely about their childhood experiences and dreams.

psychoanalytic criticism The application of the methods of Sigmund Freud's psychoanalysis to interpreting works of literature. Because this approach to literary analysis attempts to explain the how and why of human actions without developing an aesthetic theory, a variety of critical approaches such as Marxism, feminism, and New Historicism utilize psychoanalytic methods in their interpretations without violating their own theoretical assumptions.

Central to psychoanalytic criticism is Freud's assumption that all artists are neurotic. Unlike other neurotics, the artist escapes many of the outward manifestations and end results of neurosis by finding in the act of creating art a pathway back to saneness and wholeness.

Freud believes that the literary text is really an artist's dream or fantasy. A text, then, can be analyzed like a dream. For Freud this means that we must assume that the dream is a disguised wish. Just as if he were counseling a patient and trying to uncover the meaning of the disguised wish as it evidences itself in a dream, Freud believes we must apply the principles and methodology of psychoanalysis to a text to uncover its real meaning.

Although psychoanalytic criticism was founded by Freud, other critics such as Carl Jung, Northrop Frye, and Jacques Lacan have revised and expanded Freud's theories and developed their own methodologies for literary analysis. See **neurosis**.

psychobiography A method of interpreting texts that uses biographical data of an author gained through biographies, personal letters, lectures, and other sources to construct the author's personality, with all its idiosyncrasies, internal and external conflicts, and neuroses.

public symbol See **symbol**.

reader-response criticism Rising to prominence in literary analysis in the early 1970s, reader-response criticism asserts that the reader is active, not passive, during the reading process. Both the reader and the text interact or share a transactional experience: the text acts as a stimulus for eliciting various past experiences, thoughts, and ideas of the reader, those found in both real life and in past reading experiences. Simultaneously, the text shapes the reader's experiences, selecting, limiting, and ordering those ideas that best conform to the text. The resulting interpretation is thus a new creation called a *poem*. For reader-response critics, the reader + the text = meaning or the poem.

   Reader-response critics ask a variety of theoretical questions, such as, What is a text? Who is the reader? Does the reader or the text or some combination of both determine the text's interpretation? What part does the author play in a work's interpretation? and perhaps most important, What is the reading process?

   Composed of a diverse group of critics who emphasize different elements of the reading process, reader-response critics include Roland Barthes, Gerard Genette, Claude Lévi-Strauss, Wolfgang Iser, Louise Rosenblatt, Norman Holland, and David Bleich. See also **poem**.

Real Order According to Jacques Lacan, the Real Order is the third stage of psychic development and consists of the physical world, including the material universe and everything in it. It also symbolizes everything a person is not, and therefore objects within the Real Order continually function as symbols of primordial lack, leading to psychic fragmentation.

real reader A term devised by the narratologist Gerard Prince to differentiate among the three kinds of readers—**real**, virtual, and ideal—to whom the narrator is speaking, the narratee. According to Prince, the real reader is the person actually reading the book. See **virtual reader**, **ideal reader**, and **narratee**.

reality principle Introduced by Sigmund Freud in his economic model of the human psyche. Freud defines the reality principle as that part of the human psyche that holds the pleasure principle in check. The reality principle recognizes the need for societal standards and regulations on a person's desire for pleasure. See **pleasure principle**.

reception theory A term employed by reader-response critics to discuss how their theoretical assumptions are applied to textual analysis. A text's meaning, they argue, must be derived both from the present reader's personal response and from a critical examination of the history of the reception of the text through time, including contemporary critics of the author of the text in addition to critics living at the present moment.

referent In linguistics, the entity—object, state of affairs, and so on—in the external world that is represented and/or symbolized by a word or term. For example, the referent for the word *desk* is the object desk.

reflection theory One of the earliest theories developed by Marxist critics to explain the relationship between a society's base and its superstructure. A position held by Karl Marx early in his career, the reflection theory asserts that the base or economic structure of society directly affects and determines a society's values, its social, political, educational, and legal institutions, its art, and its beliefs—or, taken collectively, what Marx calls a society's superstructure. Simply put, the superstructure reflects or mirrors the base. Although a few Marxist critics still hold to this position, most now assert that the relationship between the base and the superstructure is much more complex than originally believed. The term **vulgar Marxism** is used to describe the form of Marxism that still holds to the reflection theory. See **base, Marxism,** and **superstructure.**

reflectionism See **reflection theory.**

relativistic critic One who employs various and even contradictory theories in critiquing a work of art.

rhetoric Often defined as the art of speaking and writing effectively. Founded in Greece by Corax of Syracuse in the fifth century B.C., rhetoric set forth the principles and rules of composition for speech. Today, the term is used by such critics as Kenneth Burke, Northrop Frye, Roland Barthes, and Jacques Derrida and refers to patterns of structure found within texts. It has become the basis for much modern criticism.

romanticism A literary movement that dates to the publication of William Wordsworth and Samuel Taylor Coleridge's *Lyrical Ballads* in 1798. As a reaction against the eighteenth-century Age of Reason, romanticism asserts that the world is like a living plant, ever growing, becoming, and aspiring. Denying reason as the sole path to truth, romanticists declare that intuition can lead them to an understanding of themselves and their world. Individual concerns, the emotions, and the imagination are to be valued. As an approach to a text, romanticism concerns itself with the artist's feelings and attitudes exhibited within the work of art.

schools of criticism When a variety of readers and critics assert allegiance to a similar core of assumptions concerning an approach to textual analysis, they form a school of criticism, a group of fellow believers who share common concerns about reading, writing, and interpretation. Examples of such schools are New Criticism, reader-response, structuralism, deconstruction, and New Historicism.

semantics Used in linguistics to denote the study of how words combine to make meaning within a language.

semantic features Used in linguistics to refer to those properties of words that help identify the different shades of meaning and relationships a word may have to surrounding phrases, clauses, and sentences.

semiology Proposed by the structuralist Ferdinand de Saussure, this new science would study how we create meaning through signs or codes in all our social behavioral systems. Since language was the chief and most characteristic of these systems, Saussure declared that it was to be the main branch of this new science. Although semiology never became the important new science Saussure envisioned, a similar science, semiotics, did develop and is still practiced today. See **semiotics** and **sign.**

semiotics Founded by Charles Sanders Peirce and developing at the same time as Ferdinand de Saussure's proposed science of semiology, semiotics borrows linguistic methods used by Saussure and applies them to all meaningful cultural phenomena. Semiotics declares that meaning in society can be systematically studied, both in terms of how this meaning occurs and in terms of the structures that allow it to operate. Because it uses methods employed by structuralism, semiotics and structuralism are often used interchangeably today, although the former denotes a particular field of study while the latter is more an approach to literary analysis.

sexual politics   A term introduced by Kate Millett with her publication *Sexual Politics* (1969). The term has become synonymous with the second wave of feminism, which asserts that economic inequality and ideological indoctrination have been the chief causes of women's oppression and places *patriarchy* at the center of the feminist movement. Thanks to Millet, the term also denotes distinctions between sex and gender, the first being biological and the latter being psychological. Conforming or not conforming to prescribed cultural sex roles dictated by society becomes part of what Millet dubs sexual politics.

The term has also been used by Annette Kolodny to assert that feminist critics must accept a pluralistic approach to literary criticism. Kolodny assumes that any given text has the possibility of many different readings; such an approach, she argues, is both useful and illuminating.

sentence   A group of words that expresses a complete thought and conforms to the established syntactic structures of a language.

sign   A term used in linguistics and first used by the French structuralist Ferdinand de Saussure to denote the definition for a word. According to Saussure, a word is not a symbol that equals something else, but is a sign (something that has meaning) composed of both a signifier and a signified. For Saussure, a word does not represent a referent in the objective world, but an abstract concept. See **referent**, **signifier**, and **signified**.

signification   A term used in literary criticism, theories of reading, and linguistics to denote the process by which we arrive at meaning through linguistic signs or other symbolic means.

signified   A term used by the French structuralist Ferdinand de Saussure that denotes one part of a word. Saussure proposed that all words are really signs composed of two parts: the signifier and the signified. The signified is the concept to which the signifier, a written or spoken word or sound, refers. Like the two sides of a sheet of paper, the linguistic sign is the union of the signifier and the signified. See **sign** and **signifier**.

signifier   A term used by the French structuralist Ferdinand de Saussure that denotes one part of a word. The signifier is the spoken or written constituent, such as the sound /t/ and the orthographic (written) symbol *t*. See **signified** and **sign** .

simile   A figure of speech that compares two unlike objects using the word *like* or *as*, such as "His nose is like a cherry." The objects being compared cannot be from the same class. For example, the statement "London is like Paris" contains no simile since the objects being compared are from the same class, since both are cities.

structuralism   An approach to literary analysis that flourished in the 1960s. By utilizing the techniques, methodologies, and vocabulary of linguistics as articulated by Ferdinand de Saussure, structuralism offers a scientific view of how we achieve meaning not only in literary works but in all forms of communication and social behavior.

Structuralists believe that codes, signs, and rules govern all social and cultural practices, including communication, the "language" of sports, friendships, education, and literature. They want to discover those codes that they believe give meaning to all our social and cultural customs. The proper study of meaning and therefore reality is an examination of the system behind these practices, not the individual practices themselves.

For the **structuralist critic**, the proper study of literature becomes a study of the conditions surrounding the act of interpretation itself, not an in-depth investigation of an individual work. Structuralists believe that a study of the grammar, or the system of rules that govern literary interpretation, becomes the critic's primary task.

Practiced by such critics as Jonathan Culler, Tzvetan Todorov, Roland Barthes, and Gerard Genette, structuralism challenges New Criticism's methodology for finding meaning within a text.

structuralist narratology A form of structuralism defined as the science of narrative and employed by such critics as Vladimir Propp, Tzvetan Todorov, Roland Barthes, and Gerard Genette. **Narratologists** illustrate how a story's meaning develops from its overall structure, including elements such as theme, persona, voice, style, grammatical structure, and tone.

structural linguistics A term used synonymously with linguistics, the science of language.

subaltern writers A term coined by the Marxist critic Antonio Gramsci to refer to writers among those classes of people who are not in control of a culture's ideology or its hegemony. These writers, such as African Americans, provide new ways to see and understand cultural forces at work in literature and in ourselves.

superego A term used by Sigmund Freud to designate that part of the psyche that acts like an internal censor, causing us to make moral judgments in light of social pressures.

superstructure A term used by Karl Marx to designate that part of a culture that contains the social, legal, political, and educational systems along with the religious beliefs, values, and art of a society and which embodies a society's ideology that is controlled by the dominant social class or the bourgeoisie. By controlling the base, the bourgeoisie determines a society's superstructure and thus controls and oppresses the working class or proletariat. See **base and Marxism**.

supplement A term coined by the French deconstructionist Jacques Derrida to explain the relationship between two parts of any hierarchy upon which Western culture bases its metaphysics. For example, Derrida says Western society values light over darkness. The exact relationship between light and darkness, Derrida asserts, is not totally clear. Derrida uses the term *supplement* to refer to the unstable relationship between the two elements contained in this hierarchy. Rather than being two totally separate entities, light and dark supplement each other. Who, for example, can declare it to be light or dark when it is dusk? Each term thus helps define the other and is necessary for the other to exist.

supplementation The act of supplementing. See **supplement**.

symbol An image that represents something else and that can have multiple interpretations. There are two types: a *public symbol* embodies universal meaning, such as a rose representing love or water symbolizing life; and a *private symbol* obtains its meaning from the way in which it is used in a text, such as the scarlet *A* in Nathaniel Hawthorne's romance *The Scarlet Letter*.

Symbolic Order According to Jacques Lacan, the Symbolic Order is the second phase of our psychic development, during which we learn language. In this stage, we also learn to differentiate between genders, master gender differences, and learn cultural norms and laws. Further, we learn that our fathers represent these cultural norms, and thus we master a male view of the world.

synchronic A linguistic term introduced by the French structuralist Ferdinand de Saussure and used to designate a process of language analysis that studies one language at one particular time in its evolution, emphasizing how that language functions, not its historical development through a long expanse of time. See - **diachronic**.

syntax The study of the grammatical structure of a sentence, particularly the arrangement of words or word order. Used in linguistics to describe the rules governing the arrangement of words in phrases, clauses, and sentences.

teleological The adjective of the philosophical term *teleology*, the study of the evidence of design in the natural world. It denotes a worldview or philosophy of life that asserts a purposeful going forward toward some known end, especially one relating to nature.

tension A term used in literary criticism that is synonymous with conflict. It designates the oppositions or conflicts operating with a text.

theoretical criticism Formulates the theories, principles, and tenets of the nature and value of art. By citing general aesthetic and moral principles of art, theoretical criticism provides the necessary framework for *practical criticism*. See **practical criticism**.

thick description Coined by the cultural anthropologist Clifford Geertz and brought into literary criticism via cultural poetics, this term is used by **cultural poetics critics** to describe the seemingly insignificant, but abundant details present in any cultural practice. By focusing on these details, cultural poetics critics believe they can reveal the inherent contradictory forces at work within a culture. See **cultural poetics**.

tragedy Although the term is used in many different ways, in literary criticism the term *tragedy* chiefly refers to Aristotle's definition found in the *Poetics*. Tragedy is "an imitation of a noble and complete action, having the proper magnitude; it employs language of linguistic adornment, applied separately in the various parts of the play; it is presented in dramatic, not narrative form, and achieves, through the representation of pitiable and fearful incidents, the catharsis of such pitiable and fearful incidents." See **catharsis**, **hamartia**, and *Poetics*.

transactional A term introduced by Louise M. Rosenblatt to describe the process or event that takes place at a particular time and place when a reader transacts with a text. According to Rosenblatt, the text and the reader condition each other, for the text acts as a stimulus or a blueprint for eliciting various past experiences, thoughts, and ideas of the reader—those found in both real life and in past reading experiences. The end result of this experience or "aesthetic transaction" is the creation of a poem, or what has been traditionally called the interpretation. See **aesthetic reading**, **poem**, and **transactional experience**.

transactional experience According to the reader-response critic Louise M. Rosenblatt, a reader of a text and the text itself transact during the reading process. The text acts as a stimulus for eliciting various past experiences, thoughts, and ideas from the reader, those found in both our everyday existence and in past reading experiences. Simultaneously, the text shapes the reader's experiences, selecting, limiting, and ordering the ideas that best conform to the text. This overall event or act is what Rosenblatt dubs the transactional experience. See **transactional**.

transcendental signified A term introduced into literary criticism by the French deconstructionist Jacques Derrida. In trying "to turn Western metaphysics on its head," Derrida asserts that from the time of Plato to the present, Western culture has been founded upon a classic, fundamental error: the searching for a transcendental signified, an external point of reference upon which one may build a concept or philosophy. Once found, this transcendental signified would provide ultimate meaning. It would guarantee a "center" of meaning, allowing those who believe in it to structure their ideas of reality around it. According to Derrida, Western metaphysics has invented a variety of such centers: God, reason, origin, being, truth, humanity, self, and so on.

tripartite model Sigmund Freud's most famous model of the human psyche. In this model, Freud divides the psyche into three parts: the *id*, the *ego*, and the *superego*. See **id**, **ego**, and **superego**.

trope A term synonymous with a figure of speech or a word or phrase not meant to be taken literally. The term has now been employed by several schools of criticism in a variety of specialized meanings.

typographical model A model of the human psyche devised by Sigmund Freud. In this model, Freud divides the psyche into three parts: the *conscious*, the *preconscious*, and the *unconscious*. See **conscious**, **preconscious**, and **unconscious**.

unconscious A term employed in Freudian psychoanalysis to refer to that part of the human psyche that receives and stores our hidden desires, ambitions, fears, passions, and irrational thoughts.

undecidability A term used by deconstructionists and other postmodern critics to decree that a text's meaning is always in flux, never final. Accordingly, foreclosure of meaning for any text is impossible. See **aporia**, **arche-writing**, **deconstruction**, **misspeaks**, and **poststructuralism**.

ungrammatical A term used to refer to those phrases, clauses, and sentences that do not conform to the grammatical rules of a language.

unhomeliness A term coined by the postcolonial theorist Homi K. Bhabha; it refers to the way a colonial subject perceives the world as divided between two antagonistic cultures: that of the colonizer and of the indigenous community. This "double consciousness" often leaves the colonial subject feeling caught between two cultures, with neither of them providing a sense of belonging, with the subject lacking the experience of having a "home" culture.

unprivileged A term introduced into literary criticism by the French deconstructionalist Jacques Derrida. According to Derrida, Western society bases its values and its metaphysical assumptions on opposites, such as good/bad, light/dark, true/false. In each of these pairs, Derrida asserts that Western culture values or *privileges* the first element, while devaluing or *unprivileging* the second. See **privileged** and **binary opposition**.

unvoiced In linguistics, any sound made without vibrating the vocal folds, such as /t/, /p/, /k/.

virtual reader A term devised by the narratologist Gerard Prince to differentiate among the *real, virtual,* and *ideal reader*. According to Prince, the virtual reader is the reader to whom the author believes he or she is writing.

voiced In linguistics, any sound made during which the vocal folds are brought close together and made to vibrate, causing air to pass between them, such as /b/, /d/, and /g/.

vulgar Marxism A form of Marxism that holds to the reflection theory on the relationship of the base to the superstructure. Vulgar Marxism asserts that the superstructure directly reflects or mirrors the base. See **reflection theory**.

Weltanschauung The German word for worldview. See **worldview**.

worldview According to James Sire, in his text *The Universe Next Door* (1997), a worldview is the set of assumptions or presuppositions that we all hold either consciously or unconsciously about the basic makeup of our world.

yonic symbol A term used in psychoanalytic criticism for any female symbol, such as a flower, a cup, a cave, or a vase.

References

CHAPTER 1

Beardsley, Monroe C., Robert W. Daniel, and Glenn H. Leggett. *Theme and Form: An Introduction to Literature.* Englewood Cliffs, NJ: Prentice-Hall, 1969.

Daiches, David. *Critical Approaches to Literature.* New York: Longman, 1981.

Danziger, Marlies, and W. Stacy Johnson. *An Introduction to Literary Criticism.* Boston: Heath, 1961.

Eagleton, Terry. *Literary Theory: An Introduction.* Minneapolis: U of Minnesota P, 1983.

Grebanier, Bernard. *The Enjoyment of Literature.* New York: Crown, 1975.

Holman, C. Hugh, and William Harmon. *A Handbook to Literature.* 8th ed. New York: Macmillan, 2000.

Lentricchia, Frank, and Thomas McLaughlin, eds. *Critical Terms for Literary Study.* Chicago: U of Chicago P, 1990.

Newton, K. M., ed. *Twentieth-Century Literary Criticism.* New York: Longman. 1988.

Rosenblatt, Louise M. *The Reader, the Text, the Poem: the Transactional Theory of the Literary Work.* Carbondale: Southern Illinois UP, 1978.

Sire, James W. *The Joy of Reading: A Guide to Becoming a Better Reader.* Portland, OR: Multnomah, 1978.

———. *The Universe Next Door.* 3rd. ed. Downers Grove, IL: InterVarsity, 1995.

Staton, Shirley F., ed. *Literary Theories in Praxis.* Philadelphia: U of Pennsylvania P, 1987.

Stevens, Bonnie, and Larry Stewart. *A Guide to Literary Criticism and Research.* Fort Worth: Holt, 1992.

Twain, Mark. *The Adventures of Huckleberry Finn.* New York: Harcourt, 1961.

Walder, Dennis, ed. *Literature in the Modern World: Critical Essays and Documents.* Oxford: Oxford UP, 1990.

CHAPTER 2

Alighieri, Dante. *The Divine Comedy.* Trans. by Charles S. Singleton. Princeton: Princeton UP, 1975.

———. *On the Art of Poetry.* Trans. Ingram Bywater. Oxford: Oxford UP, 1920.

———. *Eleven Letters.* Trans. Charles Sterret Latham. Boston: Houghton, 1892.

Aristotle. *Poetics.* Trans. Leon Golden. Englewood Cliffs, NJ: Prentice-Hall, 1968.

———. *Poetics.* Trans. Ingram Bywater. Oxford: Clarendon, 1920.

Arnold, Matthew. *Essays in Criticism: First Series.* New York: Macmillan, 1895.

Auerbach, Erich. *Dante: Poet of the Secular World*. Trans. Ralph Manheim. Chicago: Chicago UP, 1961.

Bate, Walter J. *From Classic to Romantic*. Cambridge, MA: Harvard UP, 1946.

Bradley, A. C. *Oxford Lectures on Poetry*. London: Macmillan, 1909.

Brody, Jules. *Boileau and Longinus*. Geneva: Droz, 1953.

Butcher, S. H. *Aristotle's Theory of Poetry and Fine Art*. 3rd ed. London: Macmillan, 1902.

Casey, John. *The Language of Criticism*. London: Methuen, 1960.

Clubbe, John, and Ernest J. Lovell. *English Romanticism: The Grounds of Belief*. London: Macmillan, 1983.

Cooper, Lane. *The Poetics of Aristotle: Its Meaning and Influence*. New York: Cooper Square, 1963.

D'Alton, J. F. *Horace and His Age*. London: Longman Green, 1917.

Daugerty, Sandi B. *The Literary Criticism of Henry James*. Athens: Ohio UP, 1981.

Devereux, James A. "The Meaning of Delight in Sidney's Defense of Poesy." *Studies in the Literary Imagination* 15 (1982): 85–97.

Eliot, T. S. *John Dryden: The Poet, the Dramatist, the Critic: Three Essays*. New York: Haskell House, 1966.

Ells, John Shepard. *The Touchstones of Matthew Arnold*. New York: Bookman, 1955.

Else, Gerald F. *Aristotle's Poetics: The Argument*. Cambridge, MA: Harvard UP, 1957.

———. *Plato and Aristotle on Poetry*. Chapel Hill: U of North Carolina P, 1986.

Fenner, Arthur, Jr. "The Unity of Pope's Essay on Criticism." *Philological Quarterly* 39 (1960) : 435–56.

Fergusson, Francis. "On the Poetics." *Tulane Drama Review* 4 (1960): 23–32.

Garrod, Deathcote William. *Poetry and the Criticism of Life*. New York: Russell, 1963.

Goad, Caroline. *Horace in the English Literature of the Eighteenth Century*. New Haven: Yale UP, 1918.

Griffin, Dustin. *Alexander Pope: The Poet in the Poems*. Princeton: Princeton UP, 1978.

Grube, G. M. *Plato's Thought*. London: Methuen, 1935.

Hamilton, Paul. *Coleridge's Poetics*. Oxford: Blackwell, 1983.

Henn, T. R. *Longinus and English Criticism*. Cambridge: Cambridge UP, 1934.

Herrick, Marvin T. *The Fusion of Horatian and Aristotelian Literary Criticism*. Urbana: U of Illinois P, 1946.

Hill, John Spencer, ed. *The Romantic Imagination: A Casebook*. London: Macmillan, 1977.

Hirsch, E. D. *Wordsworth and Schelling*. New Haven: Yale UP, 1950.

Hollander, R. *Allegory in Dante's Commedia*. Princeton: Princeton UP, 1969.

Hughes, Herbert Leland. *Theory and Practice in Henry James*. Ann Arbor, MI, Edwards, 1926.

Hume, Robert D. *Dryden's Criticism*. Ithaca, NY: Cornell UP, 1970.

James, Henry. *The Art of the Novel: Critical Prefaces*. Introduction by R. P. Blackmur. New York: Scribner's, 1932.

Jones, Henry John. *The Egotistical Sublime: A History of Wordsworth's Imagination*. London: Chatto & Windus, 1970.

Lanser, Susan S. *The Narrative Act: Point of View in Prose Fiction*. Princeton: Princeton UP, 1981.

Lodge, Rupert C. *Plato's Theory of Art*. New York: Humanities Press, 1953.

Mason, H. A. "An Introduction to Literary Criticism by Way of Sidney's Apology for Poetrie." *Cambridge Quarterly* 12. 2–3 (1984): 79–173.

Mishra, J. B. *John Dryden: His Theory and Practice of Drama.* New Delhi: Bahir, 1978.

Modrak, Deborah. *Aristotle: The Power of Perception.* Chicago: U of Chicago P, 1987.

Monk, Samuel Holt. *The Sublime: A Study of Critical Theories in XVIII-Century England.* 1935. Ann Arbor: U of Michigan P, 1960.

Olson, Elder. "The Argument of Longinus's *On the Sublime.*" *On Value Judgments in the Arts and Other Essays.* Chicago: U of Chicago P, 1976.

———. *Aristotle's Poetics and English Literature.* Chicago: U of Chicago P, 1965.

Owen, W. J. B. *Wordsworth as Critic.* Toronto: Toronto UP, 1971.

Pechter, E. *Dryden's Classical Theory of Literature.* London: Cambridge UP, 1975.

Perkins, David. "Arnold and the Function of Literature." *ELH* 18 (1951): 287–309.

Plato. *The Republic.* Trans. Benjamin Jowett. 3rd ed. Oxford: Clarendon, 1888.

Roberts, Morris. *Henry James's Criticism.* Cambridge, MA: Harvard UP, 1929.

Robinson, Forrest Glen. *The Shape of Things Known: Sidney's Apology in Its Philosophical Tradition.* Cambridge, MA: Harvard UP, 1972.

Rollinson, Philip. *Classical Theories of Allegory and Christian Culture.* Pittsburgh: Duquesne UP, 1981.

Russell, D. A., ed. *"Longinus" on the Sublime.* Oxford: Clarendon, 1964.

Sharma, L. S. *Coleridge: His Contribution to English Criticism.* New Delhi: Arnold-Heinemann, 1981.

Shorey, Paul. *What Plato Said.* Chicago: U of Chicago P, 1933.

Singleton, Charles S. *Dante Studies.* 2 vols. Cambridge, MA: Harvard UP, 1958.

Smith, Nowell C., ed. *Wordsworth's Literary Criticism.* Bristol, Eng.: Bristol Classical P, 1980.

Stack, Frank. *Pope and Horace: Studies in Imitation.* Cambridge and New York: Cambridge UP, 1985.

Taine, Hippolyte A. *The History of English Literature.* 4 vols. Trans. H. Van Laun. Philadelphia: David McKay, 1908.

Taylor, A. E. *Plato.* Ann Arbor: U of Michigan P, 1960.

Thorpe, C. D. "Coleridge as Aesthetician and Critic." *Journal of the History of Ideas 1* (1940): 387–414.

Trilling, Lionel. *Matthew Arnold.* New York: Norton, 1939.

Warren, Alba. H. *Alexander Pope as Critic and Humanist.* Princeton: Princeton UP, 1963.

———. *English Poetic Theory 1825–1865.* Princeton: Princeton UP, 1950.

———. *Pope as Critic and Humanist.* Princeton: Princeton UP, 1929.

Watson, George. *John Dryden: Of Dramatic Poesy and Other Critical Essays.* 2 vols. London: J. Dent, 1962.

Wood, Allen G. *Literary Satire and Theory: A Study of Horace, Boileau, and Pope.* New York: Garland, 1985.

CHAPTER 3

Bagwell, J. Timothy. *American Formalism and the Problem of Interpretation.* Houston: Rice UP, 1986.

Blackmur, R. P. *The Lion and the Honeycomb: Essays in Solicitude and Critique.* Harcourt, 1955.

Booth, Wayne. *The Rhetoric of Ficton*. Chicago: U of Chicago P, 1961.

Brooks, Cleanth. "In Search of the New Criticism." *American Scholar* 53 (Winter 1983-84): 41–53.

———. *Modern Poetry and The Tradition*. Chapel Hill: U of North Carolina P, 1939.

———. "My Credo: Formalist Critics." *Kenyon Review*, 13 (1951): 72–81.

———. *The Well-Thought Urn: Studies in the Structure of Poetry*. New York: Harcourt, 1947.

Brooks, Cleanth, and Robert Penn Warren. *Understanding Poetry: An Anthology for College Students*. New York: Holt, 1938.

Brooks, Cleanth, and Robert B. Heilman. *Understanding Drama: Twelve Plays*. New York: Holt, 1948.

Burke, Kenneth. *Counter-Statement*. Los Altos, CA: Hermes, 1953.

Cain, William E. *The Crisis in Criticism: Theory, Literature, and Reform in English Studies*. Baltimore: Johns Hopkins UP, 1984.

Crane, Ronald S. "Cleanth Brooks; or the Bankruptcy of Critical Monism." *Modern Philology* 45 (1948): 226–45.

Eliot, T. S. "The Function of Criticism." *Selected Essays*. New York: Harcourt, 1950.

———. *Notes Towards the Definition of Culture*. London: Faber, 1965.

———. "Tradition and the Individual Talent." *The Sacred Wood*. London: Methuen, 1928.

Empson, William. *Seven Types of Ambiguity*. New York: Noonday Press, 1958.

———. *A Glossary of the New Criticism*. Chicago: Modern Poetry Association, 1949.

Handy, William J. *Kant and the Southern New Critics*. Austin: U of Texas P, 1963.

Jancovich, Mark. *The Cultural Politics of the New Criticism*. Cambridge: Cambridge UP, 1993.

Krieger, Murray. *The New Apologists for Poetry*. Minneapolis: U of Minnesota P, 1956.

Langbaum, Robert. *The Modern Spirit: Essays on the Continuity of Nineteenth- and Twentieth-Century Literature*. Oxford and New York: Oxford UP, 1970.

Lentricchia, Frank. *After The New Criticism*. Chicago: U of Chicago P, 1980.

Patnaik, J. N. *The Aesthetics of the New Criticism*. New Delhi: Intellectual Publishing House, 1982.

Ransom, John Crowe. *Beating the Bushes: Selected Essays: 1941–1970*. New York: New Directions, 1972.

———. *The New Criticism*. New York: New Directions, 1941.

———. *The World's Body*. 1938. Baton Rouge: Louisiana State UP, 1968.

Richards, I. A. *Practical Criticism*. New York: Harcourt, 1929.

———. *Principles of Literary Criticism*. New York: Harcourt, 1924.

Schiller, Jerome P. *I. A. Richards' Theory of Literature*. New Haven: Yale UP, 1969.

Schorer, Mark. "Technique as Discovery." *Hudson Review* 1 (Spring 1948): 67–87.

Simpson, Lewis P., ed. *The Possibilities of Order: Cleanth Brooks and His Work*. Baton Rouge: Louisiana State UP, 1976.

Tate, Allen. *Reason in Madness*. New York: Putnam, 1941.

———. "What I Owe to Cleanth Brooks." *The Possibilities of Order: Cleanth Brooks and His Work*. Ed. Lewis P. Simpson. Baton Rouge: Louisiana State UP, 1976.

Warren, Robert Penn. "Pure and Impure Poetry." *Kenyon Review* 5 (Spring 1943): 229–54.

Wellek, René. "The New Criticism: Pro and Contra." *Critical Inquiry* 4 (Summer 1978): 611–24.

Wellek, René, and Austin Warren. *Theory of Literature*. 1942. San Diego: Harcourt, 1977.

Wimsatt, W. K. *The Verbal Icon*. Lexington: U of Kentucky P, 1954.

Wimsatt, W. K., and Monroe Beardsley. "The Affective Fallacy." *The Verbal Icon: Studies in the Meaning of Poetry*. Ed. W. K. Wimsatt. Lexington: U of Kentucky P, 1954. 21–39.

Wimsatt, W. K., and Cleanth Brooks. *Literary Criticism: A Short History*. New York: Knopf, 1957.

Winters, Yvor. *In Defense of Reason*. Denver: Swallow, 1947.

CHAPTER 4

Barthes, Roland. "From Work to Text." *The Rustle of Language*. Berkeley: U of California P, 1989.

Bleich, David. *Readings and Feelings: An Introduction to Subjective Criticism*. New York: Harper, 1977.

———. *Subjective Criticism*. Baltimore: Johns Hopkins UP, 1978.

Booth, Stephen. "On the Value of *Hamlet*." *Reinterpretations of Elizabethan Drama*. Ed. Norman Rabkin. New York: Columbia UP, 1969. 77–99.

Booth, Wayne C. *The Rhetoric of Fiction*. Chicago: U of Chicago P, 1978.

Eco, Umberto. *The Role of the Reader: Explorations in the Semiotics of Texts*. Bloomington: Indiana UP, 1979.

Fish, Stanley E. *Is There a Text in This Class? The Authority of Interpretive Communities*. Cambridge, MA: Harvard UP, 1980.

———. "Literature in the Reader: Affective Stylistics." *New Literary History* 2 (1970): 123–61.

———. *Self-Consuming Artifacts: The Experience of Seventeenth-Century Literature*. Berkeley: U of California P, 1972.

Freund, Elizabeth. *The Return of the Reader: Reader-Response Criticism*. New York: Methuen, 1987.

Holland, Norman N. *The Dynamics of Literary Response*. Oxford and New York: Oxford UP, 1968.

———. *Holland's Guide to Psychoanalytic Psychology and Literature-and-Psychology*. Oxford: Oxford UP, 1990.

———. *Poems in Persons: An Introduction to the Psychoanalysis of Literature*. New York: Norton, 1973.

———. "*A Portrait* as Rebellion: A Reader-Response Perspective." *A Portrait of the Artist as a Young Man: Complete, Authoritative Text with Biographical and Historical Contexts, Critical History, and Essays from Five Contemporary Critical Perspectives*. Ed. R. B. Kershner. Boston: Bedford Books–St. Martin's, 1993. 279–94.

———. "Unity, Identity, Text, Self." *PMLA* 90 (1975): 813–22.

Holub, Robert C. *Reception Theory: A Critical Introduction*. New York: Methuen, 1984.

Iser, Wolfgang. *The Act of Reading. A Theory of Aesthetic Response*. Baltimore: Johns Hopkins UP, 1978.

———. *The Implied Reader: Patterns of Communication in Prose Fiction from Bunyan to Beckett*. Baltimore: Johns Hopkins UP, 1974.

———. *Prospecting: From Reader Response to Literary Anthropology*. Baltimore: Johns Hopkins UP, 1989.

Jauss, Hans Robert. *Aesthetic Experience and Literary Hermeneutics*. Minneapolis: U of Minnesota P, 1982.

Mailloux, Steven. *Interpretive Conventions: The Reader in the Study of American Fiction*. Ithaca, NY: Cornell UP, 1982.

———. *Interpretive Conventions: The Reader in the Study of American Fiction*. Ithaca, NY: Cornell UP, 1982.

———. "Learning to Read: Interpretation and Reader-Response Criticism." *Studies in the Literary Imagination* 12 (1979): 93–108.

———. "Reader-Response Criticism?" *Genre* 10 (1977): 413–31.

Ong, Walter. *Orality and Literacy*. New York: Methuen, 1982.

Prince, Gerald. "Introduction to the Study of the Naratee." Reader-Response Criticism: From Formalism to Post-Structuralism. Ed. Jane Thompkins. Baltimore: Johns Hopkins UP, 1980. 177–96.

"Reading Interpretation, Response." Spec. sect. of *Genre* 10 (1977): 363–453.

Rosenblatt, Louise M. "Towards a Transactional Theory of Reading." *Journal of Reading Behavior* 1 (1969): 31–47.

Suleiman, Susan R., and Inge Crosman, eds. *The Reader in the Text: Essays on Audience and Interpretation*. Princeton: Princeton UP, 1980.

Thompkins, Jane, ed. *Reader-Response Criticism: From Formalism to Post-Structuralism*. Baltimore: Johns Hopkins UP, 1980.

CHAPTER 5

Bannet, Eve Tavor. *Structuralism and the Logic of Dissent*. Chicago: U of Illinois P, 1989.

Barthes, Roland. *Critical Essays*. Trans. R. Howard. Evanston, IL: Northwestern UP, 1972.

———. *Elements of Semiology*. Trans. Annette Lavers and C. Smith. London: Cape, 1967.

———. *Mythologies*. 1957. Trans. Annette Lavers. New York: Hill and Wang, 1972.

———. *Selected Writings*. London: Fontana, 1983.

———. *S/Z*. Trans. Richard Miller, New York: Hill and Wang, 1971.

Blonsky, Marshall, ed. *On Signs*. Baltimore: Johns Hopkins UP, 1985.

Connor, Steven. "Structuralism and Post-structuralism: From the Centre to the Margin." *Encyclopedia of Literature and Criticism*. Ed. Martin Coyle, Peter Garside, Malcom Kelsall, and John Peck. London: Routledge, 1990.

Crystal, David. *A Dictionary of Linguistics and Phonetics*. 2nd ed. Cambridge, MA: Basil Blackwell, 1985.

Culler, Jonathan. *Ferdinand de Saussure*. Baltimore: Penguin, 1976.

———. *The Pursuit of Signs: Semiotics, Literature, Deconstruction*. Ithaca, NY: Cornell UP, 1981.

———. *Structuralist Poetics: Structuralism, Linguistics and the Study of Literature*. London: Routledge, 1975.

De George, Richard T., and Fernande M. De George, eds. *The Structuralists: from Marx to Lévi-Strauss*. Garden City, NY: Doubleday, 1972.

Detweiler, Robert. *Story, Sign, and Self: Phenomenology and Structuralism as Literary Critical Methods*. Philadelphia: Fortress, 1978.

Ehrmann, Jacques, ed. *Structuralism*. Garden City, NY: Doubleday, 1970.

Frye, Northrop. *Anatomy of Criticism: Four Essays*. Princeton: Princeton UP, 1957.

Genette, Gerard. *Narrative Discourse*. Oxford: Blackwell, 1980.

Greimas, A. J. *On Meaning: Selected Writings in Semiotic Theory*. 1970. Trans. Paul Perron and Frank Collins. Minneapolis: U of Minnesota P, 1987.

Hawkes, Terence. *Structuralism and Semiotics*. London: Methuen, 1977.

Innes, Robert E. ed. *Semiotics: An Introductory Reader*. London: Hutchinson, 1986.

Jakobson, Roman. *Fundamentals of Language*. Paris: Mouton, 1975.

Jameson, Fredric. *The Prison-House of Language: A Critical Account of Structuralism and Russian Formalism*. Princeton: Princeton UP, 1972.

Krieger, Murray, and L. S. Dembo, eds. *Directions for Criticism: Structuralism and Its Alternatives*. Madison: U of Wisconsin P, 1977.

Lane, Michael, ed. *Introduction to Structuralism*. New York: Harper, 1972.

Lévi-Strauss, Claude. *Structural Anthropology*. Trans. Claire Jacobson and Brooke G. Schoepf. London: Allen Lanne, 1968.

———. *Tristes Tropiques*. Trans. John and Doreen Weightman. New York: Atheneum, 1974.

Lodge, David. *Working with Structuralism*. London: Routledge, 1986.

———. *Working with Structuralism: Essays and Reviews on Nineteenth- and Twentieth-Century Literature*. Boston: Routledge and Kegan Paul, 1981.

Macksey, Richard, and Eugenio Donato, eds. *The Structuralist Controversy*. Baltimore: Johns Hopkins UP, 1970.

Pratt, Annis, with Adrea Lowenstein and Andre Wyer. *Archetypal Patterns in Women's Fiction*. Bloomington: Indiana UP, 1981.

Prince, Gerald. *Narratology: The Form and Functioning of Narrative*. New York: Mouton, 1982.

Propp, Vladimir. *The Morphology of the Folktale*. Austin: Texas UP, 1968.

Robey, David, ed. *Structuralism: An Introduction*. Oxford: Clarendon, 1973.

Rowe, John Carlos. "Structure." *Critical Terms for Literary Study*. 2nd ed. Eds. Frank Lentricchia and Thomas McLaughlin. Chicago: U of Chicago P, 1995. 23–38.

Saussure, Ferdinand de. *Course in General Linguistics*. Trans. Wade Baskin. Ed. Charles Bally and Albert Reidlinger. New York: Philosophical Library, 1959.

Scholes, Robert. *Structuralism in Literature: An Introduction*. New Haven: Yale UP, 1974.

———. *Semiotics and Interpretation*. New Haven, CT: Yale UP, 1982.

Selz, Dorothy B. "Structuralism for the Non-Specialist: A Glossary and a Bibliography." *College English* 37 (1975): 160–66.

Sontag, Susan. Introduction. *Selected Writings*. By Roland Barthes. London: Fontana, 1983.

Sturrock, John. *Structuralism and Since*. New York: Oxford UP, 1979.

Tatham, Campbell. "Beyond Structuralism." *Genre* 10.1 (1977): 131–55.

Todorov, Tzvetan. *The Fantastic: A Structural Approach to a Literary Genre*. Ithaca, NY: Cornell UP, 1973.

———. *The Poetics of Prose.* Trans. Richard Howard. Ithaca, NY: Cornell UP, 1977. (Includes "The Typology of Detective Fiction")

CHAPTER 6

Abrams, M. H. "The Deconstructive Angel." *Critical Inquiry* 3 (1977): 425–38.

Anderson, Danny J. "Deconstruction: Critical Strategy/Strategic Criticism." *Contemporary Literary Theory.* Ed. G. Douglas Atkins and Laura Morrow, 137–57. Amherst: U of Massachusetts P, 1989.

Arac, Jonathan, Wlad Godzich, and Wallace Martin, eds. *The Yale Critics: Deconstruction in America.* Theory and History of Literature Ser. 6. Minneapolis: U of Minnesota Press, 1983.

Atkins, G. Douglas. *Reading Deconstruction: Deconstructive Reading.* Lexington: UP of Kentucky, 1983.

Barthes, Roland. "The Death of the Author." *Image-Music-Text.* Trans. S. Heath. New York: Hill & Wang, 1977.

———. *The Pleasure of the Text.* Trans. Richard Miller. New York: Noonday, 1976.

———. *S/Z.* Trans. Richard Miller. New York: Hill, 1974.

Belsey, Catherine. *Critical Practice.* New York: Routledge, 1980.

Bloom, Harold, Paulde Man, Jacques Derrida, Geoffrey Hartman, and J. Hillis Miller, eds. *Deconstruction and Criticism.* New York: Seabury, 1979.

Bruns, Gerald L. "Structuralism, Enconstrustion, and Hermeneutics." *Diacritics* 14 (1984): 12–23.

Cain, William E. "Deconstruction in America: The Recent Literary Criticism of J. Hillis Miller." *College English* 41 (1979): 367–82.

Caputo, John D. "The Good News about Alterity: Derrida and Theology." *Faith and Philosophy* 10.4 (Oct. 1993): 453–70.

Cascardi, A. J. "Skepticism and Deconstruction." *Philosophy and Literature* 8 (1984): 1–14.

Crowley, Sharon. *A Teacher's Introduction to Deconstruction.* Urbana, IL: National Council of Teachers of English, 1989.

Culler, Jonathan. *On Deconstruction: Theory and Criticism after Structuralism.* Ithaca, NY: Cornell UP, 1982.

———. *The Pursuit of Signs: Semiotics, Literature, Deconstruction.* Ithaca, NY: Cornell UP, 1981.

———. *Structuralist Poetics: Structuralism, Linguistics and the Study of Literature.* Ithaca, NY: Cornell UP, 1975.

Davis, Robert Con, and Ronald Schleifer, eds. *Rhetoric and Form: Deconstruction at Yale.* Norman: U of Oklahoma P, 1985.

de Man, Paul. *Allegories of Reading.* New Haven: Yale UP, 1979.

———. *Blindness and Insight.* Oxford and New York: Oxford UP, 1971.

Derrida, Jacques. *Acts of Literature.* 2nd ed. Minneapolis: U of Minnesota P, 1983.

———. *A Derrida Reader: Between the Blinds.* Ed. Peggy Kamuf. New York: Columbia UP, 1991.

———. *Dissemination.* Ed. Derek Attridge. New York: Routledge, 1992.

———. *Of Grammatology.* Trans. Gayatri Spivak. Baltimore: Johns Hopkins UP, 1974. Trans. of *De la grammatologie.* 1967.

———. "Living On: Border Lines." *Deconstruction and Criticism*. Harold Bloom et al. New York: Seabury, 1979. 75–175.

———. *Speech and Phenomena, and Other Essays on Husserl's Theory of Signs*. 1973. Trans. David B. Allison. Evanston, IL: Northwestern UP, 1978.

———. "Structure, Sign, and Play in the Discourse of the Human Sciences." *The Structuralist Controversy: The Languages of Criticism and the Sciences of Man*. Ed. Richard Macksey and Eugenio Donato. Baltimore: Johns Hopkins UP, 1970. 247–65.

———. *Writing and Difference*. 1967. Trans. Alan Bass. Chicago: U of Chicago P, 1978.

Ellis, John M. *Against Deconstruction*. Princeton: Princeton UP, 1989.

Fisher, Michael. *Does Deconstruction Make Any Difference?* Bloomington: Indiana UP, 1987.

Flores, Ralph. *The Rhetoric of Doubtful Authority: Deconstructive Readings of Self-questioning Narratives, St. Augustine to Faulkner*. Ithaca, NY: Cornell UP, 1984.

Foucault, Michel. *The Foucault Reader*. Ed. Paul Rabinow. New York: Pantheon, 1984.

Gasché, Rodolphe. "Deconstruction as Criticism." *Glyph* 6 (1979): 177–215.

———. *The Tain of the Mirror: Derrida and the Philosophy of Reflection*. Cambridge, MA: Harvard UP, 1986.

Hartman, Geoffrey. *Saving the Text: Literature/Derrida/Philosophy*. Baltimore: Johns Hopkins UP, 1981.

Johnson, Barbara. *The Critical Difference: Essays in the Contemporary Rhetoric of Reading*. Baltimore: Johns Hopkins UP, 1980.

Leitch, Vincent B. *Deconstructive Criticism: An Advanced Introduction*. New York: Columbia UP, 1983.

———. "The Laterial Dance: The Deconstructive Criticism of J. Hillis Miller." *Critical Inquiry* 6 (1980): 593–607.

Megill, Allan. *Prophets of Extremity: Nietzsche, Heidegger, Foucault, Derrida*. Berkeley and Los Angeles: U of California P, 1985.

Miller, J. Hillis. *Fiction and Repetition: Seven English Novels*. Cambridge, MA: Harvard UP, 1982.

———. Introduction. *Bleak House*. By Charles Dickens. Ed. Norman Page. Harmondsworth, Eng.: Penguin, 1971. 11–13.

———. "Narrative and History." *EHL* 41 (1974): 455–73.

———. "Tradition and Differance." *Diacritics* 2.4 (1972): 6–13.

Norris, Christopher. *Deconstruction and the Interests of Theory*. Oklahoma Project for Discourse and Theory 4. Norman: U of Oklahoma P, 1989.

———. *Deconstruction: Theory and Practice*. New York: Methuen, 1982.

———. *The Deconstructive Turn: Essays in the Rhetoric of Philosophy*. New York: Methuen, 1983.

Rajnath, ed. *Deconstruction: A Critique*. New York: Macmillan, 1989.

Rorty, Richard. *Consequences of Pragmatism*. Minneapolis: U of Minnesota P, 1982.

———. "Deconstruction and Circumvention," *Critical Inquiry* 11 (1984): 1–23.

Ryan, Michael. *Marxism and Deconstruction*. Baltimore: Johns Hopkins UP, 1982.

Said, Edward W. *The World, the Text, and the Critic*. Cambridge, MA: Harvard UP, 1983.

Saarup, Mandan. *An Introductory Guide to Post-Structuralism and Postmodernism*. Athens: U of Georgia P, 1989.

Saussure, Ferdinand de. *Course in General Linguistics.* New York: McGraw-Hill, 1966.

———. *Course in General Linguistics.* Trans. Wade Baskin. Ed. Charles Bally and Albert Reidlinger. New York: Philosophical Library, 1959.

Scholes, Robert. "Deconstruction and Criticism." *Critical Inquiry* 14, (1988): 278–95.

Spivak, Gayatri Chakravorty. "Reading the World: Literary Studies in the 1980's." *College English* 43 (1981): 671–79.

Taylor, Mark C., ed. *Deconstruction in Context: Literature and Philosophy.* Chicago: U of Chicago P, 1986.

Todorov, Tzvetan. *The Fantastic: A Structural Approach to a Literary Genre.* Trans. Richard Howard. Ithaca, NY: Cornell UP, 1975.

Young, Robert, ed. *Untying the Text: A Post-Structuralist Reader.* London: Routledge and Kegan Paul, 1981.

CHAPTER 7

Barrett, William. "Writers and Madness," *Literature and Psychoanalysis.* Ed. Edith Kurzweil and William Phillips. New York: Columbia UP, 1983.

Basler, Roy P. *Sex, Symbolism, and Psychology in Literature.* New York: Octagon, 1975.

Benvenuto, Bice, and Roger Kennedy. *The works of Jacques Lacan: An Introduction.* New York: St. Martin's, 1986.

Bodkin, Maud. *Archetypal Patterns in Poetry.* New York: Vintage, 1958.

Bonaparte, Marie. *The Life and Works of Edgar Allen Poe.* Trans. John Rodker. London: Imago, 1949.

Campbell, Joseph. *The Hero with a Thousand Faces.* New York: Pantheon, 1949.

———. *The Hero with a Thousand Faces.* 2nd ed. Princeton: Princeton UP, 1968.

———. *The Power of Myth.* With Bill Moyers. Ed. Betty Sue Flowers. New York: Doubleday, 1988.

Caroll, David. "Freud and the Myth of Origins." *New Literary History* 6 (1975): 511–28.

Cox, James M. "Remarks on the Sad Initiation of Huckleberry Finn." *Sewanee Review* 62 (1954): 389–405.

Cranfill, Thomas M., and Robert L. Clark Jr. *An Anatomy of* The Turn of the Screw. Austin: U of Texas P, 1965.

Crews, Frederick C. *Out of My System.* New York: Oxford UP, 1975.

———, ed. *Psychoanalysis and Literary Process.* Cambridge, Eng.: Winthrop, 1970.

Davis Robert Con, ed. *The Fictional Father: Lacanian Readings of the Text.* Amherst: U of Massachusetts P, 1981.

———, ed. *Lacan and Narration: The Psychoanalytic Difference in Narrative Theory.* Baltimore: Johns Hopkins UP, 1983.

———, ed. *Psychoanalysis and Pedagogy.* Spec. issue of *College English* 49–67 (1987).

Davis, Walter A. *Get the Guests: Psychoanalysis, Modern American Drama, and the Audience.* Madison: U of Wisconsin P, 1994.

Erikson, Erik. *Childhood and Society.* New York: Norton, 1963.

Feder, Lillian. *Madness in Literature.* Princeton, NJ: Princeton UP, 1980.

Felman, Shoshana. Introduction. *Literature and Psychoanalysis/The Question of Reading: Otherwise.* Spec. issue of *Yale French Studies* 55/56. 5–10.

———. *Jacques Lacan and the Adventure of Insight: Psychoanalysis in Contemporary Culture*. Cambridge, MA: Harvard UP, 1987.

———. *Writing and Madness (Literature/Philosophy/Psychoanalysis)*. 1978. Trans. Martha Noel Evans and Shoshana Felman. Ithaca, NY: Cornell UP, 1985.

———, ed. *Literature and Psychoanalysis: The Question of Reading: Otherwise*. Baltimore: Johns Hopkins UP, 1982.

Freud, Sigmund. *The Basic Writings of Sigmund Freud*. Trans. and ed. A. A. Brill. New York: Modern Library, 1938. (Includes *Psychopathology of Everyday Life, The Interpretation of Dreams, Three Contributions to the Theory of Sex, Wit and Its Relation to the Unconscious, Totem and Taboo*)

———. *The Ego and the Id*. New York: Norton, 1962.

———. *The Freud Reader*. Ed. Peter Gay. New York: Norton, 1989.

———. *Group Psychology and the Analysis of the Ego*. Trans. James Strachey. New York: Norton, 1990.

———. *The Interpretation of Dreams*. Trans. A. A. Brill. New York: Random, 1950.

———. *Introductory Lectures on Psycho-Analysis*. Trans. Joan Riviere. London: Allen, 1922.

———. *Totem and Taboo*. Trans. A. A. Brill. New York: Moffat, 1918.

Frye, Northrop. *Anatomy of Criticism*. Princeton: Princeton UP, 1957.

Gallop, Jane. *Reading Lacan*. Ithaca, NY: Cornell UP, 1985.

Gilbert, Sandra M., and Susan Gubar. *The Madwoman in the Attic: The Woman Writer and the Nineteenth-Century Literary Imagination*. New Haven, CT: Yale UP, 1979.

Gilman, Sandor. *Reading Freud's Reading*. New York: New York UP, 1994.

———, ed. *Introducing Psychoanalytic Theory*. New York: Brunner-Mazel, 1982.

Girard, René. "The Bible Is Not a Myth." *Literature and Belief* 4 (1984): 7–15.

———. *Violence and the Sacred*. Trans. Patrick Gregory. Baltimore: Johns Hopkins UP, 1977.

Gutheil, Emil. *The Handbook of Dream Analysis*. New York: Liveright, 1951.

Hartman, Geoffrey. *Psychoanalysis and the Question of the Text*. Baltimore: Johns Hopkins UP, 1979.

Hoffman, Frederick J. *Freudianism and the Literary Mind*. 2nd ed. Baton Rouge: Louisiana State UP, 1957.

Holland, Norman. *The Dynamics of Literary Response*. New York: Oxford UP, 1968.

———. *The I*. New Haven: Yale UP, 1985.

———. "Literary Interpretation and the Three Phases of Psychoanalysis," *Critical Inquiry* 3 (1976): 221–33.

———. *The Shakespearean Imagination*. Bloomington: Indiana UP, 1968.

———. "The 'Unconscious' of Literature." *Contemporary Criticism*. Ed. Norman Bradbury and David Palmer. Stratford-upon-Avon Ser. 12. New York: St. Martin's, 1970.

Jones, Ernest. *Hamlet and Oedipus*. Garden City, NY: Doubleday, 1949.

Jung, Carl G. *The Collected Works of C. J. Jung*. Ed. Herbert Read, Michael Fordhan, and Gerhard Adler. 20 vols., plus supps. New York: Bollingen Foundation, 1953–83.

Kazin, Alfred. "Freud and His Consequences." *Contemporaries*. Boston: Little, Brown, 1962.

Klein, George. *Psychoanalytic Theory: An Exploration of Essentials*. New York: International Universities P, 1976.

Klein, Melanie. *"Envy and Gratitude" and Other Works, 1946–1963*. New York: International Universities P, 1976.

———. *"Love, Guilt, and Reparation" and Other Works, 1921–1945*. New York: Delacorte, 1975.

Knapp, Bettina Liebowitz. *A Jungian Approach to Literature*. Carbondale: Southern Illinois UP, 1984.

Kramer, Samuel Noah, ed. *Mythologies of the Ancient World*. New York: Anchor-Doubleday, 1961.

Kurzweil, Edith, and William Phillips, eds. *Literature and Psychoanalysis*. New York: Columbia UP, 1983.

Lesser, Simon O. *Fiction and the Unconscious*. Boston: Beacon, 1957.

Lacan, Jacques. *The Four Fundamental Concepts of Psycho-Analysis*. Trans. Alan Sheridan. Ed. Jacques-Alain Miller. New York: Norton, 1978.

Lévi-Strauss, Claude. "The Structural Study of Myth." *Structural Anthropology*. Trans. Claire Jacobson and Brooke Grundfest Schoepf. New York: Basic, 1963. 206–31.

Lewis, C. S. "The Anthropological Approach" and "Psycho-analysis and Literary Criticism." *Selected Literary Essays*. Ed. Walter Hooper. Cambridge: Cambridge UP, 1969. 301–11, 286–300.

———. "Myth." *An Experiment in Criticism*. Cambridge: Cambridge UP, 1961. 40–49.

Meisel, Perry, ed. *Freud: A Collection of Critical Essays*. Englewood Cliffs, NJ: Prentice-Hall, 1981.

———, ed. *Freud: Twentieth Century Views*. Englewood Cliffs, NJ: Prentice-Hall, 1981.

Mitchell, Juliet. Introduction—I. *Feminine Sexuality: Jacques Lacan and the École Freudienne*. Trans. Jacqueline Rose. Ed. Juliet Mitchell and Jacqueline Rose. New York: Norton, 1982. 1–26.

Morrison, Claudia C. *Freud and the Critic*. Chapel Hill: U of North Carolina P, 1968.

Muller, John P., and William J. Richardson. *The Purloined Poe: Lacan, Derrida, and Psychoanalytic Reading*. Baltimore: Johns Hopkins UP, 1988.

Nagele, Rainer. *Reading after Freud*. New York: Columbia UP, 1987.

Natoli, Joseph, and Frederik L. Rusch, comps. *Psychocriticism: An Annotated Bibliography*. Westport, CT: Greenwood, 1984.

Paris, Bernard J. *A Psychological Approach to Fiction: Studies in Thackeray, Stendhal, George Eliot, and Dostoevsky, and Conrad*. Bloomington: Indiana UP, 1974.

Porter, Laurence M. *The Interpretation of Dreams: Freud's Theories Revisited*. Twayne's Masterwork Studies Ser. Boston: Hall, 1986.

Ragland-Sullivan, Ellie. *Jacques Lacan and the Philosophy of Psychoanalysis*. Urbana: U of Illinois P, 1986.

Reppen, Joseph, and Maurice Charney. *The Psychoanalytic Study of Literature*. Hillsdale, NJ: Analytic, 1985.

Schafer, Roy. *The Analytic Attitude*. New York: Basic Books, 1982.

———. *A New Language for Psychoanalysis*. New Haven: Yale UP, 1976.

Schwartz, Murray, and Coppelis Kahn, eds. *Presenting Shakespeare: New Psychoanalytic Essays*. Baltimore: Johns Hopkins UP, 1980.

Shumaker, Wayne. *Literature and the Irrational*. Englewood Cliffs, NJ: Prentice-Hall, 1960.

Skura, Meredith Anne. *The Literary Use of Psychoanalytic Process*. New Haven: Yale UP, 1981.

Strelka, Joseph P., ed. *Literary Criticism and Psychology*. University Park, PA: Pennsylvania State UP, 1976.

Tennenhouse, Leonard, ed. *The Practice of Psychoanalytic Criticism*. Detroit: Wayne State UP, 1976.

Trilling, Lionel. *Freud and the Crisis of Our Culture*. Boston: Beacon, 1955.

Winnicott, D. W. *The Maturational Processes and the Facilitating Environment*. New York: International UP, 1965.

———. *Playing and Reality*. Harmondworth, Eng.: Penguin, 1977.

Wright, Elizabeth. *Psychoanalytic Criticism: Theory in Practice*. London: Methuen, 1984.

Wyatt, Jean. *Reconstructing Desire: The Role of the Unconscious in Women's Reading and Writing*. Chapel Hill: U of North Carolina P, 1990.

Young, Phillip. *Ernest Hemingway*. New York: Holt, 1952.

CHAPTER 8

Abel, Elizabeth. "Editor's Introduction." *Critical Inquiry* 8 (1981): 173–78.

———, ed. *Writing and Sexual Difference*. Chicago: U of Chicago P, 1982.

Abel, Elizabeth, and Emily K. Abel. Introduction. *The Signs Reader: Women, Gender & Scholarship*. Chicago: U of Chicago P, 1983.

Anzaldúa, Gloria, ed. *Making Face, Making Soul: Haciendo Caras: Creative and Critical Perspectives of Women of Color*. San Francisco: Aunte Lute Foundation Books, 1990.

Auerbach, Nina. *Communities of Women: An Idea in Fiction*. Cambridge, MA: Harvard UP, 1978.

Barrett, Michele. *Women's Oppression Today: Problems in Marxist Feminist Analysis*. London: Verso, 1980.

Bauer, Dale M. *Feminist Dialogics: A Theory of Failed Community*. Albany: State U of New York P, 1988.

Baym, Nina. *Women's Fiction: A Guide to Novels by and about Women in America, 1820–1870*. Ithaca, NY: Cornell UP, 1978.

Beauvoir, Simone de. *The Second Sex*. 1949. Trans. and Ed. H. M. Parshley. New York: Modern Library, 1952.

Belsey, Catherine, and Jane Moore, eds. *The Feminist Reader: Essays in Gender and the Politics of Literary Criticism*. London: Macmillan, 1989.

Boone, Joseph A., and Michael Cadden, eds. *Engendering Men: The Question of Male Feminist Criticism*. New York: Routledge, 1990.

Carby, Hazel V. *Reconstructing Womanhood: The Emergence of the Afro-American Woman Novelist*. Oxford and New York: Oxford UP, 1987.

Cixous, Hélène. "Castration or Decapitation?" Trans. Annette Kuhn. *Signs* 7 (1981): 41–55.

———. "The Character of 'Character.' " *New Literary History* 5 (1974): 383–402.

————. "The Laugh of the Medusa." Trans. Keith Cohen and Paula Cohen. *Signs* 1 (1976): 875–94.

————. *Readings: The Poetics of Blanchot, Joyce, Kafka, Kleist, Lispector and Tsvetayeva*. Trans. and ed. Verena Andermatt Conley. Hemel Hempstead, Eng.: Harvester Wheatsheaf, 1992.

Cixous, Hélène, and Catherine Clement. *The Newly Born Woman*. Paris: Union Générale d'Editions, 1975.

Cohen, Ralph, ed. *Feminist Directions*. Spec. issue of *New Literary History: A Journal of Theory and Interpretation* 19.1 (Autumn 1987).

Collins, Patricai Hill. *Black Feminist Thought: Knowledge, Consciousness, and the Politics of Empowerment*. New York: Routledge, 1990.

Conley, Verena Andermatt. *Hélène Cixous*. Hemel Hempstead, Eng.: Harvester Wheatsheaf, 1992.

Daly, Mary. *Gyn/Ecology*. Boston: Beacon, 1978.

Diamond, Arlyn, and Lee R. Edwards, eds. *The Authority of Experience: Essays in Feminist Criticism*. Amherst: U of Massachusetts P, 1977.

Donovan, Josephine, ed. *Feminist Literary Criticism: Explorations in Theory*. Lexington: Kentucky UP, 1975.

Eagleton, Mary, ed. *Feminist Literary Criticism*. New York: Longman, 1991.

————, ed. *Feminist Literary Theory: A Reader*. Oxford: Basil Blackwell, 1986.

Eisenstein, Hester. *Contemporary Feminist Thought*. London: Unwin, 1984.

Eisenstein, Hester, and Alice Jardine, eds. *The Future of Difference*. Boston: G. K. Hall, 1980.

Ellmann, Mary. *Thinking About Women*. New York: Harcourt, 1968.

Felman, Shoshana. "Rereading Femininity." *Yale French Studies* 62 (1981). 19–44.

Felski, Rita. *Beyond Feminist Literature and Social Change*. Cambridge: MA: Harvard UP, 1990.

Fetterley, Judith. *The Resisting Reader: A Feminist Approach to American Fiction*. Bloomington: Indiana UP, 1978.

Fowler, Rowena. "Feminist Criticism: The Common Pursuit." *New Literary History* 19.1 (Autumn 1987): 51–62.

Flynn, Elizabeth A., and Patrocinio Schweickart, eds. *Gender and Reading: Essays on Readers, Texts, and Contexts*. Baltimore: Johns Hopkins UP, 1986.

French Feminist Theory. Spec. issue of *Signs* 7 (1981).

Frye, Marilyn. *Willful Virgin: Essays in Feminism 1976–1992*. Freddo, CA: Crossing, 1992.

Gallop, Jane. *The Daughter's Seduction: Feminism and Psychoanalysis*. Ithaca, NY: Cornell UP, 1982.

Gates, Jr., Henry Louis, ed. *Reading Black, Reading Feminist: A Critical Anthology*. New York: Meridian, 1990.

Gilbert, Sandra M., and Susan Gubar. *A Classroom Guide to Accompany the Norton Anthology of Literature by Women*. New York: Norton, 1985.

————. *The Madwoman in the Attic: The Woman Writer and the Nineteenth-Century Literary Imagination*. New Haven: Yale UP, 1979.

————. *No Man's Land: The Place of the Woman Writer in the Twentieth Century*. Vol. 1, *The War of the Words*. New Haven, Conn.: Yale UP, 1988.

————. *No Man's Land: The Place of the Woman Writer in the Twentieth Century.* Vol. 2, *Sexchanges.* New Haven, Conn.: Yale UP, 1988.

Greene, Gayle, and Coppelia Kahn, eds. *Making a Difference: Feminist Literary Criticism.* New York: Methuen, 1985.

Hansen, Karen, and Ilene J. Philipson, eds. *Women, Class and the Feminist Imagination: A Socialist-Feminist Reader.* Philadelphia: Temple UP, 1990.

Humm, Maggie, ed. *Feminisms: A Reader.* Hemel Hempstead, Eng.: Harvester Wheatsheaf, 1992.

Irigaray, Luce. *This Sex Which Is Not One.* Trans. Catherine Porter. Ithaca, NY: Cornell UP, 1985.

————. "When Our Lips Speak Together." Trans. Carolyn Burke. *Signs* 6 (1980): 69–79.

Jacobus, Mary. *Reading Woman: Essays in Feminist Criticism.* New York: Columbia UP, 1868.

————, ed. *Women Writing and Writing About Women.* London: Croom Helm, 1979.

Jardine, Alice, and Paul Smith, eds. *Men in Feminism.* New York: Methuen, 1987.

Jay, Karla, and Joanne Glasgow, eds. *Lesbian Texts and Contexts: Radical Revisions.* New York: New York UP, 1986.

Jones, Ann Rosalind. "Writing the Body: Toward an Understanding of *l'Écriture Féminine.*" *The New Feminist Criticism: Essays on Women, Literature, and Theory.* Ed. Elaine Showalter. New York: Pantheon, 1985. 361–77.

Kaplan, Cora. "Radical Feminism and Literature: Rethinking Millett's *Sexual Politics.*" 1979. Rpt. in Eagleton, 1991.

Kauffman, Linda, ed. *Gender and Theory: Dialogues on Feminist Criticism.* New York: Basil Blackwell, 1989.

Kolodny, Annette. "Dancing through the Minefield: Some Observations on the Theory, Practice, and Politics of a Feminist Literary Criticism." *Feminist Studies* 6.1 (1980): 1–25.

————. *The Lay of the Land: Metaphor as Experience in American Life and Letters.* Chapel Hill: U of North Carolina P, 1975.

————. "Some Notes on Defining a 'Feminist Literary Criticism.' " *Critical Inquiry* 2 (1975): 75–92.

Kristeva, Julia. *Desire in Language: A Semiotic Approach to Literature and Art.* Trans. Thomas Gora, Alice Jardine, and Leon S. Roudiez. Ed. Leon S. Roudiez. New York: Columbia UP, 1980.

Marks, Elaine, and Isabelle de Courtivron, eds. *New French Feminisms.* New York: Schocken, 1981.

Meese, Elizabeth. *(EX) Tensions: Re-Figuring Feminist Criticism.* Urbana: U of Illinois P, 1990.

Millett, Kate. *Sexual Politics.* New York: Doubleday, 1970.

Minnich, Elizabeth, Jean O'Barr, and Rachel Rosenfeld, eds. *Reconstructing the Academy: Women's Education and Women's Studies.* Chicago: U of Chicago P, 1988.

Moers, Ellen. *Literary Women: The Great Writers.* New York: Doubleday, 1976.

Moi, Toril. *Sexual/Textual Politics: Feminist Literary Theory.* New York: Methuen, 1985.

Mulvey, Laura. *Visual and Other Pleasures.* Bloomington: Indiana UP, 1989.

Munt, Sally, ed. *New Lesbian Criticism: Literary and Cultural Readings*. Brighton: Harvester Press, 1987.

Newton, Judith, and Deborah Rosenfelt, eds. *Feminist Criticism and Social Change: Set Class and Race in Literature and Culture*. New York: Methuen, 1985.

Nicholson, Linda J. *Feminism/Postmodernism*. New York and London: Routledge, 1990.

Pacteau, Francette. "The Impossible Referent: Representations of the Androgyne." *Formations of Fantasy*. Ed. Victor Burgin, James Donald, and Cora Kaplan. London: Methuen, 1986. 62–84.

Rich, Adrienne. *On Lies, Secrets, and Silence: Selected Prose 1966–1978*. London: Virago, 1980.

Ruthven, K. K. *Feminist Literary Studies: An Introduction*. New York: Cambridge UP, 1984.

Schriber, Mary Suzanne. *Gender and the Writer's Imagination: From Cooper to Wharton*. Lexington: UP of Kentucky, 1987.

Schuster, Marilyn R., and Susan R. Van Dyne, eds. *Women's Place in the Academy: Transforming the Liberal Arts Curriculum*. Totowa, NJ: Rowman & Allanheld, 1985.

Showalter, Elaine. *A Literature of Their Own: British Women Novelists from Brontë to Lessing*. Princeton: Princeton UP, 1977.

———. *Sexual Anarchy: Gender and Culture at the Fin de Siècle*. New York: Viking-Penguin, 1990.

———, ed. *The New Feminist Criticism: Essays on Women, Literature, Time*. New York: Pantheon, 1985.

Skandera-Trombley, Laura. *Mark Twain in the Company of Women*. Philadelphia: U of Pennsylvania P, 1994.

Spivak, Gayatri Chakravorty. *In Other Worlds: Essays in Cultural Politics*. New York: Methuen, 1987.

Suleiman, Susan Rubin. "(Re)writing the Body: The Politics and Poetics of Female Eroticism." *The Female Body in Western Culture*. Ed. Susan Rubin Suleiman. Cambridge, MA: Harvard UP, 1986. 7–29.

Todd, Janet. *Feminist Literary History*. New York: Routledge, 1988.

———. *Feminist Literary Theory: A Defence*. Oxford: Polity, 1988.

Tong, Rosemarie. *Feminist Thought: A Comprehensive Introduction*. Boulder, CO: Westview, 1989.

Walker, Alice. *Living By the Word: Selected Writings, 1973–1987*. New York: Harcourt, 1988.

Warhol, Robyn R., and Diane Price Herndl, eds. *Feminisms: An Anthology of Literary Theory and Criticism*. New Brunswick, NJ: Rutgers UP, 1991.

Waugh, Patricia. *Feminine Fictions: Revisiting the Postmodern*. New York: Routledge, 1989.

Weedon, Chris. *Feminist Practice and Poststructuralist Theory*. Oxford: Basil Blackwell, 1987.

Whitford, Margaret. *Luce Irigaray: Philosophy in the Feminine*. London: Routledge, 1991.

Wittig, Monique. *Les Guerilleres*. Trans. David Le Vay. New York: Avon, 1973.

Woolf, Virginia. *Collected Essays*. London: Hogarth, 1966.
———. *A Room of One's Own*. 1929. London: Grafton, 1987.
———. *Women and Writing*. London: Women's Press, 1979.
Wyatt, Jean. *Reconstructing Desire: The Role of the Unconscious in Women's Reading and Writing*. Chapel Hill: U of North Carolina P, 1990.

CHAPTER 9

Adorno, Theodor W. *Prisms*. London: Neville Spearman, 1967.
———. *Aesthetic Theory*. Trans. C. Lenhardt. Ed. Gretel Adorno and Rolf Tiedemann. London: Routledge and Kegan Paul, 1984.
Adorno, Theodor W., and Max Horkheimer. *The Dialectic of Enlightenment*. London: Allen Lane, 1972.
Ahearn, Edward J. *Marx and Modern Fiction*. New Haven, CT: Yale UP, 1989.
Althusser, Louis. *For Marx*. New York: Pantheon, 1969.
———. *Lenin and Philosophy and Other Essays*. Trans. Ben Brewster. New York: Monthly Review, 1971.
Arvon, Henri. *Marxist Esthetics*. Trans. Helen Lane. Ithaca, NY: Cornell UP, 1973.
Baxandall, Lee, and Stefan Morowski, eds. *Marx and Engels on Literature and Art*. New York: International General, 1973.
Benjamin, Walter. *Illuminations*. New York: Schocken, 1970
———. *The Origins of German Tragic Drama*. Trans. John Osborne. London: NLB, 1977.
———. *Reflections: Essays, Aphorisms, Autobiographical Writings*. Trans. Edmund Jephcott. Ed. Peter Dementz. New York: Harcourt, 1978.
Bennett, Tony. *Formalism and Marxism*. London: Methuen, 1979.
Caudwell, Christopher. *Further Studies in a Dying Culture*. London: Monthly Review P, 1971.
———. *Illusion and Reality*. New York: Russell, 1955.
Craig, David, ed. *Marxists on Literature*. Harmondsworth, Eng.: Penguin, 1975.
Demetz, Peter. *Marx, Engels and the Arts: Origins of Marxist Literary Criticism*. Chicago: U of Chicago P, 1967.
Dowling, William C. *Jameson, Althusser, Marx: An Introduction to the Political Unconscious*. Ithaca, NY: Cornell UP, 1984.
Eagleton, Terry. "Capitalism, Modernism, and Postmodernism." *New Left Review* 152 (1985): 60–72.
———. *Criticism and Ideology: A Study in Marxist Literary Theory*. London: New Left Books, 1976.
———. *The Function of Criticism: From* The Spectator *to Post-Structuralism*. London: Thetford, 1984.
———. *Literary Theory: An Introduction*. 2nd. Minneapolis: U of Minnesota P, 1996.
———. *Marxism and Literary Criticism*. Berkeley: U of California P, 1976.
Fekete, John. *The Critical Twilight*. Boston: Routledge & Kegan Paul, 1976.
Frow, John. *Marxism and Literary History*. Ithaca, NY: Cornell UP, 1986.
Goldmann, Lucien. *The Hidden God*. London: Routledge & Kegan Paul, 1964.

————. "Marxist Criticism." *The Philosophy of the Enlightenment*. Cambridge, MA: MIT P, 1973. 86–97.

Gottlieb, Roger S., ed. *An Anthropology of Western Marxism: From Lukács and Gramsci to Socialist-Feminism*. Oxford and New York: Oxford UP, 1989.

Gramsci, Antonio. *Selections from the Prison Notebooks*. Ed. Quintin Hoare and Geoffrey Nowell Smith. New York: International Publishers, 1971.

Hicks, Granville. *The Great Tradition*. 1931. Rev. ed. New York: Macmillan, 1935.

Horkheimer, Max, and Theodor W. Adorno. *The Dialectic of Enlightenment*. Trans. John Cumming. New York: Seabury, 1972.

James, C. Vaughan. *Soviet Socialist Realism: Origins and Theory*. New York: Macmillan, 1973.

Jameson, Fredric. *Marxism and Form: Twentieth-Century Dialectical Theories of Literature*. Princeton: Princeton UP, 1971.

————. *The Political Unconscious: Narrative as a Socially Symbolic Art*. Ithaca, NY: Cornell UP, 1981.

————. *The Prison-House of Language: A Critical Account of Structuralism and Russian Formalism*. Princeton: Princeton UP, 1972.

Jay, Martin. *The Dialectical Imagination: A History of the Frankfurt School*. London: Heinemann, 1973.

Lentricchia, Frank. *Criticism and Social Change*. Chicago: U of Chicago P, 1983.

Lukács, Georg. *Essays on Realism*. Trans. David Fernbach. Ed. Rodney Livingstone. Cambridge, MA: MIT P, 1981.

————. *The Historical Novel*. London: Merlin, 1962.

————. *The Meaning of Contemporary Realism*. London: Merlin, 1963.

————. *Writer and Critic and Other Essays*. London: Merlin, 1970.

Macherey, Pierre. *A Theory of Literary Production*. Trans. Geoffrey Wall. London: Routledge and Kegan Paul, 1978.

Marcuse, Herbert. *The Aesthetic Dimension: Toward a Critique of Marxist Aesthetics*. Boston: Beacon, 1978.

McMurtry, John. *The Structure of Marx's World-View*. Princeton: Princeton UP, 1978.

Mulhern, Francis, ed. *Contemporary Marxist Literary Criticism*. London: Longman, 1992.

Nelson, Cary, and Lawrence Grossberg, eds. *Marxism and the Interpretation of Culture*. London: Macmillan, 1980.

Prawer, S. S. *Karl Marx and World Literature*. Oxford: Oxford UP, 1978.

Sartre, Jean-Paul. *What Is Literature?* New York: Philosophical Library, 1949.

Trotsky, Leon. *Literature and Revolution*. Ann Arbor: U of Michigan P, 1971.

Wellmer, Albrecht. "Reason, Utopia, and the *Dialectic of Enlightenment*." *Habermas and Modernity*. Ed. Richard J. Bernstein. Cambridge, MA: MIT P, 1985. 35–66.

Willett, John, ed. *Brecht on Theatre*. London: Methuen, 1964.

Williams, Raymond. *Culture and Society. 1780-1950*. London: Chatto and Windus, 1958.

————. *Marxism and Literature*. Oxford: Oxford UP, 1977.

Wilson, Edmund. *Axel's Castle*. New York: Scribner's, 1961.

Wright, Elizabeth. *Postmodern Brecht: A Re-Presentation*. London: Routledge, 1988.

CHAPTER 10

Collier, Peter, and Helga Geyer-Ryan, eds. *Literary Theory Today*. Ithaca, NY: Cornell UP, 1990.

Cooper, Barry. *Michel Foucault: An Introduction to the Study of His Thought*. New York: Edwin Mellen, 1982.

Cousins, Mark, and Athar Hussain. *Michel Foucault*. New York: St. Martin's, 1984.

Cox, Jeffrey N., and Larry J. Reynolds, eds. *New Historical Literary Study: Essays on Reproducing Texts, Representing History*. Princeton, NJ: Princeton UP, 1993.

Dollimore, Jonathan. *Radical Tragedy: Religion, Ideology, and Power in the Drama of Shakespeare and his Contemporaries*. Chicago: U of Chicago P, 1984.

Dollimore, Jonathan, and Alan Sinfield, eds. *Political Shakespeare: New Essays in Cultural Materialism*. Manchester, Eng.: Manchester UP, 1985.

Foucault, Michel. *Discipline and Punish: The Birth of the Prison*. Trans. Alan Sheridan. New York: Vintage, 1979.

———. *The Foucault Reader*. Ed. Paul Rabinow. New York: Pantheon, 1984.

———. *Madness and Civilization*. Trans. Richard Howard. New York: Pantheon, 1965.

———. *The Order of Things*. New York: Pantheon, 1972.

Fox-Genovese, Elizabeth. "Literary Criticism and the Politics of the New Historicism." *The New Historicism*. Ed. H. Aram Veeser. New York: Routledge, 1989. 213–224.

Gane, Mike, ed. *Towards a Critique of Foucault*. London: Routledge and Kegan Paul, 1987.

Geertz, Clifford. *The Interpretation of Cultures: Selected Essays*. New York: Basic Books, 1973.

———. *Local Knowledge: Further Essays In Interpretive Anthropology*. New York: Basic, 1983.

———. *Negara: The Theatre State of Nineteenth-Century Bali*. Princeton, NJ: Princeton UP, 1980.

Goldberg, Jonathan. *James I and the Politics of Literature: Jonson, Shakespeare, Donne, and Their Contemporaries*. Baltimore: Johns Hopkins UP, 1983.

Graff, Gerald, and Reginald Gibbons, eds. *Criticism in the University*. Evanston, IL: Northwestern UP, 1985.

Greenblatt, Stephen. *Hamlet in Purgatory*. Princeton: Princeton UP, 2001.

———. Introduction. "The Forms of Power and the Power of Forms in the Renaissance." *Genre* 15 (Summer 1982): 3–6.

———. *Learning to Curse: Essays in Early Modern Culture*. New York: Routledge, 1991.

———. *Renaissance Self-Fashioning: From More to Shakespeare*. Chicago: U of Chicago P, 1980.

———. *Shakespearean Negotiations: The Circulation of Social Energy in Renaissance England*. Berkeley and Los Angeles: U of California P, 1988.

———. "Towards a Poetics of Culture." *The New Historicism*. Ed. H. Aram Veeser. New York: Routledge, 1989. 1–14.

Grossberg, Lawrence, Cary Nelson, and Paula Treichler, eds. *Cultural Studies*. New York: Routledge, 1992.

Howard, Jean. "The New Historicism in Renaissance Studies." *English Literary Renaissance* 16 (1986): 13–43.

Hunt, Lynn, ed. *The New Cultural History.* Berkeley and Los Angeles: U of California P, 1989.

Lindenberger, Herbert. "Toward a New History in Literary Study." *Profession: Selected Articles from the Bulletins of the Association of Departments of English and the Association of Departments of Foreign Languages.* New York: Modern Language Association, 1984. 16–23.

McGann, Jerome. *The Beauty of Inflections: Literary Investigations in Historical Method and Theory.* Oxford: Oxford UP, 1985.

———. *Historical Studies and Literary Criticism.* Madison: U of Wisconsin P, 1985.

———. *Social Values and Poetic Act: The Historical Judgment of Literary Work.* Cambridge, MA: Harvard UP, 1988.

Michaels, Walter Benn. *The Gold Standard and the Logic of Naturalism: American Literature at the Turn of the Century.* Berkeley and Los Angeles: U of California P, 1987.

Montrose, Louis. "New Historicisms." *Redrawing the Boundaries: The Transformation of English and American Literary Studies.* Ed. Stephen Greenblatt and Giles Gunn. New York: Modern Language Association, 1992. 392–418.

———. "Professing the Renaissance: The Poetics and Politics of Culture." *The New Historicism.* Ed. H. Aram Veeser. New York: Routledge, 1989. 15–36.

———. "Renaissance Literary Studies and the Subject of History." *English Literary Renaissance* 16 (1986): 5–12.

Morris, Wesley. *Toward a New Historicism.* Princeton: Princeton UP, 1972.

New Historicisms, New Histories, and Others. Spec. issue of *NLH* 21 (1990).

Orgel, Stephen. *The Illusion of Power: Political Theater in the English Renaissance.* Berkeley and Los Angeles, U of California P, 1975.

Rabinow, Paul, ed. *The Foucault Reader.* New York: Pantheon, 1984.

Robertson, D. W. "Historical Criticism." *English Institute Essays: 1950.* Ed. Alan S. Downer. New York: Columbia UP, 1951. 3–31.

Sheridan, Alan. *Michel Foucault.* New York: Horwood and Tavistock, 1985.

Thomas, Brook. "The Historical Necessity for—and Difficulties with—New Historical Analysis in Introductory Literature Courses." *College English* 49 (Sept. 1987): 509–22.

Turner, Victor. *Celebration: Studies in Festivity and Ritual.* Washington, DC: Smithsonian Institution, 1982.

Vesser, H. Aram, ed. *The New Historicism.* New York: Routledge, 1989.

Wicke, Jennifer A. *Advertising Fictions: Literature, Advertisement, and Social Reading.* New York: Columbia, 1988.

CHAPTER 11

Achebe, Chinua. "An Image of Africa: Racism in Conrad's *Heart of Darkness*." *Massachusetts Review* 18 (1977): 782–94.

Appiah, Kwame Anthony. *In My Father's House: Africa in the Philosophy of Culture.* Oxford and New York: Oxford UP, 1992.

Ashcroft, Bill, Gareth Griffiths, and Helen Tiffin. *The Empire Writes Back: Theory and Practice in Post-Colonial Literatures.* London: Routledge, 1989.

Awkward, Michael. *Inspiriting Influences: Tradition, Revision, and Afro-American Literature.* New York: Columbia UP, 1989.

Benjamin, Walter. *The Origin of German Tragic Drama.* Trans. John Osborne. London: NLB, 1997.

Bhabha, Homi K. *The Location of Culture.* London: Routledge, 1994.

———. "Postcolonial Criticism." *Redrawing the Boundaries: The Transformation of English and American Literary Studies.* Ed. Stephen Greenblatt and Giles Gunn. New York: Modern Language Association, 1992. 437–465.

———, ed. *Nation and Narration.* New York: Routledge and Kegan Paul, 1990.

Boehmer, Elleke. *Colonial and Postcolonial Literature: Migrant Metaphors.* New York: Oxford UP, 1995.

Brantlinger, Patrick. "History and Empire." *Journal of Victorian Literature and Culture* 19 (1992). 317–27.

Carby, Hazel V. *Reconstruction Womanhood: The Emergence of the Afro-American Woman Novelist.* New York: Oxford UP, 1987.

Chatterjee, Partha. "More on Modes of Power and the Peasantry." *Selected Subaltern Studies.* Ed. Ranajit Guha and Gayatri Chakravorty Spivak. New York: Oxford UP, 1988. 351–390.

Chinweizu, Onwuchekwa Jemie, and Ihechukwu Madubuike. *Toward the Decolonization of African Literature.* Vol. 1, *African Fiction and Poetry and Their Critics.* Washington, DC: Howard UP, 1983.

Cronin, Richard. *Imagining India.* London: Macmillan, 1990.

Davis, Angela Y. *Women, Race, and Class.* 1981. New York: Vintage, 1983.

Dirlik, Arif. *The Postcolonial Aura: Third World Criticism in the Age of Global Capitalism.* Boulder, Co: Westview Press, 1997.

During, Simon. "Postmodernism or Post-Colonialism Today." *Textual Practice* 1.1 (1987): 32–47.

Evans, Malcolm. *Signifying Nothing: Truth's True Contents in Shakespeare's Text.* Athens: U of Georgia P, 1986.

Fanon, Frantz. *Black Skin, White Masks.* Trans. Charles Lam Markmann. New York: Grove, 1967.

———. *A Dying Colonialism.* Trans. Haakon Chebalier. New York: Grove, 1965.

———. *Toward the African Revolution: Political Essays.* Trans. Haakon Chevalier. New York: Grove, 1967.

———. *The Wretched of the Earth.* Trans. Constance Farrington. New York: Grove, 1968.

Gates, Henry Louis, Jr. "Authority, (White) Power, and the (Black) Critic; or, It's All Greek to Me." *The Future of Literary Theory.* Ed. Raph Cohen. New York: Routledge, 1989. 324–46.

———. "Critical Fanonism." *Critical Inquiry* 17.3 (1991): 457–70.

———. *Figures in Black: Words, Signs, and the "Racial" Self.* New York: Oxford UP, 1987.

———. *Loose Canons: Notes on the Culture Wars.* New York: Oxford UP, 1992.

———. *The Signifying Monkey: A Theory of African-American Literary Criticism.* New York: Oxford UP, 1988.

————, ed. *Black Literature and Literary Theory*. New York: Methuen, 1984.

————, ed. *"Race," Writing, and Difference*. Chicago: U of Chicago P, 1986.

Gilroy, Paul. *The Black Atlantic: Modernity and Double Consciousness*. Cambridge, MA: Harvard UP, 1993.

Guha, Ranajit, and Gayatri Chakravorty Spivak, eds. *Selected Subaltern Studies*. New York: Oxford UP 1988.

Hutcheon, Linda. "Introduction: Complexities Abounding." *Colonialism and the Postcolonial Condition*. Spec. issue of *PMLA* 110.1 (1995): 7–16

Jameson, Fredic. "Third-World Literature in the Era of Multinational Capitalism." *Social Text* 15 (1986): 65–88.

JanMohamed, Abdul R. *Manichean Aesthetics: The Politics of Literature in Colonial Africa*. Amherst: U of Massachusetts P, 1983.

LaCapra, Dominick, ed. *The Bounds of Race: Perspectives on Hegemony and Resistance*. Ithaca: Cornell UP, 1991.

Lamming, George. *The Pleasure of Exile*. London: Michael Joseph, 1960.

Lazarus, Neil. *Resistance in Postcolonial African Fiction*. New Haven: Yale UP, 1990.

Llosa, Mario Vargas. *The Storyteller*. Trans. Helen Lane. New York: Penguin, 1989.

Mitchell, Angelyn, ed. *Within the Circle: An Anthology of African American Literary Criticism from the Harlem Renaissance to the Present*. Durham, NC: Duke UP, 1994.

Mitchell, W. J. T. "Postcolonial Culture, Postimperial Criticism." *Transition* 56 (1992): 11–19.

McClintock, Anne. *Imperial Leather: Race, Gender, and Sexuality in the Colonial Context*. London: Routledge, 1995.

Mohanty, Chandrda Talpade, Ann Russo, and Lourdes Torres, eds. *Third World Women and the Politics of Feminism*. Bloomington: Indiana UP, 1991.

Ngugi wa Thiong'o. *Decolonising the Mind: The Politics of Language in African Literature*. London: James Currey, 1986.

Niranjana, Tejaswine. *Sitting Translation: History, Post-Structuralism, and the Colonial Context*. Berkeley: U of California P, 1990.

Owomoyela, Oyekan, ed. *A History of Twentieth-Century African Literatures*. Lincoln: U of Nebraska P, 1993.

Richards, Thomas. *The Imperial Archive: Knowledge and the Fantasy of Empire*. London: Verso, 1993.

Rodney, Walter. *How Europe Underdeveloped Africa*. Dar es Salaam: Tanzania Publishing House, 1972.

Rushdie, Salman. *Imaginary Homelands: Essays and Criticism, 1981–91*. London: Penguin, 1991.

Said, Edward. *Culture and Imperialism*. New York: Knopf, 1993.

————. "Figures, Configurations, Transfigurations." *Race & Class* 32 (July-Sept. 1990). 1–16.

————. *Orientalism*. New York: Vintage, 1979.

————. *The World, the Text, and the Critic*. Cambridge: Harvard Up, 1983.

Spivak, Gayatri Chakravorty. "Can the Subaltern Speak?" *Marxism and the Interpetation of Culture*. Ed. Cary Nelson and Lawrence Grossberg. Urbana: U of Illinois P, 1988. 271–313.

————. *In Other Worlds: Essays in Cultural Politics*. New York: Routledge, 1988.

———. *The Post-Colonial Critic: Interviews, Strategies, Dialogues*. Ed. Sarah Harasym. New York: Routledge, 1990.

———. "Subaltern Studies: Desconstructing Historiography." *Subaltern Studies: Writings on South Asian History and Society*, vol. 4. Ed. Ranajit Guha. Delhi: Oxford UP, 1985. 330–363.

Suleri, Sarah. *The Rhetoric of English India*. Chicago: U of Chicago P, 1992.

———. "Woman Skin Deep: Feminism and the Postcolonial Condition." *Critical Inquiry* 18.4 (Summer 1992).

Taylor, Patrick. *The Narrative of Liberation*. Ithaca, NY: Cornell UP, 1989.

Trimmer, Joseph, and Tilly Warnock, eds. *Understanding Others*. Urbana: National Council of Teachers of English, 1992.

Viswanathan, Gauri. *Masks of Conquest: Literary Study and British Rule in India*. New York: Columbia UP, 1989.

Williams, Patrick, and Laura Chrisman, eds. *Colonial Discourse and Post-Colonial Theory: A Reader*. New York: Columbia UP, 1994.

Williams, Raymond. *Keywords: A Vocabulary of Culture and Society*. Rev. ed. Oxford: Oxford UP, 1983.

Wolf, Eric R. *Europe and the People without History*. Berkeley and Los Angeles: U of California P, 1982.

Zahar, Renate. *Frantz Fanon: Colonialism and Alienation*. New York: Monthly Review P, 1974.

Credits

Krista Adlhock. "Hawthorne's Understanding of History in 'The Maypole of Merry Mount'" by Krista Adlhock. Reprinted by permission.

Sandra Cisneros. From THE HOUSE ON MANGO STREET. Copyright © 1984 by Sandra Cisneros. Published by Vintage Books, a division of Random House, Inc., and in hardcover by Alfred A. Knopf in 1994. Reprinted by permission of Susan Bergholz Literary Services, New York. All rights reserved.

Jennifer Douglas. "'Ethan Brand's' Challenge to Me" by Jennifer Douglas. Reprinted by permission.

Jennifer Douglas. "Deconstructing a 'Real' House" by Jennifer Douglas. Reprinted by permission.

Tony Harrison. "Marked with D." by Tony Harrison. 1987 Penguin Selected Poems. © Tony Harrison 1987. Reprinted by permission of the author.

Lori Huth. "Throwing Off the Yoke: 'Rip Van Winkle' and Women" by Lori Huth. Reprinted by permission.

David Johnson. "A Psychoanalytic Approach to Poe's 'The City in the Sea'" by David Johnson. Reprinted by permission.

Jomo Kenyatta. Extract from FACING MOUNT KENYA by Jomo Kenyatta published by Secker & Warburg. Used by permission of The Random House Group Limited.

Conie Krause. "Will the Real Walter Mitty Please Wake Up: A Structuralist's View of 'The Secret Life of Walter Mitty'" by Conie Krause. Reprinted by permission.

John Leax. "Sacramental Vision" by John Leax from THE TASK OF ADAM, 1985. Reprinted by permission of the author.

Wendy Rader. "'The Gentlemen of the Jungle': Or Are They Beasts?" by Wendy Rader. Reprinted by permission.

Dale Schuurman. "Keats's 'To Autumn': Verses of Praise for a Malicious Season?" by Dale Schuurman. Reprinted by permission.

James Thurber. "The Secret Life of Walter Mitty" from MY WORLD—AND WELCOME TO IT © 1942 by James Thurber. Copyright renewed 1971 by James Thurber.

Index